IT'S YOUR SHOUT, MATE!

Aussie Pubs and Aussie Beers

JOHN O'GRADY

Illustrated by Benier

URE SMITH · SYDNEY

First published in Australia 1972
by Ure Smith Pty Limited
176 South Creek Road, Dee Why West 2099

Copyright © John O'Grady, 1972

National Library of Australia Card
Number and ISBN 0 7254 0093 5

Designed and produced in Australia

Printed in Australia at The Griffin
Press, Adelaide

Registered in Australia for
transmission by post as a book

First edition

Author's Note
The name James McIntosh is fictitious.
Therefore no resemblance to anybody
named McIntosh, living or dead, is
intended, or possible. The man whose
story is told herein has a different
name.

J. O'G.

CONTENTS

CHEERS!

For assistance given to me during my wanderings, I am indebted to the Australian Hotels Association, and in particular to the following 'gentlemen and scholars' who live and work and dispense hospitality and friendship in various parts of Australia:

Barry McInerney, Colin Walker, Bert Houston, Bert McPartland, Arthur Dunstan, Len Shepherd, Harry McGregor, Dolf Clowes, Harold Nevin, Bill Halligan, Bill Connelly, Peter Whallin, Jim Byfield, John Gibson, Bernie Henderson, David Watson, Arthur Wootton, Ralph Sierakowski, Doug McPhee, George Rossi, Dick Perkins, James Watt, Arthur Brooks, John Ramsay, Dennis Healey, Pat O'Neill, Cliff Volz, Lionel Anderson, Keith Smith, Sid Johnson, Laurie Gardner, Warren Wright, John van Brederode, Bill Moloney.

Although they must share the responsibility for the present shocking state of my liver, they are forgiven, and will always be remembered.

J.M.

By Way of Introduction

In the beginning . . .

Who was the person who first discovered that if one lets barley germinate and go rotten, one can swallow the mess and become 'rotten' oneself? He or she probably discovered this fact accidentally—as penicillin was discovered—and was no doubt very hungry and thirsty at the time, with only rotten barley left to assuage the pangs. We don't know who, and we don't know exactly when, but we thank him or her for passing the secret on to his or her friends.

The odds are that it was a woman, because according to historians the first brewers were female. Over six thousand years ago, women made beer in Babylon. And as early as 4,945 BC, women were brewing beer in Egypt. So the next time my wife complains because in her opinion I have been drinking too much beer, I shall remind her that ladies were the first to make it. And thank her kindly.

James McIntosh is my name, and I am writing these thoughts on the 'Australind', a very comfortable little train that runs from Perth to Bunbury, in Western Australia. And I am being ob-

7

served by a middle-aged female across the aisle who appears to disapprove of the can of Swan Lager in front of me. At least I think she disapproves. I offered her some, but she tied her face into a knot, and shook her head violently. No doubt, before she died, Eve disapproved of apples.

But her disapproval isn't worth worrying about, because the day is cool and sunny, and the grass is green, and the little stations along the line are clean and bright, and England is on the other side of the world. Here there is peace and contentment, and although the beer is much too cold, it is very good.

A much-travelled Australian told me in Perth last night, 'There's no bad beer, but some are better than others.' It was not always true, he said. 'The old Geraldton Globe, the old Rockhampton Mac's, the old Launceston Boag's, the old Mudgee Mud were lousy beers.' He said Geraldton and Mudgee are now out of business, and Boag's and Mac's have improved. 'The Lord be praised,' he said.

He told me that Australians are travelling more and more each year around their own country, and while they don't all drink beer, those who do are demanding a quality brew, served at the right temperature.

'Nearly frozen,' I said.

'Yes,' he said. 'Ice cold. And that's the way you get it now. No more warm flat stuff pulled from wooden kegs with wet bags over 'em. You can go from Perth to Darwin and Hobart and right around, and you'll get a good cold grog.'

In answer to my question, he said yes, the Australian palate distinguishes differences in taste. That, he thought, was because of regional differences in the quality of the water. I told him that a brewer can make a beer smell and taste any way he wants it. Brewers are chemists, and brewing is chemistry, and every brew is adjusted for taste.

He said, 'I wouldn't know about that. And I don't give a bugger, anyway. Australian beer is the best in the world.'

Perhaps it is. But I doubt it, although I have much more of it to taste yet. My experience teaches me that the 'best beer' is always that which a man, of his own free will, chooses to

8

drink. And I noticed in Perth that the locals chose draught, in preference to bottles or cans, at their bars. When I commented on this, I was told, 'Aw, bottles an' cans are to take home. You don't drink 'em in the bar—unless there's a carters' strike on, or something, an' there's no draught left.'

Coming out to Australia by sea, we struck up a friendship with a young doctor from Florence. The food on board was superb, and the wines very good, and this young medico was an expert on both. When we got to Fremantle, he expressed a desire to taste some 'typical Australian foods and drinks'. I told him I had the same desire.

Leaving my wife in the hands of a friendly porter, who promised to attend to the removal of baggage and its inspection by customs, the Florentine and I went to a nearby pub, as advised by the porter.

He'd said, 'Front up in the public bar. The grog's good, an' you can get a decent pie there, too.'

There were many men there, drinking beer and eating pies. And they seemed to be enjoying both. So I asked for two large beers and two pies. And I said to our friend, pretending to a knowledge which I did not possess, 'There you are. Typical Australian foods and drinks.'

He took the beer in his right hand, and a pie, doused with tomato sauce, in his left. He looked surprised—or perhaps astonished and slightly terrified would be a better description— but courageously nibbled a bit off the edge of the pie, and took a sip of the beer. Then his expression changed to one of delight. He said, and obviously meant it, 'This is magnificent foods and drinks.'

I followed his example. He was right. We each had another pie. And more beer. And then more beer.

By the time we set out to return to the ship—he was going on to Melbourne—our navigation was far from good. But there was nothing wrong with our friend's voice. The songs of Tuscany he was bellowing to the Australian sky were loud and clear. And he was loud in his praises of Australian beer. There was nothing like it in Italy, he said.

I assured him there was nothing like it in England, either.

My wife, sitting with our baggage outside customs, was of the opinion that there was nothing like either of us anywhere. We were not popular.

I am popular again today. But that day I certainly was not. I went to sleep in the taxi taking us the eleven miles up to our hotel in Perth. And went to sleep again when we reached our room. I was not fit for work until the next day. My wife said that for the rest of our Australian tour she would 'keep an eye on me'.

I am making a survey of Australian beer, its quality, distribution, consumption figures, the drinking habits and tastes of Australians in all six States, and any other pertinent information which in my opinion would interest my company. In other words, market research. Investigate and report.

My directors, in their wisdom—or lack of it—are thinking of extending their operations into the Australian market. Our alcoholic products are very popular in the UK. Perhaps they would prove popular here. I must visit breweries, and pubs, and talk, and ask questions, and listen, and sample products.

I do not need my wife's eye on me, but perhaps the work does have its 'dangers'.

'Down the hatch, mate!'

1
Western Australia

My work is finished. My report is written. And now I sit in England reviving happy memories as I sort out my many pages of notes prior to consigning them to the incinerator. But first I shall organize the events and comments, stories and legends not included in the report to my directors into a record of one 'Pommy Bastard's' introduction to Australia and her alcoholic ways.

Strictly speaking, I am not a Pommy Bastard, since McIntosh is not an English name. But I was born and educated in England, and therefore have an English accent, which branded me a Pommy in Australian circles.

I am not branded a Pommy by my friend Jock Currie, whom I first met in Melbourne. Jock, a native-born Scot, has been in Australia for several years, and regards the country as his homeland. Jock, amongst many other things, is something of a poet. With his permission I will occasionally be recording some of his verse, which I think is worth keeping. He says it is not. But, like all true Scots, he is **a** very honest man.

As already mentioned, our introduction to Australia was via Fremantle and Perth. I decided to start my work there.

Seen from the deck of a ship in the Indian Ocean, early in the morning, the coastline is not impressive. Hazy, low-lying, sandy, with a range of low hills in the background, my wife said it was depressing.

A small group of young returning Aussies—male—were noisy, making frequent use of what I learnt was called 'the great Australian adjective', although, like most of their country's profanity and slang, it was imported from England.

'Won't be long now, eh?'

'Bloody near time, too.'

'All up to the nearest rubbity, eh?'

'Bloody oath. Get some decent bloody beer for a change.'

'Yeah. Not a bad drop, the old Swan.'

'Even if it was crook, it'd be better than bloody Pommy piss.'

'Yeah. You can say that again.'

My wife's comment was low-voiced. Being a lady, she didn't want them to hear. She went below to finish packing.

I remained on deck, listening, trying to accustom my ears to the slurred flat accents.

By the time my wife returned, tugs were pushing us into our berth. She surveyed the port and delivered a one-word comment.

'Depressing,' she said.

I had to agree with her. But then all docksides are depressing, and no country should be judged by them. She brightened up considerably after a day or two in Perth. It's a beautiful little city. I expressed that opinion one evening to a rather elderly gentleman who was sitting at our table in the hotel.

'Yes,' he said. 'It's changed a lot in the last few years. The West has become civilized. And so have the people. They're not so suspicious now of anybody from the Eastern States. The first time I came over here, early in the 1930s, they could pick a man from the East just by looking at him. They reckoned we were all liars and con-men. I'm from Sydney and I remember one time I set out from Adelaide to work my way up to Darwin,

12

and then down to Perth around by the top. But I was running a bit late, and when I got to the Alice I knew I'd never make it around before the Wet. At least, that was what I was told in the Stupid Arms.'

My wife said, 'The Stupid Arms? What's that?'

'A pub,' he said. 'It's really the Stewart Arms. It was a nice little pub then, before they rebuilt it, and it went mad with the chrome and floor polish. Anyway, I didn't fancy back-tracking all the way south again, so I decided to have a go at getting across direct. On my own. No road. Straight across country. I was driving a Ford V8 then, one of the first to come out, and I had a sixty-gallon tank built into the boot. Well, I made it in a week, navigating by the sun and the Southern Cross, but what with all the petrol and water and tucker, I did in my back springs. I came out near Wiluna, with a bit of log holding the rear off the axle, and two tyres stuffed with spinifex. As far as I knew, nobody'd ever been across there before. I thought it would be a great ad. for Ford, and I'd get a new car out of it. So I limped in to the Ford agents, told the story, and said I thought the Ford people ought to give me a new car. The boss looked at my number plates, and said, "You from the East?" I said, "Yes." He said, "Come up from Kalgoorlie, did you?" I said, "No, I told you. I came straight across from Alice Springs. Direct." He just laughed at me. He said, "You blokes from the East are all the same. Good thing we don't get many of you." I had to go to the Post Office, and wire the firm to send me some funds for new tyres and tubes, and a set of springs. Nobody would cash a cheque for me. I was from the East, see. A liar. A con-man.'

We laughed at his story, and I said, 'But West Australians are different now?'

'Oh yes,' he said. 'They'll even cash a cheque for you now.' And then he added, 'If they know you.'

He asked what we had been doing that day. I told him my wife had been doing some shopping, and I had been visiting the brewery.

He said, 'Yes? How did you swing that?'

'The Secretary of the Australian Hotels Association organized it for me.'

'You must have some leverage,' he said.

I had a letter of introduction to AHA officials, but I was not going to tell him that. I was not telling anybody just why I was doing what I was doing. So I just agreed about 'leverage', and changed the subject.

The next day I started out on an investigatory 'pub crawl'. I wanted to meet some consumers of the brewery's product, and discuss it with them. This meant, of course, consuming some of the product myself. And I thought a public bar would be the best place to start, somewhere out of the inner city area.

I walked until I was really thirsty, and then went into one. There were several men there, roughly dressed, and I placed myself near two of them and asked the barmaid for a glass of beer.

When it arrived, I looked at it, and thought I could drink it in one gulp.

I said, 'Er—do you have anything bigger?'

She said, 'What's wrong with you? You asked for a glass, didn't you?'

'Yes—but—'

She said, 'Make up your mind. Do you want a middy?'

'Well—would you mind?'

'No,' she said, and there was sarcasm in her voice. 'I've got all day, an' nothing better to do.'

She poured the contents of the very small glass into one just a little larger, but not nearly large enough for my thirst, and went to the tap.

Before she began to fill the glass, I said, 'Excuse me—but I really would like something larger.'

By this time the two men had stopped talking, and we had an audience.

The barmaid's sigh was greatly exaggerated. She said to the audience, 'Wouldn't it? It's just not my day.'

And to me she said, 'If you wanted a pot, why didn't you ask for one?'

The audience was still silent. She put the pot (about a half-pint glass) in front of me and said, 'If you want anything bigger than that, bring your own bucket. But not while I'm on duty, eh?'

I drank silently. Then the man nearest me said, 'You from the East?'

Having been told that Australians were not generally fond of Englishmen, I said, 'Er—yes.'

'Thought so,' he said. 'Done up like a pox-doctor's clerk. The trouble with you bastards from the East, you always want big beers. An' you drink 'em as fast as we drink our glasses, so when it comes our turn to shout, it costs us. Bloody con-men, the whole lot of you.'

I said, 'This is what you would call a big beer?'

'Course it is. Biggest we bloody got, isn't it?'

'Is it? Well—er—thank you. Would you two gentlemen care to join me?'

'Thought you was never gunna ask,' the second man said.

They drained their very small glasses quickly, and the first one said, 'Three pots, Joannie. Eastern States shout.'

'Oh well, in that case,' the barmaid said, 'he's forgiven.'

Over the three pots, they made highly disparaging remarks about the quality of Eastern States' beer, and the habits of Eastern Staters, and then I received instructions in Western container nomenclature and comparative sizes.

'We got ponies, glasses, middies, an' pots, see,' the first man said. 'Now a pony's four ounces—'

The second man said, 'Two to four.'

'All right, two to four. But who the bloody hell drinks two's? You keep quiet while I clue him up. A glass is five ounces, a middy is seven ounces, an' a pot's ten. Got it? That's all you have to remember.'

The second man said, 'A middy's a schooner in the bush.'

'I know that. Don't confuse him. We're not *in* the bloody bush, you nong.'

I thought they would soon be fighting, and maybe it was time to go. I had not yet learnt that Australian friends habitually abuse each other in grossly insulting terms, without giving or taking offence.

I said, 'Well—thank you for the information, and for your company, gentlemen. I'm afraid I must be getting along now.'

'Oh no you don't,' the first man said. 'You can't big note yourself by shoutin' for us an' then pissin' off. You got two more pots to come yet.'

A voice behind us said, 'Drink up, fellers. The next round's on the brewery.'

Our heads turned, and the first man said, 'Another bloke done up like a pox-doctor's clerk. Gees we're honoured today.'

The owner of the voice, joining us, said, 'Wouldn't do you scruffy characters any harm to wear a suit and tie occasionally.'

'Wore one when I got married,' number two man said.

The barmaid was drawing pots. She said, 'The boss is not in, Jack.'

The newcomer Jack said, 'No matter. It's just a courtesy call.'

'Gees, you get it easy,' number one man said.

'What do you mean?'

'Travellin' for the brewery. We've only got one brewery, so you've got no opposition. Swan beer, take it or leave it. Anybody who doesn't like Swan can go an' —'

Number two man interrupted. He was belligerent. 'Who doesn't like Swan? Show me a man who doesn't like Swan.'

To me, he said, '*You* like Swan, don't you?'

'Yes. It's very nice.'

'What I mean, see? Best beer in the world, the old Swan.'

Jack the brewery man said, 'Thank you. Tell the boss I called in will you Joannie? If he's got any problems, get him to give me a ring.'

'Righto,' she said.

The first man said, 'I still reckon you've got the easiest job in the West. Only one beer an' everybody likes it. You don't have to sell it.'

The brewery man said, 'Course I don't have to sell it. I'm not here to sell. My job is to promote goodwill.'

'Why? What're you scared of? Bloody Courage?'

'Don't use that filthy word around here,' the brewery man said.

He finished his pot, and said he had to be going, because he had a lot of calls to make. I said I had to be going, too.

The first man said, 'Like bloody hell you have. You got two more pots to come yet.'

Five pots of Swan draught is fifty ounces. Two and a half pints. And I was not yet accustomed to ice-cold beer. My throat was frozen. And there is a lot of alcohol in two and a half pints of Swan draught. By the time I got away I knew that very well.

It did not make me feel better to hear one of the men say, as I was weaving towards the door, 'I don't reckon that bastard's from the East. I reckon he's a bloody Pom.'

That was the beginning of my proposed pub crawl. And the end of it. I managed to find a taxi to take me back to our hotel. And, avoiding the bars, I went up to our room.

Fortunately, my wife was out. I went to sleep.

Re-reading the notes I made—mainly technical—after my first visit to an Australian brewery, I am reminded of the head brewer who showed me around.

Those who have never met a brewer—those in England, anyway—visualize him as a large man with an enormous stomach, who wears big hob-nailed boots, has a fat red face with a walrus moustache on it, has a nose full of broken blood vessels, and, when one is down wind from him, exudes a rich aroma of sweat, malt, hops and beer.

Swan's brewer was over six feet tall, and was lean and trim. He wore a beautifully cut and fitted grey suit, highly polished black shoes, and a perfectly knotted tie. His face was alert and intelligent and his nose free of blemishes. His erect Guardsman's bearing and nimble foot work on steel gangways were a delight to watch. After weeks at sea, I was sadly out of condition, and huffed and puffed along behind him, listening with great interest.

He conducted me on a tour of the brewery from top to bot-

17

tom. 'From barley to beer'. He was justifiably proud of what he had to show me. When he discovered that I knew something about brewing, he talked chemistry, which is what brewing is.

He delivered me eventually to management, in a cosy little ground floor bar, where his product was sampled. And where I met two Australian newspaper reprobates—Paul Rigby, cartoonist, and Kerwin Ward, columnist. I was too reserved, too polite, too English, to ask them why they were there. And I had to be suitably evasive when they asked me why I was there. They told me about a kind of loosely knit faculty they had organized called the Lager Lovers' League, which conferred 'Triple L' degrees on worthy graduates.

I call them reprobates because they did their best to get me sloshed.

Management, knowing my interest in Australian beer, and gratified by my praise of Swan, asked me if I proposed to visit Kalgoorlie. I knew where it was, as I had good Australian maps, and had studied them aboard ship. I told them that we intended to travel overland by train to the Eastern States, and that I believed the train passed through Kalgoorlie.

'Oh,' management said, 'you can't just "pass through" Kalgoorlie. Stay a few days. Kalgoorlie's a must. Have a look at our brewery while you're there.'

I discussed this later with the AHA secretary, and he agreed that Kalgoorlie was a 'must'.

When I told our host that we would be leaving for the Eastern States he said, 'You won't like the beer over there after being introduced to Swan.' And he told me a story, which I have heard since in several versions, but which I accepted at the time as truth. Aussies are great leg-pullers, as I soon discovered. He said:

'One of our blokes went over to Sydney once and got a job. Knocks off at lunch time and breasts the nearest bar. "Glass o' beer, please," he says. Barmaid says, "Schooner or middy?" "Same difference," he says. "I don't care what you call it." "New or old?" she says. He says, "Eh? What's the difference?" "One's new, one's old." He says, "Oh. Well, I don't think I'd

18

like it old. She'd be pretty flat. Schooner o' new." Can't believe his eyes when he sees the size of it. Decides to give it a go, anyway. Takes a couple of swallows. "Strewth," he says. "Piss," he says. And he puts it down and walks out. Next day, same time, he's in again. And he's been told that in the East schooners and middies are not the same. "Middy o' beer," he says. "New or old?" says the barmaid. "I'll try the old," he says. He holds it up to the light. "Dark, isn't it?" He takes a couple of swallows. "Strewth," he says. "Piss," he says. And he puts it down and walks out. Next day, same time, he's in again. "Middy o' beer," he says. "New or old?" she says. And she's not very friendly. He says, "Er—half of each. An' give us a swizzle stick, will you?" He stirs it up and takes a couple of swallows. "Strewth," he says. "Piss," he says. And he puts it down and walks out. The barmaid tells the boss about him. "Comes in every day," she says. "Same time. And uses a four-letter word right in front of me." "Right," the boss says. "Next time he comes in, give me a signal. I'll fix him." Sure enough, he's in at lunch time. She spots him, and tells the boss. Big bloke, the boss. He leans over the bar and says to our fellow, "Listen

'You're about to be barred, mate!'

19

you—piss off." Our bloke laughs. He says, "Beauty. I'll have a glass o' stout." '

I gathered the impression that most West Australians are convinced that their beer is not only the best in the country, but is the best in the world. I met only one 'native' who disagreed.

It was late in the afternoon, and the bar I was in was crowded. A couple of drinkers moved apart to 'let me in'. Thinking to improve my status, I asked clearly for 'A pot of the world's best beer.'

The busy barman smiled, and while filling the pot, said, 'You like our beer?'

'Very much,' I said.

He said, 'You know your onions. It *is* the best beer in the world.'

One of the drinkers said, 'It's not, you know.'

'Now you know better than that, Charlie,' the barman said. 'You've been drinking it all your life.'

'It's the best beer in Australia,' Charlie said. 'But it's not the best in the world.'

'All right. What is?'

'Bass,' Charlie said. 'Bass. Burton-on-Trent.'

Another drinker said, 'Bass? You're bloody mad, Charlie. That's English beer.'

'I know,' Charlie said. 'Best in the world.'

There was a chorus of disagreement, including a firm statement that 'Bloody Pommy beer's only fit to wash your socks in.'

But Charlie stuck to his guns. 'I've been in England, an' I'm telling you. Bass draught is the best beer in the world.'

'An' I've been in England, an' I'm tellin' *you*. All Pommy beer is plain bloody lousy.'

Charlie was alone in his opinion. I drank my pot and left before anybody could find out that I was from England.

Later I got to know Australians better. I think that group knew that I was English. I think they would have detected my accent when I asked for a pot of the world's best beer. Aussies take great delight in what they call 'having a shot' at people.

2
Kalgoorlie

'I don't mind drinkin' with the flies, sport—but I'd like a separate glass'

We flew to Kalgoorlie and arrived in darkness, one of us still 'wi' throbbin' heid and stomach sair' from many farewell sessions in Perth with new-found friends. A 'welcome to Kalgoorlie' session on arrival produced many more potential friends, but did nothing to help the 'throbbin' heid' and the 'sair' stomach.

Upholding the honour of England amongst a bunch of hard-drinking Goldfields types, who refused to let me 'shout', was not easy. And although I switched from beer to small whiskys—a small whisky in Australia is called a 'half-Scotch'—I fell behind. There were six or seven lined up in front of me when our host said, 'Stop dragging your feet. Here, I'll make it easy.'

He emptied all the half-Scotches into one glass, and said, 'Now down that and catch up.'

I 'downed' it. For the honour of England. Which, I felt, could not remain much longer unsullied.

My wife rescued me by announcing that we were very tired, and if the gentlemen would excuse us, we would like to go to bed.

The last thing I remember was looking back from the staircase—a beautiful old cedar staircase—and shuddering to see the beginning of another round. I do not remember getting undressed and going to bed.

The bed was comfortable and any reasonable man would have remained in it until breakfast time, or later. But no matter what my condition the night before, or how late the hour of retirement, I always wake early and rise.

A cold shower temporarily relieved my hangover, but I would dearly have loved a dose of my own favourite cure. This is half a glass of vegetable juice—V8 or tomato—with ice, topped up with beer, and a few drops of tabasco gently stirred in. My wife calls it 'Red Eye'. It was unobtainable that morning. In fact, I never found a pub anywhere in Australia where it was available.

The old Colonial-type pub was as deserted and as silent as an English village at midnight. Kalgoorlie's main street, Hannan Street, was equally deserted and silent. I strolled along it, hoping that the fresh morning air would do me some good, and perhaps give me an appetite for breakfast. And I fell in love with a statue, sculpted in bronze.

Statues erected by civic authorities in memory of past great men—and Queen Victoria—are most uninteresting things. But this one was delightfully different. It honoured Irishman Paddy Hannan, the first man to discover payable gold in the area. There he sat, a dried up little bushman with dreams in his eyes, wearing an old bush hat, and offering water to passers by. His 'water-bag' was a drinking fountain, patronized, as I saw later, mainly by children. I became a patron there and then.

The clear cold water, while not as stimulating as my 'Red Eye', took care of my morning-after dehydration.

The Kalgoorlie Brewing Company Pty Ltd is a subsidiary of the Swan Brewery Company Ltd, but the beer is different. Discussing it in various Kalgoorlie-Boulder pubs—not all thirty-three of them—I was given four main reasons why Hannan's Lager is, in the opinion of those who drink it, superior to Swan.

Drinker Number One: 'It's the water, see. We get our water from Mundaring Weir, see. She's better than the Canning Dam. Perth gets Canning water, an' they supplement it with bore water, see.'

Drinker Number Two: 'Aw, it's the water. We get water from Mundaring, an' she's got fluoride in her. It's the fluoride that makes the difference, mate.'

Drinker Number Three: 'The water, mate. Because of the long pipeline, see. All the shit an' stuff sticks to the sides of the pipes, an' in the pumping stations, see. When it comes out this end, it's as pure as maiden's water.'

Drinker Number Four: 'We got a better bloody brewer, that's why. Always have had.'

The brewer, when I met him, laughed at theories one, two and three, and modestly refrained from comment on theory four. He merely said that if he didn't make beer that tasted the same as it's always tasted, the mob would throw him down the nearest bloody old mine shaft.

He had a relatively small brewery, but big enough to keep the Goldfields pubs supplied. And I was impressed by its cleanliness. And also by the quality of the product, sampled at the staff bar—free for staff during their tea breaks. I saw nobody drinking tea.

Our host and a couple of villains offered to take me out to the Sunday afternoon Two-up School.

'Oh?' I said, wondering what sort of a Sunday school would be called 'Two-up'.

The Law was present at the time. The Law said solemnly, 'There's no Two-up in Kalgoorlie.'

'Aw, that's right—we forgot. Well anyway, we'll pick you up after dinner on Sunday.'

Sunday lunch was called dinner. The pubs closed, to re-open at three o'clock. This Sunday 'dinner' was Ye Olde Englishe— soup, roast lamb and mint sauce, or roast beef and horseradish sauce, or roast pork and apple sauce, and 'sweets'. I learnt that this menu provided enough left-overs for Sunday night's 'tea'.

After a few glasses of Hannan's Lager—even though a glass is only five ounces—and a three-course meal, the sensible thing to do would be to sleep for a couple of hours, instead of careering around looking for what the Law said did not exist.

My host said, 'You'll have to slide in under the wheel. The lock's buggered on the near-side door.'

One of the two men in the back said, 'We're puttin' you in as guest spinner. We'll back you with ten bucks each.'

Not understanding a word of this, I remained silent. My host, whom everybody called 'Lurky', drove us up Hannan Street and out into the bush. When I asked him about the strange trees with their narrow, barkless trunks, almost the colour of the reddish sandy soil, he told me they were called salmon gums.

He drove into an area relatively clear of the gums, and parked among many other vehicles that were there.

I had a lot of questions on my mind, but confined myself to voicing only one of them.

'The school is here?' I asked.

'Yeah,' he said. 'Been here for years.'

We got out, and he led the way to the other side of the clearing. And there I discovered the difference between a Two-up School and a Sunday School. This was a gambling school. I was very relieved. I had not been looking forward to visiting a Sunday School.

There were many men squatting on their heels around a wide circle of smooth, hard-packed earth. We stood on one side of the circle, behind some of them.

'Ever been to a Two-up School before?' Lurky asked.

I said I had not. I refrained from mentioning my thoughts about Sunday Schools.

'You'll soon cotton on,' he said.

I 'cottoned on' when he explained the simple rules of the game, and told me what a 'ring keeper' was, and what a 'kip' was, and what a 'spinner' was.

'Reckon you can spin 'em?' he said.

24

I told him I thought I could. The technique seemed to be to turn the wrist slightly but sharply just as the coins were leaving the 'kip'.

'That's the ticket,' he said. 'I'll have a word with the keeper.'

The ring keeper was a tall, hard, tough-looking fellow, in faded blue overalls. Lurky had a word with him. He nodded, and Lurky rejoined us.

After two more spinners had 'spun out', the keeper announced, 'We've got a guest spinner.'

'Come on,' Lurky said.

He led me into the ring, and gave the keeper three ten-dollar notes.

'All yours,' he said to me, and left the ring.

The keeper gave me the kip, after ensuring that all bets were covered. He then threw down a handful of pennies, their 'tails' marked with broad white enamel crosses.

I selected two, and placed them on the kip. The keeper put the remainder in his pocket and said, 'Come in, spinner.'

I did not do too badly. The pennies didn't actually spin, but they turned over a few times in the air, before falling to the hard earth, bouncing, and settling down.

'Heads,' the keeper called.

I looked to my three sponsors for instructions. 'Send 'em up again,' they told me.

I selected two more from the handful thrown down. The keeper said, 'Centre set. All set on the side?' Then he nodded to me. I threw them up, and watched them turning slowly in the sun, and falling to earth.

'Heads,' said the keeper.

'Go again,' said my sponsors. And I threw 'heads' for the third time.

I thought that ought to be enough. The winnings were substantial. But my sponsors called, 'Let it ride.'

Well, it was their money. But I hated to lose it for them. They took some time getting 'set'.

Two more pennies spun in the sun. When they came down, one showed a head, and the other rolled around the ring, punters blowing at it. It curled over slowly, and showed its white-crossed tail.

'Ones,' said the keeper.

I threw them up again. They bounced again, rolled again, and the keeper called 'ones' again.

I was nervous. I was sure they would show tails the next time. But—'Heads' the keeper called.

Before I could ask for further instructions, my sponsors invaded the ring, gave the keeper the original stake plus another ten dollars, and with pushes and shoves propelled me out.

'What—what—what?' I said.

'Out,' they said. 'Out to the car. Come on, move—before these tail-betters kill you.'

We were followed by curses in many languages, but mainly in Australian and Yugoslav. I understood the unprintable Australian, but not the others.

Back at the pub, in time for the afternoon 'session', my sponsors divided up the loot, and over my protests insisted on splitting it four ways.

'You won it for us,' they said.

But of course I must have been dreaming. 'There's no Two-up in Kalgoorlie,' the Law had said. And the Law should know.

I was sorry to leave Kalgoorlie. Like Hannan's Lager, it was 'different'.

My wife says the kind of influenza she contracted there was also different. She was very sick the morning Lurky drove us to the station to board the east-bound train. When we thanked him for his hospitality and kindness, he just said 'Forget it' and walked back to his car, whose door lock was still 'buggered on the near side'.

3
South Australia

'What d'you have to do to get a drink round here?'

Crossing the Nullarbor Plain by train, my wife's spirits were far from strong, but the steward was very attentive, and saw to it that she was well provided for. The train was the best of all trains I have travelled in. Almost silent when running, with cabin chairs a pleasure to sit in, and beds a pleasure to sleep in, first class bar and dining-room service, good and varied food, it is a credit to the Australian Commonwealth Railways. Called the 'Indian-Pacific', it provides an unbroken journey across the big island continent, from Perth on the Indian Ocean to Sydney on the Pacific.

Sitting on the platform at Port Pirie, in South Australia, waiting for a local train to take us down to Adelaide, my wife looked even more dejected than she had outside customs at Fremantle. She was coughing and sneezing and her temperature was high. However, the management and staff of the South Australia Hotel called a doctor. He prescribed suitable medication, and advised a week in bed with 'plenty of liquids'.

She discovered Cooper's Ale. And I was free to go out and do battle.

I learnt later—in Sydney—that West Australians are called 'sandgropers', and South Australians are 'crow-eaters'. This latter libellous appellation, I was informed, derives from the days when South Australia was the poorest State in the Commonwealth.

'They don't eat crows now,' my informant told me. 'They just shoot 'em and let 'em rot. When they can sneak up close to 'em. Crows are cunning bastards.'

'We have them in England, too,' I said. 'We call them "carrion crows". To distinguish them from rooks.'

'We got plenty bloody rooks, too,' he said. 'The bastard who runs this pub is one of 'em.'

He also said that Adelaide was known as the City of Churches, the Home of Wowsers, and was 'well laid out, because it's dead'. He said, 'It's the only cemetery in Australia that's lit up at night.'

I gathered that he didn't like Adelaide very much. I liked it. I found it a very pleasant and spacious city, surrounded by parks and gardens, and inhabited by friendly and hospitable people.

My wife agrees with me about the friendly and hospitable people. She says the management and staff of our hotel couldn't have been friendlier or more hospitable.

On foot, and by taxi, I saw most of the city. And sampling the local product, called West End, I remarked to one of my casual acquaintances and temporary sampling partners, how much I liked his city.

'She's a bastard in the summer,' he said. 'Hottest capital city in the world. Holds the record—a hundred an' bloody eighteen plus.'

I agreed that that was hot.

'They built her in the wrong place,' he said. 'Same as Brisbane. Way to buggery inland. Adelaide should be down at Victor Harbor.'

The man on the other side of him said, 'Balls. If you was around here in sailing-ship days, lookin' for a good place to camp, what'd be the first two things you'd check up on?'

'Women an' grog.'

'All right, I'll give you that. What'd be the *second* two things you'd check up on?'

'I'll bite. What?'

'Safe anchorage an' fresh water, that's what. She was safe up here in the Gulf, an' there was water in the Torrens. Same goes for Brisbane. They bloody *had* to go up the river, to find fresh water.'

'Yeah, all right. I'll admit you can't make grog without fresh water.'

And so my education progressed. But I could not resist airing some of my previously acquired knowledge. I asked them, 'Do you know the origin of that word grog?'

They said they did not.

'Admiral Edward Vernon, RN, always wore a grogram cloak in foul weather. He was known as "Old Grog". He is remembered for issuing orders, in 1740, that the sailors' rum should be diluted with water.'

My nearest neighbour said, 'Yeah? The old bastard.'

The other one said, 'All Pommies are bastards. You're from Melbourne, aren't you?'

I said, 'Er—well—'

'Thought you was,' he said. 'Can tell by the way you talk.'

It was time for me to leave. And as it was not my 'shout', I drank the last inch of West End in my 'butcher', thanked them politely for their company, and went elsewhere.

That word butcher intrigued me when I first encountered it. It is peculiar to South Australia, when applied to a glass of beer. Making enquiries, I was told several stories allegedly explaining its origin, but I like to believe this one:

There was at one time a pub near the abattoirs. Employees were accustomed to visit it in their lunch hour, and because of the Australian custom of 'shouting', and the limited time available, they preferred to drink small beers. Six-ounce glasses were the smallest the publican had, and so a six-ounce glass became known as a butcher.

During my stay there I found butchers to be a popular container size in Adelaide. Others available were ponies, four ounces; schooners, nine ounces; and pints. But a pint, which is by definition twenty ounces, is not so in South Australian pubs. For some strange reason, known only to South Aussies, a pint of beer is fifteen ounces.

Here I would like to suggest to the Australian Hotels Association, that in the interests of simplicity and to avoid confusion, container sizes, and their nomenclature, should be standardized throughout the continent. No doubt this idea, because of the obvious need for it, has been proposed before, and the AHA has had good and cogent reasons for rejecting it. But I will suggest it anyway, since I would like to know what those good and cogent reasons are. The present system must be as irrational and confusing to Australian interstate travellers as it was for me.

Before continuing this saga of my liver-wrecking wanderings, I see here in my notes a quotation attributed to one John Norton, who, I presume, was an Australian of the Victorian era, and something of a 'stirrer'. I got it from a delightful and hilarious calendar which I saw hanging in an Adelaide pub. It was called the 'Down Under Calendar'. The quotation: 'Everyone knows quite well what the word wowser really means —a single, simple word, that does at once describe, deride, and denounce that numerous, noxious, pestilential, puritanical kill-joy push—the whole blasphemous, wire-whiskered brood.'

I am pleased to say that I met none of that 'puritanical kill-joy push' in Adelaide. I met Bill Cooper instead, and Bill could hardly be called a 'wowser'. He makes, amongst other beverages, Cooper's Ale, which at the time of my visit was the only true ale being made commercially in Australia.

His brewery has been a family-owned business for many years. A tall, friendly, gregarious, easy-to-get-on-with young fellow, he gave me a conducted tour, and readily answered my questions.

His ale is brewed, old English style, in oak puncheons, each

30

of 108 gallons capacity. Lying on their sides, with a valve on top, their very appearance makes a man thirsty. When fermentation is complete, the contents are refined with isinglass, and bottled. A little more sugar and yeast is added, but less sugar than the yeast needs. A second fermentation then takes place in the bottles, and the surplus yeast dies and becomes a sediment. This sediment remains in the bottle, adhering to the bottom and sides.

'Dead yeast,' he told me. 'Nourishing. Very edible. Strain it through your teeth.'

Because of this final 'brewed in the bottle' process there is no draught Cooper's Ale. And that is why, particularly in South Australia, one may see bottles on bar counters when brewery employees are *not* on strike.

I like Cooper's Ale. It is rich, and malty, and flavoursome—very different from a lager.

Nevertheless, I saw, in one city bar, a man with a bottle of Danish Tuborg in front of him. My Australian companion was horrified.

'What are you drinking that stuff for, mate?' he said. 'What's wrong with West End?'

'Danish beer,' the man said, 'is the best beer in the world.'

We ignored the Philistine, and discussed West End, which we were drinking.

'The first time I struck West End,' my companion said, 'was in Broken Hill. You been up there?'

'No,' I said.

'They go for West End in the Hill. She's in New South, but she's really a South Aus. town. Always has been. Anyway, the time I'm talking about was about—aw—thirty-five years ago. I'm coming in from Nyngan way—bastard of a road, too—and I've got a grog salesman with me. Wine and spirit bloke. His car had broken down, and he left it in Nyngan, and put the bite on me for a lift. Bloke from Scotland, he was. I could hardly understand him. Said he came from Aberdeen. "The Top o' the World," he called it. He'd been to the Hill before. I hadn't. It was dark when we got in, but they gave us a couple

31

of rooms at the Grand, and I flaked out. In the morning, about seven, when the girl brought the tea in, Scotty follows her. He's got a bottle of Scotch in his hand. "A wee dram," he says, "to put in yeer mornin' tea." I told him to get lost. It was too early. "You're a bluidy Sassenach," he says. Whatever that is.'

'He was calling you an Englishman,' I said.

'Was he? I should have clocked him. Oh, sorry. No offence?'

'No offence.'

'Goodo. Well, he went out with his bottle, and I saw him again at breakfast. Gees, he could eat porridge. He asked me what I planned to do that day. I told him first of all I was going to drive around and have a look at the place. He said he'd come with me and show me around, and I could drop him off at his first call. I forget the name of the pub now, but it was an old two-storey wooden pub, with a balcony over the footpath, held up by wooden posts on the kerb. There are still a few like it about. Well, this Scotty asked me to drive up slowly and give one of the posts a bit of a nudge with my bumper bar. I didn't want to be in that, but he said it was only for a bit of fun. He said he knew the licensee. Well, my brakes weren't too good at the time, and I gave the post a bigger nudge than I intended to. The whole pub shook. Well, you should have heard the language from inside. I was only a young bloke then, and I heard words I never even heard later when I was in the Army. And out the door charges about two tons of female, roaring, and bellowing, and waving two fists the size of legs of mutton. Scotty's laughing his head off. When she sees him, she quietens down a bit. She says, "Oh it's you, is it, you filthy drunken pox-ridden hoor of an old Scotch bastard." He says, "Good mornin', Annie." "I'll give you good mornin'," she says. "I'll kick your arse right up through your guts until it's hangin' out of your mouth. Which is where it oughta be anyway," she says. "Come in," she says, "an' wet your whistle. An' bring the boy with you —he's better lookin' than you are." I said it was too early for me, I'd just had breakfast. She said, "What's that got to do with it? Get outa there before I pull the ears off you an' hang 'em up for bloody fly traps." She would have done, too. Or at least she could have. So I went in with them. Good introduction to West End beer, eh?'

'A very good introduction,' I said. 'Was it good beer then, too?'

'Just as good then as it is now,' he said. 'The best in the world.'

Had I denied this statement perhaps my ears would now be hanging up for fly traps. So I merely asked him why, in his opinion, it was the best beer in the world.

'Because of the barley,' he said. 'You can't make good beer without good barley. And, as you know, South Australia grows the world's best barley.'

I didn't know that. 'Is that so?' I said.

'Bloody oath. We grow the world's best barley. An' we get the world's best sugar—from Queensland—an' the world's best hops—from Tasmania. A man would be a pretty poor sort of a brewer if he couldn't make the world's best beer out of that lot, wouldn't he?'

'He would indeed. But what about that other South Australian beer? Southwark. Isn't that made from the world's best barley and sugar and hops?'

'Course it is. They don't make Southwark draught, but Southwark Bitter is the best *bottled* beer you can get anywhere. I know. I've tried 'em all.'

'And what is your opinion of Cooper's?'

'Cooper's?' he said. 'Too heavy for me—except in the winter. Mind you, a lot of blokes like it, summer *and* winter. I reckon it's just a matter of getting used to it. I'll stick to West End draught and Southwark Bitter.'

Adelaide's West End and Southwark breweries—one in the city, and the other a sprawling establishment on the road to Port Adelaide—are under one management, the South Australian Brewing Company. The Southwark brewery is concerned mainly with bottles and cans.

Discussing these containers in a pub in Hindley Street, after paying my respects to SABC management nearby, an interesting argument developed following my question, 'What makes the best container for beer—glass or metal?'

I had entered the public bar and ordered a butcher. One of two men alongside me said, 'You can't drink with the flies, mate. Have one with us.'

I thanked them, and they introduced themselves as Kevin and Derek. I told them my name was James, and they said, 'Glad to know you, Jim.'

All Australians called me Jim when they discovered my name was James. Nobody does that in England.

Well, I asked my question, and was told that as long as it was good beer they 'didn't give a bugger' what it was wrapped in.

'The only thing is,' Kevin said, 'cans are more convenient to take home. They stack better in the fridge.'

Derek said, 'They were all right when you could punch a couple o' small holes in the top. What'd they want to go an' put those ring-pull things on top for? Bloody things should never have been invented. The hole's too big. Now, sometimes you don't want a whole can, do you?'

'I've never noticed you leaving any dregs in one.'

'That's because you've never seen me before breakfast,' Derek said, arguing on—both of them ignoring me. 'Suppose you have a hangover, see. There's nothing better than a glass of the old icy cold before breakfast. An' you put what's left in the fridge, an' what happens? It goes flat, that's what happens.'

'Wouldn't the old-style cans do that?'

'Where have you been all your life? With the old-style cans you just punch little holes, see. About as wide as a match. Use a nail if you can't find a can opener. Half a can'll keep for a couple of days then.'

'Well, why don't you leave the ring-pull alone, an' just punch a couple of little holes, if you want a small charge before breakfast?'

'You would think of that. Anyway, all cans should be declared illegal.'

'Why?'

34

'Litter. Pollution. That's why. What do you do with the empties? Suppose we all drank beer from cans. Wouldn't be long before there's not a square foot of dirt without a can on it. How would you go walking over empty cans all the time? Wouldn't be enough doctors in the country to mend all the broken legs an' ankles.'

'So what's your answer?'

'Bottles, mate. Returnable bottles. And don't forget you can put half a bottle in the fridge with a plastic top on it, an' she'll keep for a long time. Returnable bottles.'

'Returnable where?'

'To the pubs, where else? Take in a dozen empties, an' have a few slugs of draught on the strength of 'em.'

'The publicans wouldn't like that.'

'Too bloody bad. What do we do with our empties now? Boy Scouts an' Girl Guides come around my place an' collect 'em. Do you think it's right to have little Boy Scouts an' Girl Guides collecting bottles an' smellin' like a brewery from all the dregs they spill over themselves? Only bottles, mind you. They leave me stuck with the cans. Bottles ought to be returnable to the pubs. An' cans ought to be declared illegal.'

Kevin said, 'Matter for the publicans to work out with the brewery. An' you'd have Buckley's chance of gettin' them to agree. Anyway, would you want returnable bottles in all States?'

'Yeah. All bloody States. Returnable bottles, an' no cans.'

'There'd be problems.'

'What problems?'

'All bloody breweries export bottled beer to all bloody States, that's what problems. Now you take Guinness Stout. Made here under licence, right?'

'Right.'

'Right. An' exported to all other States. You work out how much it's gunna cost to return all the empties to Adelaide.'

'Gawd, no wonder you're not married. No woman'd have you. You got no bloody brains. What's the difference between a stout bottle an' a beer bottle? Go on, tell me.'

'All right, all right. Returnable bottles, an' no cans.'

'Yeah. Anyway, who drinks Guinness?'

'A lot of people drink Guinness. If they didn't, why would our mob be makin' it—answer me that.'

'I never saw anybody drinkin' it. Cooper's is the best stout.'

'I've never seen you drinkin' it. Listen Jim. Are you gunna stand there all bloody day lettin' us die of thirst? Hit the kick.'

It was my turn to 'shout', so I 'hit the kick'. And shortly afterwards it was time to 'hit the trail'.

My wife, still far from well, wanted to go on to Sydney, where she had friends. I told her I would first like to visit Victoria and Tasmania, then Queensland, leaving the more populous State of New South Wales until last.

She said she would go to Sydney and wait for me. She said she'd done enough travelling, and anyway there was no pleasure in 'sitting around and walking about' while I was out 'boozing' all the time.

'I am not boozing,' I told her. 'I am working. The firm wants a comprehensive report.'

'By the time you finish,' she said, 'you'll be in no condition to write it. Carry on with your disreputable pub crawl around Australia, and I'll go to Sydney and wait for you.'

She got her way, as she usually does, and I reluctantly put her on a 'plane. I caught another aircraft for Melbourne.

'Anyway, you're supposed to use champagne'

4
Victoria

'Of course, the best counter lunches are in Melbourne'

My friend Jock Currie has written a long narrative verse, set in Melbourne, which he has entitled 'Brown's Allergy'. Snowy Brown was a young bank clerk who 'suffered from a rather sad affliction—the sight of female flesh caused him to blush'. Shapely knees in a suburban train, shapely forms clad only in bikinis on a beach, and other displays of parts of the female form divine, sent his face fiery red. Consequently his only friends were men. And then one day, finding the public bar in Young and Jackson's pub overcrowded, he went into the saloon bar and 'found that he was face to face with Chloe'.

Chloe is a nude, known all over Australia as I was to discover, and when first painted she disgusted and horrified all wire-whiskered 'wowsers', of whom there appear to have been many at the time. She had an instantaneous and violent effect on Snowy Brown:

> *His face and neck at once turned blazing red;*
> *It seemed to burn him with a fiery heat;*

He threw away his glass, and turned and fled
Out through the door, and into Flinders Street.

He caused havoc. Squealing brakes, bumper to bumper crashes, cars 'banking right up Swanston Street'—'Because they thought all traffic lights were red'.

Snowy was arrested. 'They hauled him up before the local beak.' The 'beak' was sympathetic. He suggested that Snowy should 'spend a year or two in Coober Pedy; Up there it matters not how much you glow'. But, as Jock writes, 'While there are no traffic lights on bush tracks, some ladies in that region wear no clothes.'

> *So if some night when you are quietly strolling,*
> *And gazing at the sun's last afterglow,*
> *A crimson banner o'er the sky comes rolling,*
> *Just pause a while and spare a thought for Snow.*
> *It's likely that it comes from Coober Pedy,*
> *That South Australian opal centre where*
> *Young Snowy with a gin is going steady,*
> *And wastes his blushes on the desert air.*

When I met Chloe it was in late winter. Australian winter, but that day very reminiscent of an English summer. Melbourne, I was told, sometimes gets a 'beautiful day' in winter, but frequently 'she can be a bastard'.

I was pub crawling around the city, gathering impressions and information, and making notes on overheard conversations. Shameless eavesdropping, no doubt, and of no possible interest to my directors, but the Australian accent, idiom, and slang, so new to me, interested me very much. And I salved my conscience by at least sampling the local product and obtaining consumer opinions.

On this day I was walking around minus my jacket, and went into a bar somewhere on the edge of the city to sample a glass of Carlton, 'from the tap'.

I had already learnt Melbourne glass sizes and nomenclature, so different from Adelaide. One asks for a four ounce, a small beer, or a pot. There are no butchers. A request for a small beer produces seven ounces, and for a pot ten.

I asked for a small Carlton, sipped it, and listened in to a story of great trouble.

A middle-aged to elderly lady, big and fat and with a moustache, and with a voice like an English carrion crow, was talking with a man of about her own age who wore overalls, and a paint-stained cotton beret.

The lady was saying, 'He said he only had four pots. They musta been chamber pots, I reckon. Gawd, he was a mess. I had to hold him up under the shower.'

'What was he doing at your place?'

'He wasn't at my place. I wouldn't have him in my place. I was at his place, see, keepin' his wife company while he went to this bucks' barbecue.'

'How did he get home?'

'Gawd knows. He just crashed in the door an' fell flat on his puss. I reckon a couple o' blokes musta brought him home an' threw him in. Talk about a mess. He was perk from his eyebrows to his bloody toenails.'

'And you undressed him an' put him in the shower?'

'Undress him? That'll be the day. I bunged him in clothes an' all. Gees he stank. Told him to get into his pyjamas an' go to bed. Know what he said?'

'No. what?'

'He said he'd go to bed if I'd go with him. Imagine me with him. I told him, I said, I wouldn't have that big belly o' yours within four feet o' me. Besides, I said, I've got a husband at home'd make two of you.'

'What was his wife doing?'

'Goin' crook on me because she reckoned I ruined his best strides by puttin' him under the shower with 'em on. What did she expect me to do, take 'em orf? Know what she said?'

'No. What?'

'She said she wouldn't put it past me, she said. Me? With him? Can you imagine it?'

'No,' he said.

39

Neither could I. There are limits to a man's imagination. But I wondered whether this unknown had made a mess of himself on too much Carlton or Courage.

They are attractive lagers, brewed by nice people. One of these nice people at the Carlton & United Brewery gave me a tie with little gold CUBs discreetly scattered over it. I didn't wear it in Melbourne, because I discovered an undeclared war between Carlton and Courage and wished to remain neutral.

One of the nice people at Courage gave me a gleaming, silver-coloured metallic rooster. I still have it. It has now turned into a Rhode Island Red.

To return to Chloe. After jotting down the conversation between the lady and the painter, I wandered further. I discarded my tie and put it in my pocket. Finding myself in the long straight street called Elizabeth, I walked down it.

Melbourne streets are straight and parallel, as the streets in Adelaide are. One cannot become lost.

Towards the lower end of this one, I saw a pub called the London. How could I pass by a hostelry that bore that nostalgic name? I went in the main entrance and along a narrow passage which opened into a large, crowded bar.

Three barmaids were serving, two young and one matronly. I found a small space, and wedged myself in. The barmaids ignored me. I waited patiently for some time, then rapped on the bar with a coin. They still ignored me. I rapped more vigorously.

Finally the matronly type approached me, and stood in front of me, saying nothing.

I said, 'I would like a small beer, please.'

She said, 'You're not wearing a tie.'

'I beg your pardon?'

'You're not wearing a tie. I can't serve you.'

'You can't serve me? In a bar?'

'The *public* bar,' she said, as though referring to some downstairs convenience, 'is next door.'

'But—'

40

She interrupted firmly. 'I can't serve you. It's a rule of the house.'

All I could think of, in reply, was, 'The house must have a financial interest in the rag trade.'

She walked away from me to serve somebody else more suitably attired for the privilege of being permitted to buy beer, and I walked out, feeling many disapproving eyes boring small holes in my back.

So much, I thought, for Australian non-conformity. The classless society. The casual attitude to life. I knew of no bar in London where I would be refused service for not wearing a tie.

Angry and humiliated, I walked along Flinders Street to its intersection with Swanston Street. Waiting for the traffic lights to change, I saw that I was standing outside another hotel, Young and Jackson's. Very well, I said to myself, I shall enter the saloon bar here. I shall *demand* a small beer. If I am refused service for not wearing a tie, I shall take my tie from my pocket, and put it on. Then, when the beer is pulled for me, I shall take my tie off again, drink the beer, say 'good afternoon' and walk out.

I entered. There was room at the bar. I breasted it and said, truculently, 'A small beer.' I did not say please.

The barmaid said, 'One small beer coming up.'

My truculence vanished. My natural courtesy returned. I thanked the barmaid, and told her how I had been refused service in the saloon bar of the London.

She laughed and said, 'They're like that round there.'

Relaxing, and drinking my lager, I turned to survey my surroundings. And there was Chloe.

Chloe is a buxom wench. She stands, in frontal nudity, with her head turned demurely aside. It is easy to understand the antipathy she aroused in the barren breasts of Queen Victoria's devout wowsers. While I was having a good look at her, I heard a male voice from somewhere near my shoulder. 'Not bad, is she?'

41

'*Y'don't have to wear a tie in here . . .*'

I turned. There were three men, none of them wearing ties, and all three of them smiling broadly.

'Pervin' on old Chloe, eh?' one said. 'Bet it's the first time you've seen her.'

'Er—yes,' I said. 'As a matter of fact it is.'

The one nearest me said, 'I got another bet. I'm willing to bet you're English.'

'Er—yes. As a matter of fact I am. But how did you know?'

'Knew it as soon as you opened your mouth,' he said. 'I'm English meself, you know.'

His accent was unadulterated Australian. An elderly, dried up little chap of about eight or nine stone, there was a suggestion of a twinkle in his sunken, watery, little blue eyes. He was surely pulling my leg. I played along.

'Is that so?' I said. 'When did you come out?'

One of the others said, 'In time for the Eureka Stockade.'

The old chap said, 'I didn't. I came here in 1899. In time for Federation.'

'You'd have been about fifty years old then, wouldn't yer?'

'I was *two* years old. You wasn't even born then, you young squirt. You're only about fifty now.'

42

He turned to me. 'I was born in England, see. My old man was a carpenter. Bloody good one, too. A tradesman. Not like these bums we got here now. Call 'emselves tradesmen? They couldn't build a decent dunny. Without a bit o' putty an' plastic wood, they'd be lost. Jest have a look at their joints.'

'Have a look at your own. You creak like a rusty gate. You need oilin'.'

'Shut up. I'm talkin' to a gentleman. You wouldn't know what that is. May I ask how long you have been in Australia?'

'Only a few weeks,' I told him.

'That's long enough to form an opinion. What do you think of our beer?'

'I think it's very good.'

'Only the best in the world,' one of the others said. 'Which one do you like best—Carlton or Courage?'

'Well, I think I prefer Courage.'

'Why?'

'Because of its taste. It's a little more bitter than Carlton, and I prefer a bitter beer.'

'She's all right now,' his friend said. 'She started off a good brew, an' then she went lousy. But she came good again. What I like about it is she keeps the Carlton mob on their toes, see. Carlton sends out a crook batch, an' we can tell 'em to shove it, an' we drink Courage. We got a choice, see? Bloody near time too.'

The other said, 'Good name, Courage. You need courage to drink the stuff. Bloody awful. I'll stick to Carlton.'

I said, 'Well, the difference is very slight, actually. I have no complaints about either one.'

'Yeah, but you come from England. That's gin's piss country. Any kind o' beer'd be better than that English muck. Although I got to admit we got some crook beer in Australia, too. Like up in New South bloody Wales. Tooth's an' Toohey's an' Miller's. Even a thirsty horse wouldn't drink it.'

'Aw, Miller's is not bad,' his friend said.

'Don't gimme that. None of it's any good. Did you try that Toohey's urine when you was up there?'

43

'I tried 'em all—new an' old an' fifty fifty an' what have you. I reckoned Miller's was the best of a bad lot. Funny thing about Miller's though. It goes to your legs. Two pots an' your legs go wobbly—two middies, I mean. Why do they call 'em middies?'

'I dunno. S'pose because they're in the middle—halfway between a pint an' sweet Fanny Adams.'

'All right. Ask a silly question an' you get a silly answer. Where are you stayin', choom?'

'I am staying at Brighton,' I said.

'Down at Siera's?'

'Er—yes.'

'Good bloke, that feller. Runs a good pub. Did you know he was one o' the main blokes responsible for bringin' Courage into Australia?'

'He oughta be castrated,' his friend said.

'Bit too late now. He's got about nine kids.'

The old chap, who had been silent during this acrimonious debate, suddenly said, 'I'm hungry.'

'Aw, you're always bloody hungry. Dunno where you put it. You're as skinny as a half-starved kangaroo dog pup.'

'That's why I'm hungry,' the old fellow said. Then to me, 'You had your lunch yet?'

'No,' I said. 'Not yet.'

'Can't go wrong havin' it here. Good counter lunch.'

One of the others said, 'That's another thing you can't get up in New South—a decent counter lunch.'

I had a 'decent counter lunch' with them. They told me counter lunches were invented in Victoria.

'Some bloke bunged it on as bait. To get customers away from his opposition, see. Then every publican got into the act. Bigger an' better counter lunches, see, gettin' bigger an' better all the time. They winge about the cost—reckon they're doin' dough—but they make plenty out o' grog. An' we aren't complainin', are we?'

Victorian counter lunches are indeed 'bigger and better'. And astonishingly cheap. I also discovered evening meals served in bars, called, to my delight, 'counter tea'.

The most memorable lunch I had during my Victorian fact-finding mission was in the staff dining-room, off the staff bar, at the Courage brewery. I had to make a complete tour of Courage, since it was high on my directors' list of priorities.

'As far as we know,' the Chairman had told me, 'they operate only in the State of Victoria. And Victoria, as you see from the map, is a very small State by Australian standards. Geographically speaking. But it is inhabited. Its population seems to be less than half that of London. Nevertheless, Australians drink a lot of beer—approximately three hundred million gallons per annum. Which means that, on a population basis, Victorians probably consume nearly a hundred million gallons. Quite a good market. Courage has invested a lot of capital in it. Find out all you can. How have they adapted to Australian conditions? Their sources of supply—malt, hops, sugar, yeast. Try to get a breakdown on production costs. Make a survey of their retail outlets. What percentage of the market do they have? Their plans, if any, for expanding into other States. Facts and figures, my boy. But for heaven's sake don't let them suspect you are working for us.'

Industrial espionage. I went to the brewery as a spy. And I left it feeling very guilty. My letter of introduction from a Very High Personage got me almost royal treatment.

The Courage team in Australia, from management down, is young and enthusiastic, friendly and gregarious, and impressively efficient. As is their brewery. It is fully automated. The whole brewing process, from initial fermentation to final product, is controlled by just two men. The plant occupies a large area of perfectly flat land, and throughout its length and breadth it never rises above one storey. I got plenty of exercise on my tour.

The head brewer, a young Englishman, conducted me. He answered my questions freely, and without hesitation. As did management, and the PR man.

After the tour we adjourned to the staff bar for refreshment, and I was sorely in need. I froze my throat and numbed my palate by drinking the first pot too quickly.

'That,' said the brewer proudly, 'was obviously to your liking.'

'I would like it better,' I said, 'if it were not so damn cold.'

'Yes. Australians like it half frozen. It took me some time to get used to it when I first came out here. But when in Rome, you know? Apart from that, how does it appeal to you?'

'It's a very good lager,' I said.

'Have you tried Carlton?'

'Yes.'

'Any difference?'

'A little. Yours is slightly more bitter, I think.'

'You have a discerning palate. One of my major early frustrations was the necessity to produce a lager identical with Carlton.'

'Oh? Why?'

'Because when we commenced operations here, all Victorians were confirmed Carlton drinkers. Anything that didn't taste the same as Carlton was, in their opinion, undrinkable. I was full of ideas. I wanted to give them something different. I could see no point in trying to compete with Carlton by marketing an identical product. But they're a stubborn lot, these Aussies. Reactionary. They dislike change.'

I told him about the man in Western Australia who said that in his opinion the best beer in the world was Bass. Burton-on-Trent.

He was very pleased. He said, 'Did he really? Was he an Australian?'

'Yes.'

'Well, there's hope yet. I used to work for them.'

Then I told him about the man in Adelaide who liked Tuborg.

'Bloody beer snobs,' he said. 'Trying to impress other people by drinking high-priced imported beers no better than their own. In fact, not as good. Look, you probably don't know the difference between export lager and lager for home consump-

46

tion, but there *is* a difference. There has to be. Suppose we were to export, from Australia to England, a keg of beer brewed here. Identical, say, with Bass. By the time it arrived, it would be unfit to drink. Beer, without protective additives, won't travel. At least, it won't travel halfway around the world.'

'You on your hobby horse again?' a voice said.

It was lunch time. The bar was filling up. Introductions all round, conversation general, and the pots and small beers flowing. Then to tables, spotlessly arrayed, with a fine assortment of food superbly cooked, and cool red and chilled white wines.

By the time I left that brewery, burdened with my silver rooster, half-a-dozen drinking mugs, bar cloths, and a stack of literature, I was awash. Afloat. But my wife was safe in Sydney, and I was safe from reprimands.

Siera's pub at Brighton provided comfortable rest and refuge. As it seems to have done for quite a long time. When I was there it was called the Brighton Club Hotel, but was at one time known as the Brighton Inn, when it nestled in a setting far different from today's urban surroundings.

Jock Currie wrote to me recently to say that Siera has sold out to a brewery. He doesn't say which one. There are many 'tied houses' in Australia. Jock, whom I met in one of them, said, when I deplored the situation, that he 'couldn't care less'. He said he was happy to drink either Carlton or Courage, and he was not interested in the ownership of the dispensaries. Just so long as there were enough of them, and they kept the nectar flowing, he would be happy.

I said, 'They tell me Australia produces the best beer in the world.'

'If it isn't,' he said, 'I've never tasted better. Not even during my seventeen years in the Navy, boozin' in many ports.'

'RN?' I asked him.

'RN and RAN. I swallowed the anchor in Australia and I'm never going back.'

'Not even to Scotland?'

'Who wants to live in bluidy Scotland?' he said. 'The beer's

47

as bad there as it is in England, if not worse. I'm stayin' right here. I'd advise you to do the same.'

'Why?'

'It's a better world. The climate's better, the beer's better, and the people are better.'

'I agree about the climate and the beer. But the people—how does one get to know and understand them?'

'That's easy,' Jock said. 'If you can't whack 'em, join 'em.'

'Is that what you did?'

'Aye. Couldna stand 'em at first. Skitin' about their beer, and their weather, and their beaches. Couldna stand 'em.'

'What made you change your opinion?'

'I got to thinkin' one night that maybe they had something. Their beer was too bloody cold, their weather was too bloody hot, but after a few months I couldna stand the thought of goin' back to warm beer and cold weather. And I got to like their footy.'

'Oh? They play soccer here?'

'Soccer?' he said. 'Who's talkin' about soccer? I'm talkin' about football.'

I said, 'So am I. Rangers versus Celtic on New Year's Day. Arsenal. Tottenham Hotspur. Football.'

He drank some more of his Carlton draught, and looked at me. His face showed that he was thinking I was some kind of an idiot from the other side of the world. Which I was.

He said, 'Do you not ken Aussie Rules?'

'No,' I said. 'That's what I was asking you about. What rules apply to Australians?'

I was still an idiot from the other side of the world.

'Do you ken Bob Menzies?' he said.

'I have heard of him. Yes. Wasn't he Prime Minister of Australia?'

'He was,' said Jock. 'But he's not famous for that. He was a Carlton man.'

'Oh? He preferred Carlton beer to Courage?'

'God preserve us from the ignorance of emigrants,' Jock said. 'He holds Carlton Football Club's Ticket Number One.'

48

I was about to ask for clarification of this statement, but Jock said, as I opened my mouth, 'And that's got nothing to do with soccer, you ignorant bastard.'

That was the beginning of our friendship. And I learnt a lesson from Jock—'if you can't whack 'em, join 'em.'

'The lawn's vacant, mate . . .'

5
Tasmania

'Last request—a pint of Cascade . . .'

TO A FLATHEAD by Jock Currie
Ye poor wee brown and spiky fish,
I ken were ye tae hae yer wish
Ye widna be up here wi' me
But in the watter,
But since a'm gawn tae set ye free
It disna matter.

Tae tak ye hame wad be quite wrong,
Because ye'r no' ten inches long
And Fish Inspectors seem tae throng
On ilka pier,
And were I caught, some bloody nong
Wid tak ma gear.

Now haud ye still just while I look
The best way tae undo the hook,
And don't forget that bait ye took

Should be a lesson;
But I will spare ye frae the cook,
So count yer blessin'.

And noo I hope ye understand,
Stick tae the watter, not the land.
That bait ye grabbed upon the sand
Cam frae a lugger.
But noo ye've spiked ma bloody hand
Ye bad wee bugger.

Nae doot yer hert was filled wi' hate,
Tae draw some blood ye thought was great,
But I was gawn tae be yer mate
And let ye go.
But noo I'll chop ye up fer bait;
Which goes tae show.

Jock's tale of misfortune, for himself and for the poor wee flat-head, is here inserted for one reason only—I like it. My notes make mention of a late fish lunch in Hobart, tastefully cooked, moist and tender, but whether or not the fish was flathead is not mentioned. In any case I would not have known then what a flathead was. We don't have them in England.

My notes refer, however, to the batter in which this fish was cooked, and which must have impressed me because the recipe is included. A thin batter, made with flour, lemon juice, pepper and salt, and diluted with flat beer. To be deep fried in hot oil.

The beer, of course, would have been Hobart's pride—Cascade. I had tasted bottled Cascade in a pub in Melbourne. I was introduced to it by a Tasmanian expatriate who informed me that it was 'the best beer in the world'.

It was a good example of bottled lager, but, as I said at the time, no more outstanding than others I had sampled.

'Your taste is all in your feet,' he said. 'Anyway, you're going to Tassie, aren't you?'

'Yes.'

'It'd make a nice stole . . .'

'Well, wait till you have a go at the draught. If you don't reckon Cascade *draught* is the best beer in the world, you're not fit to be drinkin' beer at all. Whisky and ginger bloody ale'd be about your form.'

Well, I was on my way to gather facts and figures for the Tasmanian section of my report, and I would certainly take advantage of the opportunity to drink some Cascade draught, and form my own opinion. Probably as soon as I arrived.

What with one thing and about a dozen others—mostly in pots—I was not feeling very well that frosty morning when I left Melbourne to fly to Hobart.

It promised to be a 'perfect day'. 'But don't count on it,' my host said. 'Melbourne can get three seasons in one day. So can Hobart.'

He had joined me for an early breakfast, taken in front of a crackling log fire. I needed a glass of 'Red Eye', but settled for black coffee. He said, when I told him I was surprised to see him up so early, that he was going to drive me to Melbourne airport. He would not hear of me taking a taxi. This was a typically kind and thoughtful gesture.

Still feeling very low, I asked him would he mind stopping at a chemist's shop somewhere.

'Want something for a hangover, do you?'

'Yes.'

'I'm not surprised. You packed away quite a bit last night.'

I told the chemist that I was on my way to Hobart, where undoubtedly hospitality would be dispensed, and that because of Melbourne hospitality the night before, I was feeling low.

'Death warmed up, eh?' he said.

'Yes.'

'You'll be right,' he said. 'I'll fix you.'

He gave me some cloudy, pungent-smelling liquid in a medicine glass.

'What is it?' I asked him.

'My tried and proven recipe,' he said. 'In layman's terms, it's Sal Volatile, Nux Vomica, and Capsicum. Swallow—count down—blast off.'

I raised it cautiously to my lips.

'Don't sip it,' he said. 'Swallow it straight down.'

I accepted his advice. Reaction was instant. My eyes watered, my throat closed up, my breathing ceased, my palate caught fire, and my voice disappeared.

'It's a bit sudden,' he said. 'But that won't take long to wear off. Then you'll be on top of the world.'

I hoped he was right. A return to the top of the world would be appreciated. Just then I was in outer space, beyond earth's atmosphere, with a major fault in my oxygen apparatus.

My host said, when I rejoined him, 'Feel better now?'

I said, 'H'h—h'ar—h'm—uh—a—a,' or unintelligible sounds to that effect.

He laughed. 'What did he give you? Dry cleaning fluid?'

'H'h—h'ar—h'm.'

'Ah well,' he said, 'you can only die once.'

Death failed to claim me. Life returned before we reached the airport, where I said farewell to my charming host.

It was very cold when we landed at Hobart. Hobart is in the Roaring Forties. They were roaring. I ran for the small terminal building. It was warmer inside, out of that south-westerly Antarctic gale.

I approached a taxi driver. He approached me. We met halfway.

'City, sir?' he said.

'Thank you,' I said.

'Been to Hobart before?'

'No.'

'Best little city in the world,' he said. 'Only thing wrong with it is this old goat track in from the airport.'

I made no comment.

He said, 'Down on business or holiday?'

'Business—I think.'

'You think?'

'Yes. I have to taste some Cascade beer.'

This statement kept him quiet for a couple of winding miles. His face showed that he thought he had some kind of a nut in his cab.

On a couple of hundred yards of straight, he said, 'You from Melbourne?'

'Er—yes.'

'Well,' he said, 'I know you've got crook beer up there, but —you fly all the way down here just for a glass or two of Cascade?'

'Yes.'

'In the winter.'

'Yes.'

'M'm. Business eh? You think.'

'Yes.'

He was silent again.

On the bridge, crossing the Derwent River, he said, 'What part of the city would you like?'

'Er—I don't really know.'

'You don't really know.'

'Yes. That's right.'

'Well—you've got a fairly big bag. You stopping for a while?'

'Er—yes. I think so.'

'You think so. But you don't know where.'

'That's right.'

'It would happen to me,' he said. 'Would you like me to recommend somewhere?'

'Thank you. If you would be so kind.'

'If I would be so kind. Strewth. Well—could you tell me this —which would you sooner have, a pub or a motel?'

'Oh—a pub, please. Whichever one is, in your opinion, the best in Hobart.'

'They reckon Hadley's.'

'Very well. First take me to Hadley's. Then we will work it out from there.'

'We will, will we? And just exactly what does work it out from there mean?'

'Well—let us start there and see what happens.'

'I see. We'll start there and see what happens.'

'Yes.'

'And you'll want me to wait for you.'

'Yes, please.'

'It's none of my business,' he said, 'but if you're going to have a glass of Cascade in every pub in Hobart, I can tell you what will happen.'

'It's not that,' I said. 'It's just that I don't know exactly where I'll be staying yet.'

'I see. But you know where you are?'

'Yes. Hobart.'

'Well, that's something,' he said.

He pulled up outside the hotel. I told him I would not be long.

'Don't worry about it,' he said. 'I'm about due for a day off.'

There was a room for me at Hadley's. I was expected.

'But,' I said, 'how did you know I would be coming here? I didn't know myself.'

'Of course you would come here,' they told me. 'Where else?'

It was a good question, and no answer required. I paid off the taxi driver. He seemed pleased.

'Good luck with the tasting,' he said. 'Business, eh?'

'Yes.'

He laughed, and drove away. I could almost hear him thinking. 'A nut all right. You get all sorts in cabs.'

Before returning to the reception desk, I entered the bar for that badly needed 'hair of the dog'. I think it must have been an alsatian.

There was a barmaid on duty. 'Yes?' she said.

'A pot of beer, please.'

'A pot? You just in from Melbourne?'

'Yes.'

'We don't have pots. What you want is a ten ounce.'

'Er—thank you.'

She began to draw it. I asked her, 'What other sizes do you have?'

'Fours, sixes, and eights,' she said.

'And—er—what do you call them?'

'What do we call them? Fours, sixes, and eights. What would you call them?'

'I'll call them fours, sixes, and eights. That's a very simple system.'

'Hair of the dog, love?'

'Yes,' she said, putting my ten-ounce glass in front of me. 'Saves confusion.'

'If I were to ask for a glass of beer, without nominating the size, what would I get?'

'You'd get a six,' she said.

'Thank you.'

'Don't mention it. I like to contribute to the education of foreigners.'

'This is Cascade draught?'

'What else? If you want Carlton or Courage you'll have to go back to the mainland.'

'I want Cascade draught.'

'You've got it,' she said. She went to serve somebody else.

That ten ounces saved my miserable life. Cold as the wind outside the bar, frothy and 'spritzig' and clean and good, with enough bitterness in it to cut through the layers of Sal Volatile, Nux Vomica, and Capsicum, and reach the semi-anaesthetized palate underneath.

It was a new man who approached the reception desk. There I met the manager—a very friendly man of North Italian origin. His English, although accented, was fluent. 'Call me George,' he said.

He summoned a porter to take my bag and show me to my room.

He asked me, 'You have not yet had your lunch?'

'Not yet,' I said. 'But aren't I too late?'

'No, this is your home. Do not hurry. There will be something for you when you come down.'

A large, high-ceilinged room, tastefully furnished, in an old hotel built of stone to last forever. I would like Hadley's.

I enjoyed my late lunch, then I went out to do battle with the elements and obtain some facts and figures relative to Tasmanian Breweries Pty Ltd.

Most of those facts and figures, proudly related to me, are embodied in my report. But my notes reveal some facts not reported, and some personal impressions.

The brewing company imports from the mainland only sugar.

Hops and barley are grown on the island. Tasmania, with a climate somewhat similar to that of Kent, grows, uses and exports hops. Barley is grown in the north. It is more expensive than mainland barley, due to various production difficulties, but brewery management believe in supporting local industry.

At one time, I was told, the brewery owned the whole of Mt Wellington. It still owns a large part of it. It also owns, as a subsidiary company, the Esk brewery in Launceston, marketing a beer called Boag's, after the name of a pioneering proprietor.

The Hobart brewery is the 'prettiest' brewery I saw in Australia. It does not, from the outside, look like a brewery. It resembles more an overgrown cottage. It has an old English look about it, and I felt that it ought to be covered with ivy. It nestles at the foot of Mt Wellington, beside the 'cascade' that gives the beer its name. Clean and clear water, filtered through sand and rock, tumbles down from the heights above. The interior of the building, however, does not resemble an overgrown cottage. There all is modern, spacious and functional. And the lager it produces could easily be—a personal opinion only, perhaps prejudiced by that first delicious draught of it—'the best in the world'.

Sampling more of it the next day, in a Hobart pub crawl to obtain consumer reaction, lunch time caught up with me in a bar in Collins Street. There I made the acquaintance of a youngish man wearing gumboots, a gaudy Fair Isle sweater, and a knitted woollen multi-coloured head covering with a red pompon on it. A 'red tourie', as Jock would say. He was 'off the cray boats', he told me. He said he was going to have lunch 'down in the bistro'. He recommended it, if I had no other plans. I didn't, and thanked him.

'Goodo,' he said. 'But we can't go down there standin' on one leg. Same again?'

'Same again' it was. Or as the barman said, 'Something similar.'

In the course of conversation, over two more tens, I remarked on the fact that except for sugar, Tasmanian Breweries used all local raw materials.

'That's what makes our grog the best in the world,' he said. 'Best water, best barley, best hops. They grow a few hops in Victoria, you know, but you wouldn't piss on 'em.'

'I was told that South Australia produced the best barley.'

'Balls,' he said. 'Mob o' skites, those crow-eaters. Our north-west grows the best. But I'll tell you something—once, to our shame and sorrow, we had to import *beer* from the mainland.'

'Oh? How was that?'

'Big bush fires around Hobart. Few years back. People burnt to death. An' the brewery got burnt out. Carlton made Cascade for us for a while.'

'Was it good?'

'Anything's good enough if you're thirsty enough.'

'But what about Launceston? Wouldn't the Esk brewery come to the party?'

'Strewth,' he said. 'A man'd have to be *dyin'* o' thirst to drink bloody Boag's.'

'Couldn't they brew and bottle Cascade for you?'

'They wouldn't bloody know how. An' even if they did, she's only a small brewery, an' they wouldn't 've been able to make enough. She was stinkin' hot down here that summer, an' we were all powerful dry.'

There was enough Cascade draught for everybody when I was there, but, as I found everywhere in Australia, too many bottled and canned variations. The bottled draught was very good. But I asked did Tasmanian drinkers really need the Green, the Red, and the Blue—Pale Ale, Bitter Ale, and Light Lager—that the brewery makes for them? Yes, the drinkers said. Yes, said brewery management.

It had not been my intention to visit Launceston, Tasmania's northern city, but when brewery management told me that about half the island State 'swore by Boag's', while the southern half 'swore by Cascade', I decided that a visit was necessary. And everywhere I went, in and around Hobart—a lovely little city—any mention of Boag's beer provoked ribald or profane, but invariably adverse comment. So I had to cut Hobart short and fit Launceston into my itinerary.

It was possible to fly, provided one was prepared to rise before daybreak. I prepared carefully, by retiring early and sober.

Launceston's impressive new terminal was warm and friendly. So was the hostess at my hotel. She showed me to my room, and told me breakfast was 'on' in the dining-room.

After breakfast, I had some time to kill before keeping an appointment with a gentleman from Boag's. So I strolled around the streets of Launceston, observing an air of busyness and bustle, in contrast to Hobart's more leisurely atmosphere.

Later in the morning, when the pubs were open, I met the man from Boag's. He said his name was Ferdie Pedder. I didn't believe anybody could, or would be called Ferdie Pedder, but that's what he said his name was. He was most helpful. Was it too early for a beer? It was not.

I told him, falsely, that I was looking forward to my first taste of Boag's. Cautiously, I ordered a glass—six ounces. The colour was right; the temperature—by Australian standards, to which I was becoming accustomed—was right; the 'head' was right. I tasted it.

Ferdie Pedder said, 'Good?'

'Yes. Very good. But not quite bitter enough for me. I think it needs more hop seeds in it.'

Ferdie claimed I was wrong. So did one of two talkative gentlemen alongside us, whose eyes showed that they were recovering from a heavy night.

'You know the right place for you?' he said. 'Down in bloody Hobart drinkin' that Cascade piss. That's as bitter as a dose of cascara.'

'I like a bitter beer,' I said.

'Well go to Hobart,' he told me. 'Or bloody London. I had a pint o' bitter in London once. Took me three days to get rid o' the taste.'

'What did you drink after that—mild?'

'Yeah. Warm, weak an' sweet, like me last sheila. But it was better than cascara.'

His mate said, 'Didn't it give you the tom tits?'

'Yeah. But not as bad as cascara.'

'Aw, nothing's as bad as cascara, mate. Not even that bitter bloody stuff the Ities drink. You weren't in Italy during the war, were you?'

'No, I was lucky. Got enough bloody Ities to put up with here.'

'Aw, they're all right. But gees, the stuff they drink. Not only that vino rosso, that's bad enough, but the bitter stuff. Gawd. I got full on vino one night, an' the next morning I was as dry an' as miserable as the bloody Nullarbor. So I go into this joint that had a barman who used to live in America, an' tell him my troubles. He understood English, see. He gives me some stuff called Fernet Branca. Dark brown stuff.'

'We have it here,' the barman said, listening in.

'Well, you know what you can do with it, mate. Anyway, I reckon one sip's more than e-bloody-nough. But he starts off on a long spiel about how good it is for a hangover, an' wavin' his arms about till I thought he'd knock all the bottles off the shelf. So I down the lot, to shut him up. But he don't shut up. When I'm pullin' faces like a chimpanzee at the zoo, he persuades me to try Campari. An' then some lousy concoction called Rabarbaro. He says it's made out of rhubarb. Rhubarb an' bloody cascara, I reckon. He says I'll be all right soon. He says the stuff he's given me'll not only fix my hangover, he says it'll make me eat like a horse. He says all I needed then was a good feed. Buon apetito, he says.'

'How did you go? Did you have a feed?'

'Bloody well had to, mate. Had to get the taste out of me mouth. Spaghetti an' cheese. Don't like spaghetti an' can't stand cheese. But that's all there was. What that lousy taste needed was a real hot curry doused with Holbrook's sauce.'

'Curry's on the menu today,' the barman said. 'And I can get you a bottle of Holbrook's. Would you like a Fernet Branca first?'

'Get stuffed,' he was told.

I stayed only two days in Launceston—two days originally allotted to Hobart—absorbing Boag's and information, and acquiring another hangover. Part of the foundation for the latter was laid in what I was told was the 'oldest pub in the country'. But most of it was laid in other places equally dangerous.

In the morning, had I sought medical advice, I would have been classified as unfit for work. But work, so called, went on until it was time to go to the airport to board an afternoon 'plane for the 'mainland', with connections in Melbourne for Sydney.

My wife met me at Sydney airport. 'My God,' she said, 'you look a wreck.'

'Bags under blood-shot eyes,' she said.

'And you've put on weight,' she said. 'You're all swollen up and puffy.'

'I shouldn't have let you out of my sight,' she said. 'What you need, my lad, is a week off the booze to dry out. Starting with about twenty-four hours' sleep.'

She was so right.

'Tells his wife he doesn't touch the stuff'

6
Queensland

I did not take a week off the booze to dry out. I slept for twelve hours, dried out for a couple of days, and flew to Queensland.

There were two reasons for this decision:

One: I thought I should complete my fact-and-figure-finding mission in other areas, before investigating the situation in the more populous 'Mother State', about which I was, in any case, accumulating quite a lot of information.

Two: It would be more sensible for me, a 'cold-blooded' Englishman, to visit Queensland, so much nearer the Equator, before the advancing season made tropical and sub-tropical temperatures intolerable.

By telephone, I reserved a room in Lennon's Hotel, Brisbane.

Flying over the Newcastle area, I remarked to my seated neighbour that so many Australian place-names seemed to reflect the homesickness of early colonists.

'Yes,' he said. 'That, and crawling to top brass. Lord Sydney, Lord Melbourne, Brisbane, Hobart, and some big shot's wife named Adelaide. But we have plenty of other names for little places. How about Nevertire, Come-by-Chance, Bongongalong, Mukinbudin, Boulia, Camooweal, Warracknabeal, Bringalong—that used to be Bring Along a Bag o' Flour—there are dozens of them. Lot of Abo names, too. Our English, Scottish and Welsh ancestors weren't all homesick toadies.'

'Scots I know about,' I said. 'Perth, for example. But Welsh?'

'Sure, Welsh. Back down there in the Newcastle area is Cardiff, believe it or not. Anyway, even some of the bigger places got local names. Take Wagga Wagga, Ballarat, Kalgoorlie, Broken Hill, Toowoomba.'

'Were there any named by homesick Irish?'

'Probaby quite a lot,' he said. 'I know of a few. Ballina, Ballymore, Castlemaine, and up near the border there's even a Killarney.'

He was a very interesting travelling companion, and, as the Irish say, 'conversation shortens the road'.

Looking down as we flew farther north, it seemed to me that thousands of square miles of wooded hills and valleys were virtually uninhabited.

'I have been told,' I said, 'that the population of New South Wales is greater than that of any other State.'

'That's right,' he said.

'Well, look down there. Where are they?'

'Most of them live in and around Sydney,' he said. 'But there's plenty of room once you get out a bit. She's a big country. Room for millions more. We're just starting, really. Tokyo has nearly as many people in one city as we have in the whole of Australia. And Australia is bigger than the United States, if you take out Alaska. Couple of hundred million in the US.'

'Well,' I said. 'You may not have many people, but you drink a lot of beer.'

He said, 'It's the climate. And anyway, we've got the best beer in the world. You can take that as gospel. I've been around the world several times, and I've tried them all. Ours leaves them for dead.'

'Does that apply to all Australian beer?'

'The whole lot,' he said. 'Some's not as good as others, you know. But even Mac's at Rockhampton—and that would be our worst—is better than anything I've struck in any other country.'

It was a beautiful day for flying; cloudless, and the sky as blue as the Mediterranean sometimes is.

But stepping down from the air-conditioned 'plane on to off-white concrete was like walking fully clothed into a Turkish bath.

'This is winter?' I said.

My friend said, 'Spring up here. Beautiful. Probably like a London heat-wave to you, though. You want to get rid of that heavy English suit you're wearing.'

In the terminal building I was met by a kindly AHA gentleman who drove me to Lennon's Hotel. We made a further appointment for mid-afternoon. Although he had received a copy of my letter of introduction, he was, like others I had met, interested in the 'real purpose' of my tour.

I was not permitted to divulge the name of my Company, but my replies led him to assume that I was in some way connected with a chain of hotels in England. Which was true enough. My Company owned quite a few. If it were assumed that they were interested in acquiring a few more in Australia, the AHA would not object. Nor would the breweries. But the latter would certainly object to English competition. They would 'gang up' to keep us out.

I was told that Queensland had five breweries—two in Brisbane, and one each in Toowoomba, Rockhampton, and Cairns.

Castlemaine-Perkins, marketing XXXX beer known as Four X, was the only independent. The others were subsidiaries of Carlton & United, Melbourne.

Both Castlemaine-Perkins, and Queensland Brewery Ltd—known as QB—use modern equipment, are clean and efficient, and make good light lagers. Of the two, Four X and Bulimba, I preferred Four X, because of the slight extra bitterness in its flavour.

My room at Lennon's was modern, and very comfortable.

65

I discarded my suit coat and went down to have my first taste of Queensland beer. I discovered Lennon's 'Stockyard Bar', a most unusual and interesting place. In it were several island bars, and around and about were wooden walls and partitions, liberally decorated with cryptic letters and figures, burnt into the timber. The barmaid was decorative, too, young and mini-skirted and shapely.

I told her I would like a small glass of beer.

'One small beer,' she said, attending to me.

I said, 'I'm a stranger in Brisbane. What size beers do you serve, and what do you call them?'

She said, 'Five ounce, eight ounce, and ten ounce. We call them small beers, beers, and pots.'

'I see. Well, could you make that a beer? Five ounces is a little too small, I think.'

'No trouble,' she said.

Putting it in front of me, she said, 'There you are. Eight ounces. Mind you, in the bush you'll only get seven ounces. They call it a seven.'

'Do you know the reason for that?'

'They reckon it's the freight,' she said.

I sampled the beer, a good lager, and then gazed around trying to decipher the black hieroglyphics on the reddish-brown timber.

Two men entered from somewhere in the rear, one of them carrying, by its long shaft, an additional red-hot, wrought-iron symbol. He applied it to a vacant space. Small flames and white smoke spurted around it—and there was another black marking to puzzle me.

A man near me, with a glass in his hand, said, 'You're wondering what that's all about, are you?'

'Yes,' I said. 'I am.'

'Thought so. Heard you say you were a stranger here. They're cattle brands. Come from cattle stations all over. Stock-yard Bar, see?'

'Oh. Yes. Now I understand. Thank you.'

'That's all right,' he said. 'How about you drink that up an' have another one?'

'Thank you. It will be a pleasure.'

He ordered two pots. 'Where do you come from?' he asked.

The young barmaid said, 'Bet you he's from down south.'

He said, 'Yeah? You reckon? I'll try him out. Now I've been down in Sydney, see. Why do they call a pot a middy?'

I knew the answer to that. I said, 'Because it's midway between nothing and a pint.'

'Makes sense,' he said. 'I'd never of thought of that. Anyway, who the bloody hell drinks pints these days?'

I was learning. I said, 'Er—the bloody Poms.'

'What've they got to do with it?'

'The first fleet was full of Poms, wasn't it?'

'So what?'

'So Poms made the first beer ever made in Australia. And where did they make it? Sydney Cove. In 1796. And they liked to drink pints of it. So—'

'It wouldn't do you any good if you drank Pommy piss in gallons,' he said. 'All you'd get'd be a gutful and a headache.'

'Weak as piss, this Pommy beer . . .'

67

Another man interrupted. He said, 'I come from Sydney. You ever read Ron Saw?'

'No,' my friend said. 'Who wrote it?'

'Eh? Ron Saw is a bloke. In my opinion, the greatest newspaper columnist—'

'I get you. Well, if he's so bloody great, why doesn't he write for the *Courier Mail*?'

'Because he writes for a Sydney paper.'

'Not worth readin', mate. Sydney papers, Sydney beer. Bulldust an' Pommy piss. Not worth readin', not worth drinkin'. Give me the *Courier Mail* an' Four X.'

'If you'll listen, I'll tell you what he wrote once about what you call Pommy piss.'

'All right, I'm listenin'. But if you tell me he likes the stuff, I'm not listenin'.'

'Well, he said he likes it in England in the winter, on what he calls a good cold summer's day. But not on a hot day.'

'A hot day? When do they ever get a hot day in England? If the thermometer ever went over the ton, they'd all drop dead.'

'London can be hot. Shut up and listen. This is Ron Saw's description of a London pub on a hot day.'

'How hot? Seventy degrees?'

'In the eighties—and humid.'

'Beauty. Queensland in the winter.'

'Don't give me that. You ever been to Stanthorpe in the winter?'

'That bloody place should be in New South Wales,' my friend said. 'But excuse me—you were talkin' about this Bonsaw bloke. Is he a Frenchman?'

'A Frenchman? Oh—I see. No, he's an Aussie. Ron Saw. R for rum.'

'Listen, why is it you blokes down south go for Beenleigh rum? There's only one good rum in the world, mate, an' that's Bundy.'

'All right, all right. Bundy's a good rum. You won't buy an argument with me on that subject. Can I tell you what Ron Saw had to say about London pubs in summer?'

'Wait a sec, till we get another charge.'

I said, 'It's my shout.'

'All right. Nobody's objecting.'

The man from Sydney said, 'Now Ron Saw said—'

'Wait a sec. We haven't got it yet. Two more, love. Yeah— Four X.'

The Sydney man said, 'What's wrong with Bulimba?'

'There's nothing wrong with Bulimba—now, that is. Was you in Brizzo when that Melbourne mob took it over?'

'No. Buggered it up, did they?'

'Did they ever. Green death, we called it. Because of the green handles on the pumps, see. Of all the lousy grog—'

'Green death?'

'Yeah. Green bloody death.'

The new ice-cold pots of Four X arrived, and the Sydney man returned to his subject. 'Ron Saw said, and I think I can remember it—'

'Just a sec.' To me, my friend said, 'Cheers.'

'Cheers.'

We took a long pull. 'All right,' my friend said. 'We're listenin'.'

'Ron Saw said that in London pubs on a hot day in summer, the refrigeration consists of some elderly arthritic retainer dabbing the pipe with damp towels, because the draught lager is at blood heat, bottled lager comes straight from the shelf, soda syphons stand on the counter beside the hot pies, and even pubs which boast of having ice provide only a half gallon bucket to handle a day's business. That's what he said.'

My friend took another pull at his Four X, and said, 'Any bloody barman puts ice in my beer I'll murder the bastard.'

'The ice,' I said, 'would be for the whisky.'

'Well, bein' a Pommy yourself, you'd know.'

'How do you know I'm a Pommy?'

'Knew it all along, mate. Been havin' you on. Anyway, who wants whisky? You like whisky?'

'Yes.'

'You like Pommy piss?'

'Er—no.'

'Good on yer. *He* drinks it down in bloody Sydney.'

The Sydney man said, 'I don't.'

'You bloody do. How many pubs in Sydney refrigerate their glasses? Come on. How many?'

'Well—'

'How can you get a decent beer in a warm glass? She climbs all over the top. You get a collar a half an inch thick. This stuff is just right. A chilled glass, an' no collar. Who wants to drink bloody froth? Only Poms an' you blokes down south. You tell that North Shore mate of yours to come up here. He'll get a decent pot o' beer up here. An' if he's any bloody good as a writer he might get a job on the *Courier Mail*, too.'

'What do you mean North Shore? His name's Ron Saw.'

'So who cares? Who's ever heard of 'im?'

The Sydney man said, 'Probably nobody in this hick town. Well at least you have two papers. S'pose that's something.

'What two papers?'

'The *Courier Mail* and the *Telegraph*.'

'The Brisbane Telly? Never buy it, mate. That's only fit for arse paper.'

Queensland people, I was to learn, have strong opinions about things, and express them pungently. This includes publicans, who have strong opinions about counter lunches. If one enquires when counter lunch is likely to be 'on', one is likely to be told, in a sentence full of adjectives, that the dining-room opens at such and such a time, or there's a cafe around the whatsaname corner, or the road for down south is in that XYZ direction.

There are exceptions, but I found that Queensland publicans are not generally in favour of Melbourne-style counter lunches. They specialize in giving one an ice-cold glass, full of ice-cold beer, with little or no head on it.

I find here in my notes a copy of a lecture delivered to publicans—called 'licensed victuallers' in Queensland—by one R. A. Young of the Swan brewery in Perth. But it would be applicable to publicans in any State in Australia. It is somewhat technical, but I have been promising myself to make a summary of it. Now would be a good time.

Beer, he says, will be first class when it leaves the brewery. No licensee will be able to improve it—but he can spoil it. It comes to him with the right amount of gas in it, but by the time it gets into his cool room, the gas pressure has gone up, due to increase in temperature. So he should never broach a new keg until it has been in his cool room for a few days, to let the pressure drop back to what it was when the keg left the brewery. His job is to get the beer into the glass, with the right amount of gas in it, and at a temperature of thirty-six to thirty eight degrees F—that is nearly frozen—which is the way Australians like it. Chilled glasses are a great help. Cleanliness is essential.

How to get this delectable result is up to the licensee; his equipment; his staff's knowledge of how to operate it and keep it clean; and the rotation of his kegs, so that no keg is too old, and the temperature and gas pressure are right when he breaks into one. There should never be, he says, jugs all over the place, and froth for miles, and customers thirsty and impatient because he has just put a new keg on.

I like his summing up. He says, 'Beer dispensing is not hard. Know the fundamentals: lay down a correct procedure in your hotel. See your staff clearly understand what you want done. Have your bar staff dispense the beer one glass at a time, with one-pull operation, NO TOPPING UP. Once pressure has been applied, do not touch it until the cask is empty. Keep all dispensing equipment clean. See that your refrigeration is adequate for peak loads; make sure stocks are rotated.'

And he adds, 'Bottled and canned beer is usually taken home by your customer, so the final presentation is in *his* hands.'

This last comment is very true. I took back to my room one morning a bottle of Bulimba Pilsener. No doubt I could have asked for a glass of it in a bar, but I didn't have the courage. Nobody in Australia drinks bottled local lager in a bar if draught is available.

I left it standing there until my return fairly late in the even-

71

ing. Then I opened it. Froth and spray flew everywhere. When I had cleaned up I had less than half a bottle left for sampling purposes.

This was the fault neither of the brewery, nor of the man who sold it to me. It was entirely my own fault. There was a small refrigerator in my room, with space for bottles.

'Warm' bottled beer, however, sometimes has its uses, as I was told by an elderly gentleman in a suburban bar. He said he was 'an old bushman, retired now, not fit for work.' He said he was 'on the pension', and lived with a married daughter.

' She lets me keep enough money to have a few snorts every day,' he said.

And he told me something of his jobs and his wanderings over many years. This story I added to my notes:

'I was out in the Corner country one time,' he said. 'You know where that is?'

'No. I'm afraid I don't.'

'Out where Queensland an' New South an' South Aus. meet. On the Corner, see. There was an old post there to mark it. Stinkin' bloody hot, she was. About a hundred an' ten in me water bag. Well, I had a bottle o' beer in me swag, see. I'd been savin' her up. I reckoned right on the Corner'd be a good place to crack her. Sort o' celebrate, see. So I gets her out, an' whips the top off quick with me tobaccer tin, an' upends her into me mouth. Course I get sprayed a bit, but I got most of it down me, an' I don't pull her out till she's empty. I put her down against the post, an' I stand there lookin' at the country. Bloody awful, it is. Flat as a board whichever way you look, an' bugger all on it. Then me bladder tells me I got to have a leak. Hot beer goes just about straight through yer, you know. Well, what I did, I demonstrated me opinion of that country. I started walkin' an' pissin'. I walked right around that post, pissin' all the time. Gave me a lot o' satisfaction. In one go I pissed in three States, see. All they're fit for, out there.'

I had been told several times that I *must* visit Toowoomba —'The Queen City of the Darling Downs', one of my advisers called it.

'The brewery's a bit small and ancient, but they make a good drop. And you have to see the malt house. The only one of its kind in Australia. They send their malt everywhere. Darling Downs barley is the best in the world, you know.'

'I was told South Australian barley was—'

'Forget it. Not a patch on the Downs.'

Very well, I would go. 'How do I get there?'

'Take a bus. See a bit of the country.'

I decided to rent a car, and drive myself. So one morning I set out, travelling west, with the sun behind me. I had a companion-guide, whom I had met in a bar somewhere, and who had introduced me to 'White Lady', a colourless Bundaberg rum.

'Better than that bloody bacardi,' he said. 'Got more bite in it.'

When he heard I intended to spend a couple of days in Toowoomba, he said, 'Wouldn't mind goin' up with you. I got a brother up there. Haven't seen him for years. Born there meself.'

He was a middle-aged man, lean and leathery and weather-beaten, who was 'off on compo with a crook foot'.

He told me to call him Mick. I told him to call me James. But of course he did not. He called me Jim.

Driving along a busy bitumen road out of Brisbane, he told me the history of the Darling Downs, and the city of Too-woomba.

'The Downs,' he said, 'was discovered by Allan Cunningham in 1827. Then in eighteen forty something-or-bloody-other an Army bloke—Lieutenant—name o' Gorman—found a way up the range from this side. When they put a road up, they called it the Toll Road. They had a toll on it, see. No toll now, but. She goes up all of two thousand bloody feet. Toowoomba's right on top.'

'That word Toowoomba,' I said. 'It's an Aboriginal name?'

'Sort of. The first town was a bit further south. Where Drayton is now. They called it Drayton. That was Steele Rudd country, you know. His old man took up a selection there.

Read his book, haven't you? *On Our Selection*?'

'No, I'm sorry. I haven't.'

'Well you bloody ought to. Funniest book ever written. The old pub's still standin' there. Bull's Head Inn, she's called. Can't get a grog there now, but. Deserted, she is. Fall down one o' these days.'

'You were going to tell me about the word Toowoomba.'

'Well hold yer 'orses. I'm gettin' to it, aren't I? In the old days, where the city is now—Listen, while we're up there, don't you call it a town. They'll run you out on a rail.'

'Very well,' I said. 'I'll remember to call it a city.'

'You bloody better. She *is* a city. That's official. Anyway, where she is now was all swamp in those days. Full o' mossies. They just called it The Swamp. There were plenty of Abos about, lookin' for handouts an' tryin' to learn a bit of English. But they couldn't say The Swamp, see. All they could say was Te Wampa. That's how she gets her name. Te Wampa to Toowoomba, see?'

'I see. And how did they come to build a city in a swamp?'

'Drained the bastard, that's how. Now here's a thing—where would you reckon the first brewery in Queensland was built?'

'Well, Brisbane was the first settlement, wasn't it?'

'That's right.'

'Then I would say Brisbane.'

'An' you'd be bloody wrong. Toowoomba, that's where. Way back in the eighteen sixties. Perkins an' Co.'

'I see. Would that be the same Perkins as—'

'As in Brizzy? Yeah. Same mob.'

'And that old brewery is still functioning in Toowoomba?'

'No. Bloody Myers from Melbourne bought 'er an' knocked 'er down. Built a big store. The brewery's further out, now. Listen, talkin's thirsty work. What about pullin' in for a couple before we tackle the climb up the range?'

'Very well. Where?'

'Grantham. They'll be open now. Just keep goin'—I'll show you where.'

'That's the range we have to climb in front of us, is it?'

'Yeah, that's her. Lot o' cloud on 'er, eh?'

'Yes.'

'She's not really a range, you know. She's what they call an escarpment. Edge o' the Downs, see. They're high an' flat.'

Refreshed with a couple of 'sevens' of Bulimba draught, in a small but modern roadside pub, we came out again into the warm bright sunshine, and almost immediately began to climb. And were soon crawling in low gear through heavy fog. We crept out of it as we entered the city. I was to meet the AHA secretary there.

Mick guided me to the right street, and asked me to drop him at a nearby pub. He'd arranged to meet his brother there. And we made an appointment for the same place, same time, two days later.

The AHA man said, 'Welcome to the Garden City.'

He told me I should have delayed my visit until late in September. 'The Floral Festival,' he said. 'Place really swings. They come in from everywhere.'

He guided me to my accommodation, a hotel-motel south of the city.

I like Australian hotel-motels. Accommodation is modern, very comfortable, and isolated from dining-rooms and noisy bars. Any weary traveller who wants to retire early and sleep can do so undisturbed.

I was not permitted to do either. I was escorted to the brewery, and the malt house, and Bolton's Cobb and Co museum and the Lionel Lindsay art gallery, and to numerous pubs, all of which seemed to be owned or managed by hard-drinking wild-eyed Irishmen. Or at least of Irish descent. With one notable exception. He was a Greek. Under the influence of many sevens of Bulimba—I at any rate was so influenced—he and I performed a Zorba-style Greek dance on the footpath outside his hotel. Bulimba lager, as brewed in Toowoomba's old-style brewery, transforms normal English reserve into gregarious and uninhibited behaviour. It is a very good lager.

The malt house interested me. Called Toowoomba Maltings, it processes Darling Downs barley—'the best in the world'—

and supplies malt to all the Carlton & United breweries in Queensland. Carlton bought it, I was told, in 1952, and later spent a million dollars on additional buildings and modern equipment. Barley goes in one end, and malt comes out the other, on an automated push-button production line. But the original building was retained, and when I was there was still in use, with some of the crop being germinated in the traditional way; that is by steeping the grain, and raking it out on concrete floors. 'Spread it out and let it sprout.'

I was in dire need of two things when I left Te Wampa— a dose of 'Red Eye', and a long sleep. Mick was in the same condition.

'Dangerous bloody place,' he said. 'Man knows too many bloody people. Even if I didn't have a crook foot, I wouldn't be fit for work today. How are you goin', Jim? You fit to drive?'

I said I thought I would be able to manage.

'Well take it easy goin' down. Bloody fog's still crook.'

I took it easy. We came out into sunshine.

'Gunna call in at Grantham?' he said.

'No.'

'No. Wait till we get to town, eh? Call in there an' we might flake out an' still be there tomorrer.'

'Yes,' I said. 'That wouldn't do. I'm flying north tomorrow.'

'How far?'

'As far as Cairns.'

'Want to get rid o' that suit,' he said. 'You'll boil up there.'

'I'll get something lighter this afternoon,' I told him.

'Not another suit, but. Don't waste your money. Get shorts an' long socks. That's what they all wear up north. Shorts an' shirt.'

After saying farewell to him over Four X's, and thanking him for his company and information and advice, I returned the car, and bought two pairs of shorts and long white socks. The salesman advised short-sleeved drip-dry shirts in addition. I bought two of them.

Then I returned to my room at Lennon's, showered, changed into pyjamas, ordered an early dinner, ate it, and crashed.

7
Rockhampton and Cairns

'Of course, in Europe they have St Bernard's'

THREE WATER WORDS by Jock Currie

When I first joined the navy, a young sailor lad,
I got lots of advice from my old mum and dad,
Who had warned me so often of dangers to come
From the bright painted girls, and that old demon rum.
But I later decided 'twould be rather nice
If I looked round about for some other advice.
So while cruising around on King Neptune's dominion,
I was on the alert for a second opinion.
Well, before very long I had taken my choice—
'Twas an old three badge matelot with very gruff voice.
When I thought I had known him for quite long enough,
I had asked what was making his voice sound so gruff;
And his answer came at me as quick as a wink,
'It's the rum,' he replied. 'It's the rum that I drink.'
Then I watched him demolish his three water tot,
And I asked him what caused him to swear such a lot.
This he answered as soon as his thought he had mastered—
'It's the water—the water they put in the bastard.'

Rum—imported—was drunk in Australia at the very beginning of British occupation, my history tells me. The Aboriginals never learnt how to make alcohol, so for thousands of years before Captain Cook, the continent was teetotal.

Queenslanders, while consuming millions of gallons of Four X and Bulimba, are also recognized rum drinkers. There are many 'two-gun' men in this northern State, who drink rum with a beer chaser, or vice versa. The practice, however, as a man in Rockhampton told me, 'leaves you with a breath on you like a brewery horse's fart.' He said he did not recommend rum for honeymooners. But, he said, 'she's a quick way to get a skinful.'

I am not a 'two-gun' man. Actually, I don't like rum. I have known people in England who, on cold winter nights, drink it hot with milk or some other diluent, before going to bed. I prefer mulled ale—a preference which I only mentioned once in Australia. The expressions of undiluted horror on the faces of my companions were a sufficient deterrent.

'Stick a red hot poker in your bloody beer? Gawd.'

I was obviously insane. A mad Pom. A man to be avoided. Not fit to associate with normal human beings.

Rockhampton sits almost at sea-level on a flat alluvial plain, some twenty miles inland from the coast. It is bisected by a muddy tidal river called the Fitzroy. I was quartered in the motel section of a hotel called the Criterion, which was separated from the river by a bitumen road, and a strip of grass with trees on it. Fishing boats rode at anchor in the river.

Five miles north of the Tropic of Capricorn, the climate is hot and humid. I was glad I was not wearing a suit. I had donned my newly purchased shorts and short-sleeved open-necked shirt before leaving Brisbane. My snow-white knobbly knees and pallid forearms provoked ribald comment from the deeply-tanned citizens in the bar.

'Shit eh?—what is it?'

'Refugee from bloody Heard Island.'

'Bloody Melbourne, more like.'

'Red face, white arms an' legs—looks like a raw prawn with a cooked head.'

I decided to quell this flow of unflattering comment, and perhaps win friends, by announcing my name and origin.

I said, 'Thank you for your interest, gentlemen. Allow me to introduce myself. My name is James McIntosh, and I am from England.'

'Only just. Bloody yesterday, by the look of you.'

'That explains it. Just a poor pale Pom.'

'What're you doin' here?'

'I have been told,' I said, 'that Mac's beer is the worst beer in Australia.'

'Eh? Who told you that? Bastard wouldn't know good beer if he was swimmin' in it.'

'Mac's, I'll have you know, is the *best* bloody beer in Australia.'

'Best in the bloody world, the old Mac's.'

'Aw, take no notice of him. He's only havin' a shot.'

'No, just a minute. Listen choom—what's *your* opinion of Mac's beer? Come on. What's your opinion?'

'I have no opinion,' I said. 'I have just arrived, and I have not yet tasted it.'

'Well—we'll soon bloody fix that. Give him a big one, love.'

'Love' pulled me ten ounces. I took it to the doorway and examined it against the glaring exterior sunlight. The bar was silent. I brought the glass back and carefully savoured the aroma of its contents. I took a mouthful and rolled it around my tongue, thoughtfully gazing at the ceiling. I swallowed, drank a little more, and then drained the glass. Silence continued.

It was broken by one low-pitched voice. 'Well?'

'That,' I said reverently, 'was without doubt the best beer I have ever tasted.'

The bar erupted. There was much noise and shouting.

'You beauty.'

'Told you so.'

'You know your beer all right.'

'Can't put one over on the Poms.'

'Have another one, Jimmy. Give him another one, love.'

'Gentlemen,' I said. 'That was a memorable experience. Allow me to buy this round.'

'Not on your nelly. You came in last, you shout last.'

I had made friends. Before long I was down to sevens. Nothing smaller was permitted. They gave me some of the history of Mac's beer. They also got me drunk. Too drunk to think about a late lunch.

I retired to my air-conditioned room and slept all the afternoon.

I did not remember very much of the story of Mac's, as told to me in the bar, so was obliged to check with brewery management the next day.

'Home Brew' was made and sold in Rockhampton in the 1860s by a man named William Boldeman. Then in 1880 Russell and Co established what they called the Fitzroy Brewery, and took less than a year to go broke. That was when Thomas McLaughlin—'Mac'—with a friend, bought all the equipment and stock at an auction sale, and later built a new brewery. There was some movement from place to place, until they finally settled in Wharf Street. I was shown this old building, recently evacuated in favour of fine new modern premises, built by Carlton & United at North Rockhampton.

Mac's is not 'crook beer'. The disparaging remarks about it that I had heard came from those who had not tasted the new product. It is certainly not the best in the world, but it is a very good lager, made from Toowoomba malt, Queensland sugar, and southern hops, with enough bitterness in it to suit my palate.

My notes refer to a visit to a pub called the Crown, much frequented by Aboriginals, and over the Fitzroy River bridge to one called the Anchor, about which my only comment seems to be 'wild night'. I have rather vague memories of a lot of singing, and of witnessing a fist fight 'out the back'. But I become a bit more expansive in my references to Mount Morgan, a small mining town west of Rockhampton.

I was kidnapped and taken there by a group of Rockhampton

'licensed victuallers', who had scheduled an official lunch-hour meeting of district licensees in that small place. 'We'll be back in Rocky about three,' they said.

I did not attend the meeting, so after a taste or two in the old pub where they were to confer I wandered around the little town. Shops and houses were badly in need of repair, and paint. Somnolent under the fierce midday sun, they appeared to be waiting to die. As apparently they were. I was told, 'When the mine cuts out the town's finished.'

I wandered into a small cafe, operated by Southern Europeans—probably Greek. It was a clean and friendly place. I enjoyed a ham sandwich and black coffee and was then fit to join my hosts for a crawl around all five of the old pubs.

These pubs were dressed in several layers of old paint, and my publican hosts in one layer of clean white shirts with ties on them. They looked out of place amongst the toilers, stained with soil and oil, as also did I.

A very work-stained man, with a bent and battered old felt hat low on his brow, dog-testicle eyes, and a few teeth, said, 'What're you bastards doin' here?'

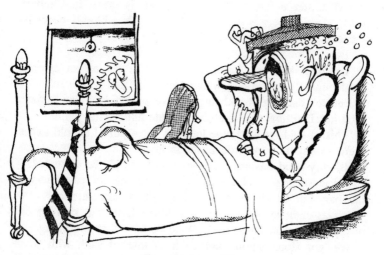

Top fermentation

81

'We've been having a meeting.'

'A meeting, eh? Gettin' your heads together to put up the price of a man's beer. Listen—you bastards've only got to put her up one more time, an' I'm pullin' the washin' machine outa the laundry an' puttin' in another tub. I'll brew me bloody own, an' send yez all broke.'

They did put up the price of their beer. And perhaps this protester has taken out his washing machine, and is brewing his own in a tub—by the age-old 'top fermentation' process—and has exploded a lot of bottles, and got himself divorced.

When I mentioned this possibility to my driver-host on the way back to Rocky he said, 'Even if he does have a go, he won't last long. He'll be back. It gets a bit lonely drinking on your own. And no home brew is ever as good as the professional product. By that I mean brewed by professionals, and dispensed by professionals. Us.'

'So you feel quite safe in increasing the price.'

'Got no bloody choice. Overheads going up all the time. We could *cut* the price to buggery if it wasn't for the excise tax. Bloody iniquitous. Shocking. Without that, beer would only cost the customer a few cents. Those bastards down in Canberra seem to think beer is a luxury. It's not. It's a bloody necessity. 'Specially in a hot climate.'

'Beer,' I said wisely, 'is a food.'

'Exactly. And any bastard who puts a tax on an essential food ought to be bloody well salted and fried in batter.'

Before reaching Rockhampton, we pulled in to an isolated little hotel, sitting all alone on the wide flat coastal plain.

'This,' I said, 'is a strange location for a pub. I should expect there would be very little business here.'

'Bloody good business,' my host said. 'You'd be surprised.'

I was surprised. Not only by the number of customers in the bar, but by the very modern and tasteful interior.

It was eight in the evening and Mac's lager was running out of my ears, when I was told, 'We'd better be getting along.'

We 'got along' about half an hour later. I said, with some difficulty, 'You were going to be back in Rocky about three.'

'That's right,' my host said. 'Queensland time. You'll get used to it.'

Airlines do not keep Queensland time. I was to fly to Cairns the next morning, Eastern Standard Time. So I begged to be excused from a further session in the Criterion's bar.

I started my breakfast next morning by drinking half the coffee, and then filling up the cup with Scotch—the best whisky in the world.

In the aircraft I went to sleep soon after fastening my seat belt for take-off, and woke when we landed for twenty minutes at Townsville.

Getting out to stretch my legs, and visit the airport toilet, I was spoken to by the man who had been sitting alongside me.

'You must have had a heavy night,' he said. 'You went to sleep as soon as you got aboard. You look as though you could use a hair of the dog.'

'Yes. Too much Mac's beer, I'm afraid.'

'Mac's? Strewth. No wonder you feel crook.'

Back aboard the aircraft, he said, 'Staying long in Cairns?'

'Just a few days.'

'You'll be right there. You'll get a good hair of the dog there. Cairns beer is the best in the world.'

'Oh? Then it must be very good. Are you from Cairns?'

'Yes. That's my home town. Can't get back quick enough. Been down doing a job in Melbourne for the last three months. Melbourne in the winter. Shouldn't happen to a dog.'

'Well,' I said. 'Their beer is good.'

'Not bad. Not a patch on Cairns, but. Where are you staying in Cairns?'

'At a place called Hides Cairns Hotel-Motel.'

'Ah,' he said. 'Best pub in the city. A home from home. Air-conditioning and the works. You'll be right there. Van Brederode knows how to run a pub.'

John van Brederode, and two of his 'licensed victualler' friends met me at the airport. Good fellows all. They briefed me on the amber fluid that provided them with a living.

Cairns Brewery, they told me, was the 'baby' of Australian breweries. There was no professional brewing in Cairns prior to 1925. The company survived for only two years. Then Northern Australian Breweries Ltd was formed, and took over in 1927. Carlton & United bought an interest in 1931, and now owns it. They call it the Great Northern Brewery. The building itself is called the R. G. Fogarty Brewhouse, Fogarty being the Carlton 'big wheel' of the period.

'She's the most modern brewery in Australia,' I was told at least a dozen times. They had a visit arranged for that afternoon.

The brewery is a fine piece of architecture. And internally it more than lives up to its external promise. I had been impressed by Courage in Melbourne, with its two-man control of the whole brewing process. But here, operating a massive isolated control panel, was only one man.

All air in the 'brewhouse' was electronically filtered. And the surprisingly young brewer who showed me around did not try to restrain his pride.

After the tour, he returned me to the manager's VIP bar. The manager, also young, was entertaining my licensee friends. He challenged my statement that there had to be some difference between his bulk draught and his bottled draught.

'Put up or shut up,' he said. 'Turn around, and I'll pour you one of each. These gentlemen will be witnesses.'

I had to put up. There was no discernible difference. I drank both, and expressed my appreciation of a very good lager indeed. The brewer smiled his pleasure.

After leaving the brewery, my 'licensed victualler' friends took me on a sampling tour of Cairns hotels. But I noticed they hustled me past a few, and these I remembered and determined to visit alone the next day. My hosts' reluctance to take me into them was understandable. They were pretty rough.

Cairns, like New South Wales beer, is a mixture of old and new. It has ultra-modern buildings, and primitive shacks. It has top class tourist hotels, and 'rough bush pubs'. The 'roughest and toughest', I was told, was the Barrier Reef, on the 'Barbary Coast'.

'Don't go down there on your own. You take your life in your hands. Bloke was knifed there the other night. Leave it to the Abos and the TI boys.'

'TI?'

'Thursday Islanders. Mad bastards when they get a few grogs in.'

I was interested. I found the place. Or rather, a taxi driver delivered me to it, with evident reluctance, and some head-shaking disapproval.

'Off a ship, are you?' he said.

'Er—yes.'

'You blokes cause more trouble than you're worth. Want me to come and pick you up later and take you back to town?'

'Er—no thank you. I think I'll walk.'

'Bloody long walk.'

'I feel I need the exercise.'

'Yeah? You might get some in there. Well, it's your funeral. If you need wheels, give us a ring.'

I headed for the bar, and, admittedly with some trepidation, entered it.

My fears were groundless. I found it to be an interesting, even exotic place. Perhaps at night it could be dangerous, but I doubted it. It was certainly safe enough in the forenoon, and pleasantly different. A percentage of clients, all coloured, were somewhat under the influence, but not objectionably so. I, still looking like a 'raw prawn with a cooked head', was not accosted, abused, or otherwise molested. 'The natives were friendly'.

The 'licensed victualler', serving behind the bar, was also friendly, and gave an appearance of being in complete control. A most unusual 'licensed victualler'. Female. Japanese. Her premises were clean, her beer good.

I walked back to town, arriving in a 'muck sweat'. More Cairns lager was indicated, to replace lost fluid. And this pleasant medication was swallowed in one of the 'rough' pubs, which also advertised counter lunch. The menu was chalked on a blackboard, and included—spelling as written—'Hot Brisket and Pickels', and 'Grilled Makeral and Salad'.

I chummed up with an old man, who walked with the aid of a knobby stick, and for whom I 'shouted'. He accused me, as the taxi driver did, of being off a ship. I did not deny it, but did not mention that I left the ship several weeks before in Fremantle.

He was a friendly old fellow. He had no objection to seamen, he said. They was all right, he said. They was welcome any time, even in the tourist season. He couldn't stand bloody tourists, but.

'They come up here in droves,' he said, 'to get away from the winter down south. More money than bloody sense. Mostly they hang around Hides an' the Northern, but sometimes they come in here. Slummin', you know. Lookin' for what they call local colour. If they come in when I'm here, I generally send 'em down to the Reef. Plenty o' colour there. Couple of 'em come in one time—business blokes by the look of 'em—big notin' 'emselves like business blokes do. One of 'em orders a gin an' it, with a cherry. The other galah wants a gin an' two, with an olive. He turns to me—I'm sittin' here on me usual stool—an' he says, "An' what would you like, old timer?" I says, "Aw, I reckon I'll just settle for a pint o' beer an' a mango." Silly bastards.'

My 'licensed victualler' friends in Cairns asked me if I planned to visit Darwin while I was in the north. It was possible to fly across, they said. All I would need would be a permit to stay overnight at Gove, which was an Aboriginal Reserve. But they said that could be arranged.

I told them my wife and I would be flying back to UK and we would break our journey and spend a couple of days in Darwin.

'Don't miss it,' they told me. 'Only one place in the world drinks more beer per head than Darwin. That's Munich. At least on last figures. Darwin could easily have passed them by now. Two breweries there—one Swan, one Carlton. Try a Darwin stubby while you're there. See if you can drink it down in one go.'

'That should not be too difficult,' I said.

'You reckon? They're not the same as our stubbies. A Darwin stubby holds forty ounces.'

I said I would not try to drink it down in one go. But I consumed more than forty ounces of Cairns lager the night before I was due to leave, thanks to local hospitality.

In the morning a banging on the door of my room woke me. And there, God bless him, was a cheerful night porter with a steaming cup of tea, and thick slices of hot buttered toast. I laced the tea with Scotch. Truly a 'home from home', Hides Cairns Hotel-Motel. I left it with regret.

8
New South Wales

'I never have a hangover'

On the long flight from Cairns to Sydney, with a brief stop at
Townsville, and a change of aircraft at Brisbane, I was thinking that so far I had no encouraging facts and figures for my
Company. In five Australian States it was my considered opinion
that a new brewery would fail. Without a string of 'tied houses'
through which to market the product, retail outlets would be
almost nil. Existing breweries 'had the game sewn up'. And in
any case, as Courage found in Victoria, the Aussie consumer's
stubborn preference for the devil he knew would take many
years to break down, if it could be done at all. Enormous
capital investment would be needed just to make a start. And the
odds against eventual success were too great for a sane investor.

This was, for me, a depressing conclusion. I had hoped to
be able to present a favourable report, and I had a further hope
—justified—that I would be offered the Australian management
job. Which I would certainly accept. I liked very much what I
had seen of Australia and its people. And I was sure my wife's
prejudices could be overcome.

There was still, however, one ray of hope, although admittedly a very small one. There was still New South Wales.

My wife met me at Sydney's airport. She said, 'Good God!'
I was still wearing my 'tropical rig' of long socks, shorts, and
an-necked shirt.

She laughed and said, 'You look—you look—'

'I know,' I said. 'I look like a raw prawn with a cooked
head.'

She laughed again. 'I wouldn't have put it just that way, but
it's a very apt description.'

'I've found us a small flat,' she said. 'I moved in today but
haven't had time to get in a supply of groceries and things.
There's only bread and butter and bacon and eggs for breakfast.'

I said, still mentally in Queensland, 'Shit, eh? No coffee, but?'

'James,' she said. 'What on earth—?'

'Sorry love. Queensland language.'

'It's high time you came back to civilization,' she said. 'I'll
have to start training you all over again. Anyway—there is
coffee, but."

'No whisky, but?'

'No whisky.'

'That's all right,' I said. 'I have some. Nothing but the best.
Mackinlay's.'

'You have it for breakfast?'

'Yes. This morning I had it in a cup of tea *before* breakfast.'

'Not only disgusting language, but disgusting habits. Things
are going to change for you, my lad.'

We took a taxi to the small flat, which was within walking
distance of King's Cross.

After I had unpacked, showered and changed, we shared
some of my remaining Mackinlay's—purchased in Cairns—
before going out to dinner. We discussed the future.

If my firm were to start brewing in Australia; and *if* they
were to set up operations in Sydney; and *if* I were to be given
the management job, she would return with me to Australia.
Three big ifs. I was not very confident.

Within a week I had no confidence left at all. 'Poms keep out' was my conclusion. I could see no hope of getting a footing in New South Wales, despite the fact that it is the most heavily populated State, with a high per capita beer consumption. My figures showed that it supported approximately 2000 hotels, about 1500 licensed clubs, numerous bottle shops, wine bars, and licensed restaurants, and that its men and women drank nearly fifty per cent of all beer consumed in Australia. And the big boys—Tooth's and Toohey's, 'had the game sewn up'.

Two independent breweries, Resch's and Miller's, had been quietly 'acquired'. Tooth's called their place the Kent Brewery, from its early founder John Tooth, who came from Kent. In certain country centres they marketed a brew called 'Old Kent', which of course, for those who drank it, was 'the best beer in the world'. Both Tooth's and Toohey's owned large numbers of 'tied houses', as outlets for their products. Drinkers had a wide choice of products—Tooth's Old or New or 'Fifty', or Resch's, or Old Kent; Toohey's Old or New or 'Fifty', or Miller's, or Grafton, and others to come; and there was a bewildering array of bottled and canned draughts and export lagers.

The various draughts were dispensed in seven, ten, fifteen, and twenty-ounce containers, called respectively sevens, middies, schooners, and pints. The timid could also get fives. Both breweries made top and bottom fermentation beers in staggering quantities. Beer made by top fermentation—the oldest brewing process known to man—they called 'new'. The bottom fermentation product, a relatively new process, they called 'old'. I don't know the reason for this reverse nomenclature, but the two products could be distinguished, the one from the other, by colour and taste. Old beer I found to be dark in colour, caused by a darker malt used in its making. This also gave it a distinctive malty flavour. The two, mixed together by bar attendants, were called 'fifty'. A middy of fifty contained half old and half new, either Tooth's, or Toohey's, depending on who owned the pub.

Although the inhabitants of other States seemed to be unanimous in their condemnation of New South Wales beers, I had no complaints. They were all good lagers, with only minor differences. Of them all, I preferred Resch's. I tried them all in city and suburban samplings, and also had my first taste of Aussie 'home brew'.

Home brewing in Australia is a popular pastime, particularly in New South Wales. Its main attraction is its low cost—no iniquitous excise duty, no brewery and bar overheads, no transportation costs, and 'empties' readily obtainable. Several manufacturers were marketing home brew kits, complete with instructions and packaged raw materials.

Legally the alcoholic content of the product was not to exceed a fixed low percentage, but neither the home brewers nor the police seemed to worry about this.

Certainly the sample I was introduced to was not low in alcohol. One bottle had a noticeable effect on me. It was brewed by a gentleman named Lionel, whom I met in a pub in Woolloomooloo — that inner suburb with the extraordinary name which no visitor can pronounce correctly until tutored. Lionel invited me to his home to sample some of his brew.

'Next Sunday,' he said. 'I'm bungin' on a barbecue lunch. Bring the wife.'

He gave me his address in Brighton, on the shores of Botany Bay.

'Got a new brew ready to crack,' he said. 'Sampled her last night. She's a beauty.'

It was a beautiful warm spring day that Sunday. I ignored my wife's protests, and wore my 'tropical rig'. And was proved to have made the right choice. Other guests, and our host, were wearing shorts. None wore a tie.

Lionel wore a tall chef's hat, and one of his wife's aprons. He barbecued steak, chops and sausages, and his supply of home brew appeared to be inexhaustible.

It was a little too sweet for my taste, but the others voted it 'a good drop o' slops'. Except one man, who said, 'If you're thirsty enough you'll drink anything.'

'No more, thanks, I'm driving'

'My best friend,' Lionel said. 'I'll have you know I'd be just about the best home brewer this side of the black stump.'

'That's what I like about the old Lionel—his modesty and humility.'

'You couldn't make a brew like that if I was to give you the recipe. Which I do not, mark you, intend to do.'

'I wouldn't want it,' best friend said. 'I like to keep my mates.'

'What, both of them? Look—we have with us today a world authority on alcoholic beverages. To wit, James McIntosh. Now tell us, Jim, in your own words, have you or have you not ever tasted a more delectable home brew?'

'I have not,' I said firmly. I had never previously tasted any.

'There you are,' Lionel said. 'A man of obvious intelligence and integrity, and the possessor of a refined and discriminating palate. I'll give *you* the recipe, Jim.'

'And may the Lord have mercy on his soul,' best friend said.

Lionel retired to write his recipe for me.

TO MANUFACTURE THE WORLD'S BEST BREW
LIONEL SPECIAL EXPORT XXXX
TOP SECRET

This recipe will self-distruct in thirty seconds. (To speed up your own self-destruction, consume recipe below in vast quantities.)

Tie four ounces hops with one teaspoonful table salt into muslin bag, and put into four-gallon honey tin containing two gallons of water. Bring to boil, and then simmer for half an hour. Pour this brew into a ten-gallon plastic garbage bin, and add two gallons cold water. Then add four pounds malt extract, and three pounds brown sugar, and stir well. Position container and contents where it will remain undisturbed by blow-ins, sticky-beaks, and amateur tasters—then top up with six gallons water, and sprinkle one ounce powdered yeast on top. Skim after twenty-four hours, and again if necessary twenty-four hours later. After seven days, syphon off into bottles, each containing a teaspoonful of white sugar. Seal, and allow to stand for at least one week.

At the end of this period, select a bottle, and grasping bottle opener between thumb and forefinger of the right hand, gingerly prize off crown seal and—STAND BACK.

This simple method, with variable quantities of hops and sugar optional, will produce a true ale, although only slightly reminiscent of Cooper's. The addition of sugar to each bottle takes care of any surplus yeast cells that may be floating about, thus producing more alcohol, and building up gas pressure. The brew is heady, frothy, and has a pronounced hop flavour. And the cost per bottle, Lionel told me, is only a few cents.

Ten gallons equals sixty bottles. But of course, Lionel said, you first have to accumulate sixty empties. The best way to do this, he advised, is to invite ten friends on a Saturday night to a bottle party, each to bring six. You provide the 'tucker' and glasses, he said. Two pounds of spaghetti, two pounds of mince steak, a tin of tomato paste, and a couple of onions will feed the lot 'cheap'. And your wife does the cooking. And there will be enough bottles left over to carry you through for a couple of weeks until your brew is ready. Then you 'bung on a Sampling Party, no charge'.

When Lionel presented me with his recipe, he said, 'There

you are, mate. Guard that with your life, and preserve it for posterity. You, and you only, are the custodian of the written evidence of my genius. Lodge it for safe keeping with your bank or solicitor. And while you live, you will never be short of a grog.'

'He won't live long,' best friend said. 'I advise him to use the paper on which that is written for other purposes. Anything would be better—metho would be better—than that. Which reminds me. When I was a commercial traveller—'

Lionel interrupted. 'Here we go again. Another bulldust anecdoty of my best friend's pre-historic past.'

Best friend ignored this remark and continued.

'I left Lake Cargelligo one morning, proceeding south to Rankin Springs, to pick up the highway for Hay. I was selling patent medicines at the time, to chemists and stores. It was in the heat of summer, and the alleged road was pot-holed, eroded, gullied, and strewn with boulders. After a couple of hours, in first and second gear, I was concentrating on my driving, when my mind registered the fact that I had passed a tin shed, bearing the sign "General Store". Now, attached to my steering column was a piece of circular celluloid, provided free of charge by my masters, on which were the words "Why am I Here?" My conscience told me that I was there to work. So at great risk to life and limb, I reversed, dismounted, and entered with my order book in hand. There was nobody there. There was an old wooden counter with some shelves behind it, and on the shelves were a few items, placed about two feet apart, of negligible total value. There was a tube of tooth paste, a tin of plum jam, a tin of peaches, a tin of pork and beans, and a couple of other things. I said to myself "Why am I Here?" And I answered "Buggered if I know."

'Whoever owned the shack wasn't there, and he had practically no stock anyway, so all I could do was to leave him a show-card and take off. I dug out a card. I was setting it up on the counter, when in walks an old bloke with a long grey beard, from somewhere out the back. I said to him, bright and breezy, "Good day." He says, "Koot tay." German, see. I say, "I'm

'I need another drink like I need a hole in the head'

just leaving you a show-card. All right?" He digs out his glasses
—they had round steel rims on them; made him look like a
mopoke with chin whiskers—and he peers at it. He says,
"Slawn's Liniment?" I say, "Yes, very goot." He says, "Ya.
Koot. You sell him?" I say, "Yes, I sell him." He says, "Koot.
I buy him." Well, that was a turn up. I get his name and
write it on my order book. I say, "Right. Sloan's Liniment.
How many would you like?" He says, "Von." I say "One?" He
says, "Ya. Von." One lousy bottle. All that reversing in the
heat, all that time wasted, order in triplicate. Bugger him. I
write one dozen. I take a chance that he won't notice when
he signs, see.'

Lionel said, 'Oh, the deception. Oh, the ruthless money-
grubbing commercial soul. Trying to take advantage of a poor
old man, a stranger in a strange land, living on a pittance in
the middle of sweet FA. Oh, how repugnant are the ways of—'

'*Will* you shut up? Do you want to hear this true story, or
don't you?'

'I don't, particularly. But unfortunately I know of no verbal device which could be used effectively as a diverting agent. Carry on.'

'Thank you. Where was I?'

'You wrote, shamefully, one dozen, in the hope that the poor old man, with his failing eyesight, would not notice the unforgivable deception.'

'Yes. Well, he did.'

'Good.'

'Shut up. Before he signs the order, he squints at it through his round glasses, and he says, "Von doz?" I know I'm gone, but I go down fighting. I say, "Yes, that's what you wanted, wasn't it?" He says, "No. Von grawss." I can't believe my ears. I don't reckon he knows what a gross is. But I write it. Quick. Before he wakes up to himself. He knows what it is, all right. He vets it and signs it. I give him his carbon copy, and thank him, and I say, "Not many people around here, are there?" He says, "No. No pipples." I say, "Well, excuse me for asking. Where do you expect to sell all that Sloan's Liniment?" Know what he says?'

'How would we know if you don't tell us?'

'He says, "Sell him? Ton't sell him. Trink him. Is koot." '

'He bought it to *drink?*

'That's what he said.'

'Strewth. Don't believe you.'

'It's as true as I stand here, weaving slightly.'

'I accidentally got some on my testicles once. Worse than blue bottles. Sat in the tub for hours before I got the sting out of it. Never been the same man since. Drink it? Strewth.'

Lionel's fine flow of language had dried up at the horrible thought.

'They were tough in the bush in those days,' best friend said. 'That old bloke would even have had a go at your home brew.'

They were inebriated, but still wrangling happily, when the party began to break up. We thanked our host and hostess, and Lionel presented us with two bottles of 'the best home brew in the world'.

With those two bottles for company we returned to our flat

and discussed our future, based on my firm conviction that the establishment of a new competitive brewery in Australia was out of the question. On the other hand, I did not want to go home. And my wife said that she was not looking forward to another English winter. But I had a good job, she said, with a good Company, and I would undoubtedly be offered a directorship one day. We couldn't think of sacrificing all that, could we?

Under the influence of Lionel's home brew, I surprised myself by asking, 'Why not?'

It was after midnight when my wife said, 'Let's go to bed. We'll talk about it again in the morning. When you're sober.'

I quietly slid out of bed very early in the morning, made myself a refreshing glass of 'Red Eye', and went for a walk. Even at that pre-sunrise hour, there were people about in King's Cross. I walked through to the small park by the Alamein Fountain, and sat on a bench, and thought about ways and means, and other things.

The 'other things' included a few thoughts on the grog situation in New South Wales, prompted by the presence of a large hotel on one side of the small park. A place whose bars had been honoured several times by my patronage. My research had disclosed that there had always been grog in New South Wales, ever since Englishmen first came to 'clutter up the place'. Cook's ship *Endeavour* carried oaken kegs of brandy—Officers and Mr Banks for the use of—and First Fleeters were making top fermentation home brew as soon as they managed to grow some spare grain.

To supplement home brew, Jamaican rum was brought 12,000 miles from England, and guarded more closely than the convicts. The 'New South Wales Rum Corps', and the 'Rum Rebellion', are part of Australia's history. For nearly 200 years, New South Welshmen have been able to find something alcoholic to drink. But not in a Macleay Street pub at six o'clock in the morning. Those pubs opened at ten. So when I returned to do verbal battle with my wife, she would not be able to accuse me of insobriety.

That there would be a verbal battle seemed to me to be inevitable. The thought of returning to England, to the day-by-day routine of boring work and traditional convention, was depressing. The Australian way of life, the Australian people, had an exhilarating effect on me; it had to be farewell to the bowler hat and furled umbrella country.

Decision irrevocable. Now for some ammunition with which to reinforce arguments pro, and defeat arguments con.

Workers were now to-ing and fro-ing, and traffic was heavy. 'The Cross' was fully awake. So was my wife.

'Good morning, darling,' she said. 'Did you have a nice walk?'

'Very nice, thank you. And you will note that I am fully sober and in my right mind. I have something important to tell you.'

'I know,' she said. 'You were up with the sparrows. You've been walking and thinking. Now you're full of words. So am I. But, like a civilized person, I do my morning thinking over a cup of coffee.'

'All right. Now sit down and listen to what—'

'Just a minute,' she said, 'pour yourself some coffee and I'll add something to it.'

Astonished and speechless, I watched her pour a double or triple whisky into my cup, and not much less into her own, which she then filled with coffee.

She raised her cup and said, 'Cheers.'

'Cheers,' I said. I knew what she was doing. Softening me up for the kill. She would not succeed.

'All right,' I said. 'Now listen.'

She said, 'No. You listen. You don't want to go back to England.'

'Check,' I said. 'And what's more, I'm not going back to England.'

'You are, my lad. We both are.'

'Look,' I said. 'I've been thinking—'

'I know. Now you're going to stop thinking and listen.'

'But—'

'No buts. You may talk after I've finished. I want a promise from you.'

'If you want me to promise—'

'I want you to promise to listen to me and not to interrupt.'

I had nothing to lose. It's always good tactics to learn the enemy's mind. I said, 'Very well. I promise.'

'Good. Last night I said that I was not looking forward to another English winter. You probably don't remember, because shortly afterwards, full of home brew, you crashed ingloriously, and kept me awake with your alcoholic snoring.'

'I remember very well. I remember—'

'Do you remember what you just promised?'

'Er—yes.'

'Thank you. So, being unable to sleep, I thought about things. And this morning, when you woke me at some ungodly hour by creeping furtively out of bed, I thought some more. We are going back to England. By air, as per schedule. On your expense account, as per arrangement. No cost to us. Shortly after arrival, and again as per arrangement, you make an appointment with the Managing Director and deliver your negative report. Have you written it yet? Your promise of silence does not apply to answers to my questions. Have you written it yet?'

'No.'

'No. Then write it. You have three days. We fly out in three days. When you deliver your report to the Managing Director, you will also deliver your written resignation. Close your mouth. You look like a fish. Then we both go to Australia House and we apply, as potential emigrants, for assisted passages back to Australia. Your vow of silence is now revoked. You may speak. Cheers.'

She drained her cup, and filled it again with coffee and whisky. My God, I thought—what's she been doing while I've been travelling around slaving for my employers? Who has been infecting her with a virus? What an unprincipled, cunning, advantage-taking—

'Cheers,' was all I could say, followed by, 'and pass the whisky.'

I said, between gulps of coffee and whisky, 'But—but—but—'

'You sound like a two-stroke engine with a mucky spark plug,' she said.

'But—are you serious?'

'Very serious,' she said, still grinning.

'Well—what about our house?'

'Sell it. That's one of the reasons why we're going back.'

'And the mortgage?'

'Pay it off after the sale. We'll keep what's left.'

'And our car?'

'That's the other reason. Sell it, and keep the lot. There are no more payments due on it, are there?'

'No. And if I can't get a good job here?'

'Then you'll have to give up your beer, won't you? And you'll have to give up whisky for breakfast, too.'

'Yes. I had no idea you were thinking—'

'I think,' she said, 'that Australia is a better country than England for bringing up children.'

'Children? What have children—? *Children*? You don't mean—?'

'That's exactly what I do mean,' she said.

'Kalgoorlie,' she said. 'Cheers.'

And I thought it was 'flu.

It is late Autumn in England. The skies are grey, the wind is cold, the trees are bare. The beer is warm, the price of whisky is prohibitive, and I have joined the ranks of the many unemployed.

Australia's hot sun, warm friendship, and cold beer are calling. We will be there shortly, our future uncertain, our capital dwindling, but our hopes high. . . .

Now you've read *It's Your Shout, Mate!* and are undoubtedly an expert on Aussie pubs and Aussie beers, may we introduce you to two more books by John O'Grady that are essential reading for the complete Aussie. The books are *Aussie English* and *Aussie Etiket*. Read on for further information . . .

AUSSiE ENGLISH

an explanation of the Australian idiom

---

by JOHN O'GRADY
(Nino Culotta)

Illustrated by WEP

Can you tell a ringer from a ring-in, a cockatoo from a galah, a blue from a bluey? This A-Z of Australian slang will show you how.

OVER 120,000 COPIES SOLD. NOW AVAILABLE IN ITS TWELFTH IMPRESSION. RECOMMENDED RETAIL PRICE $1.95.

AUSSIE ETIKET

or

Doing Things the Aussie Way

JOHN O'GRADY

Illustrated by Benier

Do you know how to do things the Aussie way? This book will show you what to do and say—also what *not* to do and say— on every occasion.

OVER 30,000 COPIES SOLD. NOW AVAILABLE IN ITS SIXTH IMPRESSION. RECOMMENDED RETAIL PRICE $1.95.

EVERYMAN'S LIBRARY

EVERYMAN,
I WILL GO WITH THEE,
AND BE THY GUIDE,
IN THY MOST NEED
TO GO BY THY SIDE

TONI MORRISON

BELOVED

WITH AN INTRODUCTION
BY A. S. BYATT

EVERYMAN'S LIBRARY
Alfred A. Knopf   New York   London   Toronto
268

THIS IS A BORZOI BOOK
PUBLISHED BY ALFRED A. KNOPF

First included in Everyman's Library, 2006
Copyright © 1987, 2004 by Toni Morrison
Originally published in a slightly different form in hardcover in the
United States by Alfred A. Knopf, a division of Random House, Inc.,
1987
First published in Great Britain by Chatto & Windus, 1987
Reprinted by permission of the Random House Group Ltd.

Introduction Copyright © 2006 by A. S. Byatt
Bibliography and Chronology Copyright © 2006 by Everyman's Library
Typography by Peter B. Willberg

US website: www.randomhouse.com/everymans

ISBN: 0-307-26488-2 (US)
1-85715-268-9 (UK)

A CIP catalogue reference for this book is available from the
British Library

Book design by Barbara de Wilde and Carol Devine Carson

Typeset in the UK by AccComputing, North Barrow, Somerset

Printed and bound in Germany by GGP Media GmbH, Pössneck

BELOVED

INTRODUCTION

I reviewed *Beloved* when it first appeared in Britain, in 1987. I
remember the experience of reading it for the first time. I wrote
then, "This novel gave me nightmares and yet I sat up late,
paradoxically smiling to myself with intense pleasure at the
exact beauty of the singing prose." I recognized it as a writer, as
one of those "fortunate" books whose forms present themselves
fluently in the writing, whose problems know their own solu-
tions. Morrison in her 2004 foreword describes how it was
written, in a rare period of freedom, when she had given up
her publishing work and was able to think about what "freedom" meant – to women, and beyond that, to people who
were, or had been, slaves. Her subject rose up at her, as the
solid female ghost rose out of the water, in a "nice hat," to
haunt the women in the house in 1873, and to embody an
American masterpiece in 1987. I reread it before writing this
introduction, with the same mixture of delight and terror and
with even more admiration for the brilliance of its art.

Beloved turns on the slaughter of a baby by her own mother.
Sethe kills her child rather than have her returned from
freedom to slavery. Sethe has escaped from Sweet Home in
Kentucky to freedom in Ohio, where she has joined her
mother-in-law, Baby Suggs, whose freedom has been bought
by the labor of Sethe's husband, Halle. Sethe's three elder
children, two boys and a "crawling-already" daughter, are
already in the free house, number 124. Sethe has given birth
to another daughter, Denver, on the way there. The harsh
Fugitive Slave Act of 1850 gave slave-owners the right to
retrieve their "property" from states that had abolished slavery.
The Act had been passed as part of a payment for Southern
support for the admission of California to the Union as a free
state, and for the ending of the slave trade in the District of
Columbia. The Act aroused anger and distress in northern
states. *Uncle Tom's Cabin,* published in 1852, dramatized the
moral distress of the abolitionists. The Act was repealed in
1864. Northern states' attempts to legislate against it led to the

secession of South Carolina in 1860, and to the American Civil War of 1861–5.

Sethe's escape is modeled on the story of Margaret Garner, who escaped from Kentucky with sixteen other slaves in January 1856. The fugitives were pursued by a posse of slave masters and sheriff's officers. They fought back. Margaret Garner cut her youngest daughter's throat with a butcher's knife and tried to kill herself and the rest of her children. There was a sensational trial, in which the slaves' lawyer paradoxically suggested that Margaret be charged with murder and the others with complicity – trying to ensure that she remained in the Free State to be judged as a person, not returned as property. She was, however, returned, and her other baby daughter was drowned when the boat returning them capsized. Margaret is reported as having "displayed frantic joy" at this death.

The tale is grim. Margaret Garner became a symbolic heroine for the abolitionists. Harriet Beecher Stowe dramatized the events in *Dred,* a novel about a slave revolution, which enacted, grimly, the lynchings and mob riots of the South, sold 100,000 copies in four weeks, and was adapted for the stage. Stowe's Cora Gordon speaks in her own justification with strong and argued rhetoric. Morrison, in her introduction to *Beloved*, speaks of the real Margaret Garner's "intellect," "ferocity," and "willingness to risk everything for what was to her the necessity of freedom." Morrison invented Sethe in order to have space to imagine history – an imagined history of slavery, both reality and myth at once.

*

Beloved is, in ways to which I shall come back, the great American nineteenth-century novel that wasn't written, about those things that were not written about, but which haunt those great novels, by Melville and Poe, that were. In American fiction of that period there is always a sense of a reality beyond realism, a reaching-out for the "myth before the myth began," as Wallace Stevens puts it in "Notes Toward a Supreme Fiction." *Beloved* has everything that makes the delight of strong realist fiction – complex, believable, admirable, and suffering characters, fully imagined places and things, food, clothes, social awkwardnesses and narrownesses, singing dialogue in real voices. It has the bleak power of true, not symbolic tragedy, the defeat of fully imagined human beings. It makes its readers, relentlessly, contemplate terrors they are really horrified by, with no Gothic thrill – mundane, unimaginative cruelties, the extremity of infanticide and its effects on everyone near it. But it has also the quality of American Gothic, the black veil of metaphor, the symbolic glitter of myth.

The two worlds are connected – indivisibly entwined – by the extraordinary solidity of the ghost of the unappeased dead baby, who is introduced in the first two brief sentences. "124 was spiteful. Full of a baby's venom." The invisible spite willfully creates her own solidity, clothes her body with real clothes, and puts shoes on her unused feet (she was only "crawling-already"), rises dripping from the water, and demands love with the unappeasable desire of a dependent baby. She becomes black and shining, lovely, greedy, and terrible. Her bodily presence anchors her in the real world of the novel. Her name, and other names, place her in a myth.

Margaret Atwood, reviewing the novel, noted the importance of its epigraph.

> *I will call them my people,*
> *which were not my people;*
> *and her beloved,*
> *which was not beloved.*

This is from St. Paul's Epistle to the Romans, and comes from a passage in which Paul is arguing that the Gentiles, as well as the Jews, are the children of God. Paul goes on:

And it shall come to pass, that in the place where it was said unto them, Ye are not my people; there shall they be called the children of the living God.

This passage is about the inclusion of the excluded, the despised and rejected of men, and can be compared to the defiant citation, by rebellious slaves, of the Declaration of Independence. "We hold these truths to be self-evident, that all men are created equal; that they are endowed by their Creator with certain unalienable rights, that among these are life, liberty and the pursuit of happiness." (Stowe's *Dred* is impressive in this context.)

The passage could also be connected to what I take to be the biblical origin of Morrison's choice of name for her heroine – Sethe. I like to think it rhymes with the classical Lethe, the river of oblivion, but I am not sure about this. What does seem clear is that Sethe was named for Adam and Eve's third child, Seth, born after the murder of Abel by Cain. This child, according to certain traditions, was presented with the staff God gave to Adam, a branch of the Tree of Life, and Kallimachus says that it is "well known...that the descendants of Cain are distinguished in Scripture by the name of the sons of man or Adam; those of Seth by the name of the sons of God." (This appears to be an allusion to those "sons of God" in Genesis 6:2 who "saw the daughters of men that they were fair.") Christ called himself the son of God, and the quotation from Romans, taken with the description of Seth, suggests that the excluded are the true inheritors.

Set, or Seth, is also an ambivalent deity, worshipped in ancient Egypt as a form of Typhon, the destroying serpent, female as well as male. Hippolytus in his refutation of heresies in the early days of Christianity says that the "Sethians" worshipped "the Eternal Logos – Darkness, and Mist, and Tempest." The divinity also became associated with the waters of the Nile and the regenerative mud that produced life from death. Some esoteric heresies identify Set or Seth with the Serpent in Paradise, the third (excluded) member of the trinity Adam, Eve, and the Serpent. Essentially what *Beloved* takes from this cluster of myths is this symbolic grouping of female, darkness, water, rejected, but secretly the source of life. There is a wonderful mythic moment when Sethe is at her lowest, battered, bleeding, crawling on her pregnant belly to hide in the grass, just before she meets Amy, the raggedy white girl.

She thinks she hears a white boy and becomes a destroyer.

She told Denver that a *something* came up out of the earth into her – like a freezing, but moving too, like jaws inside. "Look like I was just cold jaws grinding," she said. Suddenly she was eager for his eyes, to bite into them; to gnaw his cheek.

Amy is brusquely kind (her name means love, or gentleness; all the names in the novel, I think, have meanings). She speaks to Sethe.

Down in the grass, like the snake she believed she was, Sethe opened her mouth, and instead of fangs and a split tongue, out shot the truth.

And Amy massages Sethe's bleeding feet, which carries Christian associations – Christ's bleeding feet, Christ washing the feet of the disciples.

In a symbolic novel, a metaphor is as real in the reader's mind as a *thing* on the level of the primary narrative. Sethe is a snake. It is no accident that in the storytelling of the novel, the imaged snake is juxtaposed to a brief description Sethe gives her daughter Denver, named for Amy's home town, of schoolteacher, the white man at Sweet Home who inherits the slaves and is writing a book comparing the animal and human characteristics of the black people. (It was important to the argument that the Declaration of Independence didn't apply to blacks, to claim that they were part animals, in some way inferior to those "all men" [not women?] who are born free.) Sethe in the realist novel is painfully human. At her lowest moment, Paul D tells her "You got two feet, Sethe, not four," recalling the unspeakable idea of animal characteristics. The sentence goes on "and right then a forest sprang up between them; trackless and quiet." The word forest is not the word jungle, to which we shall come. But the insult carries the whole weight of the horror of being black and human and a slave.

*

Almost all readers of *Beloved*, I imagine, will associate the title more readily with the biblical Song of Solomon than with St. Paul. "I am black, but comely," says the beloved, who was perhaps the Queen of Sheba. "Look not upon me, because I am black, because the sun hath looked upon me: my mother's children were angry with me; they made me the keeper of the vineyards; but mine own vineyard have I not kept." The whole poem is dripping with sweetness, bodily pleasure, and paradisal imagery. The erotic garden of the black but comely beloved is a version of the Paradise Garden, and the beloved is the garden.

> A garden inclosed is my sister, my spouse; a spring shut up, a fountain sealed...
> A fountain of gardens, a well of living waters, and streams from Lebanon...

Almost every line of the Song of Solomon has its resonance in *Beloved*, with its triumphant sensuality, its land of milk and honey, its imagery of children as well as lovers.

> O that thou wert as my brother, that sucked the breasts of my mother! when I should find thee without, I would kiss thee; yea, I should not be despised.
> I would lead thee, and bring thee into my mother's house, who would instruct me...

Here is the voice of Denver speaking to the beloved ghost, and also the voice of Sethe, seeking out the good mother, Baby Suggs.

> ...for love is strong as death; jealousy is cruel as the grave: the coals thereof are as coals of fire, which hath a most vehement flame.
> Many waters cannot quench love, neither can the floods drown it...
> We have a little sister, and she hath no breasts: what shall we do for our sister in the day when she shall be spoken for?

The Song of Solomon is a world of shining archetypes, apple trees, milk, water, bright black flesh for which the metaphors are pomegranates and tender grapes. It is set both ironically and in a kind of yearning counterpart against the world in which Sethe, Paul D, and Baby Suggs try to live well.

There are other, more corrupt versions of the Paradise Garden. Toni Morrison's naming of the Kentucky farm, Sweet Home, is a stroke of genius. Its owners are kinder than most slave-owners and almost treat their slaves as men and women. When Sethe remembers it, she cannot recall the fields and trees without a kind of love for the beauty of the earth, followed by the immediate sense that she does not want to love it, for it is not hers, and she was not at home in it but was a slave and a captive. I think Morrison kept the original name of the

owners of Margaret Garner because it has its own wicked irony
– the owners garner the fruits of the land, the slaves bring in
the harvest. Sethe's only contact with her mother is watching
her working in the fields before she is hanged. Baby Suggs
grants that Sweet Home is an improvement on her tortured
life in Carolina. "And no matter, for the sadness was at her
center, the desolated center where the self that was no self
made its home."

The American Dream sees the New World as a paradise.
I shall come back to that.

*

It could be argued that the black people in the novel have an
almost pastoral or mythical quality of virtue and intelligence.
They are all good, patient, heroic, and defeated. There is no
malice among the Sweet Home slaves, although the venom
and spite they suppress collects and manifests itself in the swelling ghost of the baby-woman. The neighboring blacks, in the
free community around 124, feel suspicion and spite when Baby
Suggs manages to make a kind of paradisal harvest feast in the
house. That is the spite of the humiliated, unable to claim their
world for their own as bravely as she has done. Sethe's child-
killing stands out as quite different from the crime of Medea,
slaughtering her children because she is rejected as a woman.
Sethe kills out of extreme love and fear, and Paul D's horror
of her act is her worst (and just) punishment (except for the
terrible presence of the ghost). What is hard to write about is
the exact justice with which Morrison depicts these damaged
people's grown-up intelligence and dignity in a world that gives
them no home. They do not have even their own names – the
Sweet Home men are Paul D Garner, Paul F Garner and
Paul A Garner, and the wild Sixo. Baby Suggs's owner always
believed she was called "Jenny" because that was on her
papers. But she sticks to the odd and awkward Baby Suggs,
because her husband was called Suggs, and he called her
"Baby." I have wondered whether Baby Suggs carries the suggestion of the child at the breast – baby sucks. Baby is a
diminutive that makes a child of a woman, even if it is loving

– but Baby Suggs is nothing if not grown-up, wise, and generous. (And Denver, finally, feels she is a woman when Lady Jones calls her "Baby.") These are people who hardly dare love their children because they may be sold tomorrow; who will not love, or reluctantly partly love, children fathered by white masters; who do not know, as human beings need to know, who are their ancestors, where they come from. They are people who own nothing, and are themselves owned. Yet, in this tale, they are not brutalized. The chain gang rescues itself in the flood because they move together, each depending on the other.

The true representative of this goodness and dignity is Paul D. One of the most moving moments in the novel, for me, is when he thinks – clearly – about the need to restrict his love to little things.

Listening to the doves in Alfred, Georgia, and having neither the right nor the permission to enjoy it because in that place mist, doves, sunlight, copper dirt, moon – everything belonged to the men who had the guns. Little men, some of them, big men too, each one of whom he could snap like a twig if he wanted to . . . And these "men" who made even vixen laugh could, if you let them, stop you from hearing doves or loving moonlight. So you protected yourself and loved small. Picked the tiniest stars out of the sky to own . . . Grass blades, salamanders, spiders, woodpeckers, beetles, a kingdom of ants. Anything bigger wouldn't do. A woman, a child, a brother – a big love like that would split you right open in Alfred, Georgia.

Paul D has his heart in a figurative tobacco tin, rusted shut – witched open by Beloved, who seduces him, as much as by his much more cautious settling in with Sethe.

The extraordinary form of the unfolding of the tale of this novel, terrible and beautiful, is essentially constructed round what is both a survival mechanism and a profound courtesy between the survivors – the reluctance to remember the horrors, or to speak of them to others, which might bring those horrors back to life. So Paul D does not intend to damage Sethe by telling her what happened to her husband, Halle, or to Sixo. So the community does not tell Paul D what Sethe has done, at least for some time. And so, bit by bit, Toni

Morrison's readers move through a fictive present full of bear-able reminiscences to the concealed horrors – and shattered passions – embodied in Beloved. It is only on a second reading that one can see how delicately Sethe cherry-picks what can be told to Denver as the epic triumph of Denver's birth, out of the unspeakable evil that led to it happening as it did.

Connected to this, and providing a bridge back to a different discussion of the mythic dimension of this novel, is the treat-ment of the white people who appear. Whiteness in this story is blankness, emptiness. White people, on the periphery of the events, are not very much imagined – they are *unimagined* presences of the unimaginable, and also of the unimaginative. (Consider the *limitations* of the ability to talk to or understand the black people displayed by Mr. Garner as he takes Baby Suggs to liberty, or the dying Mrs. Garner, thanking Sethe, but unaware of, and uninterested in, what is distressing her.) The schoolteacher's sons who steal milk are distinguished only by their repulsive "mossy teeth." The black girl's voice in the visionary scene of the slave ship sees whites uncomprehend-ingly as incomplete, people without skins. They are ghosts, demons.

This reverses, in a wonderful way, the dangerous building of black skins into old associations of darkness with blackness, with danger, even with evil. The American nineteenth-century novel is full of lurid contrasts between black and white, based in religious and metaphysical ambiguities and questioning. I was a postgraduate student in the late 1950s, studying what was then a new subject and a new discipline – American litera-ture. American literature was in a sense defined as the attempt to define and describe America, the Brave New World of the American Dream. One of the critical books that most impressed me at the time was *The Power of Blackness* by Harry Levin. It studied images of darkness and light, blackness and whiteness in Hawthorne, Poe, and Melville, and defined a certain kind of metaphysical, allegorical, Gothic darkness as an essential characteristic of early American novels. It dis-cussed the Puritan black gloom of Hawthorne's *Scarlet Letter*, and his minister who wore a Black Veil. It discussed Poe's black Raven, and went on to look at Poe's imaginary journey to the then unexplored Antarctic, *The Narrative of Arthur Gordon Pym*, published in 1838. In that fantastic adventure Pym sails, like Coleridge's Ancient Mariner, past black ships of death, in search of the South Pole. Here is Harry Levin at the South Pole:

Curiosity is rewarded at the expense of plausibility when land is sighted beyond the ice floes, "a singular ledge of rock... bearing a strong resemblance to corded bales of cotton." But the Ultima Thule on which they eventually set foot has no "light-colored substances of any kind." "Everything is black, the flora and fauna, the dwellings and artefacts, not only the skin but the teeth of the woolly-haired inhabitants. The very water is opaque and purplish. Whereas the shirts and sails of the visitors, the pages of their books and the shells of their eggs – everything white is taboo; and an untouchable white animal with red teeth is a sort of totem." The black-skinned warriors inter the white-skinned mariners alive. They escape through grey vapour, milky water, a rain of "fine white powder resembling ashes," the flight of "many gigantic and pallidly white birds." Their last vision is a shrouded figure, huger than lifesize, blocking their path. "And the hue of the skin of the figure was of the perfect whiteness of the snow."[1]

There is a lot more of this, and of other paradoxical black-white contrasts. Levin remarks, considering Poe's loathing of abolitionists, that "in the troubled depths of Poe's unconscious, there must have been not only the fantasy of a lost heritage, but a resentment and a racial phobia."[2]

Levin also considers Melville, whose tale "Benito Cereno" dramatizes the revolt of an enslaved crew against a Spanish captain, and whose masterpiece, *Moby-Dick*, depicts a whaler with a crew of all races, with a captain with a white ivory leg, careering across all the oceans of the world in pursuit of an unmasterable demonic whale, whose impossible color is white and who can only be struck by a harpoon baptized by black magic in the blood of three dark-complexioned harpooners. Melville's Ishmael is rescued by his brotherhood with the "savage" harpooner Queequeg (as Sethe, perhaps, does need the poor white Amy, in the only scene where a white has a

1 Harry Levin, *The Power of Blackness*, Ohio University Press, 1958, 115.
2 Ibid. 121.

voice and a character). But what is remarkable about *Moby-Dick* is the extraordinary beauty of the long passage about the *horror* of the whiteness of the whale, in the chapter with that heading. It is tendentious, it is extravagant, it creates new associations for the "color of purity" and, as it says itself, "the very veil of the Christian's Deity." Melville's rhetoric rides past the horror of the white bear of the poles and the white shark of the tropics, the pale dread of the albatross and the "strangely hideous" albino human. He identifies whiteness with indifference and cruelty.

Is it that by its indefiniteness it shadows forth the heartless voids and immensities of the universe, and thus stabs us from behind with the thought of annihilation, when beholding the white depths of the milky way? Or is it, that as in essence whiteness is not so much a color as the visible absence of color, and at the same time the concrete of all colors; is it for these reasons that there is such a dumb blankness, full of meaning, in a wide landscape of snows – a colorless, all-color of atheism from which we shrink? ... pondering all this, the palsied universe lies before us a leper ..."

It is in this chapter that Melville comes to his terrible conclusion: "Though in many of its aspects this visible world seems formed in love, the invisible spheres were formed in fright." He wrote to Hawthorne of this book, "I have written a wicked book, and feel spotless as the lamb" – a traditional image of white innocence which he has compromised.

I myself read *Uncle Tom's Cabin* when I was far too young, sitting in my grandmother's garden with an old copy I had found on her shelf and feeling overwhelmed by simple horror that a way of life could have existed like the one described in that story. It was one of my very earliest experiences of real evil, and it hurt me. When I read Harry Levin in the fifties, I simply assumed that he was saying that Poe's, and Melville's, turning of the religious imagery of whiteness into horror was at some level, conscious and unconscious, an admission that the New World is contaminated by a new sin, the racial guilt of enslavement. He doesn't in fact say that – he draws back from it, though from time to time he implies it.

In *Playing in the Dark* (1992) Toni Morrison does, with considerable irony and a kind of implacable charity, discuss the absence

of the presence of the enslaved black nation in American literature. She fixes on the image white American literature gives of
the society that wants to see itself as creating a new, earthly
Paradise – democratic, just, and free of the shackles and hier-
archies of Old Europe. She remarks sharply:

Living in a nation of people who *decided* that their world view would
combine agendas for individual freedom *and* mechanisms for devastat-
ing racial oppression presents a singular landscape for a writer.[3]

*

I have suggested that the blankness of Morrison's whites can be
connected to Poe's and Melville's white horrors. The virtuoso
use of the language of colors in *Beloved* rewrites the color language of the American classics that came before it. Its mythic
and poetic images connect it to that symbolic tradition of American writing. Its realism makes the fates of real, individual people
matter, free, unfree, and in the process of claiming freedom.

Morrison is rightly fearful of what she calls "metaphorical
shortcuts." In Britain at least, enthusiastic critical moralists
have attempted to deny or prevent the use of blackness to
symbolize fear or evil or horror. Human beings of all colors
were afraid of the dark in all societies, because danger came
out of it, because it was beyond control, and this has not much
to do with skin color. Black people are afraid of the dark as
white and yellow and beige people are. Morrison writes finely,
"Neither blackness nor 'people of color' stimulates in me
notions of excessive, limitless love, anarchy, or routine dread."
But she has made a collection of "the associative language
of dread and love that accompanies blackness ... Examples I
thought of as a category of sources of imagery, like water, flight,
war, birth, religion and so on, that make up the writer's kit."

In *Beloved*, then, white is blank, and black is on the whole
invisible, because people are black, real people who inhabit
this novel are black. To be human is to be black, and to be
white is to be at least in danger of being inhuman, at the
margins. There is a religious symbolism of two connected

3 All the following quotations are from the preface to *Playing in the
Dark*, Picador, 1993.

colors, white and red, the white of milk and the red of blood, both connected with life and death at the extremes. Denver as a baby drinks her sister's blood and her mother's milk together. Paul D has shut up his red heart in his rusted tobacco box. The source of Baby Suggs's life and her religious calling in the green Clearing is the life in her red heart. Red is the color of the ribbon that Stamp Paid thought was a cardinal feather in the river but that turns out to be "a red ribbon knotted around a curl of wet woolly hair, clinging still to its bit of scalp." "Red" is what Baby Suggs slips in, trying to wrest Denver from the wild and murderous Sethe. "Red" is also the color of the innocent velvet Amy is traveling to Boston in search of, but the word she uses is the rich word "carmine."

It is in this context that we need to read Baby Suggs's pre-occupation with color, as she lies in bed, defeated, we later learn, by Sethe's blow for freedom.

Her past had been like her present – intolerable – and since she knew death was anything but forgetfulness, she used the little energy left her for pondering color.

"Bring a little lavender in, if you got any. Pink, if you don't."

Pink is a dubious color – it is the pleasing flesh of a pink tongue, pondered by Baby. It is the tombstone "pink as a fingernail," that Sethe leans on to pay with sex to have the word Beloved chiseled on the baby's headstone. It is also the wonderfully described blossom on tree after tree, in American orchard after American orchard, that Paul D follows north after the Civil War to find a new place to be, waiting until one tree fades and hunting out the next one, in a cooler and later climate. This is a different version of the Paradise Garden, half-wild, half-cultivated, entered but not owned, full of birds that can be heard singing, and must be eaten raw to survive.

Color is the scraps of material that Baby Suggs makes into an American quilt, in 124, where she is free and defeated. Two patches of orange among the drab. She tells Stamp Paid she needs to fix on something harmless in this world. "Blue ... don't hurt nobody. Yellow neither." Stamp Paid later fingers his talismanic ribbon and "hoped she stuck to blue, yellow, maybe green, and never fixed on red."

Color is Denver thinking about her years of shocked speechlessness and the return of the solid ghost.

Anything is better than the silence in which she answered to hands gesturing and was indifferent to the movement of lips. When she saw every little thing and colors leaped smoldering into view. She will forgo the most violent of sunsets, stars as fat as dinner plates and all the blood of autumn, and settle for the palest yellow if it comes from her Beloved.

Color is Denver, going to find work, only half hearing Miss Bodwin "because she was stepping on something soft and blue. All around her was thick, soft and blue." It is her first experience of a carpet.

Color is connected in a very complex way to flesh and blood. Baby Suggs, free, listening to her great heart, calls the people and tells them to love their flesh because

the only grace they could have was the grace they could imagine. That if they could not see it, they would not have it.

"Here," she said, "in this here place, we flesh; flesh that weeps, laughs; flesh that dances on bare feet in grass. Love it. Love it hard. Yonder they do not love your flesh..."

Flesh is solid in this novel, tortured flesh, damaged flesh, tentatively loving flesh, the willed flesh of the too solid ghost, the bodily fluids of birth and death, spit, blood, piss, milk, and water. When Baby Suggs is strong, she can love flesh in a clearing. When she is defeated, she retreats,

dismissed her great heart and lay in the keeping-room bed roused once in a while by a craving for color and not for another thing.

"Those white things have taken all I had or dreamed," she said, "and broke my heartstrings too. There is no bad luck in the world but whitefolks."

Stamp Paid, in his way, also reverses both the paradisal imagery and its opposing image, the savage jungle from which black cannibals, in white mythology, come. He broods.

Whitepeople believed that whatever the manners, under every dark skin was a jungle...The more coloredpeople spent their strength trying to convince them how gentle they were, how clever and loving, how human, the more they used themselves up to persuade whites of something Negroes believed could not be questioned, the deeper and more tangled the jungle grew inside. But it wasn't the jungle blacks brought with them to this place from the other (livable) place. It was the jungle whitefolks planted in them. And it grew ... until it invaded the whites who had made it ... Made them bloody, silly, worse than even they wanted to be, so scared were they of the jungle they had made. The screaming baboon lived under their own white skin; the red gums were their own.

T. S. Eliot, in "Tradition and the Individual Talent," said that every new work of literature altered the literature of the past – in a sense reread that literature. *Beloved* enacts this alteration more forcefully than most classics. But the book does also have that gentler quality of seeming to be something that, while entirely new, was always there to be discovered, has always existed. I tried to describe that feeling in a novel (*Possession*.) I was moved to find Toni Morrison quoting my sentence in *Playing in the Dark*, as an example of the way in which "writing and reading are not all that distinct for a writer." Morrison quotes my passage as "an example of certain kinds of readings that seem to me inextricable from certain experiences of writing." It goes:

... when the knowledge that we *shall know* the writing differently or better or satisfactorily runs ahead of any capacity to say what we know, or how. In these readings, a sense that the text has appeared to be wholly new, never before seen, is followed, almost immediately, by the sense that it was *always there*, that we, the readers, knew it was always there, and have *always known* it was as it was, though we have now for the first time recognized, become fully cognizant of, our knowledge.

Beloved is the novel I think of first, when I think of this kind of reading, this kind of writing.

A. S. Byatt

SELECT BIBLIOGRAPHY

FICTION
The Bluest Eye, Holt, Rinehart, and Winston, New York, 1970; Chatto & Windus, London, 1979.
Sula, Alfred A. Knopf, New York, 1973; Allen Lane, London, 1974.
Song of Solomon, Alfred A. Knopf, New York, 1977; Chatto & Windus, London, 1978.
Tar Baby, Alfred A. Knopf, New York, 1981; Chatto & Windus, London, 1981.
Beloved, Alfred A. Knopf, New York, 1987; Chatto & Windus, London, 1987.
Jazz, Alfred A. Knopf, New York, 1992; Chatto & Windus, London, 1992.
Paradise, Alfred A. Knopf, New York, 1997; Chatto & Windus, London, 1998.
Love, Alfred A. Knopf, New York, 2003; Chatto & Windus, London, 2003.

NONFICTION
Playing in the Dark: Whiteness and the Literary Imagination, Harvard University Press, Cambridge, 1992.
Race-ing Justice, En-Gendering Power: Essays on Anita Hill, Clarence Thomas, and the Construction of Social Reality, editor, Pantheon, New York, 1992.
Conversations with Toni Morrison, University Press of Mississippi, 1994.
The Nobel Lecture in Literature, Alfred A. Knopf, 1994.
The Dancing Mind, Alfred A. Knopf, 1996.
Birth of a Nation'hood: Gaze, Script, and Spectacle in the O. J. Simpson Case, editor, Pantheon, New York, 1997.

CRITICISM
ANDREAS, WILLIAM L. and NELLIE Y. MCKAY, *Toni Morrison*, Oxford University Press, New York, 1999.
BJORK, PATRICK BRYCE, *The Novels of Toni Morrison*, P. Lang, New York, 1994.
FURMAN, MARVA JANNETT, *Toni Morrison's Fiction*, University of South Carolina Press, Columbia, 1996.
GATES, JR., HENRY LOUIS and KWAME ANTHONY APPIAH, editors, *Toni Morrison: Critical Perspectives Past and Present*, Amistad, New York, 1993.
GREWAL, GURLEEN, *Circles of Sorrow, Lines of Struggle: The Novels of Toni Morrison*, Louisiana State University Press, Baton Rouge, 1998.

HARRIS, TRUDIER, *Fiction and Folklore: The Novels of Toni Morrison*, University of Tennessee Press, Knoxville, 1991.

JONES, BESSIE W. and VINSON, AUDREY L., *The World of Toni Morrison: Explorations in Literary Criticism*, Kendall/Hunt, Dubuque, 1985.

KOLMERTON, CAROL M., ROSS, STEPHEN M. and WITTENBERG, JUDITH BRYANT, editors, *Unflinching Gaze: Morrison and Faulkner Re-envisioned*, University Press of Mississippi, Jackson, 1997.

KUBITSCHEK, MISSY DEHN, *Toni Morrison: A Critical Companion*, Greenwood Press, Westport, 1998.

MCKAY, NELLIE Y., *Critical Essays on Toni Morrison*, G. K. Hall, Boston, 1988.

MCKAY, NELLIE Y. and EARLE, KATHRYN, editors, *Approaches to Teaching the Novels of Toni Morrison*, MLA of America, New York, 1997.

MIDDLETON, DAVID L., *Toni Morrison: An Annotated Bibliography*, Garland, New York, 1987.

MIDDLETON, DAVID L., *Toni Morrison's Fiction: Contemporary Criticism*, Garland, New York, 1997.

PEACH, LINDEN, *Toni Morrison*, St. Martins Press, New York, 1995.

RIGNEY, BARBARA HILL, *The Voices of Toni Morrison*, Ohio State University Press, Columbus, 1991.

SAMUELS, WILFRED D. and HUDSON-WEEMS, CLENORA, *Toni Morrison*, Twayne Publishers, Boston, 1990.

CHRONOLOGY

———

DATE	AUTHOR'S LIFE	LITERARY CONTEXT
1931	Birth of Toni Morrison (Chloe Anthony Morrison, née Woodford) in Lorain, Ohio (18 February).	
		1932 Huxley: *Brave New World.* Faulkner: *Light in August.*
		1934 Fitzgerald: *Tender is the Night.* Miller: *Tropic of Cancer.* 1935 Lewis: *It Can't Happen Here.* 1936 Faulkner: *Absalom, Absalom!* Eliot: *Collected Poems.*
		1937 Steinbeck: *Of Mice and Men.* Hemingway: *To Have and Have Not.* 1938 Sartre: *Nausea.* 1939 Steinbeck: *The Grapes of Wrath.* Joyce: *Finnegans Wake.* 1940 Hemingway: *For Whom the Bell Tolls.* Greene: *The Power and the Glory.* 1941 Fitzgerald: *The Last Tycoon.*
		1942 Eliot: *Four Quartets.* Camus: *The Stranger.*
		1945 Orwell: *Animal Farm.* Waugh: *Brideshead Revisited.* Borges: *Fictions.* 1948 Greene: *The Heart of the Matter.* 1949 Orwell: *Nineteen Eighty-Four.* de Beauvoir: *The Second Sex.*
		1951 Frost: *Complete Poems.* Salinger: *The Catcher in the Rye.* 1952 Beckett: *Waiting for Godot.*
1953	Awarded BA from Howard University, Washington, DC.	1953 Bellow: *The Adventures of Augie March.*

1932 Election of Roosevelt in US. Nazis become largest party in German Reichstag.
1933 Roosevelt announces "New Deal." Hitler becomes German Chancellor.

1936 Outbreak of Spanish Civil War. Hitler and Mussolini form Rome–Berlin Axis. Stalin's "Great Purge" of the Communist Party (to 1938). Edward VIII abdicates; George VI crowned in UK.
1937 Japanese invasion of China.

1938 Germany annexes Austria; Munich crisis.
1939 World War II.

1940 Fall of France; Battle of Britain.

1941 Japanese attack on Pearl Harbor; US enters war. Hitler invades USSR.

1944 Allied landings in Normandy.
1945 Roosevelt dies; Truman becomes President. Surrender of Germany. US drops atomic bombs on Hiroshima and Nagasaki. End of World War II.

1948 Jewish state of Israel comes into existence. Russian blockade of West Berlin.
1949 Communists win Chinese civil war. North Atlantic Treaty signed.

1950 Korean War begins.

1952 Eisenhower elected US President. Accession of Elizabeth II in UK.
1953 Korean War ends.

DATE	AUTHOR'S LIFE	LITERARY CONTEXT
		1954 Amis: *Lucky Jim*.
1955	Awarded MA from Cornell University, New York. Begins teaching English at Texas Southern University, Houston (to 1957).	1955 Nabokov: *Lolita*. 1956 Osborne: *Look Back in Anger*.
1957–64	Teaches English at Howard University.	1957 Kerouac: *On the Road*. 1958 Pasternak: *Doctor Zhivago*. Achebe: *Things Fall Apart*. 1959 Burroughs: *Naked Lunch*. Bellow: *Henderson the Rain King*. 1960 Updike: *Rabbit, Run*. 1961 Heller: *Catch-22*. Naipaul: *A House for Mr Biswas*. 1962 Nabokov: *Pale Fire*. Solzhenitsyn: *One Day in the Life of Ivan Denisovich*. 1964 Bellow: *Herzog*.
1965	Begins work for Random House publishers, New York, as Senior Editor.	1965 Calvino: *Cosmicomics*. 1967 Márquez: *One Hundred Years of Solitude*. 1968 Solzhenitsyn: *Cancer Ward*.
1970	*The Bluest Eye*.	
1973	*Sula*.	1971 Updike: *Rabbit Redux*. 1973 Pynchon: *Gravity's Rainbow*. Solzhenitsyn: *The Gulag Archipelago* (to 1975).
1975–7	Teaches English at Bard College, New York.	1975 Levi: *The Periodic Table*.
1976–7	Visiting Lecturer, Yale University, New Haven.	
1977	*Song of Solomon* wins National Book Critics Circle Award.	
1979	Receives American Academy of Arts and Letters Distinguished Writer Award.	1979 Calvino: *If on a winter's night a traveler*. 1980 Eco: *The Name of the Rose*.

CHRONOLOGY

HISTORICAL EVENTS

1954 Vietnam War begins.

1956 Soviet invasion of Hungary. Suez crisis.

1957 Civil Rights Commission established in US to safeguard voting rights.

1959 Castro seizes power in Cuba.

1960 Kennedy elected US President.
1961 Erection of Berlin Wall.

1962 Cuban missile crisis.

1963 Assassination of Kennedy. Johnson becomes US President.
1964 Civil Rights Act prohibits discrimination in US. Brezhnev becomes Communist Party General Secretary in USSR.

1968 Student unrest in US and throughout Europe. Assassination of Martin Luther King, Jr. Soviet invasion of Czechoslovakia. Nixon elected US President.
1970 Death of de Gaulle.

1974 Nixon resigns in wake of Watergate scandal; Ford becomes US President.
1975 Vietnam War ends.

1976 Death of Mao Tse-Tung. Carter elected US President.

1978 P. W. Botha comes to power in South Africa.
1979 Margaret Thatcher first woman Prime Minister in UK. Carter and Brezhnev sign SALT-2 arms treaty. Soviet occupation of Afghanistan.

1980 Lech Walesa leads strikes in Gdansk, Poland. Reagan elected US President.

DATE	AUTHOR'S LIFE	LITERARY CONTEXT
1981	*Tar Baby.*	1981 Updike: *Rabbit Is Rich.* Rushdie: *Midnight's Children.* Márquez: *Chronicle of a Death Foretold.* 1982 Levi: *If not Now, When?* Walker: *The Color Purple.*
1983–84	Visiting professor, Rutgers University, New Jersey.	
1984	Retires from Random House. Schweitzer Professor of the Humanities, State University of New York.	
1985	*Dreaming Emmett,* play commissioned by New York State Writers Institute of the State University of New York.	1985 Márquez: *Love in the Time of Cholera.*
		1986: Levi: *The Drowned and the Saved.* Atwood: *The Handmaid's Tale.*
1987	Regents Lecturer, University of California and Santagata Lecturer, Bowdoin College. *Beloved* wins Pulitzer Prize.	
		1988 Rushdie: *The Satanic Verses.*
1989	Appointed Robert F. Goheen Professor in the Council of the Humanities at Princeton University. Modern Language Association of America Commonwealth Award in Literature.	
		1990 Updike: *Rabbit at Rest.* Pynchon: *Vineland.*
1992	*Jazz: Playing in the Dark: Whiteness and the Literary Imagination:* and *Race-ing Justice, En-Gendering Power: Essays on Anita Hill, Clarence Thomas, and the Construction of Social Reality.* Premiere of *Honey and Rue,* lyrics commissioned by Carnegie Hall. set to music by André Previn.	1992 McCarthy: *The Border Trilogy* (to 1998).

CHRONOLOGY

DATE	AUTHOR'S LIFE	LITERARY CONTEXT
1993	Awarded the Nobel Prize for Literature.	
1994	Wins the Pearl Buck Award.	1994 Heller: *Closing Time.*
1996	Awarded the National Book Foundation Medal for Distinguished Contribution to American Letters.	
1997	*Paradise.*	1997 Roth: *American Pastoral.*
1998		1998 Munro: *The Love of a Good Woman.* DeLillo: *Underworld.* Roth: *I Married a Communist.*
2001		2001 Franzen: *The Corrections.*
2003	*Love.*	2003 DeLillo: *Cosmopolis.*
2006	A *New York Times* poll of 200 critics, writers and editors selects *Beloved* as "the single best work of American fiction published in the last twenty-five years."	

CHRONOLOGY

BELOVED

Sixty Million and more

I will call them my people,
which were not my people;
and her beloved,
which was not beloved.

ROMANS 9:25

I

124 WAS SPITEFUL. Full of a baby's venom. The women in the house knew it and so did the children. For years each put up with the spite in his own way, but by 1873 Sethe and her daughter Denver were its only victims. The grandmother, Baby Suggs, was dead, and the sons, Howard and Buglar, had run away by the time they were thirteen years old – as soon as merely looking in a mirror shattered it (that was the signal for Buglar); as soon as two tiny hand prints appeared in the cake (that was it for Howard). Neither boy waited to see more; another kettleful of chickpeas smoking in a heap on the floor; soda crackers crumbled and strewn in a line next to the door-sill. Nor did they wait for one of the relief periods: the weeks, months even, when nothing was disturbed. No. Each one fled at once – the moment the house committed what was for him the one insult not to be borne or witnessed a second time. Within two months, in the dead of winter, leaving their grandmother, Baby Suggs; Sethe, their mother; and their little sister, Denver, all by themselves in the gray and white house on Bluestone Road. It didn't have a number then, because Cincinnati didn't stretch that far. In fact, Ohio had been calling itself a state only seventy years when first one brother and then the next stuffed quilt packing into his hat, snatched up his shoes, and crept away from the lively spite the house felt for them.

Baby Suggs didn't even raise her head. From her sickbed she heard them go but that wasn't the reason she lay still. It was a wonder to her that her grandsons had taken so long to realize that every house wasn't like the one on Bluestone

Road. Suspended between the nastiness of life and the meanness of the dead, she couldn't get interested in leaving life or living it, let alone the fright of two creeping-off boys. Her past had been like her present – intolerable – and since she knew death was anything but forgetfulness, she used the little energy left her for pondering color.

"Bring a little lavender in, if you got any. Pink, if you don't."

And Sethe would oblige her with anything from fabric to her own tongue. Winter in Ohio was especially rough if you had an appetite for color. Sky provided the only drama, and counting on a Cincinnati horizon for life's principal joy was reckless indeed. So Sethe and the girl Denver did what they could, and what the house permitted, for her. Together they waged a perfunctory battle against the outrageous behavior of that place; against turned-over slop jars, smacks on the behind, and gusts of sour air. For they understood the source of the outrage as well as they knew the source of light.

Baby Suggs died shortly after the brothers left, with no interest whatsoever in their leave-taking or hers, and right afterward Sethe and Denver decided to end the persecution by calling forth the ghost that tried them so. Perhaps a conversation, they thought, an exchange of views or something would help. So they held hands and said, "Come on. Come on. You may as well just come on."

The sideboard took a step forward but nothing else did.

"Grandma Baby must be stopping it," said Denver. She was ten and still mad at Baby Suggs for dying.

Sethe opened her eyes. "I doubt that," she said.

"Then why don't it come?"

"You forgetting how little it is," said her mother. "She wasn't even two years old when she died. Too little to understand. Too little to talk much even."

"Maybe she don't want to understand," said Denver.

"Maybe. But if she'd only come, I could make it clear to her." Sethe released her daughter's hand and together they pushed the sideboard back against the wall. Outside a driver whipped his horse into the gallop local people felt necessary when they passed 124.

"For a baby she throws a powerful spell," said Denver.

"No more powerful than the way I loved her," Sethe answered and there it was again. The welcoming cool of un-chiseled headstones; the one she selected to lean against on tiptoe, her knees wide open as any grave. Pink as a fingernail it was, and sprinkled with glittering chips. Ten minutes, he said. You got ten minutes I'll do it for free.

Ten minutes for seven letters. With another ten could she have gotten "Dearly" too? She had not thought to ask him and it bothered her still that it might have been possible – that for twenty minutes, a half hour, say, she could have had the whole thing, every word she heard the preacher say at the funeral (and all there was to say, surely) engraved on her baby's headstone: Dearly Beloved. But what she got, settled for, was the one word that mattered. She thought it would be enough, rutting among the headstones with the engraver, his young son looking on, the anger in his face so old; the appetite in it quite new. That should certainly be enough. Enough to answer one more preacher, one more abolitionist and a town full of disgust.

Counting on the stillness of her own soul, she had forgot-ten the other one: the soul of her baby girl. Who would have thought that a little old baby could harbor so much rage? Rutting among the stones under the eyes of the engraver's son was not enough. Not only did she have to live out her years in a house palsied by the baby's fury at having its throat cut, but those ten minutes she spent pressed up against dawn-colored stone studded with star chips, her knees wide open as the grave, were longer than life, more alive, more pulsating than the baby blood that soaked her fingers like oil.

"We could move," she suggested once to her mother-in-law.

"What'd be the point?" asked Baby Suggs. "Not a house in the country ain't packed to its rafters with some dead Negro's grief. We lucky this ghost is a baby. My husband's spirit was to come back in here? or yours? Don't talk to me. You lucky. You got three left. Three pulling at your skirts and just one raising hell from the other side. Be thankful, why don't you? I had eight. Every one of them gone away from me. Four taken, four chased, and all, I expect, worrying somebody's house into evil." Baby Suggs rubbed her eyebrows. "My first-born. All I can remember of her is how she loved the burned bottom of bread. Can you beat that? Eight children and that's all I remember."

"That's all you let yourself remember," Sethe had told her, but she was down to one herself – one alive, that is – the boys chased off by the dead one, and her memory of Buglar was fading fast. Howard at least had a head shape nobody could forget. As for the rest, she worked hard to remember as close to nothing as was safe. Unfortunately her brain was devious. She might be hurrying across a field, running practically, to get to the pump quickly and rinse the chamomile sap from her legs. Nothing else would be in her mind. The picture of the men coming to nurse her was as lifeless as the nerves in her back where the skin buckled like a washboard. Nor was there the faintest scent of ink or the cherry gum and oak bark from which it was made. Nothing. Just the breeze cooling her face as she rushed toward water. And then sopping the chamomile away with pump water and rags, her mind fixed on getting every last bit of sap off – on her carelessness in taking a shortcut across the field just to save a half mile, and not noticing how high the weeds had grown until the itching was all the way to her knees. Then something. The plash of water, the sight of her shoes and stockings awry on the path where she had flung them; or Here Boy lapping in the puddle near her feet, and suddenly there was Sweet Home rolling, rolling, rolling out before her eyes, and although there was not a leaf on that farm that did not make her want to scream, it rolled itself out before her in shameless beauty. It never looked as terrible as it was and it made her wonder if hell was a pretty place too. Fire and brimstone all right, but hidden in lacy groves. Boys hanging from the most beautiful sycamores in the world. It shamed her – remembering the wonderful soughing trees rather than the boys. Try as she might to make it otherwise, the sycamores beat out the children every time and she could not forgive her memory for that.

When the last of the chamomile was gone, she went around to the front of the house, collecting her shoes and stockings on the way. As if to punish her further for her terrible memory, sitting on the porch not forty feet away was Paul D, the last of the Sweet Home men. And although she could never mistake his face for another's, she said, "Is that you?"

"What's left." He stood up and smiled. "How you been, girl, besides barefoot?"

When she laughed it came out loose and young. "Messed up my legs back yonder. Chamomile."

He made a face as though tasting a teaspoon of something bitter. "I don't want to even hear 'bout it. Always did hate that stuff."

Sethe balled up her stockings and jammed them into her pocket. "Come on in."

"Porch is fine, Sethe. Cool out here." He sat back down and looked at the meadow on the other side of the road, knowing the eagerness he felt would be in his eyes.

"Eighteen years," she said softly.

"Eighteen," he repeated. "And I swear I been walking every one of em. Mind if I join you?" He nodded toward her feet and began unlacing his shoes.

"You want to soak them? Let me get you a basin of water." She moved closer to him to enter the house.

"No, uh uh. Can't baby feet. A whole lot more tramping they got to do yet."

"You can't leave right away, Paul D. You got to stay awhile."

"Well, long enough to see Baby Suggs, anyway. Where is she?"

"Dead."

"Aw no. When?"

"Eight years now. Almost nine."

"Was it hard? I hope she didn't die hard."

Sethe shook her head. "Soft as cream. Being alive was the hard part. Sorry you missed her though. Is that what you came by for?"

"That's some of what I came for. The rest is you. But if all the truth be known, I go anywhere these days. Anywhere they let me sit down."

"You looking good."

"Devil's confusion. He lets me look good long as I feel bad." He looked at her and the word "bad" took on another meaning.

Sethe smiled. This is the way they were – had been. All of the Sweet Home men, before and after Halle, treated her to a mild brotherly flirtation, so subtle you had to scratch for it.

Except for a heap more hair and some waiting in his eyes, he looked the way he had in Kentucky. Peachstone skin; straight-backed. For a man with an immobile face it was amazing how ready it was to smile, or blaze or be sorry with you. As though all you had to do was get his attention and right away he produced the feeling you were feeling. With less than a blink, his face seemed to change – underneath it lay the activity.

"I wouldn't have to ask about him, would I? You'd tell me if there was anything to tell, wouldn't you?" Sethe looked down at her feet and saw again the sycamores.

"I'd tell you. Sure I'd tell you. I don't know any more now than I did then." Except for the churn, he thought, and you don't need to know that. "You must think he's still alive."

"No. I think he's dead. It's not being sure that keeps him alive."

"What did Baby Suggs think?"

"Same, but to listen to her, all her children is dead. Claimed she felt each one go the very day and hour."

"When she say Halle went?"

"Eighteen fifty-five. The day my baby was born."

"You had that baby, did you? Never thought you'd make it." He chuckled. "Running off pregnant."

"Had to. Couldn't be no waiting." She lowered her head and thought, as he did, how unlikely it was that she had made it. And if it hadn't been for that girl looking for velvet, she never would have.

"All by yourself too." He was proud of her and annoyed by her. Proud she had done it; annoyed that she had not needed Halle or him in the doing.

"Almost by myself. Not all by myself. A whitegirl helped me."

"Then she helped herself too, God bless her."

"You could stay the night, Paul D."

"You don't sound too steady in the offer."

Sethe glanced beyond his shoulder toward the closed door. "Oh it's truly meant. I just hope you'll pardon my house. Come on in. Talk to Denver while I cook you something."

Paul D tied his shoes together, hung them over his shoulder and followed her through the door straight into a pool of red and undulating light that locked him where he stood.

"You got company?" he whispered, frowning.

"Off and on," said Sethe.

"Good God." He backed out the door onto the porch. "What kind of evil you got in here?"

"It's not evil, just sad. Come on. Just step through."

He looked at her then, closely. Closer than he had when she first rounded the house on wet and shining legs, holding her shoes and stockings up in one hand, her skirts in the other. Halle's girl – the one with iron eyes and backbone to match. He had never seen her hair in Kentucky. And though her face was eighteen years older than when last he saw her, it was softer now. Because of the hair. A face too still for comfort; irises the same color as her skin, which, in that still face, used to make him think of a mask with mercifully punched-out eyes. Halle's woman. Pregnant every year including the year she sat by the fire telling him she was going to run. Her three children she had already packed into a wagonload of others in a caravan of Negroes crossing the river. They were to be left with Halle's mother near Cincinnati. Even in that tiny shack, leaning so close to the fire you could smell the heat in her dress, her eyes did not pick up a flicker of light. They were like two wells into which he had trouble gazing. Even punched out they needed to be covered, lidded, marked with some sign to warn folks of what that emptiness held. So he looked instead at the fire while she told him, because her husband was not there for the telling. Mr. Garner was dead and his wife had a lump in her neck the size of a sweet potato and unable to speak to anyone. She leaned as close to the fire as her pregnant belly allowed and told him, Paul D, the last of the Sweet Home men.

There had been six of them who belonged to the farm, Sethe the only female. Mrs. Garner, crying like a baby, had sold his brother to pay off the debts that surfaced the minute she was widowed. Then schoolteacher arrived to put things in order. But what he did broke three more Sweet Home men and punched the glittering iron out of Sethe's eyes, leaving two open wells that did not reflect firelight.

Now the iron was back but the face, softened by hair,

made him trust her enough to step inside her door smack into a pool of pulsing red light.

She was right. It was sad. Walking through it, a wave of grief soaked him so thoroughly he wanted to cry. It seemed a long way to the normal light surrounding the table, but he made it – dry-eyed and lucky.

"You said she died soft. Soft as cream," he reminded her.

"That's not Baby Suggs," she said.

"Who then?"

"My daughter. The one I sent ahead with the boys."

"She didn't live?"

"No. The one I was carrying when I run away is all I got left. Boys gone too. Both of em walked off just before Baby Suggs died."

Paul D looked at the spot where the grief had soaked him. The red was gone but a kind of weeping clung to the air where it had been.

Probably best, he thought. If a Negro got legs he ought to use them. Sit down too long, somebody will figure out a way to tie them up. Still . . . if her boys were gone . . .

"No man? You here by yourself?"

"Me and Denver," she said.

"That all right by you?"

"That's all right by me."

She saw his skepticism and went on. "I cook at a restaurant in town. And I sew a little on the sly."

Paul D smiled then, remembering the bedding dress. Sethe was thirteen when she came to Sweet Home and already iron-eyed. She was a timely present for Mrs. Garner who had lost Baby Suggs to her husband's high principles. The five Sweet Home men looked at the new girl and decided to let her be. They were young and so sick with the absence of women they had taken to calves. Yet they let the iron-eyed girl be, so she could choose in spite of the fact that each one would have beaten the others to mush to have her.

It took her a year to choose – a long, tough year of thrashing on pallets eaten up with dreams of her. A year of yearning, when rape seemed the solitary gift of life. The restraint they had exercised possible only because they were Sweet Home men – the ones Mr. Garner bragged about while other farmers shook their heads in warning at the phrase.

"Y'all got boys," he told them. "Young boys, old boys, picky boys, stroppin boys. Now at Sweet Home, my niggers is men every one of em. Bought em thataway, raised em thataway. Men every one."

"Beg to differ, Garner. Ain't no nigger men."

"Not if you scared, they ain't." Garner's smile was wide. "But if you a man yourself, you'll want your niggers to be men too."

"I wouldn't have no nigger men round my wife."

It was the reaction Garner loved and waited for. "Neither would I," he said. "Neither would I," and there was always a pause before the neighbor, or stranger, or peddler, or brother-in-law or whoever it was got the meaning. Then a fierce argument, sometimes a fight, and Garner came home bruised and pleased, having demonstrated one more time what a real Kentuckian was: one tough enough and smart enough to make and call his own niggers men.

And so they were: Paul D Garner, Paul F Garner, Paul A Garner, Halle Suggs and Sixo, the wild man. All in their twenties, minus women, fucking cows, dreaming of rape, thrashing on pallets, rubbing their thighs and waiting for the new girl – the one who took Baby Suggs' place after Halle bought her with five years of Sundays. Maybe that was why she chose him. A twenty-year-old man so in love with his mother he gave up five years of Sabbaths just to see her sit down for a change was a serious recommendation.

She waited a year. And the Sweet Home men abused cows while they waited with her. She chose Halle and for their first bedding she sewed herself a dress on the sly.

"Won't you stay on awhile? Can't nobody catch up on eighteen years in a day."

Out of the dimness of the room in which they sat, a white staircase climbed toward the blue-and-white wallpaper of the second floor. Paul D could see just the beginning of the paper; discreet flecks of yellow sprinkled among a blizzard of snowdrops all backed by blue. The luminous white of the railing and steps kept him glancing toward it. Every sense he had told him the air above the stairwell was charmed and very thin. But the girl who walked down out of that air was round and brown with the face of an alert doll.

Paul D looked at the girl and then at Sethe who smiled saying, "Here she is my Denver. This is Paul D, honey, from Sweet Home."

"Good morning, Mr. D."

"Garner, baby. Paul D Garner."

"Yes sir."

"Glad to get a look at you. Last time I saw your mama, you were pushing out the front of her dress."

"Still is," Sethe smiled, "provided she can get in it."

Denver stood on the bottom step and was suddenly hot and shy. It had been a long time since anybody (good-willed whitewoman, preacher, speaker or newspaperman) sat at their table, their sympathetic voices called liar by the revulsion in their eyes. For twelve years, long before Grandma Baby died, there had been no visitors of any sort and certainly no friends. No coloredpeople. Certainly no hazelnut man with too long hair and no notebook, no charcoal, no oranges, no questions. Someone her mother wanted to talk to and would even consider talking to while barefoot. Looking, in fact acting, like a girl instead of the quiet, queenly woman Denver had known all her life. The one who never looked away, who when a man got stomped to death by a mare right in front of Sawyer's restaurant did not look away; and when a sow began eating her own litter did not look away then either. And when the baby's spirit picked up Here Boy and slammed him into the wall hard enough to break two of his legs and dislocate his eye, so hard he went into convulsions and chewed up his tongue, still her mother had not looked away. She had taken a hammer, knocked the dog unconscious, wiped away the blood and saliva, pushed his eye back in his head and set his leg bones. He recovered, mute and off-balance, more because of his untrustworthy eye than his bent legs, and winter, summer, drizzle or dry, nothing could persuade him to enter the house again.

Now here was this woman with the presence of mind to repair a dog gone savage with pain rocking her crossed ankles and looking away from her own daughter's body. As though the size of it was more than vision could bear. And neither she nor he had on shoes. Hot, shy, now Denver was lonely. All that leaving: first her brothers, then her grandmother – serious losses since there were no children willing to circle her in a game or hang by their knees from her porch railing. None of that had mattered as long as her mother did not look away as she was doing now, making Denver long, downright *long*, for a sign of spite from the baby ghost.

"She's a fine-looking young lady," said Paul D. "Fine-looking. Got her daddy's sweet face."

"You know my father?"

"Knew him. Knew him well."

"Did he, Ma'am?" Denver fought an urge to realign her affection.

"Of course he knew your daddy. I told you, he's from Sweet Home."

Denver sat down on the bottom step. There was nowhere else gracefully to go. They were a twosome, saying "Your daddy" and "Sweet Home" in a way that made it clear both belonged to them and not to her. That her own father's absence was not hers. Once the absence had belonged to Grandma Baby – a son, deeply mourned because he was the one who had bought her out of there. Then it was her mother's absent husband. Now it was this hazelnut stranger's absent friend. Only those who knew him ("knew him well") could claim his absence for themselves. Just as only those who lived in Sweet Home could remember it, whisper it and glance sideways at one another while they did. Again she wished for the baby ghost – its anger thrilling her now where it used to wear her out. Wear her out.

"We have a ghost in here," she said, and it worked. They were not a twosome anymore. Her mother left off swinging her feet and being girlish. Memory of Sweet Home dropped away from the eyes of the man she was being girlish for. He looked quickly up the lightning-white stairs behind her.

"So I hear," he said. "But sad, your mama said. Not evil."

"No sir," said Denver, "not evil. But not sad either."

"What then?"

"Rebuked. Lonely and rebuked."

"Is that right?" Paul D turned to Sethe.

"I don't know about lonely," said Denver's mother. "Mad, maybe, but I don't see how it could be lonely spending every minute with us like it does."

"Must be something you got it wants."

Sethe shrugged. "It's just a baby."

"My sister," said Denver. "She died in this house."

Paul D scratched the hair under his jaw. "Reminds me of that headless bride back behind Sweet Home. Remember that, Sethe? Used to roam them woods regular."

"How could I forget? Worrisome . . ."

"How come everybody run off from Sweet Home can't stop talking about it? Look like if it was so sweet you would have stayed."

"Girl, who you talking to?"

Paul D laughed. "True, true. She's right, Sethe. It wasn't sweet and it sure wasn't home." He shook his head.

"But it's where we were," said Sethe. "All together. Comes

back whether we want it to or not." She shivered a little. A light ripple of skin on her arm, which she caressed back into sleep. "Denver," she said, "start up that stove. Can't have a friend stop by and don't feed him."

"Don't go to any trouble on my account," Paul D said.

"Bread ain't trouble. The rest I brought back from where I work. Least I can do, cooking from dawn to noon, is bring dinner home. You got any objections to pike?"

"If he don't object to me I don't object to him."

At it again, thought Denver. Her back to them, she jostled the kindlin and almost lost the fire. "Why don't you spend the night, Mr. Garner? You and Ma'am can talk about Sweet Home all night long."

Sethe took two swift steps to the stove, but before she could yank Denver's collar, the girl leaned forward and began to cry.

"What is the matter with you? I never knew you to behave this way."

"Leave her be," said Paul D. "I'm a stranger to her."

"That's just it. She got no cause to act up with a stranger. Oh baby, what is it? Did something happen?"

But Denver was shaking now and sobbing so she could not speak. The tears she had not shed for nine years wetting her far too womanly breasts.

"I can't no more. I can't no more."

"Can't what? What can't you?"

"I can't live here. I don't know where to go or what to do, but I can't live here. Nobody speaks to us. Nobody comes by. Boys don't like me. Girls don't either."

"Honey, honey."

"What's she talking 'bout nobody speaks to you?" asked Paul D.

"It's the house. People don't —"

"It's not! It's not the house. It's us! And it's you!"

"Denver!"

"Leave off, Sethe. It's hard for a young girl living in a haunted house. That can't be easy."

"It's easier than some other things."

"Think, Sethe. I'm a grown man with nothing new left to see or do and I'm telling you it ain't easy. Maybe you all ought to move. Who owns this house?"

Over Denver's shoulder Sethe shot Paul D a look of snow. "What you care?"

"They won't let you leave?"

"No."

"Sethe."

"No moving. No leaving. It's all right the way it is."

"You going to tell me it's all right with this child half out of her mind?"

Something in the house braced, and in the listening quiet that followed Sethe spoke.

"I got a tree on my back and a haint in my house, and nothing in between but the daughter I am holding in my arms. No more running – from nothing. I will never run from another thing on this earth. I took one journey and I paid for the ticket, but let me tell you something, Paul D Garner: it cost too much! Do you hear me? It cost too much. Now sit down and eat with us or leave us be."

Paul D fished in his vest for a little pouch of tobacco – concentrating on its contents and the knot of its string while Sethe led Denver into the keeping room that opened off the large room he was sitting in. He had no smoking papers, so he fiddled with the pouch and listened through the open door to Sethe quieting her daughter. When she came back she avoided his look and went straight to a small table next to the stove. Her back was to him and he could see all the hair he wanted without the distraction of her face.

"What tree on your back?"

"Huh." Sethe put a bowl on the table and reached under it for flour.

23

"What tree on your back? Is something growing on your back? I don't see nothing growing on your back."

"It's there all the same."

"Who told you that?"

"Whitegirl. That's what she called it. I've never seen it and never will. But that's what she said it looked like. A choke-cherry tree. Trunk, branches, and even leaves. Tiny little chokecherry leaves. But that was eighteen years ago. Could have cherries too now for all I know."

Sethe took a little spit from the tip of her tongue with her forefinger. Quickly, lightly she touched the stove. Then she trailed her fingers through the flour, parting, separating small hills and ridges of it, looking for mites. Finding none, she poured soda and salt into the crease of her folded hand and tossed both into the flour. Then she reached into a can and scooped half a handful of lard. Deftly she squeezed the flour through it, then with her left hand sprinkling water, she formed the dough.

"I had milk," she said. "I was pregnant with Denver but I had milk for my baby girl. I hadn't stopped nursing her when I sent her on ahead with Howard and Buglar."

Now she rolled the dough out with a wooden pin. "Anybody could smell me long before he saw me. And when he saw me he'd see the drops of it on the front of my dress. Nothing I could do about that. All I knew was I had to get my milk to my baby girl. Nobody was going to nurse her like me. Nobody was going to get it to her fast enough, or take it away when she had enough and didn't know it. Nobody knew that she couldn't pass her air if you held her up on your shoulder, only if she was lying on my knees. Nobody knew that but me and nobody had her milk but me. I told that to the women in the wagon. Told them to put sugar water in cloth to suck from so when I got there in a few days she wouldn't have forgot me. The milk would be there and I would be there with it."

"Men don't know nothing much," said Paul D, tucking his pouch back into his vest pocket, "but they do know a suckling can't be away from its mother for long."

"Then they know what it's like to send your children off when your breasts are full."

"We was talking 'bout a tree, Sethe."

"After I left you, those boys came in there and took my milk. That's what they came in there for. Held me down and took it. I told Mrs. Garner on em. She had that lump and couldn't speak but her eyes rolled out tears. Them boys found out I told on em. Schoolteacher made one open up my back, and when it closed it made a tree. It grows there still."

"They used cowhide on you?"

"And they took my milk."

"They beat you and you was pregnant?"

"And they took my milk!"

The fat white circles of dough lined the pan in rows. Once more Sethe touched a wet forefinger to the stove. She opened the oven door and slid the pan of biscuits in. As she raised up from the heat she felt Paul D behind her and his hands under her breasts. She straightened up and knew, but could not feel, that his cheek was pressing into the branches of her chokecherry tree.

Not even trying, he had become the kind of man who could walk into a house and make the women cry. Because with him, in his presence, they could. There was something blessed in his manner. Women saw him and wanted to weep – to tell him that their chest hurt and their knees did too. Strong women and wise saw him and told him things they only told each other: that way past the Change of Life, desire in them had suddenly become enormous, greedy, more savage than when they were fifteen, and that it embarrassed them and made them sad; that secretly they longed to die – to be quit of it – that sleep was more precious to them than any waking day. Young girls sidled up to him to confess or describe how well-dressed the visitations were that had followed them straight from their dreams. Therefore, although he did not understand why this was so, he was not surprised when Denver dripped tears into the stovefire. Nor, fifteen minutes later, after telling him about her stolen milk, her mother wept as well. Behind her, bending down, his body an arc of kindness, he held her breasts in the palms of his hands. He rubbed his cheek on her back and learned that way her sorrow, the roots of it; its wide trunk and intricate branches. Raising his fingers to the hooks of her dress, he knew without seeing them or hearing any sigh that the tears were coming fast. And when the top of her dress was around her hips and he saw the sculpture her back had become, like the decorative work of an ironsmith too passionate for display, he could think but not say, "Aw, Lord, girl." And he would tolerate no peace until he had touched every ridge and leaf of it with his mouth, none of which Sethe could feel because her back skin had been dead for years. What she knew was that the responsibility for her breasts, at last, was in somebody else's hands.

Would there be a little space, she wondered, a little time, some way to hold off eventfulness, to push busyness into the corners of the room and just stand there a minute or two, naked from shoulder blade to waist, relieved of the weight of her breasts, smelling the stolen milk again and the pleasure of baking bread? Maybe this one time she could stop dead still in the middle of a cooking meal – not even leave the stove – and feel the hurt her back ought to. Trust things and remember things because the last of the Sweet Home men was there to catch her if she sank?

The stove didn't shudder as it adjusted to its heat. Denver wasn't stirring in the next room. The pulse of red light hadn't come back and Paul D had not trembled since 1856 and then for eighty-three days in a row. Locked up and chained down, his hands shook so bad he couldn't smoke or even scratch properly. Now he was trembling again but in the legs this time. It took him a while to realize that his legs were not shaking because of worry, but because the floorboards were and the grinding, shoving floor was only part of it. The house itself was pitching. Sethe slid to the floor and struggled to get back into her dress. While down on all fours, as though she were holding her house down on the ground, Denver burst from the keeping room, terror in her eyes, a vague smile on her lips.

"God damn it! Hush up!" Paul D was shouting, falling, reaching for anchor. "Leave the place alone! Get the hell out!" A table rushed toward him and he grabbed its leg. Somehow he managed to stand at an angle and, holding the table by two legs, he bashed it about, wrecking everything, screaming back at the screaming house. "You want to fight, come on! God damn it! She got enough without you. She got enough!"

The quaking slowed to an occasional lurch, but Paul D did not stop whipping the table around until everything was rock quiet. Sweating and breathing hard, he leaned against the wall in the space the sideboard left. Sethe was still crouched next to the stove, clutching her salvaged shoes to her chest. The three of them, Sethe, Denver, and Paul D, breathed to the same beat, like one tired person. Another breathing was just as tired.

It was gone. Denver wandered through the silence to the stove. She ashed over the fire and pulled the pan of biscuits from the oven. The jelly cupboard was on its back, its contents lying in a heap in the corner of the bottom shelf. She took out a jar, and, looking around for a plate, found half of one by the door. These things she carried out to the porch steps, where she sat down.

The two of them had gone up there. Stepping lightly, easy-footed, they had climbed the white stairs, leaving her

27

down below. She pried the wire from the top of the jar and then the lid. Under it was cloth and under that a thin cake of wax. She removed it all and coaxed the jelly onto one half of the half a plate. She took a biscuit and pulled off its black top. Smoke curled from the soft white insides.

She missed her brothers. Buglar and Howard would be twenty-two and twenty-three now. Although they had been polite to her during the quiet time and gave her the whole top of the bed, she remembered how it was before: the pleasure they had sitting clustered on the white stairs – she between the knees of Howard or Buglar – while they made up die-witch! stories with proven ways of killing her dead. And Baby Suggs telling her things in the keeping room. She smelled like bark in the day and leaves at night, for Denver would not sleep in her old room after her brothers ran away.

Now her mother was upstairs with the man who had gotten rid of the only other company she had. Denver dipped a bit of bread into the jelly. Slowly, methodically, miserably she ate it.

NOT QUITE IN a hurry, but losing no time, Sethe and Paul D climbed the white stairs. Overwhelmed as much by the downright luck of finding her house and her in it as by the certainty of giving her his sex, Paul D dropped twenty-five years from his recent memory. A stair step before him was Baby Suggs' replacement, the new girl they dreamed of at night and fucked cows for at dawn while waiting for her to choose. Merely kissing the wrought iron on her back had shook the house, had made it necessary for him to beat it to pieces. Now he would do more.

She led him to the top of the stairs, where light came straight from the sky because the second-story windows of that house had been placed in the pitched ceiling and not the walls. There were two rooms and she took him into one of them, hoping he wouldn't mind the fact that she was not prepared; that though she could remember desire, she had forgotten how it worked; the clutch and helplessness that resided in the hands; how blindness was altered so that what leapt to the eye were places to lie down, and all else – doorknobs, straps, hooks, the sadness that crouched in corners, and the passing of time – was interference.

It was over before they could get their clothes off. Half-dressed and short of breath, they lay side by side resentful of one another and the skylight above them. His dreaming of her had been too long and too long ago. Her deprivation had been not having any dreams of her own at all. Now they were sorry and too shy to make talk.

Sethe lay on her back, her head turned from him. Out of

the corner of his eye, Paul D saw the float of her breasts and disliked it, the spread-away, flat roundness of them that he could definitely live without, never mind that downstairs he had held them as though they were the most expensive part of himself. And the wrought-iron maze he had explored in the kitchen like a gold miner pawing through pay dirt was in fact a revolting clump of scars. Not a tree, as she said. Maybe shaped like one, but nothing like any tree he knew because trees were inviting; things you could trust and be near; talk to if you wanted to as he frequently did since way back when he took the midday meal in the fields of Sweet Home. Always in the same place if he could, and choosing the place had been hard because Sweet Home had more pretty trees than any farm around. His choice he called Brother, and sat under it, alone sometimes, sometimes with Halle or the other Pauls, but more often with Sixo, who was gentle then and still speaking English. Indigo with a flame-red tongue, Sixo experimented with night-cooked potatoes, trying to pin down exactly when to put smoking-hot rocks in a hole, potatoes on top, and cover the whole thing with twigs so that by the time they broke for the meal, hitched the animals, left the field and got to Brother, the potatoes would be at the peak of perfection. He might get up in the middle of the night, go all the way out there, start the earth-over by starlight; or he would make the stones less hot and put the next day's potatoes on them right after the meal. He never got it right, but they ate those undercooked, over-cooked, dried-out or raw potatoes anyway, laughing, spitting and giving him advice.

Time never worked the way Sixo thought, so of course he never got it right. Once he plotted down to the minute a thirty-mile trip to see a woman. He left on a Saturday when the moon was in the place he wanted it to be, arrived at her cabin before church on Sunday and had just enough time to say good morning before he had to start back again so he'd make the field call on time Monday morning. He had walked for seventeen hours, sat down for one, turned around and walked seventeen more. Halle and the Pauls spent the whole day covering Sixo's fatigue from Mr. Garner. They ate no potatoes that day, sweet or white. Sprawled near Brother, his flame-red tongue hidden from them, his indigo face closed, Sixo slept through dinner like a corpse. Now *there* was a man, and *that* was a tree. Himself lying in the bed and the "tree" lying next to him didn't compare.

Paul D looked through the window above his feet and folded his hands behind his head. An elbow grazed Sethe's shoulder. The touch of cloth on her skin startled her. She had forgotten he had not taken off his shirt. Dog, she thought, and then remembered that she had not allowed him the time for taking it off. Nor herself time to take off her petticoat, and considering she had begun undressing before she saw him on the porch, that her shoes and stockings were already in her hand and she had never put them back on; that he had looked at her wet bare feet and asked to join her; that when she rose to cook he had undressed her further; con-sidering how quickly they had started getting naked, you'd think by now they would be. But maybe a man was nothing but a man, which is what Baby Suggs always said. They encouraged you to put some of your weight in their hands and soon as you felt how light and lovely that was, they studied your scars and tribulations, after which they did what he had done: ran her children out and tore up the house.

She needed to get up from there, go downstairs and piece it all back together. This house he told her to leave as though a house was a little thing – a shirtwaist or a sewing basket you could walk off from or give away any old time. She who had never had one but this one; she who left a dirt floor to come to this one; she who had to bring a fistful of salsify into Mrs. Garner's kitchen every day just to be able to work in it, feel like some part of it was hers, because she wanted to love the work she did, to take the ugly out of it, and the only way she could feel at home on Sweet Home was if she picked some pretty growing thing and took it with her. The day she forgot was the day butter wouldn't come or the brine in the barrel blistered her arms.

At least it seemed so. A few yellow flowers on the table, some myrtle tied around the handle of the flatiron holding the door open for a breeze calmed her, and when Mrs. Garner and she sat down to sort bristle, or make ink, she felt fine. Fine. Not scared of the men beyond. The five who slept in quarters near her, but never came in the night. Just touched their raggedy hats when they saw her and stared. And if she brought food to them in the fields, bacon and bread wrapped in a piece of clean sheeting, they never took it from her hands. They stood back and waited for her to put it on the ground (at the foot of a tree) and leave. Either they did not want to take anything from her, or did not want her to see them eat. Twice or three times she lingered. Hidden behind honeysuckle she watched them. How different they were without her, how they laughed and played and urinated and sang. All but Sixo, who laughed once – at the very end. Halle, of course, was the nicest. Baby Suggs' eighth and last child, who rented himself out all over the county to buy her away from there. But he too, as it turned out, was nothing but a man.

"A man ain't nothing but a man," said Baby Suggs. "But a son? Well now, that's *somebody*."

It made sense for a lot of reasons because in all of Baby's life, as well as Sethe's own, men and women were moved around like checkers. Anybody Baby Suggs knew, let alone loved, who hadn't run off or been hanged, got rented out, loaned out, bought up, brought back, stored up, mortgaged, won, stolen or seized. So Baby's eight children had six fathers. What she called the nastiness of life was the shock she received upon learning that nobody stopped playing checkers just because the pieces included her children. Halle she was able to keep the longest. Twenty years. A lifetime. Given to her, no doubt, to make up for *hearing* that her two girls, neither of whom had their adult teeth, were sold and gone and she had not been able to wave goodbye. To make up for coupling with a straw boss for four months in exchange for keeping her third child, a boy, with her – only to have him traded for lumber in the spring of the next year and to find herself pregnant by the man who promised not to and did. That child she could not love and the rest she would not. "God take what He would," she said. And He did, and He did, and He did and then gave her Halle who gave her freedom when it didn't mean a thing.

Sethe had the amazing luck of six whole years of marriage to that "somebody" son who had fathered every one of her children. A blessing she was reckless enough to take for granted, lean on, as though Sweet Home really was one. As though a handful of myrtle stuck in the handle of a pressing iron propped against the door in a whitewoman's kitchen could make it hers. As though mint sprig in the mouth changed the breath as well as its odor. A bigger fool never lived.

Sethe started to turn over on her stomach but changed her mind. She did not want to call Paul D's attention back to her, so she settled for crossing her ankles.

But Paul D noticed the movement as well as the change in her breathing. He felt obliged to try again, slower this time, but the appetite was gone. Actually it was a good feeling – not wanting her. Twenty-five years and blip! The kind of thing Sixo would do – like the time he arranged a meeting with Patsy the Thirty-Mile Woman. It took three months and two thirty-four-mile round trips to do it. To persuade her to walk one-third of the way toward him, to a place he knew. A deserted stone structure that Redmen used way back when they thought the land was theirs. Sixo discovered it on one of his night creeps, and asked its permission to enter. Inside, having felt what it felt like, he asked the Redmen's Presence if he could bring his woman there. It said yes and Sixo painstakingly instructed her how to get there, exactly when to start out, how his welcoming or warning whistles would sound. Since neither could go any-where on business of their own, and since the Thirty-Mile Woman was already fourteen and scheduled for somebody's arms, the danger was real. When he arrived, she had not. He whistled and got no answer. He went into the Redmen's deserted lodge. She was not there. He returned to the meet-ing spot. She was not there. He waited longer. She still did not come. He grew frightened for her and walked down the road in the direction she should be coming from. Three or four miles, and he stopped. It was hopeless to go on that way, so he stood in the wind and asked for help. Listening close for some sign, he heard a whimper. He turned toward it, waited and heard it again. Uncautious now, he hollered her name. She answered in a voice that sounded like life to him – not death. "Not move!" he shouted. "Breathe hard I can find you." He did. She believed she was already at the meeting place and was crying because she thought he had not kept his promise. Now it was too late for the rendezvous to happen at the Redmen's house, so they dropped where they were. Later he punctured her calf to simulate snakebite so she could use it in some way as an excuse for not being on time to shake worms from tobacco leaves. He gave her detailed directions about following the stream as a shortcut back, and saw her off. When he got to the road it was very light and he had his clothes in his hands. Suddenly from around a bend a wagon trundled toward him. Its driver, wide-eyed, raised a whip while the woman seated beside him covered her face. But Sixo had already melted into the woods before the lash could unfurl itself on his indigo behind.

He told the story to Paul F, Halle, Paul A and Paul D in the peculiar way that made them cry-laugh. Sixo went among trees at night. For dancing, he said, to keep his bloodlines open, he said. Privately, alone, he did it. None of the rest of them had seen him at it, but they could imagine it, and the picture they pictured made them eager to laugh at him – in daylight, that is, when it was safe.

But that was before he stopped speaking English because there was no future in it. Because of the Thirty-Mile Woman Sixo was the only one not paralyzed by yearning for Sethe. Nothing could be as good as the sex with her Paul D had been imagining off and on for twenty-five years. His foolishness made him smile and think fondly of himself as he turned over on his side, facing her. Sethe's eyes were closed, her hair a mess. Looked at this way, minus the polished eyes, her face was not so attractive. So it must have been her eyes that kept him both guarded and stirred up. Without them her face was manageable – a face he could handle. Maybe if she would keep them closed like that . . . But no, there was her mouth. Nice. Halle never knew what he had.

Although her eyes were closed, Sethe knew his gaze was on her face, and a paper picture of just how bad she must look raised itself up before her mind's eye. Still, there was no mockery coming from his gaze. Soft. It felt soft in a waiting kind of way. He was not judging her – or rather he was judging but not comparing her. Not since Halle had a man looked at her that way: not loving or passionate, but interested, as though he were examining an ear of corn for quality. Halle was more like a brother than a husband. His care suggested a family relationship rather than a man's laying claim. For years they saw each other in full daylight only on Sundays. The rest of the time they spoke or touched or ate in darkness. Predawn darkness and the afterlight of sunset. So looking at each other intently was a Sunday-morning pleasure and Halle examined her as though storing up what he saw in sunlight for the shadow he saw the rest of the week. And he had so little time. After his Sweet Home work and on Sunday afternoons was the debt work he owed for his mother. When he asked her to be his wife, Sethe happily agreed and then was stuck not knowing the next step. There should be a ceremony, shouldn't there? A preacher, some dancing, a party, a something. She and Mrs. Garner were the only women there, so she decided to ask her.

"Halle and me want to be married, Mrs. Garner."

"So I heard." She smiled. "He talked to Mr. Garner about it. Are you already expecting?"

"No, ma'am."

"Well, you will be. You know that, don't you?"

"Yes, ma'am."

"Halle's nice, Sethe. He'll be good to you."

"But I mean we want to get married."

"You just said so. And I said all right."

"Is there a wedding?"

Mrs. Garner put down her cooking spoon. Laughing a little, she touched Sethe on the head, saying, "You are one sweet child." And then no more.

Sethe made a dress on the sly and Halle hung his hitching rope from a nail on the wall of her cabin. And there on top of a mattress on top of the dirt floor of the cabin they coupled for the third time, the first two having been in the tiny cornfield Mr. Garner kept because it was a crop animals could use as well as humans. Both Halle and Sethe were under the impression that they were hidden. Scrunched down among the stalks they couldn't see anything, including the corn tops waving over their heads and visible to everyone else.

Sethe smiled at her and Halle's stupidity. Even the crows knew and came to look. Uncrossing her ankles, she managed not to laugh aloud.

The jump, thought Paul D, from a calf to a girl wasn't all that mighty. Not the leap Halle believed it would be. And taking her in the corn rather than her quarters, a yard away

36

from the cabins of the others who had lost out, was a gesture of tenderness. Halle wanted privacy for her and got public display. Who could miss a ripple in a cornfield on a quiet cloudless day? He, Sixo and both of the Pauls sat under Brother pouring water from a gourd over their heads, and through eyes streaming with well water, they watched the confusion of tassels in the field below. It had been hard, hard, hard sitting there erect as dogs, watching corn stalks dance at noon. The water running over their heads made it worse.

Paul D sighed and turned over. Sethe took the opportunity afforded by his movement to shift as well. Looking at Paul D's back, she remembered that some of the corn stalks broke, folded down over Halle's back, and among the things her fingers clutched were husk and cornsilk hair.

How loose the silk. How jailed down the juice.

The jealous admiration of the watching men melted with the feast of new corn they allowed themselves that night. Plucked from the broken stalks that Mr. Garner could not doubt was the fault of the raccoon. Paul F wanted his roasted; Paul A wanted his boiled and now Paul D couldn't remember how finally they'd cooked those ears too young to eat. What he did remember was parting the hair to get to the tip, the edge of his fingernail just under, so as not to graze a single kernel.

The pulling down of the tight sheath, the ripping sound always convinced her it hurt.

As soon as one strip of husk was down, the rest obeyed and the ear yielded up to him its shy rows, exposed at last. How loose the silk. How quick the jailed-up flavor ran free.

No matter what all your teeth and wet fingers anticipated, there was no accounting for the way that simple joy could shake you.

How loose the silk. How fine and loose and free.

DENVER'S SECRETS WERE SWEET. Accompanied every time by wild veronica until she discovered cologne. The first bottle was a gift, the next she stole from her mother and hid among boxwood until it froze and cracked. That was the year winter came in a hurry at suppertime and stayed eight months. One of the War years when Miss Bodwin, the whitewoman, brought Christmas cologne for her mother and herself, oranges for the boys and another good wool shawl for Baby Suggs. Talking of a war full of dead people, she looked happy – flush-faced, and although her voice was heavy as a man's, she smelled like a roomful of flowers – excitement that Denver could have all for herself in the boxwood. Back beyond 124 was a narrow field that stopped itself at a wood. On the yonder side of these woods, a stream. In these woods, between the field and the stream, hidden by post oaks, five boxwood bushes, planted in a ring, had started stretching toward each other four feet off the ground to form a round, empty room seven feet high, its walls fifty inches of murmuring leaves.

Bent low, Denver could crawl into this room, and once there she could stand all the way up in emerald light.

It began as a little girl's houseplay, but as her desires changed, so did the play. Quiet, private and completely secret except for the noisome cologne signal that thrilled the rabbits before it confused them. First a playroom (where the silence was softer), then a refuge (from her brothers' fright), soon the place became the point. In that bower, closed off from the hurt of the hurt world, Denver's imagination produced its own hunger and its own food, which she badly needed

38

because loneliness wore her out. *Wore her out.* Veiled and protected by the live green walls, she felt ripe and clear, and salvation was as easy as a wish.

Once when she was in the boxwood, an autumn long before Paul D moved into the house with her mother, she was made suddenly cold by a combination of wind and the perfume on her skin. She dressed herself, bent down to leave and stood up in snowfall: a thin and whipping snow very like the picture her mother had painted as she described the circumstances of Denver's birth in a canoe straddled by a whitegirl for whom she was named.

Shivering, Denver approached the house, regarding it, as she always did, as a person rather than a structure. A person that wept, sighed, trembled and fell into fits. Her steps and her gaze were the cautious ones of a child approaching a nervous, idle relative (someone dependent but proud). A breastplate of darkness hid all the windows except one. Its dim glow came from Baby Suggs' room. When Denver looked in, she saw her mother on her knees in prayer, which was not unusual. What was unusual (even for a girl who had lived all her life in a house peopled by the living activity of the dead) was that a white dress knelt down next to her mother and had its sleeve around her mother's waist. And it was the tender embrace of the dress sleeve that made Denver remember the details of her birth — that and the thin, whipping snow she was standing in, like the fruit of common flowers. The dress and her mother together looked like two friendly grown-up women — one (the dress) helping out the other. And the magic of her birth, its miracle in fact, testified to that friendliness as did her own name.

Easily she stepped into the told story that lay before her eyes on the path she followed away from the window. There was only one door to the house and to get to it from the back you had to walk all the way around to the front of 124, past the storeroom, past the cold house, the privy, the shed, on around to the porch. And to get to the part of the story she liked best, she had to start way back: hear the birds in the thick woods, the crunch of leaves underfoot; see her mother making her way up into the hills where no houses were likely to be. How Sethe was walking on two feet meant for standing still. How they were so swollen she could not see her arch or feel her ankles. Her leg shaft ended in a loaf of flesh scalloped by five toenails. But she could not, would not, stop, for when she did the little antelope rammed her with horns and pawed the ground of her womb with impatient hooves. While she was walking, it seemed to graze, quietly – so she walked, on two feet meant, in this sixth month of pregnancy, for standing still. Still, near a kettle; still, at the churn; still, at the tub and ironing board. Milk, sticky and sour on her dress, attracted every small flying thing from gnats to grasshoppers. By the time she reached the hill skirt she had long ago stopped waving them off. The clanging in her head, begun as a churchbell heard from a distance, was by then a tight cap of pealing bells around her ears. She sank and had to look down to see whether she was in a hole or kneeling. Nothing was alive but her nipples and the little antelope. Finally, she was horizontal – or must have been because blades of wild onion were scratching her temple and her cheek. Concerned as she was for the life of her children's mother, Sethe told Denver, she remembered thinking: Well, at least I don't have to take another step. A dying thought if ever there was one, and she waited for the little antelope to protest, and why she thought of an antelope Sethe could not imagine since she had never seen one. She guessed it must have been an invention held on to from before Sweet Home, when she was very young. Of that place where she was born (Carolina maybe? or was it Louisiana?) she remembered only song and dance. Not even her own mother, who was pointed out to her by the eight-year-old child who watched over the young ones – pointed out as the one among many backs turned away from her, stooping in a watery field. Patiently Sethe waited for this particular back to gain the row's end and stand. What she saw was a cloth hat as opposed to a straw one, singularity enough in that world of cooing women each of whom was called Ma'am.

"Seth – thuh."

"Ma'am."

"Hold on to the baby."

"Yes, Ma'am."

"Seth – thuh."

"Ma'am."

"Get some kindlin in here."

"Yes, Ma'am."

Oh but when they sang. And oh but when they danced and sometimes they danced the antelope. The men as well as the ma'ams, one of whom was certainly her own. They shifted shapes and became something other. Some unchained, demanding other whose feet knew her pulse better than she did. Just like this one in her stomach.

"I believe this baby's ma'am is gonna die in wild onions on the bloody side of the Ohio River." That's what was on her mind and what she told Denver. Her exact words. And it didn't seem such a bad idea, all in all, in view of the step she would not have to take, but the thought of herself stretched out dead while the little antelope lived on – an hour? a day? a day and a night? – in her lifeless body grieved her so she made the groan that made the person walking on a path not ten yards away halt and stand right still. Sethe had not heard the walking, but suddenly she heard the standing still and then she smelled the hair. The voice, saying, "Who's in there?" was all she needed to know that she was about to be discovered by a whiteboy. That he too had mossy teeth, an appetite. That on a ridge of pine near the Ohio River, trying to get to her three children, one of whom was starving for the food she carried; that after her

41

husband had disappeared; that after her milk had been stolen, her back pulped, her children orphaned, she was not to have an easeful death. No.

She told Denver that a *something* came up out of the earth into her – like a freezing, but moving too, like jaws inside. "Look like I was just cold jaws grinding," she said. Suddenly she was eager for his eyes, to bite into them; to gnaw his cheek.

"I was hungry," she told Denver, "just as hungry as I could be for his eyes. I couldn't wait."

So she raised up on her elbow and dragged herself, one pull, two, three, four, toward the young white voice talking about "Who that back in there?"

" 'Come see,' I was thinking. 'Be the last thing you behold,' and sure enough here come the feet so I thought well that's where I'll have to start God do what He would, I'm gonna eat his feet off. I'm laughing now, but it's true. I wasn't just set to do it. I was hungry to do it. Like a snake. All jaws and hungry.

"It wasn't no whiteboy at all. Was a girl. The raggediest-looking trash you ever saw saying, 'Look there. A nigger. If that don't beat all.' "

And now the part Denver loved the best:

Her name was Amy and she needed beef and pot liquor like nobody in this world. Arms like cane stalks and enough hair for four or five heads. Slow-moving eyes. She didn't look at anything quick. Talked so much it wasn't clear how she could breathe at the same time. And those cane-stalk arms, as it turned out, were as strong as iron.

"You 'bout the scariest-looking something I ever seen. What you doing back up in here?"

Down in the grass, like the snake she believed she was, Sethe opened her mouth, and instead of fangs and a split tongue, out shot the truth.

"Running," Sethe told her. It was the first word she had

spoken all day and it came out thick because of her tender tongue.

"Them the feet you running on? My Jesus my." She squatted down and stared at Sethe's feet. "You got anything on you, gal, pass for food?"

"No." Sethe tried to shift to a sitting position but couldn't.

"I like to die I'm so hungry." The girl moved her eyes slowly, examining the greenery around her. "Thought there'd be huckleberries. Look like it. That's why I come up in here. Didn't expect to find no nigger woman. If they was any, birds ate em. You like huckleberries?"

"I'm having a baby, miss."

Amy looked at her. "That mean you don't have no appetite? Well I got to eat me something."

Combing her hair with her fingers, she carefully surveyed the landscape once more. Satisfied nothing edible was around, she stood up to go and Sethe's heart stood up too at the thought of being left alone in the grass without a fang in her head.

"Where you on your way to, miss?"

She turned and looked at Sethe with freshly lit eyes. "Boston. Get me some velvet. It's a store there called Wilson. I seen the pictures of it and they have the prettiest velvet. They don't believe I'm a get it, but I am."

Sethe nodded and shifted her elbow. "Your ma'am know you on the lookout for velvet?"

The girl shook her hair out of her face. "My mama worked for these here people to pay for her passage. But then she had me and since she died right after, well, they said I had to work for em to pay it off. I did, but now I want me some velvet."

They did not look directly at each other, not straight into the eyes anyway. Yet they slipped effortlessly into yard chat about nothing in particular – except one lay on the ground.

"Boston," said Sethe. "Is that far?"

"Ooooh, yeah. A hundred miles. Maybe more."

"Must be velvet closer by."

"Not like in Boston. Boston got the best. Be so pretty on me. You ever touch it?"

"No, miss. I never touched no velvet." Sethe didn't know if it was the voice, or Boston or velvet, but while the whitegirl talked, the baby slept. Not one butt or kick, so she guessed her luck had turned.

"Ever see any?" she asked Sethe. "I bet you never even seen any."

"If I did I didn't know it. What's it like, velvet?"

Amy dragged her eyes over Sethe's face as though she would never give out so confidential a piece of information as that to a perfect stranger.

"What they call you?" she asked.

However far she was from Sweet Home, there was no point in giving out her real name to the first person she saw. "Lu," said Sethe. "They call me Lu."

"Well, Lu, velvet is like the world was just born. Clean and new and so smooth. The velvet I seen was brown, but in Boston they got all colors. Carmine. That means red but when you talk about velvet you got to say 'carmine.'" She raised her eyes to the sky and then, as though she had wasted enough time away from Boston, she moved off saying, "I gotta go."

Picking her way through the brush she hollered back to Sethe, "What you gonna do, just lay there and foal?"

"I can't get up from here," said Sethe.

"What?" She stopped and turned to hear.

"I said I can't get up."

Amy drew her arm across her nose and came slowly back to where Sethe lay. "It's a house back yonder," she said.

"A house?"

"Mmmmm. I passed it. Ain't no regular house with people in it though. A lean-to, kinda."

44

"How far?"

"Make a difference, does it? You stay the night here snake get you."

"Well he may as well come on. I can't stand up let alone walk and God help me, miss, I can't crawl."

"Sure you can, Lu. Come on," said Amy and, with a toss of hair enough for five heads, she moved toward the path.

So she crawled and Amy walked alongside her, and when Sethe needed to rest, Amy stopped too and talked some more about Boston and velvet and good things to eat. The sound of that voice, like a sixteen-year-old boy's, going on and on and on, kept the little antelope quiet and grazing. During the whole hateful crawl to the lean-to, it never bucked once.

Nothing of Sethe's was intact by the time they reached it except the cloth that covered her hair. Below her bloody knees, there was no feeling at all; her chest was two cushions of pins. It was the voice full of velvet and Boston and good things to eat that urged her along and made her think that maybe she wasn't, after all, just a crawling graveyard for a six-month baby's last hours.

The lean-to was full of leaves, which Amy pushed into a pile for Sethe to lie on. Then she gathered rocks, covered them with more leaves and made Sethe put her feet on them, saying: "I know a woman had her feet cut off they was so swole." And she made sawing gestures with the blade of her hand across Sethe's ankles. "Zzz Zzz Zzz Zzz."

"I used to be a good size. Nice arms and everything. Wouldn't think it, would you? That was before they put me in the root cellar. I was fishing off the Beaver once. Catfish in Beaver River sweet as chicken. Well I was just fishing there and a nigger floated right by me. I don't like drowned people, you? Your feet remind me of him. All swole like."

Then she did the magic: lifted Sethe's feet and legs and massaged them until she cried salt tears.

"It's gonna hurt, now," said Amy. "Anything dead coming back to life hurts."

A truth for all times, thought Denver. Maybe the white dress holding its arm around her mother's waist was in pain. If so, it could mean the baby ghost had plans. When she opened the door, Sethe was just leaving the keeping room.

"I saw a white dress holding on to you," Denver said.

"White? Maybe it was my bedding dress. Describe it to me."

"Had a high neck. Whole mess of buttons coming down the back."

"Buttons. Well, that lets out my bedding dress. I never had a button on nothing."

"Did Grandma Baby?"

Sethe shook her head. "She couldn't handle them. Even on her shoes. What else?"

"A bunch at the back. On the sit-down part."

"A bustle? It had a bustle?"

"I don't know what it's called."

"Sort of gathered-like? Below the waist in the back?"

"Um hm."

"A rich lady's dress. Silk?"

"Cotton, look like."

"Lisle probably. White cotton lisle. You say it was holding on to me. How?"

"Like you. It looked just like you. Kneeling next to you while you were praying. Had its arm around your waist."

"Well, I'll be."

"What were you praying for, Ma'am?"

"Not *for* anything. I don't pray anymore. I just talk."

"What were you talking about?"

"You won't understand, baby."

"Yes, I will."

"I was talking about time. It's so hard for me to believe in it. Some things go. Pass on. Some things just stay. I used to think it was my rememory. You know. Some things you forget. Other things you never do. But it's not. Places, places are still there. If a house burns down, it's gone, but the place – the picture of it – stays, and not just in my rememory, but out there, in the world. What I remember is a picture floating around out there outside my head. I mean, even if I don't think it, even if I die, the picture of what I did, or knew, or saw is still out there. Right in the place where it happened."

"Can other people see it?" asked Denver.

"Oh, yes. Oh, yes, yes, yes. Someday you be walking down the road and you hear something or see something going on. So clear. And you think it's you thinking it up. A thought picture. But no. It's when you bump into a rememory that belongs to somebody else. Where I was before I came here, that place is real. It's never going away. Even if the whole farm – every tree and grass blade of it dies. The picture is still there and what's more, if you go there – you who never was there – if you go there and stand in the place where it was, it will happen again; it will be there for you, waiting for you. So, Denver, you can't never go there. Never. Because even though it's all over – over and done with – it's going to always be there waiting for you. That's how come I had to get all my children out. No matter what."

Denver picked at her fingernails. "If it's still there, waiting, that must mean that nothing ever dies."

Sethe looked right in Denver's face. "Nothing ever does," she said.

"You never told me all what happened. Just that they whipped you and you run off, pregnant. With me."

"Nothing to tell except schoolteacher. He was a little man. Short. Always wore a collar, even in the fields. A school-teacher, she said. That made her feel good that her husband's sister's husband had book learning and was willing to come farm Sweet Home after Mr. Garner passed. The men could have done it, even with Paul F sold. But it was like Halle

47

said. She didn't want to be the only white person on the farm and a woman too. So she was satisfied when the schoolteacher agreed to come. He brought two boys with him. Sons or nephews. I don't know. They called him Onka and had pretty manners, all of em. Talked soft and spit in handkerchiefs. Gentle in a lot of ways. You know, the kind who know Jesus by His first name, but out of politeness never use it even to His face. A pretty good farmer, Halle said. Not strong as Mr. Garner but smart enough. He liked the ink I made. It was her recipe, but he preferred how I mixed it and it was important to him because at night he sat down to write in his book. It was a book about us but we didn't know that right away. We just thought it was his manner to ask us questions. He commenced to carry round a notebook and write down what we said. I still think it was them questions that tore Sixo up. Tore him up for all time."

She stopped.

Denver knew that her mother was through with it – for now anyway. The single slow blink of her eyes; the bottom lip sliding up slowly to cover the top; and then a nostril sigh, like the snuff of a candle flame – signs that Sethe had reached the point beyond which she would not go.

"Well, I think the baby got plans," said Denver.

"What plans?"

"I don't know, but the dress holding on to you got to mean something."

"Maybe," said Sethe. "Maybe it does have plans."

Whatever they were or might have been, Paul D messed them up for good. With a table and a loud male voice he had rid 124 of its claim to local fame. Denver had taught herself to take pride in the condemnation Negroes heaped on them; the assumption that the haunting was done by an evil thing looking for more. None of them knew the downright pleasure of enchantment, of not suspecting but *knowing*

48

the things behind things. Her brothers had known, but it scared them; Grandma Baby knew, but it saddened her. None could appreciate the safety of ghost company. Even Sethe didn't love it. She just took it for granted – like a sudden change in the weather.

But it was gone now. Whooshed away in the blast of a hazelnut man's shout, leaving Denver's world flat, mostly, with the exception of an emerald closet standing seven feet high in the woods. Her mother had secrets – things she wouldn't tell; things she halfway told. Well, Denver had them too. And hers were sweet – sweet as lily-of-the-valley cologne.

Sethe had given little thought to the white dress until Paul D came, and then she remembered Denver's interpretation: plans. The morning after the first night with Paul D, Sethe smiled just thinking about what the word could mean. It was a luxury she had not had in eighteen years and only that once. Before and since, all her effort was directed not on avoiding pain but on getting through it as quickly as possible. The one set of plans she had made – getting away from Sweet Home – went awry so completely she never dared life by making more.

Yet the morning she woke up next to Paul D, the word her daughter had used a few years ago did cross her mind and she thought about what Denver had seen kneeling next to her, and thought also of the temptation to trust and remember that gripped her as she stood before the cooking stove in his arms. Would it be all right? Would it be all right to go ahead and feel? Go ahead and *count on something*?

She couldn't think clearly, lying next to him listening to his breathing, so carefully, carefully, she had left the bed.

Kneeling in the keeping room where she usually went to talk-think it was clear why Baby Suggs was so starved for color. There wasn't any except for two orange squares in a quilt that made the absence shout. The walls of the room were slate-colored, the floor earth-brown, the wooden dresser the color of itself, curtains white, and the dominating feature, the quilt over an iron cot, was made up of scraps of blue serge, black, brown and gray wool – the full range of the dark and the muted that thrift and modesty allowed. In that sober field, two patches of orange looked wild – like life in the raw.

Sethe looked at her hands, her bottle-green sleeves, and thought how little color there was in the house and how strange that she had not missed it the way Baby did. Deliberate, she thought, it must be deliberate, because the last color she remembered was the pink chips in the headstone of her baby girl. After that she became as color conscious as a hen. Every dawn she worked at fruit pies, potato dishes and vegetables while the cook did the soup, meat and all the rest. And she could not remember remembering a molly apple or a yellow squash. Every dawn she saw the dawn, but never acknowledged or remarked its color. There was something wrong with that. It was as though one day she saw red baby blood, another day the pink gravestone chips, and that was the last of it.

124 was so full of strong feeling perhaps she was oblivious to the loss of anything at all. There was a time when she scanned the fields every morning and every evening for her boys. When she stood at the open window, unmindful of flies, her head cocked to her left shoulder, her eyes searching to the right for them. Cloud shadow on the road, an old woman, a wandering goat untethered and gnawing bramble – each one looked at first like Howard – no, Buglar. Little by little she stopped and their thirteen-year-old faces faded completely into their baby ones, which came to her only in sleep. When her dreams roamed outside 124, anywhere they wished, she saw them sometimes in beautiful trees, their little

legs barely visible in the leaves. Sometimes they ran along the railroad track laughing, too loud, apparently, to hear her because they never did turn around. When she woke the house crowded in on her: there was the door where the soda crackers were lined up in a row; the white stairs her baby girl loved to climb; the corner where Baby Suggs mended shoes, a pile of which were still in the cold room; the exact place on the stove where Denver burned her fingers. And of course the spite of the house itself. There was no room for any other thing or body until Paul D arrived and broke up the place, making room, shifting it, moving it over to some-place else, then standing in the place he had made.

So, kneeling in the keeping room the morning after Paul D came, she was distracted by the two orange squares that signaled how barren 124 really was.

He was responsible for that. Emotions sped to the surface in his company. Things became what they were: drabness looked drab; heat was hot. Windows suddenly had view. And wouldn't you know he'd be a singing man.

> *Little rice, little bean,*
> *No meat in between.*
> *Hard work ain't easy,*
> *Dry bread ain't greasy.*

He was up now and singing as he mended things he had broken the day before. Some old pieces of song he'd learned on the prison farm or in the War afterward. Nothing like what they sang at Sweet Home, where yearning fashioned every note.

The songs he knew from Georgia were flat-headed nails for pounding and pounding and pounding.

> *Lay my head on the railroad line,*
> *Train come along, pacify my mind.*
> *If I had my weight in lime,*

> *I'd whip my captain till he went stone blind.*
> *Five-cent nickel,*
> *Ten-cent dime,*
> *Busting rocks is busting time.*

But they didn't fit, these songs. They were too loud, had too much power for the little house chores he was engaged in – resetting table legs; glazing.

He couldn't go back to "Storm upon the Waters" that they sang under the trees of Sweet Home, so he contented himself with mmmmmmmmmm, throwing in a line if one occurred to him, and what occurred over and over was "Bare feet and chamomile sap,/Took off my shoes; took off my hat."

It was tempting to change the words (Gimme back my shoes; gimme back my hat), because he didn't believe he could live with a woman – any woman – for over two out of three months. That was about as long as he could abide one place. After Delaware and before that Alfred, Georgia, where he slept underground and crawled into sunlight for the sole purpose of breaking rock, walking off when he got ready was the only way he could convince himself that he would no longer have to sleep, pee, eat or swing a sledge hammer in chains.

But this was not a normal woman in a normal house. As soon as he had stepped through the red light he knew that, compared to 124, the rest of the world was bald. After Alfred he had shut down a generous portion of his head, operating on the part that helped him walk, eat, sleep, sing. If he could do those things – with a little work and a little sex thrown in – he asked for no more, for more required him to dwell on Halle's face and Sixo laughing. To recall trembling in a box built into the ground. Grateful for the daylight spent doing mule work in a quarry because he did not tremble when he had a hammer in his hands. The box had done what Sweet Home had not, what working like an ass and living like a dog had not: drove him crazy so he would not lose his mind.

By the time he got to Ohio, then to Cincinnati, then to Halle Suggs' mother's house, he thought he had seen and felt it all. Even now as he put back the window frame he had smashed, he could not account for the pleasure in his surprise at seeing Halle's wife alive, barefoot with uncovered hair — walking around the corner of the house with her shoes and stockings in her hands. The closed portion of his head opened like a greased lock.

"I was thinking of looking for work around here. What you think?"

"Ain't much. River mostly. And hogs."

"Well, I never worked on water, but I can pick up anything heavy as me, hogs included."

"Whitepeople better here than Kentucky but you may have to scramble some."

"It ain't whether I scramble; it's where. You saying it's all right to scramble here?"

"Better than all right."

"Your girl, Denver. Seems to me she's of a different mind."

"Why you say that?"

"She's got a waiting way about her. Something she's expecting and it ain't me."

"I don't know what it could be."

"Well, whatever it is, she believes I'm interrupting it."

"Don't worry about her. She's a charmed child. From the beginning."

"Is that right?"

"Uh huh. Nothing bad can happen to her. Look at it. Everybody I knew dead or gone or dead and gone. Not her. Not my Denver. Even when I was carrying her, when it got clear that I wasn't going to make it — which meant she wasn't going to make it either — she pulled a whitegirl out of the hill. The last thing you'd expect to help. And when the schoolteacher found us and came busting in here with the law and a shotgun —"

"Schoolteacher found you?"

"Took a while, but he did. Finally."

"And he didn't take you back?"

"Oh, no. I wasn't going back there. I don't care who found who. Any life but not that one. I went to jail instead. Denver was just a baby so she went right along with me. Rats bit everything in there but her."

Paul D turned away. He wanted to know more about it, but jail talk put him back in Alfred, Georgia.

"I need some nails. Anybody around here I can borrow from or should I go to town?"

"May as well go to town. You'll need other things."

One night and they were talking like a couple. They had skipped love and promise and went directly to "You saying it's all right to scramble here?"

To Sethe, the future was a matter of keeping the past at bay. The "better life" she believed she and Denver were living was simply not that other one.

The fact that Paul D had come out of "that other one" into her bed was better too; and the notion of a future with him, or for that matter without him, was beginning to stroke her mind. As for Denver, the job Sethe had of keeping her from the past that was still waiting for her was all that mattered.

PLEASANTLY TROUBLED, Sethe avoided the keeping room and Denver's sidelong looks. As she expected, since life was like that – it didn't do any good. Denver ran a mighty interference and on the third day flat-out asked Paul D how long he was going to hang around.

The phrase hurt him so much he missed the table. The coffee cup hit the floor and rolled down the sloping boards toward the front door.

"Hang around?" Paul D didn't even look at the mess he had made.

"Denver! What's got into you?" Sethe looked at her daughter, feeling more embarrassed than angry.

Paul D scratched the hair on his chin. "Maybe I should make tracks."

"No!" Sethe was surprised by how loud she said it.

"He know what he needs," said Denver.

"Well, you don't," Sethe told her, "and you must not know what you need either. I don't want to hear another word out of you."

"I just asked if –"

"Hush! *You* make tracks. Go somewhere and sit down."

Denver picked up her plate and left the table but not before adding a chicken back and more bread to the heap she was carrying away. Paul D leaned over to wipe the spilled coffee with his blue handkerchief.

"I'll get that." Sethe jumped up and went to the stove. Behind it various cloths hung, each in some stage of drying. In silence she wiped the floor and retrieved the cup. Then she poured him another cupful, and set it carefully before him. Paul D touched its rim but didn't say anything – as though even "thank you" was an obligation he could not meet and the coffee itself a gift he could not take.

Sethe resumed her chair and the silence continued. Finally she realized that if it was going to be broken she would have to do it.

"I didn't train her like that."

Paul D stroked the rim of the cup.

"And I'm as surprised by her manners as you are hurt by em."

Paul D looked at Sethe. "Is there history to her question?"

"History? What you mean?"

"I mean, did she have to ask that, or want to ask it, of anybody else before me?"

Sethe made two fists and placed them on her hips. "You as bad as she is."

"Come on, Sethe."

"Oh, I am coming on. I am!"

"You know what I mean."

"I do and I don't like it."

"Jesus," he whispered.

"Who?" Sethe was getting loud again.

"Jesus! I said Jesus! All I did was sit down for supper! and I get cussed out twice. Once for being here and once for asking why I was cussed in the first place!"

"She didn't cuss."

"No? Felt like it."

"Look here. I apologize for her. I'm real –"

"You can't do that. You can't apologize for nobody. She got to do that."

"Then I'll see that she does." Sethe sighed.

"What I want to know is, is she asking a question that's on your mind too?"

"Oh no. No, Paul D. Oh no."

"Then she's of one mind and you another? If you can call whatever's in her head a mind, that is."

"Excuse me, but I can't hear a word against her. I'll chastise her. You leave her alone."

Risky, thought Paul D, very risky. For a used-to-be-slave woman to love anything that much was dangerous, especially if it was her children she had settled on to love. The best thing, he knew, was to love just a little bit; everything, just a little bit, so when they broke its back, or shoved it in a croaker sack, well, maybe you'd have a little love left over for the next one. "Why?" he asked her. "Why you think you have to take up for her? Apologize for her? She's grown."

"I don't care what she is. Grown don't mean nothing to a mother. A child is a child. They get bigger, older, but grown? What's that supposed to mean? In my heart it don't mean a thing."

"It means she has to take it if she acts up. You can't protect her every minute. What's going to happen when you die?"

"Nothing! I'll protect her while I'm live and I'll protect her when I ain't."

"Oh well, I'm through," he said. "I quit."

"That's the way it is, Paul D. I can't explain it to you no better than that, but that's the way it is. If I have to choose – well, it's not even a choice."

"That's the point. The whole point. I'm not asking you to choose. Nobody would. I thought – well, I thought you could – there was some space for me."

"She's asking me."

"You can't go by that. You got to say it to her. Tell her it's not about choosing somebody over her – it's making space for somebody along with her. You got to say it. And if you say it and mean it, then you also got to know you can't gag me. There's no way I'm going to hurt her or not take care of what she need if I can, but I can't be told to

57

keep my mouth shut if she's acting ugly. You want me here, don't put no gag on me."

"Maybe I should leave things the way they are," she said.

"How are they?"

"We get along."

"What about inside?"

"I don't go inside."

"Sethe, if I'm here with you, with Denver, you can go anywhere you want. Jump, if you want to, 'cause I'll catch you, girl. I'll catch you 'fore you fall. Go as far inside as you need to, I'll hold your ankles. Make sure you get back out. I'm not saying this because I need a place to stay. That's the last thing I need. I told you, I'm a walking man, but I been heading in this direction for seven years. Walking all around this place. Upstate, downstate, east, west; I been in territory ain't got no name, never staying nowhere long. But when I got here and sat out there on the porch, waiting for you, well, I knew it wasn't the place I was heading toward; it was you. We can make a life, girl. A life."

"I don't know. I don't know."

"Leave it to me. See how it goes. No promises, if you don't want to make any. Just see how it goes. All right?"

"All right."

"You willing to leave it to me?"

"Well – some of it."

"Some?" he smiled. "Okay. Here's some. There's a carnival in town. Thursday, tomorrow, is for coloreds and I got two dollars. Me and you and Denver gonna spend every penny of it. What you say?"

"No" is what she said. At least what she started out saying (what would her boss say if she took a day off?), but even when she said it she was thinking how much her eyes enjoyed looking in his face.

*

The crickets were screaming on Thursday and the sky, stripped of blue, was white hot at eleven in the morning. Sethe was badly dressed for the heat, but this being her first social outing in eighteen years, she felt obliged to wear her one good dress, heavy as it was, and a hat. Certainly a hat. She didn't want to meet Lady Jones or Ella with her head wrapped like she was going to work. The dress, a good-wool castoff, was a Christmas present to Baby Suggs from Miss Bodwin, the whitewoman who loved her. Denver and Paul D fared better in the heat since neither felt the occasion required special clothing. Denver's bonnet knocked against her shoulder blades; Paul D wore his vest open, no jacket and his shirt sleeves rolled above his elbows. They were not holding hands, but their shadows were. Sethe looked to her left and all three of them were gliding over the dust holding hands. Maybe he was right. A life. Watching their hand-holding shadows, she was embarrassed at being dressed for church. The others, ahead and behind them, would think she was putting on airs, letting them know that she was different because she lived in a house with two stories; tougher, because she could do and survive things they believed she should neither do nor survive. She was glad Denver had resisted her urgings to dress up – rebraid her hair at least. But Denver was not doing anything to make this trip a pleasure. She agreed to go – sullenly – but her attitude was "Go 'head. Try and make me happy." The happy one was Paul D. He said howdy to everybody within twenty feet. Made fun of the weather and what it was doing to him, yelled back at the crows, and was the first to smell the doomed roses. All the time, no matter what they were doing – whether Denver wiped perspiration from her forehead or stooped to retie her shoes; whether Paul D kicked a stone or reached over to meddle a child's face leaning on its mother's shoulder – all the time the three shadows that shot out of their feet to the left held hands. Nobody noticed but Sethe and she stopped looking after she decided that it was a good sign. A life. Could be.

Up and down the lumberyard fence old roses were dying. The sawyer who had planted them twelve years ago to give his workplace a friendly feel – something to take the sin out of slicing trees for a living – was amazed by their abundance; how rapidly they crawled all over the stake-and-post fence that separated the lumberyard from the open field next to it where homeless men slept, children ran and, once a year, carnival people pitched tents. The closer the roses got to death, the louder their scent, and everybody who attended the carnival associated it with the stench of the rotten roses. It made them a little dizzy and very thirsty but did nothing to extinguish the eagerness of the colored people filing down the road. Some walked on the grassy shoulders, others dodged the wagons creaking down the road's dusty center. All, like Paul D, were in high spirits, which the smell of dying roses (that Paul D called to everybody's attention) could not dampen. As they pressed to get to the rope entrance they were lit like lamps. Breathless with the excitement of seeing whitepeople loose: doing magic, clowning, without heads or with two heads, twenty feet tall or two feet tall, weighing a ton, completely tattooed, eating glass, swallowing fire, spitting ribbons, twisted into knots, forming pyramids, playing with snakes and beating each other up.

All of this was advertisement, read by those who could and heard by those who could not, and the fact that none of it was true did not extinguish their appetite a bit. The barker called them and their children names ("Pickaninnies free!") but the food on his vest and the hole in his pants rendered it fairly harmless. In any case it was a small price to pay for the fun they might not ever have again. Two pennies and an insult were well spent if it meant seeing the spectacle of whitefolks making a spectacle of themselves. So, although the carnival was a lot less than mediocre (which is why it agreed to a Colored Thursday), it gave the four hundred black people in its audience thrill upon thrill upon thrill.

One-Ton Lady spit at them, but her bulk shortened her aim and they got a big kick out of the helpless meanness in her little eyes. Arabian Nights Dancer cut her performance to three minutes instead of the usual fifteen she normally did – earning the gratitude of the children, who could hardly wait for Abu Snake Charmer, who followed her.

Denver bought horehound, licorice, peppermint and lemonade at a table manned by a little whitegirl in ladies' high-topped shoes. Soothed by sugar, surrounded by a crowd of people who did not find her the main attraction, who, in fact, said, "Hey, Denver," every now and then, pleased her enough to consider the possibility that Paul D wasn't all that bad. In fact there was something about him – when the three of them stood together watching Midget dance – that made the stares of other Negroes kind, gentle, something Denver did not remember seeing in their faces. Several even nodded and smiled at her mother, no one, apparently, able to withstand sharing the pleasure Paul D was having. He slapped his knees when Giant danced with Midget; when Two-Headed Man talked to himself. He bought everything Denver asked for and much she did not. He teased Sethe into tents she was reluctant to enter. Stuck pieces of candy she didn't want between her lips. When Wild African Savage shook his bars and said wa wa, Paul D told everybody he knew him back in Roanoke.

Paul D made a few acquaintances; spoke to them about what work he might find. Sethe returned the smiles she got. Denver was swaying with delight. And on the way home, although leading them now, the shadows of three people still held hands.

A FULLY DRESSED WOMAN walked out of the water. She barely gained the dry bank of the stream before she sat down and leaned against a mulberry tree. All day and all night she sat there, her head resting on the trunk in a position abandoned enough to crack the brim in her straw hat. Everything hurt but her lungs most of all. Sopping wet and breathing shallow she spent those hours trying to negotiate the weight of her eyelids. The day breeze blew her dress dry; the night wind wrinkled it. Nobody saw her emerge or came accidentally by. If they had, chances are they would have hesitated before approaching her. Not because she was wet, or dozing or had what sounded like asthma, but because amid all that she was smiling. It took her the whole of the next morning to lift herself from the ground and make her way through the woods past a giant temple of boxwood to the field and then the yard of the slate-gray house. Exhausted again, she sat down on the first handy place – a stump not far from the steps of 124. By then keeping her eyes open was less of an effort. She could manage it for a full two minutes or more. Her neck, its circumference no wider than a parlor-service saucer, kept bending and her chin brushed the bit of lace edging her dress.

Women who drink champagne when there is nothing to celebrate can look like that: their straw hats with broken brims are often askew; they nod in public places; their shoes are undone. But their skin is not like that of the woman breathing near the steps of 124. She had new skin, lineless and smooth, including the knuckles of her hands.

By late afternoon when the carnival was over, and the

Negroes were hitching rides home if they were lucky –
walking if they were not – the woman had fallen asleep again.
The rays of the sun struck her full in the face, so that when
Sethe, Denver and Paul D rounded the curve in the road all
they saw was a black dress, two unlaced shoes below it, and
Here Boy nowhere in sight.

"Look," said Denver. "What is that?"

And, for some reason she could not immediately account
for, the moment she got close enough to see the face, Sethe's
bladder filled to capacity. She said, "Oh, excuse me," and
ran around to the back of 124. Not since she was a baby girl,
being cared for by the eight-year-old girl who pointed out
her mother to her, had she had an emergency that unmanageable. She never made the outhouse. Right in front of its door
she had to lift her skirts, and the water she voided was endless.
Like a horse, she thought, but as it went on and on she
thought, No, more like flooding the boat when Denver was
born. So much water Amy said, "Hold on, Lu. You going
to sink us you keep that up." But there was no stopping
water breaking from a breaking womb and there was no
stopping now. She hoped Paul D wouldn't take it upon
himself to come looking for her and be obliged to see her
squatting in front of her own privy making a mudhole too
deep to be witnessed without shame. Just about the time she
started wondering if the carnival would accept another freak,
it stopped. She tidied herself and ran around to the porch.
No one was there. All three were inside – Paul D and Denver
standing before the stranger, watching her drink cup after
cup of water.

"She said she was thirsty," said Paul D. He took off his
cap. "Mighty thirsty look like."

The woman gulped water from a speckled tin cup and held
it out for more. Four times Denver filled it, and four times
the woman drank as though she had crossed a desert. When
she was finished a little water was on her chin, but she did

not wipe it away. Instead she gazed at Sethe with sleepy eyes. Poorly fed, thought Sethe, and younger than her clothes suggested – good lace at the throat, and a rich woman's hat. Her skin was flawless except for three vertical scratches on her forehead so fine and thin they seemed at first like hair, baby hair before it bloomed and roped into the masses of black yarn under her hat.

"You from around here?" Sethe asked her.

She shook her head no and reached down to take off her shoes. She pulled her dress up to the knees and rolled down her stockings. When the hosiery was tucked into the shoes, Sethe saw that her feet were like her hands, soft and new. She must have hitched a wagon ride, thought Sethe. Probably one of those West Virginia girls looking for something to beat a life of tobacco and sorghum. Sethe bent to pick up the shoes.

"What might your name be?" asked Paul D.

"Beloved," she said, and her voice was so low and rough each one looked at the other two. They heard the voice first – later the name.

"Beloved. You use a last name, Beloved?" Paul D asked her.

"Last?" She seemed puzzled. Then "No," and she spelled it for them, slowly as though the letters were being formed as she spoke them.

Sethe dropped the shoes; Denver sat down and Paul D smiled. He recognized the careful enunciation of letters by those, like himself, who could not read but had memorized the letters of their name. He was about to ask who her people were but thought better of it. A young coloredwoman drifting was drifting from ruin. He had been in Rochester four years ago and seen five women arriving with fourteen female children. All their men – brothers, uncles, fathers, husbands, sons – had been picked off one by one by one. They had a single piece of paper directing them to a preacher on DeVore Street. The War had been over four or five years then, but nobody white or black seemed to know it. Odd clusters and strays of Negroes wandered the back roads and cowpaths from Schenectady to Jackson. Dazed but insistent, they searched each other out for word of a cousin, an aunt, a friend who once said, "Call on me. Anytime you get near Chicago, just call on me." Some of them were running from family that could not support them, some to family; some were running from dead crops, dead kin, life threats, and took-over land. Boys younger than Buglar and Howard; configurations and blends of families of women and children, while elsewhere, solitary, hunted and hunting for, were men, men, men. Forbidden public transportation, chased by debt and filthy "talking sheets," they followed secondary routes, scanned the horizon for signs and counted heavily on each other. Silent, except for social courtesies, when they met one another they neither described nor asked about the sorrow that drove them from one place to another. The whites didn't bear speaking on. Everybody knew.

So he did not press the young woman with the broken hat about where from or how come. If she wanted them to know and was strong enough to get through the telling, she would. What occupied them at the moment was what it might be that she needed. Underneath the major question, each harbored another. Paul D wondered at the newness of her shoes. Sethe was deeply touched by her sweet name; the remembrance of glittering headstone made her feel especially kindly toward her. Denver, however, was shaking. She looked at this sleepy beauty and wanted more.

Sethe hung her hat on a peg and turned graciously toward the girl. "That's a pretty name, Beloved. Take off your hat, why don't you, and I'll make us something. We just got back from the carnival over near Cincinnati. Everything in there is something to see."

Bolt upright in the chair, in the middle of Sethe's welcome, Beloved had fallen asleep again.

"Miss. Miss." Paul D shook her gently. "You want to lay down a spell?"

She opened her eyes to slits and stood up on her soft new feet which, barely capable of their job, slowly bore her to the keeping room. Once there, she collapsed on Baby Suggs' bed. Denver removed her hat and put the quilt with two squares of color over her feet. She was breathing like a steam engine.

"Sounds like croup," said Paul D, closing the door.

"Is she feverish? Denver, could you tell?"

"No. She's cold."

"Then she is. Fever goes from hot to cold."

"Could have the cholera," said Paul D.

"Reckon?"

"All that water. Sure sign."

"Poor thing. And nothing in this house to give her for it. She'll just have to ride it out. That's a hateful sickness if ever there was one."

"She's not sick!" said Denver, and the passion in her voice made them smile.

Four days she slept, waking and sitting up only for water. Denver tended her, watched her sound sleep, listened to her labored breathing and, out of love and a breakneck posses-siveness that charged her, hid like a personal blemish Beloved's incontinence. She rinsed the sheets secretly, after Sethe went to the restaurant and Paul D went scrounging for barges to help unload. She boiled the underwear and soaked it in bluing, praying the fever would pass without damage. So intent was her nursing, she forgot to eat or visit the emerald closet.

"Beloved?" Denver would whisper. "Beloved?" and when the black eyes opened a slice all she could say was "I'm here. I'm still here."

Sometimes, when Beloved lay dreamy-eyed for a very long time, saying nothing, licking her lips and heaving deep sighs, Denver panicked. "What is it?" she would ask.

"Heavy," murmured Beloved. "This place is heavy."

"Would you like to sit up?"

"No," said the raspy voice.

It took three days for Beloved to notice the orange patches in the darkness of the quilt. Denver was pleased because it kept her patient awake longer. She seemed totally taken with those faded scraps of orange, even made the effort to lean on her elbow and stroke them. An effort that quickly exhausted her, so Denver rearranged the quilt so its cheeriest part was in the sick girl's sight line.

Patience, something Denver had never known, overtook her. As long as her mother did not interfere, she was a model of compassion, turning waspish, though, when Sethe tried to help.

"Did she take a spoonful of anything today?" Sethe inquired.

"She shouldn't eat with cholera."

"You sure that's it? Was just a hunch of Paul D's."

"I don't know, but she shouldn't eat anyway just yet."

"I think cholera people puke all the time."

"That's even more reason, ain't it?"

"Well she shouldn't starve to death either, Denver."

"Leave us alone, Ma'am. I'm taking care of her."

"She say anything?"

"I'd let you know if she did."

Sethe looked at her daughter and thought, Yes, she has been lonesome. Very lonesome.

"Wonder where Here Boy got off to?" Sethe thought a change of subject was needed.

"He won't be back," said Denver.

"How you know?"

"I just know." Denver took a square of sweet bread off the plate.

Back in the keeping room, Denver was about to sit down when Beloved's eyes flew wide open. Denver felt her heart race. It wasn't that she was looking at that face for the first time with no trace of sleep in it, or that the eyes were big and black. Nor was it that the whites of them were much too white – blue-white. It was that deep down in those big black eyes there was no expression at all.

"Can I get you something?"

Beloved looked at the sweet bread in Denver's hands and Denver held it out to her. She smiled then and Denver's heart stopped bouncing and sat down – relieved and easeful like a traveler who had made it home.

From that moment and through everything that followed, sugar could always be counted on to please her. It was as though sweet things were what she was born for. Honey as well as the wax it came in, sugar sandwiches, the sludgy molasses gone hard and brutal in the can, lemonade, taffy and any type of dessert Sethe brought home from the res- taurant. She gnawed a cane stick to flax and kept the strings in her mouth long after the syrup had been sucked away. Denver laughed, Sethe smiled and Paul D said it made him sick to his stomach.

Sethe believed it was a recovering body's need – after an illness – for quick strength. But it was a need that went on and on into glowing health because Beloved didn't go anywhere. There didn't seem anyplace for her to go. She didn't mention one, or have much of an idea of what she was doing in that part of the country or where she had been. They believed the fever had caused her memory to fail just as it kept her slow-moving. A young woman, about nineteen or twenty, and slender, she moved like a heavier one or an older one, holding on to furniture, resting her head in the palm of her hand as though it was too heavy for a neck alone.

"You just gonna feed her? From now on?" Paul D, feeling ungenerous, and surprised by it, heard the irritability in his voice.

"Denver likes her. She's no real trouble. I thought we'd

BELOVED

wait till her breath was better. She still sounds a little lumbar to me."

"Something funny 'bout that gal," Paul D said, mostly to himself.

"Funny how?"

"Acts sick, sounds sick, but she don't look sick. Good skin, bright eyes and strong as a bull."

"She's not strong. She can hardly walk without holding on to something."

"That's what I mean. Can't walk, but I seen her pick up the rocker with one hand."

"You didn't."

"Don't tell *me*. Ask Denver. She was right there with her."

"Denver! Come in here a minute."

Denver stopped rinsing the porch and stuck her head in the window.

"Paul D says you and him saw Beloved pick up the rocking chair single-handed. That so?"

Long, heavy lashes made Denver's eyes seem busier than they were; deceptive, even when she held a steady gaze as she did now on Paul D. "No," she said. "I didn't see no such thing."

Paul D frowned but said nothing. If there had been an open latch between them, it would have closed.

RAINWATER HELD ON to pine needles for dear life and Beloved could not take her eyes off Sethe. Stooping to shake the damper, or snapping sticks for kindlin, Sethe was licked, tasted, eaten by Beloved's eyes. Like a familiar, she hovered, never leaving the room Sethe was in unless required and told to. She rose early in the dark to be there, waiting, in the kitchen when Sethe came down to make fast bread before she left for work. In lamplight, and over the flames of the cooking stove, their two shadows clashed and crossed on the ceiling like black swords. She was in the window at two when Sethe returned, or the doorway; then the porch, its steps, the path, the road, till finally, surrendering to the habit, Beloved began inching down Bluestone Road further and further each day to meet Sethe and walk her back to 124. It was as though every afternoon she doubted anew the older woman's return.

Sethe was flattered by Beloved's open, quiet devotion. The same adoration from her daughter (had it been forthcoming) would have annoyed her; made her chill at the thought of having raised a ridiculously dependent child. But the company of this sweet, if peculiar, guest pleased her the way a zealot pleases his teacher.

Time came when lamps had to be lit early because night arrived sooner and sooner. Sethe was leaving for work in the dark; Paul D was walking home in it. On one such evening dark and cool, Sethe cut a rutabaga into four pieces and left them stewing. She gave Denver a half peck of peas to sort and soak overnight. Then she sat herself down to rest.

The heat of the stove made her drowsy and she was sliding into sleep when she felt Beloved touch her. A touch no heavier than a feather but loaded, nevertheless, with desire. Sethe stirred and looked around. First at Beloved's soft new hand on her shoulder, then into her eyes. The longing she saw there was bottomless. Some plea barely in control. Sethe patted Beloved's fingers and glanced at Denver, whose eyes were fixed on her pea-sorting task.

"Where your diamonds?" Beloved searched Sethe's face.

"Diamonds? What would I be doing with diamonds?"

"On your ears."

"Wish I did. I had some crystal once. A present from a lady I worked for."

"Tell me," said Beloved, smiling a wide happy smile. "Tell me your diamonds."

It became a way to feed her. Just as Denver discovered and relied on the delightful effect sweet things had on Beloved, Sethe learned the profound satisfaction Beloved got from storytelling. It amazed Sethe (as much as it pleased Beloved) because every mention of her past life hurt. Everything in it was painful or lost. She and Baby Suggs had agreed without saying so that it was unspeakable; to Denver's inquiries Sethe gave short replies or rambling incomplete reveries. Even with Paul D, who had shared some of it and to whom she could talk with at least a measure of calm, the hurt was always there – like a tender place in the corner of her mouth that the bit left.

But, as she began telling about the earrings, she found herself wanting to, liking it. Perhaps it was Beloved's distance from the events itself, or her thirst for hearing it – in any case it was an unexpected pleasure.

Above the patter of the pea sorting and the sharp odor of cooking rutabaga, Sethe explained the crystal that once hung from her ears.

"That lady I worked for in Kentucky gave them to me

when I got married. What they called married back there and back then. I guess she saw how bad I felt when I found out there wasn't going to be no ceremony, no preacher. Nothing. I thought there should be something – something to say it was right and true. I didn't want it to be just me moving over a bit of pallet full of corn husks. Or just me bringing my night bucket into his cabin. I thought there should be some ceremony. Dancing maybe. A little sweet william in my hair." Sethe smiled. "I never saw a wedding, but I saw Mrs. Garner's wedding gown in the press, and heard her go on about what it was like. Two pounds of currants in the cake, she said, and four whole sheep. The people were still eating the next day. That's what I wanted. A meal maybe, where me and Halle and all the Sweet Home men sat down and ate something special. Invite some of the other coloredpeople from over by Covington or High Trees – those places Sixo used to sneak off to. But it wasn't going to be nothing. They said it was all right for us to be husband and wife and that was it. All of it.

"Well, I made up my mind to have at the least a dress that wasn't the sacking I worked in. So I took to stealing fabric, and wound up with a dress you wouldn't believe. The top was from two pillow cases in her mending basket. The front of the skirt was a dresser scarf a candle fell on and burnt a hole in, and one of her old sashes we used to test the flatiron on. Now the back was a problem for the longest time. Seem like I couldn't find a thing that wouldn't be missed right away. Because I had to take it apart afterwards and put all the pieces back where they were. Now Halle was patient, waiting for me to finish it. He knew I wouldn't go ahead without having it. Finally I took the mosquito netting from a nail out the barn. We used it to strain jelly through. I washed it and soaked it best I could and tacked it on for the back of the skirt. And there I was, in the worst-looking gown you could imagine. Only my wool shawl kept me from looking like a haint peddling. I wasn't but fourteen years old, so I reckon that's why I was so proud of myself.

"Anyhow, Mrs. Garner must have seen me in it. I thought I was stealing smart, and she knew everything I did. Even our honeymoon: going down to the cornfield with Halle. That's where we went first. A Saturday afternoon it was. He begged sick so he wouldn't have to go work in town that day. Usually he worked Saturdays and Sundays to pay off Baby Suggs' freedom. But he begged sick and I put on my dress and we walked into the corn holding hands. I can still smell the ears roasting yonder where the Pauls and Sixo was. Next day Mrs. Garner crooked her finger at me and took me upstairs to her bedroom. She opened up a wooden box and took out a pair of crystal earrings. She said, 'I want you to have these, Sethe.' I said, 'Yes, ma'am.' 'Are your ears pierced?' she said. I said, 'No, ma'am.' 'Well do it,' she said, 'so you can wear them. I want you to have them and I want you and Halle to be happy.' I thanked her but I never did put them on till I got away from there. One day after I walked into this here house Baby Suggs unknotted my underskirt and took em out. I sat right here by the stove with Denver in my arms and let her punch holes in my ears for to wear them."

"I never saw you in no earrings," said Denver. "Where are they now?"

"Gone," said Sethe. "Long gone," and she wouldn't say another word. Until the next time when all three of them ran through the wind back into the house with rainsoaked sheets and petticoats. Panting, laughing, they draped the laundry over the chairs and table. Beloved filled herself with water from the bucket and watched while Sethe rubbed Denver's hair with a piece of toweling.

"Maybe we should unbraid it?" asked Sethe.

"Uh uh. Tomorrow." Denver crouched forward at the thought of a fine-tooth comb pulling her hair.

"Today is always here," said Sethe. "Tomorrow, never."

"It hurts," Denver said.

"Comb it every day, it won't."

"Ouch."

"Your woman she never fix up your hair?" Beloved asked.

Sethe and Denver looked up at her. After four weeks they still had not got used to the gravelly voice and the song that seemed to lie in it. Just outside music it lay, with a cadence not like theirs.

"Your woman she never fix up your hair?" was clearly a question for Sethe, since that's who she was looking at.

"My woman? You mean my mother? If she did, I don't remember. I didn't see her but a few times out in the fields and once when she was working indigo. By the time I woke up in the morning, she was in line. If the moon was bright they worked by its light. Sunday she slept like a stick. She must of nursed me two or three weeks – that's the way the others did. Then she went back in rice and I sucked from another woman whose job it was. So to answer you, no. I reckon not. She never fixed my hair nor nothing. She didn't even sleep in the same cabin most nights I remember. Too far from the line-up, I guess. One thing she did do. She picked me up and carried me behind the smokehouse. Back there she opened up her dress front and lifted her breast and pointed under it. Right on her rib was a circle and a cross burnt right in the skin. She said, 'This is your ma'am. This,' and she pointed. 'I am the only one got this mark now. The rest dead. If something happens to me and you can't tell me by my face, you can know me by this mark.' Scared me so. All I could think of was how important this was and how I needed to have something important to say back, but I couldn't think of anything so I just said what I thought. 'Yes, Ma'am,' I said. 'But how will you know me? How will you know me? Mark me, too,' I said. 'Mark the mark on me too.'" Sethe chuckled.

"Did she?" asked Denver.

"She slapped my face."

"What for?"

"I didn't understand it then. Not till I had a mark of my own."

"What happened to her?"

"Hung. By the time they cut her down nobody could tell whether she had a circle and a cross or not, least of all me and I did look." Sethe gathered hair from the comb and leaning back tossed it into the fire. It exploded into stars and the smell infuriated them. "Oh, my Jesus," she said and stood up so suddenly the comb she had parked in Denver's hair fell to the floor.

"Ma'am? What's the matter with you, Ma'am?"

Sethe walked over to a chair, lifted a sheet and stretched it as wide as her arms would go. Then she folded, refolded and double-folded it. She took another. Neither was completely dry but the folding felt too fine to stop. She had to do something with her hands because she was remembering something she had forgotten she knew. Something privately shameful that had seeped into a slit in her mind right behind the slap on her face and the circled cross.

"Why they hang your ma'am?" Denver asked. This was the first time she had heard anything about her mother's mother. Baby Suggs was the only grandmother she knew.

"I never found out. It was a lot of them," she said, but what was getting clear and clearer as she folded and refolded damp laundry was the woman called Nan who took her hand and yanked her away from the pile before she could make out the mark. Nan was the one she knew best, who was around all day, who nursed babies, cooked, had one good arm and half of another. And who used different words. Words Sethe understood then but could neither recall nor repeat now. She believed that must be why she remembered so little before Sweet Home except singing and dancing and how crowded it was. What Nan told her she had forgotten, along with the language she told it in. The same language her ma'am spoke, and which would never come back. But the message – that was and had been there all along. Holding the damp white sheets against her chest, she was picking meaning out of a code she no longer understood. Nighttime. Nan holding her with her good arm, waving the stump of the other in the air. "Telling you. I am telling you, small girl Sethe," and she did that. She told Sethe that her mother and Nan were together from the sea. Both were taken up many times by the crew. "She threw them all away but you. The one from the crew she threw away on the island. The others from more whites she also threw away. Without names, she threw them. You she gave the name of the black man. She put her arms around him. The others she did not put her arms around. Never. Never. Telling you. I am telling you, small girl Sethe."

As small girl Sethe, she was unimpressed. As grown-up woman Sethe she was angry, but not certain at what. A mighty wish for Baby Suggs broke over her like surf. In the quiet following its splash, Sethe looked at the two girls sitting by the stove: her sickly, shallow-minded boarder, her irritable, lonely daughter. They seemed little and far away.

"Paul D be here in a minute," she said.

Denver sighed with relief. For a minute there, while her mother stood folding the wash lost in thought, she clamped her teeth and prayed it would stop. Denver hated the stories her mother told that did not concern herself, which is why Amy was all she ever asked about. The rest was a gleaming, powerful world made more so by Denver's absence from it. Not being in it, she hated it and wanted Beloved to hate it too, although there was no chance of that at all. Beloved took every opportunity to ask some funny question and get Sethe going. Denver noticed how greedy she was to hear Sethe talk. Now she noticed something more. The questions

Beloved asked: "Where your diamonds?" "Your woman she never fix up your hair?" And most perplexing: Tell me your earrings.

How did she know?

BELOVED WAS SHINING and Paul D didn't like it. Women did what strawberry plants did before they shot out their thin vines: the quality of the green changed. Then the vine threads came, then the buds. By the time the white petals died and the mint-colored berry poked out, the leaf shine was gilded tight and waxy. That's how Beloved looked – gilded and shining. Paul D took to having Sethe on waking, so that later, when he went down the white stairs where she made bread under Beloved's gaze, his head was clear.

In the evening when he came home and the three of them were all there fixing the supper table, her shine was so pronounced he wondered why Denver and Sethe didn't see it. Or maybe they did. Certainly women could tell, as men could, when one of their number was aroused. Paul D looked carefully at Beloved to see if she was aware of it but she paid him no attention at all – frequently not even answering a direct question put to her. She would look at him and not open her mouth. Five weeks she had been with them, and they didn't know any more about her than they did when they found her asleep on the stump.

They were seated at the table Paul D had broken the day he arrived at 124. Its mended legs stronger than before. The cabbage was all gone and the shiny ankle bones of smoked pork were pushed in a heap on their plates. Sethe was dishing up bread pudding, murmuring her hopes for it, apologizing in advance the way veteran cooks always do, when something in Beloved's face, some petlike adoration that took hold of her as she looked at Sethe, made Paul D speak.

"Ain't you got no brothers or sisters?"

Beloved diddled her spoon but did not look at him. "I don't have nobody."

"What was you looking for when you came here?" he asked her.

"This place. I was looking for this place I could be in."

"Somebody tell you about this house?"

"She told me. When I was at the bridge, she told me."

"Must be somebody from the old days," Sethe said. The days when 124 was a way station where messages came and then their senders. Where bits of news soaked like dried beans in spring water – until they were soft enough to digest.

"How'd you come? Who brought you?"

Now she looked steadily at him, but did not answer.

He could feel both Sethe and Denver pulling in, holding their stomach muscles, sending out sticky spiderwebs to touch one another. He decided to force it anyway.

"I asked you who brought you here?"

"I walked here," she said. "A long, long, long, long way. Nobody bring me. Nobody help me."

"You had new shoes. If you walked so long why don't your shoes show it?"

"Paul D, stop picking on her."

"I want to know," he said, holding the knife handle in his fist like a pole.

"I take the shoes! I take the dress! The shoe strings don't fix!" she shouted and gave him a look so malevolent Denver touched her arm.

"I'll teach you," said Denver, "how to tie your shoes," and got a smile from Beloved as a reward.

Paul D had the feeling a large, silver fish had slipped from his hands the minute he grabbed hold of its tail. That it was streaming back off into dark water now, gone but for the glistening marking its route. But if her shining was not for him, who then? He had never known a woman who lit up for nobody in particular, who just did it as a general announcement. Always, in his experience, the light appeared when there was focus. Like the Thirty-Mile Woman, dulled to smoke while he waited with her in the ditch, and starlight when Sixo got there. He never knew himself to mistake it. It was there the instant he looked at Sethe's wet legs, otherwise he never would have been bold enough to enclose her in his arms that day and whisper into her back.

This girl Beloved, homeless and without people, beat all, though he couldn't say exactly why, considering the colored-people he had run into during the last twenty years. During, before and after the War he had seen Negroes so stunned, or hungry, or tired or bereft it was a wonder they recalled or said anything. Who, like him, had hidden in caves and fought owls for food; who, like him, stole from pigs; who, like him, slept in trees in the day and walked by night; who, like him, had buried themselves in slop and jumped in wells to avoid regulators, raiders, paterollers, veterans, hill men, posses and merrymakers. Once he met a Negro about fourteen years old who lived by himself in the woods and said he couldn't remember living anywhere else. He saw a witless coloredwoman jailed and hanged for stealing ducks she believed were her own babies.

Move. Walk. Run. Hide. Steal and move on. Only once had it been possible for him to stay in one spot – with a woman, or a family – for longer than a few months. That once was almost two years with a weaver lady in Delaware, the meanest place for Negroes he had ever seen outside Pulaski County, Kentucky, and of course the prison camp in Georgia.

From all those Negroes, Beloved was different. Her shining, her new shoes. It bothered him. Maybe it was just the fact that he didn't bother her. Or it could be timing. She had appeared and been taken in on the very day Sethe and he had patched up their quarrel, gone out in public and had a right good time – like a family. Denver had come around, so to speak; Sethe was laughing; he had a promise of steady work, 124 was cleared up from spirits. It had begun to look like a life. And damn! a water-drinking woman fell sick, got took in, healed, and hadn't moved a peg since.

He wanted her out, but Sethe had let her in and he couldn't put her out of a house that wasn't his. It was one thing to beat up a ghost, quite another to throw a helpless coloredgirl out in territory infected by the Klan. Desperately thirsty for black blood, without which it could not live, the dragon swam the Ohio at will.

Sitting at table, chewing on his after-supper broom straw, Paul D decided to place her. Consult with the Negroes in town and find her her own place.

No sooner did he have the thought than Beloved strangled on one of the raisins she had picked out of the bread pudding. She fell backward and off the chair and thrashed around holding her throat. Sethe knocked her on the back while Denver pried her hands away from her neck. Beloved, on her hands and knees, vomited up her food and struggled for breath.

When she was quiet and Denver had wiped up the mess, she said, "Go to sleep now."

"Come in my room," said Denver. "I can watch out for you up there."

No moment could have been better. Denver had worried herself sick trying to think of a way to get Beloved to share her room. It was hard sleeping above her, wondering if she was going to be sick again, fall asleep and not wake, or (God, please don't) get up and wander out of the yard just the way she wandered in. They could have their talks easier there: at night when Sethe and Paul D were asleep; or in the daytime before either came home. Sweet, crazy conversations full of half sentences, daydreams and misunderstandings more thrilling than understanding could ever be.

When the girls left, Sethe began to clear the table. She stacked the plates near a basin of water.

"What is it about her vex you so?"

Paul D frowned, but said nothing.

"We had one good fight about Denver. Do we need one about her too?" asked Sethe.

"I just don't understand what the hold is. It's clear why she holds on to you, but I just can't see why you holding on to her."

Sethe turned away from the plates toward him. "What you care who's holding on to who? Feeding her is no trouble. I pick up a little extra from the restaurant is all. And she's nice girl company for Denver. You know that and I know you know it, so what is it got your teeth on edge?"

"I can't place it. It's a feeling in me."

"Well, feel this, why don't you? Feel how it feels to have a bed to sleep in and somebody there not worrying you to death about what you got to do each day to deserve it. Feel how that feels. And if that don't get it, feel how it feels to be a coloredwoman roaming the roads with anything God made liable to jump on you. Feel that."

"I know every bit of that, Sethe. I wasn't born yesterday and I never mistreated a woman in my life."

"That makes one in the world," Sethe answered.

"Not two?"

"No. Not two."

"What Halle ever do to you? Halle stood by you. He never left you."

"What'd he leave then if not me?"

"I don't know, but it wasn't you. That's a fact."

"Then he did worse; he left his children."

"You don't know that."

"He wasn't there. He wasn't where he said he would be."

"He was there."

"Then why didn't he show himself? Why did I have to pack my babies off and stay behind to look for him?"

"He couldn't get out the loft."

"Loft? What loft?"

"The one over your head. In the barn."

Slowly, slowly, taking all the time allowed, Sethe moved toward the table.

"He saw?"

"He saw."

"He told you?"

"You told me."

"What?"

"The day I came in here. You said they stole your milk. I never knew what it was that messed him up. That was it, I guess. All I knew was that something broke him. Not a one of them years of Saturdays, Sundays and nighttime extra never touched him. But whatever he saw go on in that barn that day broke him like a twig."

"He saw?" Sethe was gripping her elbows as though to keep them from flying away.

"He saw. Must have."

"He saw them boys do that to me and let them keep on breathing air? He saw? He saw? He saw?"

"Hey! Hey! Listen up. Let me tell you something. A man ain't a goddamn ax. Chopping, hacking, busting every god-damn minute of the day. Things get to him. Things he can't chop down because they're inside."

Sethe was pacing up and down, up and down in the lamp-light. "The underground agent said, By Sunday. They took my milk and he saw it and didn't come down? Sunday came and he didn't. Monday came and no Halle. I thought he was dead, that's why; then I thought they caught him, that's why. Then I thought, No, he's not dead because if he was I'd know it, and then you come here after all this time and you didn't say he was dead, because you didn't know either, so I thought, Well, he just found him another better way to live. Because if he was anywhere near here, he'd come to Baby Suggs, if not to me. But I never knew he saw."

"What does that matter now?"

"If he is alive, and saw that, he won't step foot in my door. Not Halle."

"It broke him, Sethe." Paul D looked up at her and sighed. "You may as well know it all. Last time I saw him he was sitting by the churn. He had butter all over his face."

Nothing happened, and she was grateful for that. Usually she could see the picture right away of what she heard. But she could not picture what Paul D said. Nothing came to mind. Carefully, carefully, she passed on to a reasonable question.

"What did he say?"

"Nothing."

"Not a word?"

"Not a word."

"Did you speak to him? Didn't you say anything to him? Something!"

"I couldn't, Sethe. I just ... couldn't."

"Why!"

"I had a bit in my mouth."

Sethe opened the front door and sat down on the porch steps. The day had gone blue without its sun, but she could still make out the black silhouettes of trees in the meadow beyond. She shook her head from side to side, resigned to her rebellious brain. Why was there nothing it refused? No misery, no regret, no hateful picture too rotten to accept? Like a greedy child it snatched up everything. Just once, could it say, No thank you? I just ate and can't hold another bite? I am full God damn it of two boys with mossy teeth, one sucking on my breast the other holding me down, their book-reading teacher watching and writing it up. I am still full of that, God damn it, I can't go back and add more. Add my husband to it, watching, above me in the loft – hiding close by – the one place he thought no one would look for him, looking down on what I couldn't look at at all. And not stopping them – looking and letting it happen. But my greedy brain says, Oh thanks, I'd love more – so I add more. And no sooner than I do, there is no stopping. There is also my husband squatting by the churn smearing the butter as well as its clabber all over his face because the milk they took is on his mind. And as far as he is concerned, the world may as well know it. And if he was that broken then, then he is also and certainly dead now. And if Paul D saw him and could not save or comfort him because the iron bit was in his mouth, then there is still more that Paul D could tell me and my brain would go right ahead and take it and never say, No thank you. I don't want to know or have to remember that. I have other things to do: worry, for example, about tomorrow, about Denver, about Beloved, about age and sickness not to speak of love.

But her brain was not interested in the future. Loaded with the past and hungry for more, it left her no room to imagine, let alone plan for, the next day. Exactly like that afternoon in the wild onions – when one more step was the most she could see of the future. Other people went crazy, why couldn't she? Other people's brains stopped, turned around and went on to something new, which is what must have happened to Halle. And how sweet that would have been: the two of them back by the milk shed, squatting by the churn, smashing cold, lumpy butter into their faces with not a care in the world. Feeling it slippery, sticky – rubbing it in their hair, watching it squeeze through their fingers. What a relief to stop it right there. Close. Shut. Squeeze the butter. But her three children were chewing sugar teat under a blanket on their way to Ohio and no butter play would change that.

Paul D stepped through the door and touched her shoulder.

"I didn't plan on telling you that."

"I didn't plan on hearing it."

"I can't take it back, but I can leave it alone," Paul D said.

He wants to tell me, she thought. He wants me to ask him about what it was like for him – about how offended the tongue is, held down by iron, how the need to spit is so deep you cry for it. She already knew about it, had seen it time after time in the place before Sweet Home. Men, boys, little girls, women. The wildness that shot up into the eye the moment the lips were yanked back. Days after it was taken out, goose fat was rubbed on the corners of the mouth but nothing to soothe the tongue or take the wildness out of the eye.

Sethe looked up into Paul D's eyes to see if there was any trace left in them.

"People I saw as a child," she said, "who'd had the bit always looked wild after that. Whatever they used it on them for, it couldn't have worked, because it put a wildness where before there wasn't any. When I look at you, I don't see it. There ain't no wildness in your eye nowhere."

"There's a way to put it there and there's a way to take it out. I know em both and I haven't figured out yet which is worse." He sat down beside her. Sethe looked at him. In that unlit daylight his face, bronzed and reduced to its bones, smoothed her heart down.

"You want to tell me about it?" she asked him.

"I don't know. I never have talked about it. Not to a soul. Sang it sometimes, but I never told a soul."

"Go ahead. I can hear it."

"Maybe. Maybe you can hear it. I just ain't sure I can say it. Say it right, I mean, because it wasn't the bit – that wasn't it."

"What then?" Sethe asked.

"The roosters," he said. "Walking past the roosters looking at them look at me."

Sethe smiled. "In that pine?"

"Yeah." Paul D smiled with her. "Must have been five of them perched up there, and at least fifty hens."

"Mister, too?"

"Not right off. But I hadn't took twenty steps before I seen him. He come down off the fence post there and sat on the tub."

"He loved that tub," said Sethe, thinking, No, there is no stopping now.

"Didn't he? Like a throne. Was me took him out the shell, you know. He'd a died if it hadn't been for me. The hen had walked on off with all the hatched peeps trailing behind her. There was this one egg left. Looked like a blank, but then I saw it move so I tapped it open and here come Mister, bad feet and all. I watched that son a bitch grow up and whup everything in the yard."

"He always was hateful," Sethe said.

"Yeah, he was hateful all right. Bloody too, and evil. Crooked feet flapping. Comb as big as my hand and some kind of red. He sat right there on the tub looking at me. I swear he smiled. My head was full of what I'd seen of Halle a while back. I wasn't even thinking about the bit. Just Halle and before him Sixo, but when I saw Mister I knew it was me too. Not just them, me too. One crazy, one sold, one missing, one burnt and me licking iron with my hands crossed behind me. The last of the Sweet Home men.

"Mister, he looked so . . . free. Better than me. Stronger, tougher. Son a bitch couldn't even get out the shell by hisself but he was still king and I was . . ." Paul D stopped and squeezed his left hand with his right. He held it that way long enough for it and the world to quiet down and let him go on.

"Mister was allowed to be and stay what he was. But

87

I wasn't allowed to be and stay what I was. Even if you cooked him you'd be cooking a rooster named Mister. But wasn't no way I'd ever be Paul D again, living or dead. Schoolteacher changed me. I was something else and that something was less than a chicken sitting in the sun on a tub."

Sethe put her hand on his knee and rubbed.

Paul D had only begun, what he was telling her was only the beginning when her fingers on his knee, soft and reassuring, stopped him. Just as well. Just as well. Saying more might push them both to a place they couldn't get back from. He would keep the rest where it belonged: in that tobacco tin buried in his chest where a red heart used to be. Its lid rusted shut. He would not pry it loose now in front of this sweet sturdy woman, for if she got a whiff of the contents it would shame him. And it would hurt her to know that there was no red heart bright as Mister's comb beating in him.

Sethe rubbed and rubbed, pressing the work cloth and the stony curves that made up his knee. She hoped it calmed him as it did her. Like kneading bread in the half-light of the restaurant kitchen. Before the cook arrived when she stood in a space no wider than a bench is long, back behind and to the left of the milk cans. Working dough. Working, working dough. Nothing better than that to start the day's serious work of beating back the past.

UPSTAIRS BELOVED WAS dancing. A little two-step, two-step, make-a-new-step, slide, slide and strut on down.

Denver sat on the bed smiling and providing the music.

She had never seen Beloved this happy. She had seen her pouty lips open wide with the pleasure of sugar or some piece of news Denver gave her. She had felt warm satisfaction radiating from Beloved's skin when she listened to her mother talk about the old days. But gaiety she had never seen. Not ten minutes had passed since Beloved had fallen backward to the floor, pop-eyed, thrashing and holding her throat. Now, after a few seconds lying in Denver's bed, she was up and dancing.

"Where'd you learn to dance?" Denver asked her.

"Nowhere. Look at me do this." Beloved put her fists on her hips and commenced to skip on bare feet. Denver laughed.

"Now you. Come on," said Beloved. "You may as well just come on." Her black skirt swayed from side to side.

Denver grew ice-cold as she rose from the bed. She knew she was twice Beloved's size but she floated up, cold and light as a snowflake.

Beloved took Denver's hand and placed another on Denver's shoulder. They danced then. Round and round the tiny room and it may have been dizziness, or feeling light and icy at once, that made Denver laugh so hard. A catching laugh that Beloved caught. The two of them, merry as kittens, swung to and fro, to and fro, until exhausted they sat on the floor. Beloved let her head fall back on the edge of

89

the bed while she found her breath and Denver saw the tip of the thing she always saw in its entirety when Beloved undressed to sleep. Looking straight at it she whispered, "Why you call yourself Beloved?"

Beloved closed her eyes. "In the dark my name is Beloved."

Denver scooted a little closer. "What's it like over there, where you were before? Can you tell me?"

"Dark," said Beloved. "I'm small in that place. I'm like this here." She raised her head off the bed, lay down on her side and curled up.

Denver covered her lips with her fingers. "Were you cold?"

Beloved curled tighter and shook her head. "Hot. Nothing to breathe down there and no room to move in."

"You see anybody?"

"Heaps. A lot of people is down there. Some is dead."

"You see Jesus? Baby Suggs?"

"I don't know. I don't know the names." She sat up.

"Tell me, how did you get here?"

"I wait; then I got on the bridge. I stay there in the dark, in the daytime, in the dark, in the daytime. It was a long time."

"All this time you were on a bridge?"

"No. After. When I got out."

"What did you come back for?"

Beloved smiled. "To see her face."

"Ma'am's? Sethe?"

"Yes, Sethe."

Denver felt a little hurt, slighted that she was not the main reason for Beloved's return. "Don't you remember we played together by the stream?"

"I was on the bridge," said Beloved. "You see me on the bridge?"

"No, by the stream. The water back in the woods."

"Oh, I was in the water. I saw her diamonds down there. I could touch them."

"What stopped you?"

"She left me behind. By myself," said Beloved. She lifted her eyes to meet Denver's and frowned, perhaps. Perhaps not. The tiny scratches on her forehead may have made it seem so.

Denver swallowed. "Don't," she said. "Don't. You won't leave us, will you?"

"No. Never. This is where I am."

Suddenly Denver, who was sitting cross-legged, lurched forward and grabbed Beloved's wrist. "Don't tell her. Don't let Ma'am know who you are. Please, you hear?"

"Don't tell me what to do. Don't you never never tell me what to do."

"But I'm on your side, Beloved."

"She is the one. She is the one I need. You can go but she is the one I have to have." Her eyes stretched to the limit, black as the all-night sky.

"I didn't do anything to you. I never hurt you. I never hurt anybody," said Denver.

"Me either. Me either."

"What you gonna do?"

"Stay here. I belong here."

"I belong here too."

"Then stay, but don't never tell me what to do. Don't never do that."

"We were dancing. Just a minute ago we were dancing together. Let's."

"I don't want to." Beloved got up and lay down on the bed. Their quietness boomed about on the walls like birds in panic. Finally Denver's breath steadied against the threat of an unbearable loss.

"Tell me," Beloved said. "Tell me how Sethe made you in the boat."

"She never told me all of it," said Denver.

"Tell me."

Denver climbed up on the bed and folded her arms under her apron. She had not been in the tree room once since Beloved sat on their stump after the carnival, and had not remembered that she hadn't gone there until this very desperate moment. Nothing was out there that this sister-girl did not provide in abundance: a racing heart, dreaminess, society, danger, beauty. She swallowed twice to prepare for the telling, to construct out of the strings she had heard all her life a net to hold Beloved.

"She had good hands, she said. The whitegirl, she said, had thin little arms but good hands. She saw that right away, she said. Hair enough for five heads and good hands, she said. I guess the hands made her think she could do it: get us both across the river. But the mouth was what kept her from being scared. She said there ain't nothing to go by with whitepeople. You don't know how they'll jump. Say one thing, do another. But if you looked at the mouth sometimes you could tell by that. She said this girl talked a storm, but there wasn't no meanness around her mouth. She took Ma'am to that lean-to and rubbed her feet for her, so that was one thing. And Ma'am believed she wasn't going to turn her over. You could get money if you turned a runaway over, and she wasn't sure this girl Amy didn't need money more than anything, especially since all she talked about was getting hold of some velvet."

"What's velvet?"

"It's a cloth, kind of deep and soft."

"Go ahead."

"Anyway, she rubbed Ma'am's feet back to life, and she cried, she said, from how it hurt. But it made her think she could make it on over to where Grandma Baby Suggs was and . . ."

"Who is that?"

"I just said it. My grandmother."

"Is that Sethe's mother?"

"No. My father's mother."

"Go ahead."

"That's where the others was. My brothers and . . . the baby girl. She sent them on before to wait for her at Grandma Baby's. So she had to put up with everything to get there. And this here girl Amy helped."

Denver stopped and sighed. This was the part of the story she loved. She was coming to it now, and she loved it because it was all about herself; but she hated it too because it made her feel like a bill was owing somewhere and she, Denver, had to pay it. But who she owed or what to pay it with eluded her. Now, watching Beloved's alert and hungry face, how she took in every word, asking questions about the color of things and their size, her downright craving to know, Denver began to see what she was saying and not just to hear it: there is this nineteen-year-old slavegirl – a year older than herself – walking through the dark woods to get to her children who are far away. She is tired, scared maybe, and maybe even lost. Most of all she is by herself and inside her is another baby she has to think about too. Behind her dogs, perhaps; guns probably; and certainly mossy teeth. She is not so afraid at night because she is the color of it, but in the day every sound is a shot or a tracker's quiet step.

Denver was seeing it now and feeling it – through Beloved. Feeling how it must have felt to her mother. Seeing how it must have looked. And the more fine points she made, the more detail she provided, the more Beloved liked it. So she anticipated the questions by giving blood to the scraps her mother and grandmother had told her – and a heartbeat. The monologue became, in fact, a duet as they lay down together, Denver nursing Beloved's interest like a lover whose pleasure was to overfeed the loved. The dark quilt with two orange patches was there with them because Beloved wanted it near her when she slept. It was smelling like grass and feeling like hands – the unrested hands of busy women: dry, warm, prickly. Denver spoke, Beloved listened, and the two did the best they could to create what really happened, how it really was, something only Sethe knew because she alone had the mind for it and the time afterward to shape it: the quality of Amy's voice, her breath like burning wood. The quick-change weather up in those hills – cool at night, hot in the day, sudden fog. How recklessly she behaved with this whitegirl – a recklessness born of desperation and encouraged by Amy's fugitive eyes and her tenderhearted mouth.

"You ain't got no business walking round these hills, miss."

"Looka here who's talking. I got more business here 'n you got. They catch you they cut your head off. Ain't nobody after me but I know somebody after you." Amy pressed her fingers into the soles of the slavewoman's feet. "Whose baby that?"

Sethe did not answer.

"You don't even know. Come here, Jesus," Amy sighed and shook her head. "Hurt?"

"A touch."

"Good for you. More it hurt more better it is. Can't nothing heal without pain, you know. What you wiggling for?"

Sethe raised up on her elbows. Lying on her back so long had raised a ruckus between her shoulder blades. The fire in her feet and the fire on her back made her sweat.

"My back hurt me," she said.

"Your back? Gal, you a mess. Turn over here and let me see."

In an effort so great it made her sick to her stomach, Sethe turned onto her right side. Amy unfastened the back of her dress and said, "Come here, Jesus," when she saw. Sethe guessed it must be bad because after that call to Jesus Amy didn't speak for a while. In the silence of an Amy struck dumb for a change, Sethe felt the fingers of those good hands lightly touch her back. She could hear her breathing but still the whitegirl said nothing. Sethe could not move. She couldn't lie on her stomach or her back, and to keep on her side meant pressure on her screaming feet. Amy spoke at last in her dreamwalker's voice.

"It's a tree, Lu. A chokecherry tree. See, here's the trunk – it's red and split wide open, full of sap, and this here's the parting for the branches. You got a mighty lot of branches. Leaves, too, look like, and dern if these ain't blossoms. Tiny little cherry blossoms, just as white. Your back got a whole tree on it. In bloom. What God have in mind, I wonder. I had me some whippings, but I don't remember nothing like this. Mr. Buddy had a right evil hand too. Whip you for looking at him straight. Sure would. I looked right at him one time and he hauled off and threw the poker at me. Guess he knew what I was a-thinking."

Sethe groaned and Amy cut her reverie short – long enough to shift Sethe's feet so the weight, resting on leaf-covered stones, was above the ankles.

"That better? Lord what a way to die. You gonna die in here, you know. Ain't no way out of it. Thank your Maker I come along so's you wouldn't have to die outside in them weeds. Snake come along he bite you. Bear eat you up. Maybe you should of stayed where you was, Lu. I can see by your back why you didn't ha ha. Whoever planted that tree beat Mr. Buddy by a mile. Glad I ain't you. Well, spiderwebs is 'bout all I can do for you. What's in here ain't enough. I'll look outside. Could use moss, but sometimes bugs and things is in it. Maybe I ought to break them blossoms open. Get that pus to running, you think? Wonder what God had in mind. You must of did something. Don't run off nowhere now."

Sethe could hear her humming away in the bushes as she hunted spiderwebs. A humming she concentrated on because as soon as Amy ducked out the baby began to stretch. Good question, she was thinking. What did He have in mind? Amy had left the back of Sethe's dress open and now a tail of wind hit it, taking the pain down a step. A relief that let her feel the lesser pain of her sore tongue. Amy returned with two palm-fuls of web, which she cleaned of prey and then draped on Sethe's back, saying it was like stringing a tree for Christmas.

"We got a old nigger girl come by our place. She don't know nothing. Sews stuff for Mrs. Buddy – real fine lace but can't barely stick two words together. She don't know nothing, just like you. You don't know a thing. End up dead, that's what. Not me. I'm a get to Boston and get myself some velvet. Carmine. You don't even know about that, do you? Now you never will. Bet you never even sleep with the sun in your face. I did it a couple of times. Most times I'm feeding stock before light and don't get to sleep till way after dark comes. But I was in the back of the wagon once and fell asleep. Sleeping with the sun in your face is the best old feeling. Two times I did it. Once when I was little. Didn't nobody bother me then. Next time, in back of the wagon, it happened again and doggone if the chickens didn't get loose. Mr. Buddy whipped my tail. Kentucky ain't no good place to be in. Boston's the place to be in. That's where my mother was before she was give to Mr. Buddy. Joe Nathan said Mr. Buddy is my daddy but I don't believe that, you?"

Sethe told her she didn't believe Mr. Buddy was her daddy.

"You know your daddy, do you?"

"No," said Sethe.

"Neither me. All I know is it ain't him." She stood up then, having finished her repair work, and weaving about the lean-to, her slow-moving eyes pale in the sun that lit her hair, she sang:

> *"When the busy day is done*
> *And my weary little one*

Rocketh gently to and fro;
When the night winds softly blow,
And the crickets in the glen
Chirp and chirp and chirp again;
Where 'pon the haunted green
Fairies dance around their queen,
Then from yonder misty skies
Cometh Lady Button Eyes."

Suddenly she stopped weaving and rocking and sat down, her skinny arms wrapped around her knees, her good good hands cupping her elbows. Her slow-moving eyes stopped and peered into the dirt at her feet. "That's my mama's song. She taught me it."

"Through the muck and mist and gloam
To our quiet cozy home,
Where to singing sweet and low
Rocks a cradle to and fro.
Where the clock's dull monotone
Telleth of the day that's done,
Where the moonbeams hover o'er
Playthings sleeping on the floor,
Where my weary wee one lies
Cometh Lady Button Eyes.

"Layeth she her hands upon
My dear weary little one,
And those white hands overspread
Like a veil the curly head,
Seem to fondle and caress
Every little silken tress.
Then she smooths the eyelids down
Over those two eyes of brown
In such soothing tender wise
Cometh Lady Button Eyes."

Amy sat quietly after her song, then repeated the last line before she stood, left the lean-to and walked off a little ways to lean against a young ash. When she came back the sun was in the valley below and they were way above it in blue Kentucky light.

"You ain't dead yet, Lu? Lu?"

"Not yet."

"Make you a bet. You make it through the night, you make it all the way." Amy rearranged the leaves for comfort and knelt down to massage the swollen feet again. "Give these one more real good rub," she said, and when Sethe sucked air through her teeth, she said, "Shut up. You got to keep your mouth shut."

Careful of her tongue, Sethe bit down on her lips and let the good hands go to work to the tune of "So bees, sing soft and bees, sing low." Afterward, Amy moved to the other side of the lean-to where, seated, she lowered her head toward her shoulder and braided her hair, saying, "Don't up and die on me in the night, you hear? I don't want to see your ugly black face hankering over me. If you do die, just go on off somewhere where I can't see you, hear?"

"I hear," said Sethe. "I'll do what I can, miss."

Sethe never expected to see another thing in this world, so when she felt toes prodding her hip it took a while to come out of a sleep she thought was death. She sat up, stiff and shivery, while Amy looked in on her juicy back.

"Looks like the devil," said Amy. "But you made it through. Come down here, Jesus, Lu made it through. That's because of me. I'm good at sick things. Can you walk, you think?"

"I have to let my water some kind of way."

"Let's see you walk on em."

It was not good, but it was possible, so Sethe limped, holding on first to Amy, then to a sapling.

"Was me did it. I'm good at sick things ain't I?"

"Yeah," said Sethe, "you good."

"We got to get off this here hill. Come on. I'll take you down to the river. That ought to suit you. Me, I'm going to the Pike. Take me straight to Boston. What's that all over your dress?"

"Milk."

"You one mess."

Sethe looked down at her stomach and touched it. The baby was dead. She had not died in the night, but the baby had. If that was the case, then there was no stopping now. She would get that milk to her baby girl if she had to swim.

"Ain't you hungry?" Amy asked her.

"I ain't nothing but in a hurry, miss."

"Whoa. Slow down. Want some shoes?"

"Say what?"

"I figured how," said Amy and so she had. She tore two pieces from Sethe's shawl, filled them with leaves and tied them over her feet, chattering all the while.

"How old are you, Lu? I been bleeding for four years but I ain't having nobody's baby. Won't catch me sweating milk cause . . ."

"I know," said Sethe. "You going to Boston."

At noon they saw it; then they were near enough to hear it. By late afternoon they could drink from it if they wanted to. Four stars were visible by the time they found, not a riverboat to stow Sethe away on, or a ferryman willing to take on a fugitive passenger – nothing like that – but a whole boat to steal. It had one oar, lots of holes and two bird nests.

"There you go, Lu. Jesus looking at you."

Sethe was looking at one mile of dark water, which would have to be split with one oar in a useless boat against a current dedicated to the Mississippi hundreds of miles away. It looked like home to her, and the baby (not dead in the least) must have thought so too. As soon as Sethe got close to the river her own water broke loose to join it. The break, followed by the redundant announcement of labor, arched her back.

"What you doing that for?" asked Amy. "Ain't you got a brain in your head? Stop that right now. I said stop it, Lu. You the dumbest thing on this here earth. Lu! Lu!"

Sethe couldn't think of anywhere to go but in. She waited for the sweet beat that followed the blast of pain. On her knees again, she crawled into the boat. It waddled under her and she had just enough time to brace her leaf-bag feet on the bench when another rip took her breath away. Panting under four summer stars, she threw her legs over the sides, because here come the head, as Amy informed her as though she did not know it — as though the rip was a breakup of walnut logs in the brace, or of lightning's jagged tear through a leather sky.

It was stuck. Face up and drowning in its mother's blood. Amy stopped begging Jesus and began to curse His daddy.

"Push!" screamed Amy.

"Pull," whispered Sethe.

And the strong hands went to work a fourth time, none too soon, for river water, seeping through any hole it chose, was spreading over Sethe's hips. She reached one arm back and grabbed the rope while Amy fairly clawed at the head. When a foot rose from the river bed and kicked the bottom of the boat and Sethe's behind, she knew it was done and permitted herself a short faint. Coming to, she heard no cries, just Amy's encouraging coos. Nothing happened for so long they both believed they had lost it. Sethe arched suddenly and the afterbirth shot out. Then the baby whimpered and Sethe looked. Twenty inches of cord hung from its belly and it trembled in the cooling evening air. Amy wrapped her skirt around it and the wet sticky women clambered ashore to see what, indeed, God had in mind.

Spores of bluefern growing in the hollows along the riverbank float toward the water in silver-blue lines hard to see unless you are in or near them, lying right at the river's edge when the sunshots are low and drained. Often they are mistook for insects – but they are seeds in which the whole generation sleeps confident of a future. And for a moment it is easy to believe each one has one – will become all of what is contained in the spore: will live out its days as planned. This moment of certainty lasts no longer than that; longer, perhaps, than the spore itself.

On a riverbank in the cool of a summer evening two women struggled under a shower of silvery blue. They never expected to see each other again in this world and at the moment couldn't care less. But there on a summer night surrounded by bluefern they did something together appropriately and well. A pateroller passing would have sniggered to see two throw-away people, two lawless outlaws – a slave and a barefoot whitewoman with unpinned hair – wrapping a ten-minute-old baby in the rags they wore. But no pateroller came and no preacher. The water sucked and swallowed itself beneath them. There was nothing to disturb them at their work. So they did it appropriately and well.

Twilight came on and Amy said she had to go; that she wouldn't be caught dead in daylight on a busy river with a runaway. After rinsing her hands and face in the river, she stood and looked down at the baby wrapped and tied to Sethe's chest.

"She's never gonna know who I am. You gonna tell her? Who brought her into this here world?" She lifted her chin, looked off into the place where the sun used to be. "You better tell her. You hear? Say Miss Amy Denver. Of Boston."

Sethe felt herself falling into a sleep she knew would be deep. On the lip of it, just before going under, she thought, "That's pretty. Denver. Real pretty."

IT WAS TIME to lay it all down. Before Paul D came and sat on her porch steps, words whispered in the keeping room had kept her going. Helped her endure the chastising ghost; refurbished the baby faces of Howard and Buglar and kept them whole in the world because in her dreams she saw only their parts in trees; and kept her husband shadowy but *there* – somewhere. Now Halle's face between the butter press and the churn swelled larger and larger, crowding her eyes and making her head hurt. She wished for Baby Suggs' fingers molding her nape, reshaping it, saying, "Lay em down, Sethe. Sword and shield. Down. Down. Both of em down. Down by the riverside. Sword and shield. Don't study war no more. Lay all that mess down. Sword and shield." And under the pressing fingers and the quiet instructive voice, she would. Her heavy knives of defense against misery, regret, gall and hurt, she placed one by one on a bank where clear water rushed on below.

Nine years without the fingers or the voice of Baby Suggs was too much. And words whispered in the keeping room were too little. The butter-smeared face of a man God made none sweeter than demanded more: an arch built or a robe sewn. Some fixing ceremony. Sethe decided to go to the Clearing, back where Baby Suggs had danced in sunlight.

Before 124 and everybody in it had closed down, veiled over and shut away; before it had become the plaything of spirits and the home of the chafed, 124 had been a cheerful, buzzing house where Baby Suggs, holy, loved, cautioned, fed, chastised and soothed. Where not one but two pots simmered on the stove; where the lamp burned all night long. Strangers rested there while children tried on their shoes. Messages were left there, for whoever needed them was sure to stop in one day soon. Talk was low and to the point – for Baby Suggs, holy, didn't approve of extra. "Everything depends on knowing how much," she said, and "Good is knowing when to stop."

It was in front of *that* 124 that Sethe climbed off a wagon, her newborn tied to her chest, and felt for the first time the wide arms of her mother-in-law, who had made it to Cincinnati. Who decided that, because slave life had "busted her legs, back, head, eyes, hands, kidneys, womb and tongue," she had nothing left to make a living with but her heart – which she put to work at once. Accepting no title of honor before her name, but allowing a small caress after it, she became an unchurched preacher, one who visited pulpits and opened her great heart to those who could use it. In winter and fall she carried it to AME's and Baptists, Holinesses and Sanctifieds, the Church of the Redeemer and the Redeemed. Uncalled, unrobed, unanointed, she let her great heart beat in their presence. When warm weather came, Baby Suggs, holy, followed by every black man, woman and child who could make it through, took her great heart to the Clearing – a wide-open place cut deep in the woods nobody knew for what at the end of a path known only to deer and whoever cleared the land in the first place. In the heat of every Saturday afternoon, she sat in the clearing while the people waited among the trees.

After situating herself on a huge flat-sided rock, Baby Suggs bowed her head and prayed silently. The company watched her from the trees. They knew she was ready when she put her stick down. Then she shouted, "Let the children come!" and they ran from the trees toward her.

"Let your mothers hear you laugh," she told them, and

the woods rang. The adults looked on and could not help smiling.

Then "Let the grown men come," she shouted. They stepped out one by one from among the ringing trees.

"Let your wives and your children see you dance," she told them, and groundlife shuddered under their feet.

Finally she called the women to her. "Cry," she told them. "For the living and the dead. Just cry." And without covering their eyes the women let loose.

It started that way: laughing children, dancing men, crying women and then it got mixed up. Women stopped crying and danced; men sat down and cried; children danced, women laughed, children cried until, exhausted and riven, all and each lay about the Clearing damp and gasping for breath. In the silence that followed, Baby Suggs, holy, offered up to them her great big heart.

She did not tell them to clean up their lives or to go and sin no more. She did not tell them they were the blessed of the earth, its inheriting meek or its glorybound pure.

She told them that the only grace they could have was the grace they could imagine. That if they could not see it, they would not have it.

"Here," she said, "in this here place, we flesh; flesh that weeps, laughs; flesh that dances on bare feet in grass. Love it. Love it hard. Yonder they do not love your flesh. They despise it. They don't love your eyes; they'd just as soon pick em out. No more do they love the skin on your back. Yonder they flay it. And O my people they do not love your hands. Those they only use, tie, bind, chop off and leave empty. Love your hands! Love them. Raise them up and kiss them. Touch others with them, pat them together, stroke them on your face 'cause they don't love that either. *You* got to love it, *you!* And no, they ain't in love with your mouth. Yonder, out there, they will see it broken and break it again. What you say out of it they will not heed. What you scream from it they do not hear. What you put into it to nourish your body they will snatch away and give you leavins instead. No, they don't love your mouth. *You* got to love it. This is flesh I'm talking about here. Flesh that needs to be loved. Feet that need to rest and to dance; backs that need support; shoulders that need arms, strong arms I'm telling you. And O my people, out yonder, hear me, they do not love your neck unnoosed and straight. So love your neck; put a hand on it, grace it, stroke it and hold it up. And all your inside parts that they'd just as soon slop for hogs, you got to love them. The dark, dark liver – love it, love it, and the beat and beating heart, love that too. More than eyes or feet. More than lungs that have yet to draw free air. More than your life-holding womb and your life-giving private parts, hear me now, love your heart. For this is the prize." Saying no more, she stood up then and danced with her twisted hip the rest of what her heart had to say while the others opened their mouths and gave her the music. Long notes held until the four-part harmony was perfect enough for their deeply loved flesh.

Sethe wanted to be there now. At the least to listen to the spaces that the long-ago singing had left behind. At the most to get a clue from her husband's dead mother as to what she should do with her sword and shield now, dear Jesus, now nine years after Baby Suggs, holy, proved herself a liar, dismissed her great heart and lay in the keeping-room bed roused once in a while by a craving for color and not for another thing.

"Those white things have taken all I had or dreamed," she said, "and broke my heartstrings too. There is no bad luck in the world but whitefolks." 124 shut down and put up with the venom of its ghost. No more lamp all night long, or neighbors dropping by. No low conversations after supper. No watched barefoot children playing in the shoes of strangers. Baby Suggs, holy, believed she had lied. There was no grace – imaginary or real – and no sunlit dance in a

Clearing could change that. Her faith, her love, her imagination and her great big old heart began to collapse twenty-eight days after her daughter-in-law arrived.

Yet it was to the Clearing that Sethe determined to go – to pay tribute to Halle. Before the light changed, while it was still the green blessed place she remembered: misty with plant steam and the decay of berries.

She put on a shawl and told Denver and Beloved to do likewise. All three set out late one Sunday morning, Sethe leading, the girls trotting behind, not a soul in sight.

When they reached the woods it took her no time to find the path through it because big-city revivals were held there regularly now, complete with food-laden tables, banjos and a tent. The old path was a track now, but still arched over with trees dropping buckeyes onto the grass below.

There was nothing to be done other than what she had done, but Sethe blamed herself for Baby Suggs' collapse. However many times Baby denied it, Sethe knew the grief at 124 started when she jumped down off the wagon, her newborn tied to her chest in the underwear of a whitegirl looking for Boston.

Followed by the two girls, down a bright green corridor of oak and horse chestnut, Sethe began to sweat a sweat just like the other one when she woke, mud-caked, on the banks of the Ohio.

Amy was gone. Sethe was alone and weak, but alive, and so was her baby. She walked a ways downriver and then stood gazing at the glimmering water. By and by a flatbed slid into view, but she could not see if the figures on it were whitepeople or not. She began to sweat from a fever she thanked God for since it would certainly keep her baby warm. When the flatbed was beyond her sight she stumbled on and found herself near three coloredpeople fishing – two boys and an older man. She stopped and waited to be spoken to. One of the boys pointed and the man looked over his shoulder at her

— a quick look since all he needed to know about her he could see in no time.

No one said anything for a while. Then the man said, "Headin' 'cross?"

"Yes, sir," said Sethe.

"Anybody know you coming?"

"Yes, sir."

He looked at her again and nodded toward a rock that stuck out of the ground above him like a bottom lip. Sethe walked to it and sat down. The stone had eaten the sun's rays but was nowhere near as hot as she was. Too tired to move, she stayed there, the sun in her eyes making her dizzy. Sweat poured over her and bathed the baby completely. She must have slept sitting up, because when next she opened her eyes the man was standing in front of her with a smoking-hot piece of fried eel in his hands. It was an effort to reach for, more to smell, impossible to eat. She begged him for water and he gave her some of the Ohio in a jar. Sethe drank it all and begged more. The clanging was back in her head but she refused to believe that she had come all that way, endured all she had, to die on the wrong side of the river.

The man watched her streaming face and called one of the boys over.

"Take off that coat," he told him.

"Sir?"

"You heard me."

The boy slipped out of his jacket, whining, "What you gonna do? What I'm gonna wear?"

The man untied the baby from her chest and wrapped it in the boy's coat, knotting the sleeves in front.

"What I'm gonna wear?"

The old man sighed and, after a pause, said, "You want it back, then go head and take it off that baby. Put the baby naked in the grass and put your coat back on. And if you can do it, then go on 'way somewhere and don't come back."

The boy dropped his eyes, then turned to join the other. With eel in her hand, the baby at her feet, Sethe dozed, dry-mouthed and sweaty. Evening came and the man touched her shoulder.

Contrary to what she expected they poled upriver, far away from the rowboat Amy had found. Just when she thought he was taking her back to Kentucky, he turned the flatbed and crossed the Ohio like a shot. There he helped her up the steep bank, while the boy without a jacket carried the baby who wore it. The man led her to a brush-covered hutch with a beaten floor.

"Wait here. Somebody be here directly. Don't move. They'll find you."

"Thank you," she said. "I wish I knew your name so I could remember you right."

"Name's Stamp," he said. "Stamp Paid. Watch out for that there baby, you hear?"

"I hear. I hear," she said, but she didn't. Hours later a woman was right up on her before she heard a thing. A short woman, young, with a croaker sack, greeted her.

"Saw the sign a while ago," she said. "But I couldn't get here no quicker."

"What sign?" asked Sethe.

"Stamp leaves the old sty open when there's a crossing. Knots a white rag on the post if it's a child too."

She knelt and emptied the sack. "My name's Ella," she said, taking a wool blanket, cotton cloth, two baked sweet potatoes and a pair of men's shoes from the sack. "My husband, John, is out yonder a ways. Where you heading?"

Sethe told her about Baby Suggs where she had sent her three children.

Ella wrapped a cloth strip tight around the baby's navel as she listened for the holes – the things the fugitives did not say; the questions they did not ask. Listened too for the unnamed, unmentioned people left behind. She shook gravel from the men's shoes and tried to force Sethe's feet into them. They would not go. Sadly, they split them down the heel, sorry indeed to ruin so valuable an item. Sethe put on the boy's jacket, not daring to ask whether there was any word of the children.

"They made it," said Ella. "Stamp ferried some of that party. Left them on Bluestone. It ain't too far."

Sethe couldn't think of anything to do, so grateful was she, so she peeled a potato, ate it, spit it up and ate more in quiet celebration.

"They be glad to see you," said Ella. "When was this one born?"

"Yesterday," said Sethe, wiping sweat from under her chin. "I hope she makes it."

Ella looked at the tiny, dirty face poking out of the wool blanket and shook her head. "Hard to say," she said. "If anybody was to ask me I'd say, 'Don't love nothing.' " Then, as if to take the edge off her pronouncement, she smiled at Sethe. "You had that baby by yourself?"

"No. Whitegirl helped."

"Then we better make tracks."

Baby Suggs kissed her on the mouth and refused to let her see the children. They were asleep she said and Sethe was too ugly-looking to wake them in the night. She took the newborn and handed it to a young woman in a bonnet, telling her not to clean the eyes till she got the mother's urine.

"Has it cried out yet?" asked Baby.

"A little."

"Time enough. Let's get the mother well."

She led Sethe to the keeping room and, by the light of a spirit lamp, bathed her in sections, starting with her face. Then, while waiting for another pan of heated water, she sat next to her and stitched gray cotton. Sethe dozed and woke to the washing of her hands and arms. After each bathing, Baby covered her with a quilt and put another pan on in the kitchen. Tearing sheets, stitching the gray cotton, she supervised the woman in the bonnet who tended the baby and cried into her cooking. When Sethe's legs were done, Baby looked at her feet and wiped them lightly. She cleaned between Sethe's legs with two separate pans of hot water and then tied her stomach and vagina with sheets. Finally she attacked the unrecognizable feet.

"You feel this?"

"Feel what?" asked Sethe.

"Nothing. Heave up." She helped Sethe to a rocker and lowered her feet into a bucket of salt water and juniper. The rest of the night Sethe sat soaking. The crust from her nipples Baby softened with lard and then washed away. By dawn the silent baby woke and took her mother's milk.

"Pray God it ain't turned bad," said Baby. "And when you through, call me." As she turned to go, Baby Suggs caught a glimpse of something dark on the bed sheet. She frowned and looked at her daughter-in-law bending toward the baby. Roses of blood blossomed in the blanket covering Sethe's shoulders. Baby Suggs hid her mouth with her hand. When the nursing was over and the newborn was asleep – its eyes half open, its tongue dream-sucking – wordlessly the older woman greased the flowering back and pinned a double thickness of cloth to the inside of the newly stitched dress.

It was not real yet. Not yet. But when her sleepy boys and crawling-already? girl were brought in, it didn't matter whether it was real or not. Sethe lay in bed under, around, over, among but especially with them all. The little girl dribbled clear spit into her face, and Sethe's laugh of delight was so loud the crawling-already? baby blinked. Buglar and Howard played with her ugly feet, after daring each other to be the first to touch them. She kept kissing them. She kissed the backs of their necks, the tops of their heads and the centers of their palms, and it was the boys who decided enough was enough when she lifted their shirts to kiss their tight round bellies. She stopped when and because they said, "Pappie come?"

She didn't cry. She said "soon" and smiled so they would think the brightness in her eyes was love alone. It was some time before she let Baby Suggs shoo the boys away so Sethe could put on the gray cotton dress her mother-in-law had started stitching together the night before. Finally she lay back and cradled the crawling-already? girl in her arms. She enclosed her left nipple with two fingers of her right hand and the child opened her mouth. They hit home together.

Baby Suggs came in and laughed at them, telling Sethe how strong the baby girl was, how smart, already crawling. Then she stooped to gather up the ball of rags that had been Sethe's clothes.

"Nothing worth saving in here," she said.

Sethe lifted her eyes. "Wait," she called. "Look and see if there's something still knotted up in the petticoat."

Baby Suggs inched the spoiled fabric through her fingers and came upon what felt like pebbles. She held them out toward Sethe. "Going-away present?"

"Wedding present."

"Be nice if there was a groom to go with it." She gazed into her hand. "What you think happened to him?"

"I don't know," said Sethe. "He wasn't where he said to meet him at. I had to get out. Had to." Sethe watched the drowsy eyes of the sucking girl for a moment then looked at Baby Suggs' face. "He'll make it. If I made it, Halle sure can."

"Well, put these on. Maybe they'll light his way." Convinced her son was dead, she handed the stones to Sethe.

"I need holes in my ears."

"I'll do it," said Baby Suggs. "Soon's you up to it."

Sethe jingled the earrings for the pleasure of the crawling-already? girl, who reached for them over and over again.

*

In the Clearing, Sethe found Baby's old preaching rock and remembered the smell of leaves simmering in the sun, thunderous feet and the shouts that ripped pods off the limbs of the chestnuts. With Baby Suggs' heart in charge, the people let go.

Sethe had had twenty-eight days – the travel of one whole moon – of unslaved life. From the pure clear stream of spit that the little girl dribbled into her face to her oily blood was twenty-eight days. Days of healing, ease and real-talk. Days of company: knowing the names of forty, fifty other Negroes, their views, habits; where they had been and what done; of feeling their fun and sorrow along with her own, which made it better. One taught her the alphabet; another a stitch. All taught her how it felt to wake up at dawn and *decide* what to do with the day. That's how she got through the waiting for Halle. Bit by bit, at 124 and in the Clearing, along with the others, she had claimed herself. Freeing yourself was one thing; claiming ownership of that freed self was another.

Now she sat on Baby Suggs' rock, Denver and Beloved watching her from the trees. There will never be a day, she thought, when Halle will knock on the door. Not knowing it was hard; knowing it was harder.

Just the fingers, she thought. Just let me feel your fingers again on the back of my neck and I will lay it all down, make a way out of this no way. Sethe bowed her head and sure enough – they were there. Lighter now, no more than the strokes of bird feather, but unmistakably caressing fingers. She had to relax a bit to let them do their work, so light was the touch, childlike almost, more finger kiss than kneading. Still she was grateful for the effort; Baby Suggs' long-distance love was equal to any skin-close love she had known. The desire, let alone the gesture, to meet her needs was good enough to lift her spirits to the place where she could take the next step: ask for some clarifying word; some advice about how to keep on with a brain greedy for news nobody could live with in a world happy to provide it.

She knew Paul D was adding something to her life – something she wanted to count on but was scared to. Now he had added more: new pictures and old rememories that broke her heart. Into the empty space of not knowing about Halle – a space sometimes colored with righteous resentment at what could have been his cowardice, or stupidity or bad luck – that empty place of no definite news was filled now with a brand-new sorrow and who could tell how many more on the way. Years ago – when 124 was alive – she had women friends, men friends from all around to share grief with. Then there was no one, for they would not visit her while the baby ghost filled the house, and she returned their disapproval with the potent pride of the mistreated. But now there was someone to share it, and he had beat the spirit away the very day he entered her house and no sign of it since. A blessing, but in its place he brought another kind of haunting: Halle's face smeared with butter and the clabber too; his own mouth jammed full of iron, and Lord knows what else he could tell her if he wanted to.

The fingers touching the back of her neck were stronger now – the strokes bolder as though Baby Suggs were gathering strength. Putting the thumbs at the nape, while the fingers pressed the sides. Harder, harder, the fingers moved slowly around toward her windpipe, making little circles on the way. Sethe was actually more surprised than frightened to find that she was being strangled. Or so it seemed. In any case, Baby Suggs' fingers had a grip on her that would not let her breathe. Tumbling forward from her seat on the rock, she clawed at the hands that were not there. Her feet were thrashing by the time Denver got to her and then Beloved.

"Ma'am! Ma'am!" Denver shouted. "Ma'ammy!" and turned her mother over on her back.

The fingers left off and Sethe had to swallow huge draughts of air before she recognized her daughter's face next to her own and Beloved's hovering above.

"You all right?"

"Somebody choked me," said Sethe.

"Who?"

Sethe rubbed her neck and struggled to a sitting position. "Grandma Baby, I reckon. I just asked her to *rub* my neck, like she used to and she was doing fine and then just got crazy with it, I guess."

"She wouldn't do that to you, Ma'am. Grandma Baby? Uh uh."

"Help me up from here."

"Look." Beloved was pointing at Sethe's neck.

"What is it? What you see?" asked Sethe.

"Bruises," said Denver.

"On my neck?"

"Here," said Beloved. "Here and here, too." She reached out her hand and touched the splotches, gathering color darker than Sethe's dark throat, and her fingers were mighty cool.

"That don't help nothing," Denver said, but Beloved was leaning in, her two hands stroking the damp skin that felt like chamois and looked like taffeta.

Sethe moaned. The girl's fingers were so cool and knowing. Sethe's knotted, private, walk-on-water life gave in a bit, softened, and it seemed that the glimpse of happiness she caught in the shadows swinging hands on the road to the carnival was a likelihood – if she could just manage the news Paul D brought and the news he kept to himself. Just manage it. Not break, fall or cry each time a hateful picture drifted in front of her face. Not develop some permanent craziness like Baby Suggs' friend, a young woman in a bonnet whose food was full of tears. Like Aunt Phyllis, who slept with her eyes wide open. Like Jackson Till, who slept under the bed.

All she wanted was to go on. As she had. Alone with her daughter in a haunted house she managed every damn thing. Why now, with Paul D instead of the ghost, was she breaking up? getting scared? needing Baby? The worst was over, wasn't it? She had already got through, hadn't she? With the ghost in 124 she could bear, do, solve anything. Now a hint of what had happened to Halle and she cut out like a rabbit looking for its mother.

Beloved's fingers were heavenly. Under them and breathing evenly again, the anguish rolled down. The peace Sethe had come there to find crept into her.

We must look a sight, she thought, and closed her eyes to see it: the three women in the middle of the Clearing, at the base of the rock where Baby Suggs, holy, had loved. One seated, yielding up her throat to the kind hands of one of the two kneeling before her.

Denver watched the faces of the other two. Beloved watched the work her thumbs were doing and must have loved what she saw because she leaned over and kissed the tenderness under Sethe's chin.

They stayed that way for a while because neither Denver nor Sethe knew how not to: how to stop and not love the look or feel of the lips that kept on kissing. Then Sethe, grabbing Beloved's hair and blinking rapidly, separated herself. She later believed that it was because the girl's breath was exactly like new milk that she said to her, stern and frowning, "You too old for that."

She looked at Denver, and seeing panic about to become something more, stood up quickly, breaking the tableau apart.

"Come on up! Up!" Sethe waved the girls to their feet. As they left the Clearing they looked pretty much the same as they had when they had come: Sethe in the lead, the girls a ways back. All silent as before, but with a difference. Sethe was bothered, not because of the kiss, but because, just before it, when she was feeling so fine letting Beloved massage away the pain, the fingers she was loving and the ones that had soothed her before they strangled her had reminded her of something that now slipped her mind. But one thing for sure, Baby Suggs had not choked her as first she thought. Denver was right, and walking in the dappled tree-light, clearer-headed now – away from the enchantment of the Clearing – Sethe remembered the touch of those fingers that she knew better than her own. They had bathed her in sections, wrapped her womb, combed her hair, oiled her nipples, stitched her clothes, cleaned her feet, greased her back and dropped just about anything they were doing to massage Sethe's nape when, especially in the early days, her spirits fell down under the weight of the things she remembered and those she did not: schoolteacher writing in ink she herself had made while his nephews played on her; the face of the woman in a felt hat as she rose to stretch in the field. If she lay among all the hands in the world, she would know Baby Suggs' just as she did the good hands of the whitegirl looking for velvet. But for eighteen years she had lived in a house full of touches from the other side. And the thumbs that pressed her nape were the same. Maybe that was where it had gone to. After Paul D beat it out of 124, maybe it collected itself in the Clearing. Reasonable, she thought.

Why she had taken Denver and Beloved with her didn't puzzle her now – at the time it seemed impulse, with a vague wish for protection. And the girls had saved her, Beloved so agitated she behaved like a two-year-old.

Like a faint smell of burning that disappears when the fire is cut off or the window opened for a breeze, the suspicion that the girl's touch was also exactly like the baby's ghost dissipated. It was only a tiny disturbance anyway – not strong enough to divert her from the ambition welling in her now: she wanted Paul D. No matter what he told and knew, she wanted him in her life. More than commemorating Halle, that is what she had come to the Clearing to figure out, and now it *was* figured. Trust and rememory, yes, the way she believed it could be when he cradled her before the cooking stove. The weight and angle of him; the true-to-life beard hair on him; arched back, educated hands. His waiting eyes and awful human power. The mind of him that knew her own. Her story was bearable because it was his as well – to tell, to refine and tell again. The things neither knew about the other – the things neither had word-shapes for – well, it would come in time: where they led him off to sucking iron; the perfect death of her crawling-already? baby.

She wanted to get back – fast. Set these idle girls to some work that would fill their wandering heads. Rushing through the green corridor, cooler now because the sun had moved, it occurred to her that the two were alike as sisters. Their obedience and absolute reliability shot through with surprise. Sethe understood Denver. Solitude had made her secretive – self-manipulated. Years of haunting had dulled her in ways you wouldn't believe and sharpened her in ways you wouldn't believe either. The consequence was a timid but hard-headed daughter Sethe would die to protect. The other, Beloved, she knew less, nothing, about – except that there was nothing she wouldn't do for Sethe and that Denver and she liked each other's company. Now she thought she knew why. They spent up or held on to their feelings in harmonious ways. What one had to give the other was pleased to take. They hung back in the trees that ringed the Clearing, then rushed into it with screams and kisses when Sethe choked – anyhow that's how she explained it to herself for she noticed neither competition between the two nor domination by one. On her mind was the supper she wanted to fix for Paul D – something difficult to do, something she would do just so – to launch her newer, stronger life with a tender man. Those litty bitty potatoes browned on all sides, heavy on the pepper; snap beans seasoned with rind; yellow squash sprinkled with vinegar and sugar. Maybe corn cut from the cob and fried with green onions and butter. Raised bread, even.

Her mind, searching the kitchen before she got to it, was so full of her offering she did not see right away, in the space under the white stairs, the wooden tub and Paul D sitting in it. She smiled at him and he smiled back.

"Summer must be over," she said.

"Come on in here."

"Uh uh. Girls right behind me."

"I don't hear nobody."

"I have to cook, Paul D."

"Me too." He stood up and made her stay there while he held her in his arms. Her dress soaked up the water from his body. His jaw was near her ear. Her chin touched his shoulder.

"What you gonna cook?"

"I thought some snap beans."

"Oh, yeah."

"Fry up a little corn?"

"Yeah."

There was no question but that she could do it. Just like the day she arrived at 124 – sure enough, she had milk enough for all.

Beloved came through the door and they ought to have heard her tread, but they didn't.

Breathing and murmuring, breathing and murmuring. Beloved heard them as soon as the door banged shut behind her. She jumped at the slam and swiveled her head toward the whispers coming from behind the white stairs. She took a step and felt like crying. She had been so close, then closer. And it was so much better than the anger that ruled when Sethe did or thought anything that excluded herself. She could bear the hours – nine or ten of them each day but one – when Sethe was gone. Bear even the nights when she was close but out of sight, behind walls and doors lying next to him. But now – even the daylight time that Beloved had counted on, disciplined herself to be content with, was being reduced, divided by Sethe's willingness to pay attention to other things. Him mostly. Him who said something to her that made her run out into the woods and talk to herself on a rock. Him who kept her hidden at night behind doors. And him who had hold of her now whispering behind the stairs after Beloved had rescued her neck and was ready now to put her hand in that woman's own.

Beloved turned around and left. Denver had not arrived, or else she was waiting somewhere outside. Beloved went to look, pausing to watch a cardinal hop from limb to branch. She followed the blood spot shifting in the leaves until she lost it and even then she walked on, backward, still hungry for another glimpse.

She turned finally and ran through the woods to the stream. Standing close to its edge she watched her reflection there. When Denver's face joined hers, they stared at each other in the water.

"You did it, I saw you," said Denver.

"What?"

"I saw your face. You made her choke."

"I didn't do it."

"You told me you loved her."

"I fixed it, didn't I? Didn't I fix her neck?"

"After. After you choked her neck."

"I kissed her neck. I didn't choke it. The circle of iron choked it."

"I saw you." Denver grabbed Beloved's arm.

"Look out, girl," said Beloved and, snatching her arm away, ran ahead as fast as she could along the stream that sang on the other side of the woods.

Left alone, Denver wondered if, indeed, she had been

wrong. She and Beloved were standing in the trees whispering, while Sethe sat on the rock. Denver knew that the Clearing used to be where Baby Suggs preached, but that was when she was a baby. She had never been there herself to remember it. 124 and the field behind it were all the world she knew or wanted.

Once upon a time she had known more and wanted to. Had walked the path leading to a real other house. Had stood outside the window listening. Four times she did it on her own – crept away from 124 early in the afternoon when her mother and grandmother had their guard down, just before supper, after chores; the blank hour before gears changed to evening occupations. Denver had walked off looking for the house other children visited but not her. When she found it she was too timid to go to the front door so she peeped in the window. Lady Jones sat in a straight-backed chair; several children sat cross-legged on the floor in front of her. Lady Jones had a book. The children had slates. Lady Jones was saying something too soft for Denver to hear. The children were saying it after her. Four times Denver went to look. The fifth time Lady Jones caught her and said, "Come in the front door, Miss Denver. This is not a side show."

So she had almost a whole year of the company of her peers and along with them learned to spell and count. She was seven, and those two hours in the afternoon were precious to her. Especially so because she had done it on her own and was pleased and surprised by the pleasure and surprise it created in her mother and her brothers. For a nickel a month, Lady Jones did what whitepeople thought unnecessary if not illegal: crowded her little parlor with the colored children who had time for and interest in book learning. The nickel, tied to a handkerchief knot, tied to her belt, that she carried to Lady Jones, thrilled her. The effort to handle chalk expertly and avoid the scream it would make; the capital w, the little i, the beauty of the letters in her name, the deeply mournful sentences from the Bible Lady Jones used as a textbook. Denver practiced every morning; starred every afternoon. She was so happy she didn't even know she was being avoided by her classmates – that they made excuses and altered their pace not to walk with her. It was Nelson Lord – the boy as smart as she was – who put a stop to it; who asked her the question about her mother that put chalk, the little *i* and all the rest that those afternoons held, out of reach forever. She should have laughed when he said it, or pushed him down, but there was no meanness in his face or his voice. Just curiosity. But the thing that leapt up in her when he asked it was a thing that had been lying there all along.

She never went back. The second day she didn't go, Sethe asked her why not. Denver didn't answer. She was too scared to ask her brothers or anyone else Nelson Lord's question because certain odd and terrifying feelings about her mother were collecting around the thing that leapt up inside her. Later on, after Baby Suggs died, she did not wonder why Howard and Buglar had run away. She did not agree with Sethe that they left because of the ghost. If so, what took them so long? They had lived with it as long as she had. But if Nelson Lord was right – no wonder they were sulky, staying away from home as much as they could.

Meanwhile the monstrous and unmanageable dreams about Sethe found release in the concentration Denver began to fix on the baby ghost. Before Nelson Lord, she had been barely interested in its antics. The patience of her mother and grandmother in its presence made her indifferent to it. Then it began to irritate her, wear her out with its mischief. That was when she walked off to follow the children to Lady Jones' house-school. Now it held for her all the anger, love and fear she didn't know what to do with. Even when she did muster the courage to ask Nelson Lord's question, she could not hear Sethe's answer, nor Baby Suggs' words, nor anything at all thereafter. For two years she walked in a silence too solid for penetration but which gave her eyes a power even she found hard to believe. The black nostrils of a sparrow sitting on a branch sixty feet above her head, for instance. For two years she heard nothing at all and then she heard close thunder crawling up the stairs. Baby Suggs thought it was Here Boy padding into places he never went. Sethe thought it was the India-rubber ball the boys played with bounding down the stairs.

"Is that damn dog lost his mind?" shouted Baby Suggs.

"He's on the porch," said Sethe. "See for yourself."

"Well, what's that I'm hearing then?"

Sethe slammed the stove lid. "Buglar! Buglar! I told you all not to use that ball in here." She looked at the white stairs and saw Denver at the top.

"She was trying to get upstairs."

"What?" The cloth she used to handle the stove lid was balled in Sethe's hand.

"The baby," said Denver. "Didn't you hear her crawling?"

What to jump on first was the problem: that Denver heard anything at all or that the crawling-already? baby girl was still at it but more so.

The return of Denver's hearing, cut off by an answer she could not bear to hear, cut on by the sound of her dead sister trying to climb the stairs, signaled another shift in the fortunes of the people of 124. From then on the presence was full of spite. Instead of sighs and accidents there was pointed and deliberate abuse. Buglar and Howard grew furious at the company of the women in the house, and spent in sullen reproach any time they had away from their odd work in town carrying water and feed at the stables. Until the spite became so personal it drove each off. Baby Suggs grew tired, went to bed and stayed there until her big old heart quit. Except for an occasional request for color she said practically nothing – until the afternoon of the last day of her life when she got out of bed, skipped slowly to the door of the keeping room and announced to Sethe and Denver the lesson she had learned from her sixty years a slave and ten years free: that there was no bad luck in the world but whitepeople. "They don't know when to stop," she said, and returned to her bed, pulled up the quilt and left them to hold that thought forever.

Shortly afterward Sethe and Denver tried to call up and reason with the baby ghost, but got nowhere. It took a man, Paul D, to shout it off, beat it off and take its place for himself. And carnival or no carnival, Denver preferred the venomous baby to him any day. During the first days after Paul D moved in, Denver stayed in her emerald closet as long as she could, lonely as a mountain and almost as big, thinking everybody had somebody but her; thinking even a ghost's company was denied her. So when she saw the black dress with two unlaced shoes beneath it she trembled with secret thanks. Whatever her power and however she used it, Beloved was *hers*. Denver was alarmed by the harm she thought Beloved planned for Sethe, but felt helpless to thwart it, so unrestricted was her need to love another. The display she witnessed at the Clearing shamed her because the choice between Sethe and Beloved was without conflict.

Walking toward the stream, beyond her green bush house, she let herself wonder what if Beloved really decided to choke her mother. Would she let it happen? Murder, Nelson Lord had said. "Didn't your mother get locked away for murder? Wasn't you in there with her when she went?"

It was the second question that made it impossible for so long to ask Sethe about the first. The thing that leapt up had been coiled in just such a place: a darkness, a stone, and some other thing that moved by itself. She went deaf rather than hear the answer, and like the little four o'clocks that searched openly for sunlight, then closed themselves tightly when it left, Denver kept watch for the baby and withdrew from everything else. Until Paul D came. But the damage he did came undone with the miraculous resurrection of Beloved.

Just ahead, at the edge of the stream, Denver could see her silhouette, standing barefoot in the water, lifting her black skirts up above her calves, the beautiful head lowered in rapt attention.

Blinking fresh tears Denver approached her – eager for a word, a sign of forgiveness.

Denver took off her shoes and stepped into the water with her. It took a moment for her to drag her eyes from the spectacle of Beloved's head to see what she was staring at.

A turtle inched along the edge, turned and climbed to dry ground. Not far behind it was another one, headed in the same direction. Four placed plates under a hovering motion-less bowl. Behind her in the grass the other one moving quickly, quickly to mount her. The impregnable strength of him – earthing his feet near her shoulders. The embracing necks – hers stretching up toward his bending down, the pat pat pat of their touching heads. No height was beyond her yearning neck, stretched like a finger toward his, risking everything outside the bowl just to touch his face. The gravity of their shields, clashing, countered and mocked the floating heads touching.

Beloved dropped the folds of her skirt. It spread around her. The hem darkened in the water.

OUT OF SIGHT of Mister's sight, away, praise His name, from the smiling boss of roosters, Paul D began to tremble. Not all at once and not so anyone could tell. When he turned his head, aiming for a last look at Brother, turned it as much as the rope that connected his neck to the axle of a buckboard allowed, and, later on, when they fastened the iron around his ankles and clamped the wrists as well, there was no outward sign of trembling at all. Nor eighteen days after that when he saw the ditches; the one thousand feet of earth – five feet deep, five feet wide, into which wooden boxes had been fitted. A door of bars that you could lift on hinges like a cage opened into three walls and a roof of scrap lumber and red dirt. Two feet of it over his head; three feet of open trench in front of him with anything that crawled or scurried welcome to share that grave calling itself quarters. And there were forty-five more. He was sent there after trying to kill Brandywine, the man schoolteacher sold him to. Brandywine was leading him, in a coffle with ten others, through Kentucky into Virginia. He didn't know exactly what prompted him to try – other than Halle, Sixo, Paul A, Paul F and Mister. But the trembling was fixed by the time he knew it was there.

Still no one else knew it, because it began inside. A flutter of a kind, in the chest, then the shoulder blades. It felt like rippling – gentle at first and then wild. As though the further south they led him the more his blood, frozen like an ice pond for twenty years, began thawing, breaking into pieces that, once melted, had no choice but to swirl and eddy.

Sometimes it was in his leg. Then again it moved to the base of his spine. By the time they unhitched him from the wagon and he saw nothing but dogs and two shacks in a world of sizzling grass, the roiling blood was shaking him to and fro. But no one could tell. The wrists he held out for the bracelets that evening were steady as were the legs he stood on when chains were attached to the leg irons. But when they shoved him into the box and dropped the cage door down, his hands quit taking instruction. On their own, they traveled. Nothing could stop them or get their attention. They would not hold his penis to urinate or a spoon to scoop lumps of lima beans into his mouth. The miracle of their obedience came with the hammer at dawn.

All forty-six men woke to rifle shot. All forty-six. Three whitemen walked along the trench unlocking the doors one by one. No one stepped through. When the last lock was opened, the three returned and lifted the bars, one by one. And one by one the blackmen emerged – promptly and without the poke of a rifle butt if they had been there more than a day; promptly with the butt if, like Paul D, they had just arrived. When all forty-six were standing in a line in the trench, another rifle shot signaled the climb out and up to the ground above, where one thousand feet of the best hand-forged chain in Georgia stretched. Each man bent and waited. The first man picked up the end and threaded it through the loop on his leg iron. He stood up then, and, shuffling a little, brought the chain tip to the next prisoner, who did likewise. As the chain was passed on and each man stood in the other's place, the line of men turned around, facing the boxes they had come out of. Not one spoke to the other. At least not with words. The eyes had to tell what there was to tell: "Help me this mornin; 's bad"; "I'm a make it"; "New man"; "Steady now steady."

Chain-up completed, they knelt down. The dew, more likely than not, was mist by then. Heavy sometimes and if the dogs were quiet and just breathing you could hear doves. Kneeling in the mist they waited for the whim of a guard, or two, or three. Or maybe all of them wanted it. Wanted it from one prisoner in particular or none – or all.

"Breakfast? Want some breakfast, nigger?"

"Yes, sir."

"Hungry, nigger?"

"Yes, sir."

"Here you go."

Occasionally a kneeling man chose gunshot in his head as the price, maybe, of taking a bit of foreskin with him to Jesus. Paul D did not know that then. He was looking at his palsied hands, smelling the guard, listening to his soft grunts so like the doves', as he stood before the man kneeling in mist on his right. Convinced he was next, Paul D retched – vomiting up nothing at all. An observing guard smashed his shoulder with the rifle and the engaged one decided to skip the new man for the time being lest his pants and shoes got soiled by nigger puke.

"Hiiii!"

It was the first sound, other than "Yes, sir," a black man was allowed to speak each morning, and the lead chain gave it everything he had. "Hiiii!" It was never clear to Paul D how he knew when to shout that mercy. They called him Hi Man and Paul D thought at first the guards told him when to give the signal that let the prisoners rise up off their knees and dance two-step to the music of hand-forged iron. Later he doubted it. He believed to this day that the "Hiiii!" at dawn and the "Hoooo!" when evening came were the responsibility Hi Man assumed because he alone knew what was enough, what was too much, when things were over, when the time had come.

They chain-danced over the fields, through the woods to a trail that ended in the astonishing beauty of feldspar, and there Paul D's hands disobeyed the furious rippling of his blood and paid attention. With a sledge hammer in his hands and Hi Man's lead, the men got through. They sang it out and beat it up, garbling the words so they could not be understood; tricking the words so their syllables yielded up other meanings. They sang the women they knew; the children they had been; the animals they had tamed themselves or seen others tame. They sang of bosses and masters and misses; of mules and dogs and the shamelessness of life. They sang lovingly of graveyards and sisters long gone. Of pork in the woods; meal in the pan; fish on the line; cane, rain and rocking chairs.

And they beat. The women for having known them and no more, no more; the children for having been them but never again. They killed a boss so often and so completely they had to bring him back to life to pulp him one more time. Tasting hot mealcake among pine trees, they beat it away. Singing love songs to Mr. Death, they smashed his head. More than the rest, they killed the flirt whom folks called Life for leading them on. Making them think the next sunrise would be worth it; that another stroke of time would do it at last. Only when she was dead would they be safe. The successful ones – the ones who had been there enough years to have maimed, mutilated, maybe even buried her – kept watch over the others who were still in her cock-teasing hug, caring and looking forward, remembering and looking back. They were the ones whose eyes said, "Help me, 's bad"; or "Look out," meaning *this might be the day I bay or eat my own mess or run*, and it was this last that had to be guarded against, for if one pitched and ran – all, all forty-six, would be yanked by the chain that bound them and no telling who or how many would be killed. A man could risk his own life, but not his brother's. So the eyes said, "Steady now," and "Hang by me."

Eighty-six days and done. Life was dead. Paul D beat her butt all day every day till there was not a whimper in her.

Eighty-six days and his hands were still, waiting serenely each rat-rustling night for "Hiiii!" at dawn and the eager clench on the hammer's shaft. Life rolled over dead. Or so he thought.

It rained.

Snakes came down from short-leaf pine and hemlock.

It rained.

Cypress, yellow poplar, ash and palmetto drooped under five days of rain without wind. By the eighth day the doves were nowhere in sight, by the ninth even the salamanders were gone. Dogs laid their ears down and stared over their paws. The men could not work. Chain-up was slow, breakfast abandoned, the two-step became a slow drag over soupy grass and unreliable earth.

It was decided to lock everybody down in the boxes till it either stopped or lightened up so a whiteman could walk, damnit, without flooding his gun and the dogs could quit shivering. The chain was threaded through forty-six loops of the best hand-forged iron in Georgia.

It rained.

In the boxes the men heard the water rise in the trench and looked out for cottonmouths. They squatted in muddy water, slept above it, peed in it. Paul D thought he was screaming; his mouth was open and there was this loud throat-splitting sound – but it may have been somebody else. Then he thought he was crying. Something was running down his cheeks. He lifted his hands to wipe away the tears and saw dark brown slime. Above him rivulets of mud slid through the boards of the roof. When it come down, he thought, gonna crush me like a tick bug. It happened so quick he had no time to ponder. Somebody yanked the chain – once – hard enough to cross his legs and throw him into the mud. He never figured out how he knew – how anybody did – but he did know – he did – and he took both hands and yanked the length of chain at his left, so the next man would know too. The water was above his ankles, flowing over the wooden plank he slept on. And then it wasn't water anymore. The ditch was caving in and mud oozed under and through the bars.

They waited – each and every one of the forty-six. Not screaming, although some of them must have fought like the devil not to. The mud was up to his thighs and he held on to the bars. Then it came – another yank – from the left this time and less forceful than the first because of the mud it passed through.

It started like the chain-up but the difference was the power of the chain. One by one, from Hi Man back on down the line, they dove. Down through the mud under the bars, blind, groping. Some had sense enough to wrap their heads in their shirts, cover their faces with rags, put on their shoes. Others just plunged, simply ducked down and pushed out, fighting up, reaching for air. Some lost direction and their neighbors, feeling the confused pull of the chain, snatched them around. For one lost, all lost. The chain that held them would save all or none, and Hi Man was the Delivery. They talked through that chain like Sam Morse and, Great God, they all came up. Like the unshriven dead, zombies on the loose, holding the chains in their hands, they trusted the rain and the dark, yes, but mostly Hi Man and each other.

Past the sheds where the dogs lay in deep depression; past the two guard shacks, past the stable of sleeping horses, past the hens whose bills were bolted into their feathers, they waded. The moon did not help because it wasn't there. The field was a marsh, the track a trough. All Georgia seemed to be sliding, melting away. Moss wiped their faces as they fought the live-oak branches that blocked their way. Georgia took up all of Alabama and Mississippi then, so there was no state line to cross and it wouldn't have mattered anyway. If they had known about it, they would have avoided not only Alfred and the beautiful feldspar, but Savannah too and headed for the Sea Islands on the river that slid down from the Blue Ridge Mountains. But they didn't know.

Daylight came and they huddled in a copse of redbud trees. Night came and they scrambled up to higher ground, praying the rain would go on shielding them and keeping folks at home. They were hoping for a shack, solitary, some distance from its big house, where a slave might be making rope or heating potatoes at the grate. What they found was a camp of sick Cherokee for whom a rose was named.

Decimated but stubborn, they were among those who chose a fugitive life rather than Oklahoma. The illness that swept them now was reminiscent of the one that had killed half their number two hundred years earlier. In between that calamity and this, they had visited George III in London, published a newspaper, made baskets, led Oglethorpe through forests, helped Andrew Jackson fight Creek, cooked maize, drawn up a constitution, petitioned the King of Spain, been experimented on by Dartmouth, established asylums, wrote their language, resisted settlers, shot bear and translated scripture. All to no avail. The forced move to the Arkansas River, insisted upon by the same president they fought for against the Creek, destroyed another quarter of their already shattered number.

That was it, they thought, and removed themselves from those Cherokee who signed the treaty, in order to retire into the forest and await the end of the world. The disease they suffered now was a mere inconvenience compared to the devastation they remembered. Still, they protected each other as best they could. The healthy were sent some miles away; the sick stayed behind with the dead – to survive or join them.

The prisoners from Alfred, Georgia, sat down in semicircle near the encampment. No one came and still they sat. Hours passed and the rain turned soft. Finally a woman stuck her head out of her house. Night came and nothing happened.

At dawn two men with barnacles covering their beautiful skin approached them. No one spoke for a moment, then Hi Man raised his hand. The Cherokee saw the chains and went away. When they returned each carried a handful of small axes. Two children followed with a pot of mush cooling and thinning in the rain.

Buffalo men, they called them, and talked slowly to the prisoners scooping mush and tapping away at their chains. Nobody from a box in Alfred, Georgia, cared about the illness the Cherokee warned them about, so they stayed, all forty-six, resting, planning their next move. Paul D had no idea of what to do and knew less than anybody, it seemed. He heard his co-convicts talk knowledgeably of rivers and states, towns and territories. Heard Cherokee men describe the beginning of the world and its end. Listened to tales of other Buffalo men they knew – three of whom were in the healthy camp a few miles away. Hi Man wanted to join them; others wanted to join him. Some wanted to leave; some to stay on. Weeks later Paul D was the only Buffalo man left – without a plan. All he could think of was tracking dogs, although Hi Man said the rain they left in gave that no chance of success. Alone, the last man with buffalo hair among the ailing Cherokee, Paul D finally woke up and, admitting his ignorance, asked how he might get North. Free North. Magical North. Welcoming, benevolent North. The Cherokee smiled and looked around. The flood rains of a month ago had turned everything to steam and blossoms.

"That way," he said, pointing. "Follow the tree flowers," he said. "Only the tree flowers. As they go, you go. You will be where you want to be when they are gone."

So he raced from dogwood to blossoming peach. When they thinned out he headed for the cherry blossoms, then magnolia, chinaberry, pecan, walnut and prickly pear. At last he reached a field of apple trees whose flowers were just becoming tiny knots of fruit. Spring sauntered north, but he had to run like hell to keep it as his traveling companion. From February to July he was on the lookout for blossoms. When he lost them, and found himself without so much as a petal to guide him, he paused, climbed a tree on a hillock and scanned the horizon for a flash of pink or white in the leaf world that surrounded him. He did not touch them or stop to smell. He merely followed in their wake, a dark ragged figure guided by the blossoming plums.

The apple field turned out to be Delaware where the weaver lady lived. She snapped him up as soon as he finished the sausage she fed him and he crawled into her bed crying. She passed him off as her nephew from Syracuse simply by calling him that nephew's name. Eighteen months and he was looking out again for blossoms only this time he did the looking on a dray.

It was some time before he could put Alfred, Georgia, Sixo, schoolteacher, Halle, his brothers, Sethe, Mister, the taste of iron, the sight of butter, the smell of hickory, notebook paper, one by one, into the tobacco tin lodged in his chest. By the time he got to 124 nothing in this world could pry it open.

SHE MOVED HIM.

Not the way he had beat off the baby's ghost – all bang and shriek with windows smashed and jelly jars rolled in a heap. But she moved him nonetheless, and Paul D didn't know how to stop it because it looked like he was moving himself. Imperceptibly, downright reasonably, he was moving out of 124.

The beginning was so simple. One day, after supper, he sat in the rocker by the stove, bone-tired, river-whipped, and fell asleep. He woke to the footsteps of Sethe coming down the white stairs to make breakfast.

"I thought you went out somewhere," she said.

Paul D moaned, surprised to find himself exactly where he was the last time he looked.

"Don't tell me I slept in this chair the whole night."

Sethe laughed. "Me? I won't say a word to you."

"Why didn't you rouse me?"

"I did. Called you two or three times. I gave it up around midnight and then I thought you went out somewhere."

He stood, expecting his back to fight it. But it didn't. Not a creak or a stiff joint anywhere. In fact he felt refreshed. Some things are like that, he thought, good-sleep places. The base of certain trees here and there; a wharf, a bench, a rowboat once, a haystack usually, not always bed, and here, now, a rocking chair, which was strange because in his experience furniture was the worst place for a good-sleep sleep.

The next evening he did it again and then again. He was accustomed to sex with Sethe just about every day, and to avoid the confusion Beloved's shining caused him he still made it his business to take her back upstairs in the morning, or lie down with her after supper. But he found a way and a reason to spend the longest part of the night in the rocker. He told himself it must be his back – something supportive it needed for a weakness left over from sleeping in a box in Georgia.

It went on that way and might have stayed that way but one evening, after supper, after Sethe, he came downstairs, sat in the rocker and didn't want to be there. He stood up and realized he didn't want to go upstairs either. Irritable and longing for rest, he opened the door to Baby Suggs' room and dropped off to sleep on the bed the old lady died in. That settled it – so it seemed. It became his room and Sethe didn't object – her bed made for two had been occupied by one for eighteen years before Paul D came to call. And maybe it was better this way, with young girls in the house and him not being her true-to-life husband. In any case, since there was no reduction in his before-breakfast or after-supper appetites, he never heard her complain.

It went on that way and might have stayed that way, except one evening, after supper, after Sethe, he came downstairs and lay on Baby Suggs' bed and didn't want to be there.

He believed he was having house-fits, the glassy anger men sometimes feel when a woman's house begins to bind them, when they want to yell and break something or at least run off. He knew all about that – felt it lots of times – in the Delaware weaver's house, for instance. But always he associated the house-fit with the woman in it. This nervousness had nothing to do with the woman, whom he loved a little bit more every day: her hands among vegetables, her mouth when she licked a thread end before guiding it through a needle or bit it in two when the seam was done, the blood in her eye when she defended her girls (and Beloved was hers now) or any coloredwoman from a slur. Also in this house-fit there was no anger, no suffocation, no yearning to be elsewhere. He just could not, would not, sleep upstairs or in the rocker or, now, in Baby Suggs' bed. So he went to the storeroom.

It went on that way and might have stayed that way except one evening, after supper, after Sethe, he lay on a pallet in the storeroom and didn't want to be there. Then it was the cold house and it was out there, separated from the main part of 124, curled on top of two croaker sacks full of sweet potatoes, staring at the sides of a lard can, that he realized the moving was involuntary. He wasn't being nervous; he was being prevented.

So he waited. Visited Sethe in the morning; slept in the cold room at night and waited.

She came, and he wanted to knock her down.

In Ohio seasons are theatrical. Each one enters like a prima donna, convinced its performance is the reason the world has people in it. When Paul D had been forced out of 124 into a shed behind it, summer had been hooted offstage and autumn with its bottles of blood and gold had everybody's attention. Even at night, when there should have been a restful intermission, there was none because the voices of a dying landscape were insistent and loud. Paul D packed newspaper under himself and over, to give his thin blanket some help. But the chilly night was not on his mind. When he heard the door open behind him he refused to turn and look.

"What you want in here? What you want?" He should have been able to hear her breathing.

"I want you to touch me on the inside part and call me my name."

Paul D never worried about his little tobacco tin anymore. It was rusted shut. So, while she hoisted her skirts and turned her head over her shoulder the way the turtles had, he just looked at the lard can, silvery in moonlight, and spoke quietly.

"When good people take you in and treat you good, you ought to try to be good back. You don't . . . Sethe loves you. Much as her own daughter. You know that."

Beloved dropped her skirts as he spoke and looked at him with empty eyes. She took a step he could not hear and stood close behind him.

"She don't love me like I love her. I don't love nobody but her."

"Then what you come in here for?"

"I want you to touch me on the inside part."

"Go on back in that house and get to bed."

"You have to touch me. On the inside part. And you have to call me my name."

As long as his eyes were locked on the silver of the lard can he was safe. If he trembled like Lot's wife and felt some womanish need to see the nature of the sin behind him; feel a sympathy, perhaps, for the cursing cursed, or want to hold it in his arms out of respect for the connection between them, he too would be lost.

"Call me my name."

"No."

"Please call it. I'll go if you call it."

"Beloved." He said it, but she did not go. She moved closer with a footfall he didn't hear and he didn't hear the whisper that the flakes of rust made either as they fell away from the seams of his tobacco tin. So when the lid gave he didn't know it. What he knew was that when he reached the inside part he was saying, "Red heart. Red heart," over and over again. Softly and then so loud it woke Denver, then Paul D himself. "Red heart. Red heart. Red heart."

TO GO BACK to the original hunger was impossible. Luckily for Denver, looking was food enough to last. But to be looked at in turn was beyond appetite; it was breaking through her own skin to a place where hunger hadn't been discovered. It didn't have to happen often, because Beloved seldom looked right at her, or when she did, Denver could tell that her own face was just the place those eyes stopped while the mind behind it walked on. But sometimes – at moments Denver could neither anticipate nor create – Beloved rested cheek on knuckles and looked at Denver with attention.

It was lovely. Not to be stared at, not seen, but being pulled into view by the interested, uncritical eyes of the other. Having her hair examined as a part of her self, not as material or a style. Having her lips, nose, chin caressed as they might be if she were a moss rose a gardener paused to admire. Denver's skin dissolved under that gaze and became soft and bright like the lisle dress that had its arm around her mother's waist. She floated near but outside her own body, feeling vague and intense at the same time. Needing nothing. Being what there was.

At such times it seemed to be Beloved who needed something – wanted something. Deep down in her wide black eyes, back behind the expressionlessness, was a palm held out for a penny which Denver would gladly give her, if only she knew how or knew enough about her, a knowledge not to be had by the answers to the questions Sethe occasionally put to her: "You disremember everything? I never knew my mother neither, but I saw her a couple of times. Did you never see yours? What kind of whites was they? You don't remember none?"

Beloved, scratching the back of her hand, would say she remembered a woman who was hers, and she remembered being snatched away from her. Other than that, the clearest memory she had, the one she repeated, was the bridge – standing on the bridge looking down. And she knew one whiteman.

Sethe found that remarkable and more evidence to support her conclusions, which she confided to Denver.

"Where'd you get the dress, them shoes?"

Beloved said she took them.

"Who from?"

Silence and a faster scratching of her hand. She didn't know; she saw them and just took them.

"Uh huh," said Sethe, and told Denver that she believed Beloved had been locked up by some whiteman for his own purposes, and never let out the door. That she must have escaped to a bridge or someplace and rinsed the rest out of her mind. Something like that had happened to Ella except it was two men – a father and son – and Ella remembered every bit of it. For more than a year, they kept her locked in a room for themselves.

"You couldn't think up," Ella had said, "what them two done to me."

Sethe thought it explained Beloved's behavior around Paul D, whom she hated so.

Denver neither believed nor commented on Sethe's speculations, and she lowered her eyes and never said a word about the cold house. She was certain that Beloved was the white dress that had knelt with her mother in the keeping room, the true-to-life presence of the baby that had kept her company most of her life. And to be looked at by her, however briefly, kept her grateful for the rest of the time when she was merely the looker. Besides, she had her own set of questions which had nothing to do with the past. The present alone interested Denver, but she was careful to appear uninquisitive about the things she was dying to ask Beloved, for if she pressed too hard, she might lose the penny that the held-out palm wanted, and lose, therefore, the place beyond appetite. It was better to feast, to have permission to be the looker, because the old hunger – the before-Beloved hunger that drove her into boxwood and cologne for just a taste of a life, to feel it bumpy and not flat – was out of the question. Looking kept it at bay.

So she did not ask Beloved how she knew about the earrings, the night walks to the cold house or the tip of the thing she saw when Beloved lay down or came undone in her sleep. The look, when it came, came when Denver had been careful, had explained things, or participated in things, or told stories to keep her occupied when Sethe was at the restaurant. No given chore was enough to put out the licking fire that seemed always to burn in her. Not when they wrung out sheets so tight the rinse water ran back up their arms. Not when they shoveled snow from the path to the outhouse. Or broke three inches of ice from the rain barrel; scoured and boiled last summer's canning jars, packed mud in the cracks of the hen house and warmed the chicks with their skirts. All the while Denver was obliged to talk about what they were doing – the how and why of it. About people Denver knew once or had seen, giving them more life than life had: the sweet-smelling whitewoman who brought her oranges and cologne and good wool skirts; Lady Jones who taught them songs to spell and count by; a beautiful boy as smart as she was with a birthmark like a nickel on his cheek. A white preacher who prayed for their souls while Sethe peeled potatoes and Grandma Baby sucked air. And she told her about Howard and Buglar: the parts of the bed that belonged to each (the top reserved for herself); that before she transferred to Baby Suggs' bed she never knew them to sleep without holding hands. She described them to Beloved slowly, to keep her attention, dwelling on their habits, the games they taught her and not the fright that drove them increasingly out of the house – anywhere – and finally far away.

This day they are outside. It's cold and the snow is hard as packed dirt. Denver has finished singing the counting song Lady Jones taught her students. Beloved is holding her arms steady while Denver unclasps frozen underwear and towels from the line. One by one she lays them in Beloved's arms until the pile, like a huge deck of cards, reaches her chin. The rest, aprons and brown stockings, Denver carries herself. Made giddy by the cold, they return to the house. The clothes will thaw slowly to a dampness perfect for the pressing iron, which will make them smell like hot rain. Dancing around the room with Sethe's apron, Beloved wants to know if there are flowers in the dark. Denver adds sticks to the stovefire and assures her there are. Twirling, her face framed by the neckband, her waist in the apron strings' embrace, she says she is thirsty.

Denver suggests warming up some cider, while her mind races to something she might do or say to interest and entertain the dancer. Denver is a strategist now and has to keep Beloved by her side from the minute Sethe leaves for work until the hour of her return when Beloved begins to hover at the window, then work her way out the door, down the steps and near the road. Plotting has changed Denver markedly. Where she was once indolent, resentful of every task, now she is spry, executing, even extending the assignments Sethe leaves for them. All to be able to say "We got to" and "Ma'am said for us to." Otherwise Beloved gets private and dreamy, or quiet and sullen, and Denver's chances of being looked at by her go down to nothing. She has no control over the evenings. When her mother is anywhere around, Beloved has eyes only for Sethe. At night, in bed, anything might happen. She might want to be told a story in the dark when Denver can't see her. Or she might get up and go into the cold house where Paul D has begun to sleep. Or she might cry, silently. She might even sleep like a brick, her breath sugary from fingerfuls of molasses or sand-cookie crumbs. Denver will turn toward her then, and if Beloved faces her, she will inhale deeply the sweet air from her mouth. If not, she will have to lean up and over her, every once in a while, to catch a sniff. For anything is better than the original hunger – the time when, after a year of the wonderful little *i*, sentences rolling out like pie dough and the company of other children, there was no sound coming through. Anything is better than the silence when she answered to hands gesturing and was indifferent to the movement of lips. When she saw every little thing and colors leaped smoldering into view. She will forgo the most violent of sunsets, stars as fat as dinner plates and all the blood of autumn and settle for the palest yellow if it comes from her Beloved.

The cider jug is heavy, but it always is, even when empty. Denver can carry it easily, yet she asks Beloved to help her. It is in the cold house next to the molasses and six pounds of cheddar hard as bone. A pallet is in the middle of the floor covered with newspaper and a blanket at the foot. It has been slept on for almost a month, even though snow has come and, with it, serious winter.

It is noon, quite light outside; inside it is not. A few cuts of sun break through the roof and walls but once there they are too weak to shift for themselves. Darkness is stronger and swallows them like minnows.

The door bangs shut. Denver can't tell where Beloved is standing.

"Where are you?" she whispers in a laughing sort of way.

"Here," says Beloved.

"Where?"

"Come find me," says Beloved.

Denver stretches out her right arm and takes a step or two. She trips and falls down onto the pallet. Newspaper crackles under her weight. She laughs again. "Oh, shoot. Beloved?"

No one answers. Denver waves her arms and squinches her eyes to separate the shadows of potato sacks, a lard can and a side of smoked pork from the one that might be human.

"Stop fooling," she says and looks up toward the light to check and make sure this is still the cold house and not something going on in her sleep. The minnows of light still swim there; they can't make it down to where she is.

"You the one thirsty. You want cider or don't you?" Denver's voice is mildly accusatory. Mildly. She doesn't want to offend and she doesn't want to betray the panic that is creeping over her like hairs. There is no sight or sound of Beloved. Denver struggles to her feet amid the crackling newspaper. Holding her palm out, she moves slowly toward the door. There is no latch or knob – just a loop of wire to catch a nail. She pushes the door open. Cold sunlight displaces the dark. The room is just as it was when they entered – except Beloved is not there. There is no point in looking further, for everything in the place can be seen at first sight. Denver looks anyway because the loss is ungovernable. She steps back into the shed, allowing the door to close quickly behind her. Darkness or not, she moves rapidly around, reaching, touching cobwebs, cheese, slanting shelves, the pallet interfering with each step. If she stumbles, she is not aware of it because she does not know where her body stops, which part of her is an arm, a foot or a knee. She feels like an ice cake torn away from the solid surface of the stream, floating on darkness, thick and crashing against the edges of things around it. Breakable, meltable and cold.

It is hard to breathe and even if there were light she wouldn't be able to see anything because she is crying. Just as she thought it might happen, it has. Easy as walking into a room. A magical appearance on a stump, the face wiped out by sunlight, and a magical disappearance in a shed, eaten alive by the dark.

"Don't," she is saying between tough swallows. "Don't. Don't go back."

This is worse than when Paul D came to 124 and she cried helplessly into the stove. This is worse. Then it was for herself. Now she is crying because she has no self. Death is a skipped meal compared to this. She can feel her thickness thinning, dissolving into nothing. She grabs the hair at her temples to get enough to uproot it and halt the melting for a while. Teeth clamped shut, Denver brakes her sobs. She doesn't move to open the door because there is no world out there. She decides to stay in the cold house and let the dark swallow her like the minnows of light above. She won't put up with another leaving, another trick. Waking up to find one brother then another not at the bottom of the bed, his foot jabbing her spine. Sitting at the table eating turnips and saving the liquor for her grandmother to drink; her mother's hand on the keeping-room door and her voice saying, "Baby Suggs is gone, Denver." And when she got around to worrying about what would be the case if Sethe died or Paul D took her away, a dream-come-true comes true just to leave her on a pile of newspaper in the dark.

No footfall announces her, but there she is, standing where before there was nobody when Denver looked. And smiling.

Denver grabs the hem of Beloved's skirt. "I thought you left me. I thought you went back."

Beloved smiles, "I don't want that place. This the place I am." She sits down on the pallet and, laughing, lies back looking at the cracklights above.

Surreptitiously, Denver pinches a piece of Beloved's skirt between her fingers and holds on. A good thing she does because suddenly Beloved sits up.

"What is it?" asks Denver.

"Look," she points to the sunlit cracks.

"What? I don't see nothing." Denver follows the pointing finger.

Beloved drops her hand. "I'm like this."

Denver watches as Beloved bends over, curls up and rocks. Her eyes go to no place; her moaning is so small Denver can hardly hear it.

"You all right? Beloved?"

Beloved focuses her eyes. "Over there. Her face."

Denver looks where Beloved's eyes go; there is nothing but darkness there.

"Whose face? Who is it?"

"Me. It's me."

She is smiling again.

THE LAST OF the Sweet Home men, so named and called by one who would know, believed it. The other four believed it too, once, but they were long gone. The sold one never returned, the lost one never found. One, he knew, was dead for sure; one he hoped was, because butter and clabber was no life or reason to live it. He grew up thinking that, of all the Blacks in Kentucky, only the five of them were men. Allowed, encouraged to correct Garner, even defy him. To invent ways of doing things; to see what was needed and attack it without permission. To buy a mother, choose a horse or a wife, handle guns, even learn reading if they wanted to – but they didn't want to since nothing important to them could be put down on paper.

Was that it? Is that where the manhood lay? In the naming done by a whiteman who was supposed to know? Who gave them the privilege not of working but of deciding how to? No. In their relationship with Garner was true metal: they were believed and trusted, but most of all they were listened to.

He thought what they said had merit, and what they felt was serious. Deferring to his slaves' opinions did not deprive him of authority or power. It was schoolteacher who taught them otherwise. A truth that waved like a scarecrow in rye: they were only Sweet Home men at Sweet Home. One step off that ground and they were trespassers among the human race. Watchdogs without teeth; steer bulls without horns; gelded workhorses whose neigh and whinny could not be translated into a language responsible humans spoke. His strength had lain in knowing that schoolteacher was wrong. Now he wondered. There was Alfred, Georgia, there was Delaware, there was Sixo and still he wondered. If schoolteacher was right it explained how he had come to be a rag doll – picked up and put back down anywhere any time by a girl young enough to be his daughter. Fucking her when he was convinced he didn't want to. Whenever she turned her behind up, the calves of his youth (was that it?) cracked his resolve. But it was more than appetite that humiliated him and made him wonder if schoolteacher was right. It was being moved, placed where she wanted him, and there was nothing he was able to do about it. For his life he could not walk up the glistening white stairs in the evening; for his life he could not stay in the kitchen, in the keeping room, in the storeroom at night. And he tried. Held his breath the way he had when he ducked into the mud; steeled his heart the way he had when the trembling began. But it was worse than that, worse than the blood eddy he had controlled with a sledge hammer. When he stood up from the supper table at 124 and turned toward the stairs, nausea was first, then repulsion. He, he. He who had eaten raw meat barely dead, who under plum trees bursting with blossoms had crunched through a dove's breast before its heart stopped beating. Because he was a man and a man could do what he would: be still for six hours in a dry well while night dropped; fight raccoon with his hands and win; watch another man, whom he loved better than his brothers, roast without a tear just so the roasters would know what a man was like. And it was he, *that* man, who had walked from Georgia to Delaware, who could not go or stay put where he wanted to in 124 – shame.

Paul D could not command his feet, but he thought he could still talk and he made up his mind to break out that way. He would tell Sethe about the last three weeks: catch her alone coming from work at the beer garden she called a restaurant and tell it all.

He waited for her. The winter afternoon looked like dusk as he stood in the alley behind Sawyer's Restaurant. Rehearsing, imagining her face and letting the words flock in his head like kids before lining up to follow the leader.

"Well, ah, this is not the, a man can't, see, but aw listen here, it ain't that, it really ain't, Ole Garner, what I mean is, it ain't a weakness, the kind of weakness I can fight 'cause 'cause something is happening to me, that girl is doing it, I know you think I never liked her nohow, but she is doing it to me. Fixing me. Sethe, she's fixed me and I can't break it."

What? A grown man fixed by a girl? But what if the girl was not a girl, but something in disguise? A lowdown something that looked like a sweet young girl and fucking her or not was not the point, it was not being able to stay or go where he wished in 124, and the danger was in losing Sethe because he was not man enough to break out, so he needed her, Sethe, to help him, to know about it, and it shamed him to have to ask the woman he wanted to protect to help him do it, God damn it to hell.

Paul D blew warm breath into the hollow of his cupped hands. The wind raced down the alley so fast it sleeked the fur of four kitchen dogs waiting for scraps. He looked at the dogs. The dogs looked at him.

Finally the back door opened and Sethe stepped through holding a scrap pan in the crook of her arm. When she saw him, she said Oh, and her smile was both pleasure and surprise.

Paul D believed he smiled back but his face was so cold he wasn't sure.

"Man, you make me feel like a girl, coming by to pick me up after work. Nobody ever did that before. You better watch out, I might start looking forward to it." She tossed the largest bones into the dirt rapidly so the dogs would know there was enough and not fight each other. Then she dumped the skins of some things, heads of other things and the insides of still more things – what the restaurant could not use and she would not – in a smoking pile near the animals' feet.

"Got to rinse this out," she said, "and then I'll be right with you."

He nodded as she returned to the kitchen.

The dogs ate without sound and Paul D thought they at least got what they came for, and if she had enough for them –

The cloth on her head was brown wool and she edged it down over her hairline against the wind.

"You get off early or what?"

"I took off early."

"Anything the matter?"

"In a way of speaking," he said and wiped his lips.

"Not cut back?"

"No, no. They got plenty work. I just –"

"Hm?"

"Sethe, you won't like what I'm 'bout to say."

She stopped then and turned her face toward him and the hateful wind. Another woman would have squinted or at least teared if the wind whipped her face as it did Sethe's. Another woman might have shot him a look of apprehension, pleading, anger even, because what he said sure sounded like part one of Goodbye, I'm gone.

Sethe looked at him steadily, calmly, already ready to accept, release or excuse an in-need-or-trouble man. Agreeing, saying okay, all right, in advance, because she didn't believe any of them – over the long haul – could measure up. And whatever the reason, it was all right. No fault. Nobody's fault.

He knew what she was thinking and even though she was wrong – he was not leaving her, wouldn't ever – the thing he had in mind to tell her was going to be worse. So, when he saw the diminished expectation in her eyes, the melancholy without blame, he could not say it. He could not say to this woman who did not squint in the wind, "I am not a man."

"Well, say it, Paul D, whether I like it or not."

Since he could not say what he planned to, he said something he didn't know was on his mind. "I want you pregnant, Sethe. Would you do that for me?"

Now she was laughing and so was he.

"You came by here to ask me that? You are one crazy-headed man. You right; I don't like it. Don't you think I'm too old to start that all over again?" She slipped her fingers in his hand for all the world like the hand-holding shadows on the side of the road.

"Think about it," he said. And suddenly it was a solution: a way to hold on to her, document his manhood and break out of the girl's spell – all in one. He put the tips of Sethe's fingers on his cheek. Laughing, she pulled them away lest somebody passing the alley see them misbehaving in public, in daylight, in the wind.

Still, he'd gotten a little more time, bought it, in fact, and hoped the price wouldn't wreck him. Like paying for an afternoon in the coin of life to come.

They left off playing, let go hands and hunched forward as they left the alley and entered the street. The wind was quieter there but the dried-out cold it left behind kept pedestrians fast-moving, stiff inside their coats. No men leaned against door frames or storefront windows. The wheels of wagons delivering feed or wood screeched as though they hurt. Hitched horses in front of the saloons shivered and closed their eyes. Four women, walking two abreast, approached, their shoes loud on the wooden walkway. Paul D touched Sethe's elbow to guide her as they stepped from the slats to the dirt to let the women pass.

Half an hour later, when they reached the city's edge, Sethe and Paul D resumed catching and snatching each other's fingers, stealing quick pats on the behind. Joyfully embarrassed to be that grown-up and that young at the same time.

Resolve, he thought. That was all it took, and no motherless gal was going to break it up. No lazy, stray pup of a woman could turn him around, make him doubt himself, wonder, plead or confess. Convinced of it, that he could do it, he threw his arm around Sethe's shoulders and squeezed. She let her head touch his chest, and since the moment was valuable to both of them, they stopped and stood that way – not breathing, not even caring if a passerby passed them by. The winter light was low. Sethe closed her eyes. Paul D looked at the black trees lining the roadside, their defending arms raised against attack. Softly, suddenly, it began to snow, like a present come down from the sky. Sethe opened her eyes to it and said, "Mercy." And it seemed to Paul D that it was – a little mercy – something given to them on purpose to mark what they were feeling so they would remember it later on when they needed to.

Down came the dry flakes, fat enough and heavy enough to crash like nickels on stone. It always surprised him, how quiet it was. Not like rain, but like a secret.

"Run!" he said.

"You run," said Sethe. "I been on my feet all day."

"Where I been? Sitting down?" and he pulled her along.

"Stop! Stop!" she said. "I don't have the legs for this."

"Then give em to me," he said and before she knew it he had backed into her, hoisted her on his back and was running down the road past brown fields turning white.

Breathless at last, he stopped and she slid back down on her own two feet, weak from laughter.

"You *need* some babies, somebody to play with in the snow." Sethe secured her headcloth.

Paul D smiled and warmed his hands with his breath. "I sure would like to give it a try. Need a willing partner though."

"I'll say," she answered. "Very, very willing."

It was nearly four o'clock now and 124 was half a mile ahead. Floating toward them, barely visible in the drifting snow, was a figure, and although it was the same figure that had been meeting Sethe for four months, so complete was the attention she and Paul D were paying to themselves they both felt a jolt when they saw her close in.

Beloved did not look at Paul D; her scrutiny was for Sethe. She had no coat, no wrap, nothing on her head, but she held in her hands a long shawl. Stretching out her arms she tried to circle it around Sethe.

"Crazy girl," said Sethe. "You the one out here with nothing on." And stepping away and in front of Paul D, Sethe took the shawl and wrapped it around Beloved's head and shoulders. Saying, "You got to learn more sense than that," she enclosed her in her left arm. Snowflakes stuck now. Paul D felt icy cold in the place Sethe had been before Beloved came. Trailing a yard or so behind the women, he fought the anger that shot through his stomach all the way home. When he saw Denver silhouetted in the lamplight at the window, he could not help thinking, "And whose ally you?"

It was Sethe who did it. Unsuspecting, surely, she solved everything with one blow.

"Now I know you not sleeping out there tonight, are you, Paul D?" She smiled at him, and like a friend in need, the chimney coughed against the rush of cold shooting into it from the sky. Window sashes shuddered in a blast of winter air.

Paul D looked up from the stew meat.

"You come upstairs. Where you belong," she said, ". . . and stay there."

The threads of malice creeping toward him from Beloved's side of the table were held harmless in the warmth of Sethe's smile.

Once before (and only once) Paul D had been grateful to

a woman. Crawling out of the woods, cross-eyed with hunger and loneliness, he knocked at the first back door he came to in the colored section of Wilmington. He told the woman who opened it that he'd appreciate doing her woodpile, if she could spare him something to eat. She looked him up and down.

"A little later on," she said and opened the door wider. She fed him pork sausage, the worst thing in the world for a starving man, but neither he nor his stomach objected. Later, when he saw pale cotton sheets and two pillows in her bedroom, he had to wipe his eyes quickly, quickly so she would not see the thankful tears of a man's first time. Soil, grass, mud, shucking, leaves, hay, cobs, seashells – all that he'd slept on. White cotton sheets had never crossed his mind. He fell in with a groan and the woman helped him pretend he was making love to her and not her bed linen. He vowed that night, full of pork, deep in luxury, that he would never leave her. She would have to kill him to get him out of that bed. Eighteen months later, when he had been purchased by Northpoint Bank and Railroad Company, he was still thankful for that introduction to sheets.

Now he was grateful a second time. He felt as though he had been plucked from the face of a cliff and put down on sure ground. In Sethe's bed he knew he could put up with two crazy girls – as long as Sethe made her wishes known. Stretched out to his full length, watching snowflakes stream past the window over his feet, it was easy to dismiss the doubts that took him to the alley behind the restaurant: his expectations for himself were high, too high. What he might call cowardice other people called common sense.

Tucked into the well of his arm, Sethe recalled Paul D's face in the street when he asked her to have a baby for him. Although she laughed and took his hand, it had frightened her. She thought quickly of how good the sex would be if that is what he wanted, but mostly she was frightened by the thought of having a baby once more. Needing to be good enough, alert enough, strong enough, *that* caring – again. Having to stay alive just that much longer. O Lord, she thought, deliver me. Unless carefree, motherlove was a killer. What did he want her pregnant for? To hold on to her? have a sign that he passed this way? He probably had children everywhere anyway. Eighteen years of roaming, he would have to have dropped a few. No. He resented the children she had, that's what. Child, she corrected herself. Child plus Beloved whom she thought of as her own, and that is what he resented. Sharing her with the girls. Hearing the three of them laughing at something he wasn't in on. The code they used among themselves that he could not break. Maybe even the time spent on their needs and not his. They were a family somehow and he was not the head of it.

Can you stitch this up for me, baby?

Um hm. Soon's I finish this petticoat. She just got the one she came here in and everybody needs a change.

Any pie left?

I think Denver got the last of it.

And not complaining, not even minding that he slept all over and around the house now, which she put a stop to this night out of courtesy.

Sethe sighed and placed her hand on his chest. She knew she was building a case against him in order to build a case against getting pregnant, and it shamed her a little. But she had all the children she needed. If her boys came back one day, and Denver and Beloved stayed on – well, it would be the way it was supposed to be, no? Right after she saw the shadows holding hands at the side of the road hadn't the picture altered? And the minute she saw the dress and shoes sitting in the front yard, she broke water. Didn't even have to see the face burning in the sunlight. She had been dreaming it for years.

Paul D's chest rose and fell, rose and fell under her hand.

DENVER FINISHED WASHING the dishes and sat down at the table. Beloved, who had not moved since Sethe and Paul D left the room, sat sucking her forefinger. Denver watched her face awhile and then said, "She likes him here."

Beloved went on probing her mouth with her finger. "Make him go away," she said.

"She might be mad at you if he leaves."

Beloved, inserting a thumb in her mouth along with the forefinger, pulled out a back tooth. There was hardly any blood, but Denver said, "Ooooh, didn't that hurt you?"

Beloved looked at the tooth and thought, This is it. Next would be her arm, her hand, a toe. Pieces of her would drop maybe one at a time, maybe all at once. Or on one of those mornings before Denver woke and after Sethe left she would fly apart. It is difficult keeping her head on her neck, her legs attached to her hips when she is by herself. Among the things she could not remember was when she first knew that she could wake up any day and find herself in pieces. She had two dreams: exploding, and being swallowed. When her tooth came out – an odd fragment, last in the row – she thought it was starting.

"Must be a wisdom," said Denver. "Don't it hurt?"

"Yes."

"Then why don't you cry?"

"What?"

"If it hurts, why don't you cry?"

And she did. Sitting there holding a small white tooth in the palm of her smooth smooth hand. Cried the way she wanted to when turtles came out of the water, one behind the other, right after the blood-red bird disappeared back into the leaves. The way she wanted to when Sethe went to him standing in the tub under the stairs. With the tip of her tongue she touched the salt water that slid to the corner of her mouth and hoped Denver's arm around her shoulders would keep them from falling apart.

The couple upstairs, united, didn't hear a sound, but below them, outside, all around 124 the snow went on and on and on. Piling itself, burying itself. Higher. Deeper.

IN THE BACK of Baby Suggs' mind may have been the thought that if Halle made it, God do what He would, it would be a cause for celebration. If only this final son could do for himself what he had done for her and for the three children John and Ella delivered to her door one summer night. When the children arrived and no Sethe, she was afraid and grateful. Grateful that the part of the family that survived was her own grandchildren – the first and only she would know: two boys and a little girl who was crawling already. But she held her heart still, afraid to form questions: What about Sethe and Halle; why the delay? Why didn't Sethe get on board too? Nobody could make it alone. Not only because trappers picked them off like buzzards or netted them like rabbits, but also because you couldn't run if you didn't know how to go. You could be lost forever, if there wasn't nobody to show you the way.

So when Sethe arrived – all mashed up and split open, but with another grandchild in her arms – the idea of a whoop moved closer to the front of her brain. But since there was still no sign of Halle and Sethe herself didn't know what had happened to him, she let the whoop lie – not wishing to hurt his chances by thanking God too soon.

It was Stamp Paid who started it. Twenty days after Sethe got to 124 he came by and looked at the baby he had tied up in his nephew's jacket, looked at the mother he had handed a piece of fried eel to and, for some private reason of his own, went off with two buckets to a place near the river's edge that only he knew about where blackberries grew, tasting so good and happy that to eat them was like being in church. Just one of the berries and you felt anointed. He walked six miles to the riverbank; did a slide-run-slide down into a ravine made almost inaccessible by brush. He reached through brambles lined with blood-drawing thorns thick as knives that cut through his shirt sleeves and trousers. All the while suffering mosquitoes, bees, hornets, wasps and the meanest lady spiders in the state. Scratched, raked and bitten, he maneuvered through and took hold of each berry with fingertips so gentle not a single one was bruised. Late in the afternoon he got back to 124 and put two full buckets down on the porch. When Baby Suggs saw his shredded clothes, bleeding hands, welted face and neck she sat down laughing out loud.

Buglar, Howard, the woman in the bonnet and Sethe came to look and then laughed along with Baby Suggs at the sight of the sly, steely old black man: agent, fisherman, boatman, tracker, savior, spy, standing in broad daylight whipped finally by two pails of blackberries. Paying them no mind he took a berry and put it in the three-week-old Denver's mouth. The women shrieked.

"She's too little for that, Stamp."

"Bowels be soup."

"Sickify her stomach."

But the baby's thrilled eyes and smacking lips made them follow suit, sampling one at a time the berries that tasted like church. Finally Baby Suggs slapped the boys' hands away from the bucket and sent Stamp around to the pump to rinse himself. She had decided to do something with the fruit worthy of the man's labor and his love. That's how it began.

She made the pastry dough and thought she ought to tell Ella and John to stop on by because three pies, maybe four, were too much to keep for one's own. Sethe thought they might as well back it up with a couple of chickens. Stamp allowed that perch and catfish were jumping into the boat – didn't even have to drop a line.

From Denver's two thrilled eyes it grew to a feast for ninety people. 124 shook with their voices far into the night. Ninety people who ate so well, and laughed so much, it made them angry. They woke up the next morning and remembered the meal-fried perch that Stamp Paid handled with a hickory twig, holding his left palm out against the spit and pop of the boiling grease; the corn pudding made with cream; tired, overfed children asleep in the grass, tiny bones of roasted rabbit still in their hands – and got angry.

Baby Suggs' three (maybe four) pies grew to ten (maybe twelve). Sethe's two hens became five turkeys. The one block of ice brought all the way from Cincinnati – over which they poured mashed watermelon mixed with sugar and mint to make a punch – became a wagonload of ice cakes for a washtub full of strawberry shrug. 124, rocking with laughter, goodwill and food for ninety, made them angry. Too much, they thought. Where does she get it all, Baby Suggs, holy? Why is she and hers always the center of things? How come she always knows exactly what to do and when? Giving advice; passing messages; healing the sick, hiding fugitives, loving, cooking, cooking, loving, preaching, singing, dancing and loving everybody like it was her job and hers alone.

Now to take two buckets of blackberries and make ten, maybe twelve, pies; to have turkey enough for the whole town pretty near, new peas in September, fresh cream but no cow, ice *and* sugar, batter bread, bread pudding, raised bread, shortbread – it made them mad. Loaves and fishes were His powers – they did not belong to an ex-slave who had probably never carried one hundred pounds to the scale, or picked okra with a baby on her back. Who had never been lashed by a ten-year-old whiteboy as God knows they had. Who had not even escaped slavery – had, in fact, been *bought out* of it by a doting son and *driven* to the Ohio River in a wagon – free papers folded between her breasts (driven by the very man who had been her master, who also paid her resettlement fee – name of Garner), and rented a house with *two* floors *and* a well from the Bodwins – the white brother and sister who gave Stamp Paid, Ella and John clothes, goods and gear for runaways because they hated slavery worse than they hated slaves.

It made them furious. They swallowed baking soda, the morning after, to calm the stomach violence caused by the bounty, the reckless generosity on display at 124. Whispered to each other in the yards about fat rats, doom and uncalled-for pride.

The scent of their disapproval lay heavy in the air. Baby Suggs woke to it and wondered what it was as she boiled hominy for her grandchildren. Later, as she stood in the garden, chopping at the tight soil over the roots of the pepper plants, she smelled it again. She lifted her head and looked around. Behind her some yards to the left Sethe squatted in the pole beans. Her shoulders were distorted by the greased flannel under her dress to encourage the healing of her back. Near her in a bushel basket was the three-week-old baby. Baby Suggs, holy, looked up. The sky was blue and clear. Not one touch of death in the definite green of the leaves. She could hear birds and, faintly, the stream way down in the meadow. The puppy, Here Boy, was burying the last bones from yesterday's party. From somewhere at the side of the house came the voices of Buglar, Howard and the crawling girl. Nothing seemed amiss – yet the smell of disapproval was sharp. Back beyond the vegetable garden, closer to the stream but in full sun, she had planted corn. Much as they'd picked for the party, there were still ears ripening, which she could see from where she stood. Baby Suggs leaned back into the peppers and the squash vines with her hoe. Carefully, with the blade at just the right angle, she cut through a stalk of insistent rue. Its flowers she stuck through a split in her hat; the rest she tossed aside. The quiet clok clok clok of wood splitting reminded her that Stamp was doing the chore he promised to the night before. She sighed at her work and, a moment later, straightened up to sniff the disapproval once again. Resting on the handle of the hoe, she concentrated. She was accustomed to the knowledge that nobody prayed for her – but this free-floating repulsion was new. It wasn't whitefolks – that much she could tell – so it must be colored ones. And then she knew. Her friends and neighbors were angry at her because she had overstepped, given too much, offended them by excess.

Baby closed her eyes. Perhaps they were right. Suddenly, behind the disapproving odor, way way back behind it, she smelled another thing. Dark and coming. Something she couldn't get at because the other odor hid it.

She squeezed her eyes tight to see what it was but all she could make out was high-topped shoes she didn't like the look of.

Thwarted yet wondering, she chopped away with the hoe. What could it be? This dark and coming thing. What was left to hurt her now? News of Halle's death? No. She had been prepared for that better than she had for his life. The last of her children, whom she barely glanced at when he was born because it wasn't worth the trouble to try to learn features you would never see change into adulthood anyway. Seven times she had done that: held a little foot; examined the fat fingertips with her own – fingers she never saw become the male or female hands a mother would recognize anywhere. She didn't know to this day what their permanent teeth looked like; or how they held their heads when they walked. Did Patty lose her lisp? What color did Famous' skin finally take? Was that a cleft in Johnny's chin or just a dimple that would disappear soon's his jawbone changed? Four girls, and the last time she saw them there was no hair under their arms. Does Ardelia still love the burned bottom of bread? All seven were gone or dead. What would be the point of looking too hard at that youngest one? But for some reason they let her keep him. He was with her – everywhere.

When she hurt her hip in Carolina she was a real bargain (costing less than Halle, who was ten then) for Mr. Garner, who took them both to Kentucky to a farm he called Sweet Home. Because of the hip she jerked like a three-legged dog when she walked. But at Sweet Home there wasn't a rice field or tobacco patch in sight, and nobody, but nobody, knocked her down. Not once. Lillian Garner called her Jenny for some reason but she never pushed, hit or called her mean names. Even when she slipped in cow dung and broke every egg in her apron, nobody said you-black-bitch-what's-the-matter-with-you and nobody knocked her down.

Sweet Home was tiny compared to the places she had been. Mr. Garner, Mrs. Garner, herself, Halle, and four boys, over half named Paul, made up the entire population. Mrs. Garner hummed when she worked; Mr. Garner acted like the world was a toy he was supposed to have fun with. Neither wanted her in the field – Mr. Garner's boys, including Halle, did all of that – which was a blessing since she could not have managed it anyway. What she did was stand beside the humming Lillian Garner while the two of them cooked, preserved, washed, ironed, made candles, clothes, soap and cider; fed chickens, pigs, dogs and geese; milked cows, churned butter, rendered fat, laid fires . . . Nothing to it. And nobody knocked her down.

Her hip hurt every single day – but she never spoke of it. Only Halle, who had watched her movements closely for the last four years, knew that to get in and out of bed she had to lift her thigh with both hands, which was why he spoke to Mr. Garner about buying her out of there so she could sit down for a change. Sweet boy. The one person who did something hard for her: gave her his work, his life and now his children, whose voices she could just make out as she stood in the garden wondering what was the dark and coming thing behind the scent of disapproval. Sweet Home was a marked improvement. No question. And no matter, for the sadness was at her center, the desolated center where the self that was no self made its home. Sad as it was that she did not know where her children were buried or what they looked like if alive, fact was she knew more about them than she knew about herself, having never had the map to discover what she was like.

Could she sing? (Was it nice to hear when she did?) Was she pretty? Was she a good friend? Could she have been a loving mother? A faithful wife? Have I got a sister and does she favor me? If my mother knew me would she like me?

In Lillian Garner's house, exempted from the field work that broke her hip and the exhaustion that drugged her mind; in Lillian Garner's house where nobody knocked her down (or up), she listened to the whitewoman humming at her work; watched her face light up when Mr. Garner came in and thought, It's better here, but I'm not. The Garners, it seemed to her, ran a special kind of slavery, treating them like paid labor, listening to what they said, teaching what they wanted known. And he didn't stud his boys. Never brought them to her cabin with directions to "lay down with her," like they did in Carolina, or rented their sex out on other farms. It surprised and pleased her, but worried her too. Would he pick women for them or what did he think was going to happen when those boys ran smack into their nature? Some danger he was courting and he surely knew it. In fact, his order for them not to leave Sweet Home, except in his company, was not so much because of the law, but the danger of men-bred slaves on the loose.

Baby Suggs talked as little as she could get away with because what was there to say that the roots of her tongue could manage? So the whitewoman, finding her new slave excellent if silent help, hummed to herself while she worked.

When Mr. Garner agreed to the arrangements with Halle, and when Halle looked like it meant more to him that she go free than anything in the world, she let herself be taken 'cross the river. Of the two hard things – standing on her feet till she dropped or leaving her last and probably only living child – she chose the hard thing that made him happy, and never put to him the question she put to herself: What for? What does a sixty-odd-year-old slavewoman who walks like a three-legged dog need freedom for? And when she stepped foot on free ground she could not believe that Halle knew what she didn't; that Halle, who had never drawn one free breath, knew that there was nothing like it in this world. It scared her.

Something's the matter. What's the matter? What's the matter? she asked herself. She didn't know what she looked like and was not curious. But suddenly she saw her hands and thought with a clarity as simple as it was dazzling, "These hands belong to me. These *my* hands." Next she felt a knocking in her chest and discovered something else new: her own heartbeat. Had it been there all along? This pounding thing? She felt like a fool and began to laugh out loud. Mr. Garner looked over his shoulder at her with wide brown eyes and smiled himself. "What's funny, Jenny?"

She couldn't stop laughing. "My heart's beating," she said.

And it was true.

Mr. Garner laughed. "Nothing to be scared of, Jenny. Just keep your same ways, you'll be all right."

She covered her mouth to keep from laughing too loud.

"These people I'm taking you to will give you what help you need. Name of Bodwin. A brother and a sister. Scots. I been knowing them for twenty years or more."

Baby Suggs thought it was a good time to ask him something she had long wanted to know.

"Mr. Garner," she said, "why you all call me Jenny?"

" 'Cause that what's on your sales ticket, gal. Ain't that your name? What you call yourself?"

"Nothing," she said. "I don't call myself nothing."

Mr. Garner went red with laughter. "When I took you out of Carolina, Whitlow called you Jenny and Jenny Whitlow is what his bill said. Didn't he call you Jenny?"

"No, sir. If he did I didn't hear it."

"What did you answer to?"

"Anything, but Suggs is what my husband name."

"You got married, Jenny? I didn't know it."

"Manner of speaking."

"You know where he is, this husband?"

"No, sir."

"Is that Halle's daddy?"

"No, sir."

"Why you call him Suggs, then? His bill of sale says Whitlow too, just like yours."

"Suggs is my name, sir. From my husband. He didn't call me Jenny."

"What he call you?"

"Baby."

"Well," said Mr. Garner, going pink again, "if I was you I'd stick to Jenny Whitlow. Mrs. Baby Suggs ain't no name for a freed Negro."

Maybe not, she thought, but Baby Suggs was all she had left of the "husband" she claimed. A serious, melancholy man who taught her how to make shoes. The two of them made a pact: whichever one got a chance to run would take it; together if possible, alone if not, and no looking back. He got his chance, and since she never heard otherwise she believed he made it. Now how could he find or hear tell of her if she was calling herself some bill-of-sale name?

She couldn't get over the city. More people than Carolina and enough whitefolks to stop the breath. Two-story buildings everywhere, and walkways made of perfectly cut slats of wood. Roads wide as Garner's whole house.

"This is a city of water," said Mr. Garner. "Everything travels by water and what the rivers can't carry the canals take. A queen of a city, Jenny. Everything you ever dreamed of, they make it right here. Iron stoves, buttons, ships, shirts, hairbrushes, paint, steam engines, books. A sewer system make your eyes bug out. Oh, this is a city, all right. If you have to live in a city – this is it."

The Bodwins lived right in the center of a street full of houses and trees. Mr. Garner leaped out and tied his horse to a solid iron post.

"Here we are."

Baby picked up her bundle and with great difficulty, caused by her hip and the hours of sitting in a wagon, climbed down. Mr. Garner was up the walk and on the porch before she touched ground, but she got a peep at a Negro girl's face at the open door before she followed a path to the back of the house. She waited what seemed a long time before this same girl opened the kitchen door and offered her a seat by the window.

"Can I get you anything to eat, ma'am?" the girl asked.

"No, darling. I'd look favorable on some water though." The girl went to the sink and pumped a cupful of water. She placed it in Baby Suggs' hand. "I'm Janey, ma'am."

Baby, marveling at the sink, drank every drop of water although it tasted like a serious medicine. "Suggs," she said, blotting her lips with the back of her hand. "Baby Suggs."

"Glad to meet you, Mrs. Suggs. You going to be staying here?"

"I don't know where I'll be. Mr. Garner – that's him what brought me here – he say he arrange something for me." And then, "I'm free, you know."

Janey smiled. "Yes, ma'am."

"Your people live around here?"

"Yes, ma'am. All us live out on Bluestone."

"We scattered," said Baby Suggs, "but maybe not for long."

Great God, she thought, where do I start? Get somebody to write old Whitlow. See who took Patty and Rosa Lee. Somebody name Dunn got Ardelia and went West, she heard. No point in trying for Tyree or John. They cut thirty years ago and, if she searched too hard and they were hiding, finding them would do them more harm than good. Nancy and Famous died in a ship off the Virginia coast before it set sail for Savannah. That much she knew. The overseer at Whitlow's place brought her the news, more from a wish to have his way with her than from the kindness of his heart. The captain waited three weeks in port, to get a full cargo before setting off. Of the slaves in the hold who didn't make it, he said, two were Whitlow pickaninnies name of . . .

But she knew their names. She knew, and covered her ears with her fists to keep from hearing them come from his mouth.

Janey heated some milk and poured it in a bowl next to a plate of cornbread. After some coaxing, Baby Suggs came to the table and sat down. She crumbled the bread into the hot milk and discovered she was hungrier than she had ever been in her life and that was saying something.

"They going to miss this?"

"No," said Janey. "Eat all you want; it's ours."

"Anybody else live here?"

"Just me. Mr. Woodruff, he does the outside chores. He comes by two, three days a week."

"Just you two?"

"Yes, ma'am. I do the cooking and washing."

"Maybe your people know of somebody looking for help."

"I be sure to ask, but I know they take women at the slaughterhouse."

"Doing what?"

"I don't know."

"Something men don't want to do, I reckon."

"My cousin say you get all the meat you want, plus twenty-five cents the hour. She make summer sausage."

Baby Suggs lifted her hand to the top of her head. Money? Money? They would pay her money every single day? Money?

"Where is this here slaughterhouse?" she asked.

Before Janey could answer, the Bodwins came in to the kitchen with a grinning Mr. Garner behind. Undeniably brother and sister, both dressed in gray with faces too young for their snow-white hair.

"Did you give her anything to eat, Janey?" asked the brother.

"Yes, sir."

"Keep your seat, Jenny," said the sister, and that good news got better.

When they asked what work she could do, instead of reeling off the hundreds of tasks she had performed, she asked about the slaughterhouse. She was too old for that, they said.

"She's the best cobbler you ever see," said Mr. Garner.

"Cobbler?" Sister Bodwin raised her black thick eyebrows. "Who taught you that?"

"Was a slave taught me," said Baby Suggs.

"New boots, or just repair?"

"New, old, anything."

"Well," said Brother Bodwin, "that'll be something, but you'll need more."

"What about taking in wash?" asked Sister Bodwin.

"Yes, ma'am."

"Two cents a pound."

"Yes, ma'am. But where's the in?"

"What?"

"You said 'take in wash.' Where is the 'in'? Where I'm going to be."

"Oh, just listen to this, Jenny," said Mr. Garner. "These two angels got a house for you. Place they own out a ways."

It had belonged to their grandparents before they moved in town. Recently it had been rented out to a whole parcel of Negroes, who had left the state. It was too big a house for Jenny alone, they said (two rooms upstairs, two down), but it was the best and the only thing they could do. In return for laundry, some seamstress work, a little canning and so on (oh shoes, too), they would permit her to stay there. Provided she was clean. The past parcel of colored wasn't. Baby Suggs agreed to the situation, sorry to see the money go but excited about a house with steps – never mind she couldn't climb them. Mr. Garner told the Bodwins that she was a right fine cook as well as a fine cobbler and showed his belly and the sample on his feet. Everybody laughed.

"Anything you need, let us know," said the sister. "We don't hold with slavery, even Garner's kind."

"Tell em, Jenny. You live any better on any place before mine?"

"No, sir," she said. "No place."

"How long was you at Sweet Home?"

"Ten year, I believe."

"Ever go hungry?"

"No, sir."

"Cold?"

"No, sir."

"Anybody lay a hand on you?"

"No, sir."

"Did I let Halle buy you or not?"

"Yes, sir, you did," she said, thinking, But you got my boy and I'm all broke down. You be renting him out to pay for me way after I'm gone to Glory.

Woodruff, they said, would carry her out there, they said, and all three disappeared through the kitchen door.

"I have to fix the supper now," said Janey.

"I'll help," said Baby Suggs. "You too short to reach the fire."

It was dark when Woodruff clicked the horse into a trot. He was a young man with a heavy beard and a burned place on his jaw the beard did not hide.

"You born up here?" Baby Suggs asked him.

"No, ma'am. Virginia. Been here a couple years."

"I see."

"You going to a nice house. Big too. A preacher and his family was in there. Eighteen children."

"Have mercy. Where they go?"

"Took off to Illinois. Bishop Allen gave him a congregation up there. Big."

"What churches around here? I ain't set foot in one in ten years."

"How come?"

"Wasn't none. I dislike the place I was before this last one, but I did get to church every Sunday some kind of way. I bet the Lord done forgot who I am by now."

"Go see Reverend Pike, ma'am. He'll reacquaint you."

"I won't need him for that. I can make my own acquaintance. What I need him for is to reacquaint me with my children. He can read and write, I reckon?"

"Sure."

"Good, 'cause I got a lot of digging up to do." But the news they dug up was so pitiful she quit. After two years of messages written by the preacher's hand, two years of washing, sewing, canning, cobbling, gardening, and sitting in churches, all she found out was that the Whitlow place was gone and that you couldn't write to "a man named Dunn" if all you knew was that he went West. The good news, however, was that Halle got married and had a baby coming. She fixed on that and her own brand of preaching, having made up her mind about what to do with the heart that started beating the minute she crossed the Ohio River. And it worked out, worked out just fine, until she got proud and let herself be overwhelmed by the sight of her daughter-in-law and Halle's children – one of whom was born on the way – and have a celebration of blackberries that put Christmas to shame. Now she stood in the garden smelling disapproval, feeling a dark and coming thing, and seeing high-topped shoes that she didn't like the look of at all. At all.

WHEN THE FOUR horsemen came – schoolteacher, one nephew, one slave catcher and a sheriff – the house on Bluestone Road was so quiet they thought they were too late. Three of them dismounted, one stayed in the saddle, his rifle ready, his eyes trained away from the house to the left and to the right, because likely as not the fugitive would make a dash for it. Although sometimes, you could never tell, you'd find them folded up tight somewhere: beneath floorboards, in a pantry – once in a chimney. Even then care was taken, because the quietest ones, the ones you pulled from a press, a hayloft, or, that once, from a chimney, would go along nicely for two or three seconds. Caught red-handed, so to speak, they would seem to recognize the futility of outsmarting a whiteman and the hopelessness of outrunning a rifle. Smile even, like a child caught dead with his hand in the jelly jar, and when you reached for the rope to tie him, well, even then you couldn't tell. The very nigger with his head hanging and a little jelly-jar smile on his face could all of a sudden roar, like a bull or some such, and commence to do disbelievable things. Grab the rifle at its mouth; throw himself at the one holding it – anything. So you had to keep back a pace, leave the tying to another. Otherwise you ended up killing what you were paid to bring back alive. Unlike a snake or a bear, a dead nigger could not be skinned for profit and was not worth his own dead weight in coin.

Six or seven Negroes were walking up the road toward the house: two boys from the slave catcher's left and some women from his right. He motioned them still with his rifle

and they stood where they were. The nephew came back
from peeping inside the house, and after touching his lips
for silence, pointed his thumb to say that what they were
looking for was round back. The slave catcher dismounted
then and joined the others. Schoolteacher and the nephew
moved to the left of the house; himself and the sheriff to the
right. A crazy old nigger was standing in the woodpile with
an ax. You could tell he was crazy right off because he was
grunting – making low, cat noises like. About twelve yards
beyond that nigger was another one – a woman with a flower
in her hat. Crazy too, probably, because she too was standing
stock-still – but fanning her hands as though pushing cobwebs out of her way. Both, however, were staring at the
same place – a shed. Nephew walked over to the old nigger
boy and took the ax from him. Then all four started toward
the shed.

Inside, two boys bled in the sawdust and dirt at the feet of
a nigger woman holding a blood-soaked child to her chest
with one hand and an infant by the heels in the other. She
did not look at them; she simply swung the baby toward the
wall planks, missed and tried to connect a second time, when
out of nowhere – in the ticking time the men spent staring
at what there was to stare at – the old nigger boy, still mewing,
ran through the door behind them and snatched the baby
from the arc of its mother's swing.

Right off it was clear, to schoolteacher especially, that
there was nothing there to claim. The three (now four –
because she'd had the one coming when she cut) pickaninnies they had hoped were alive and well enough to take
back to Kentucky, take back and raise properly to do the
work Sweet Home desperately needed, were not. Two were
lying open-eyed in sawdust; a third pumped blood down
the dress of the main one – the woman schoolteacher
bragged about, the one he said made fine ink, damn good
soup, pressed his collars the way he liked besides having at

least ten breeding years left. But now she'd gone wild, due to the mishandling of the nephew who'd overbeat her and made her cut and run. Schoolteacher had chastised that nephew, telling him to think – just think – what would his own horse do if you beat it beyond the point of education. Or Chipper, or Samson. Suppose you beat the hounds past that point thataway. Never again could you trust them in the woods or anywhere else. You'd be feeding them maybe, holding out a piece of rabbit in your hand, and the animal would revert – bite your hand clean off. So he punished that nephew by not letting him come on the hunt. Made him stay there, feed stock, feed himself, feed Lillian, tend crops. See how he liked it; see what happened when you overbeat creatures God had given you the responsibility of – the trouble it was, and the loss. The whole lot was lost now. Five. He could claim the baby struggling in the arms of the mewing old man, but who'd tend her? Because the woman – something was wrong with her. She was looking at him now, and if his other nephew could see that look he would learn the lesson for sure: you just can't mishandle creatures and expect success.

The nephew, the one who had nursed her while his brother held her down, didn't know he was shaking. His uncle had warned him against that kind of confusion, but the warning didn't seem to be taking. What she go and do that for? On account of a beating? Hell, he'd been beat a million times and he was white. Once it hurt so bad and made him so mad he'd smashed the well bucket. Another time he took it out on Samson – a few tossed rocks was all. But no beating ever made him . . . I mean no way he could have . . . What she go and do that for? And that is what he asked the sheriff, who was standing there amazed like the rest of them, but not shaking. He was swallowing hard, over and over again. "What she want to go and do that for?"

The sheriff turned, then said to the other three, "You all

better go on. Look like your business is over. Mine's started now."

Schoolteacher beat his hat against his thigh and spit before leaving the woodshed. Nephew and the catcher backed out with him. They didn't look at the woman in the pepper plants with the flower in her hat. And they didn't look at the seven or so faces that had edged closer in spite of the catcher's rifle warning. Enough nigger eyes for now. Little nigger-boy eyes open in sawdust; little nigger-girl eyes staring between the wet fingers that held her face so her head wouldn't fall off; little nigger-baby eyes crinkling up to cry in the arms of the old nigger whose own eyes were nothing but slivers looking down at his feet. But the worst ones were those of the nigger woman who looked like she didn't have any. Since the whites in them had disappeared and since they were as black as her skin, she looked blind.

They unhitched from schoolteacher's horse the borrowed mule that was to carry the fugitive woman back to where she belonged, and tied it to the fence. Then, with the sun straight up over their heads, they trotted off, leaving the sheriff behind among the damnedest bunch of coons they'd ever seen. All testimony to the results of a little so-called freedom imposed on people who needed every care and guidance in the world to keep them from the cannibal life they preferred.

The sheriff wanted to back out too. To stand in the sunlight outside of that place meant for housing wood, coal, kerosene – fuel for cold Ohio winters, which he thought of now, while resisting the urge to run into the August sunlight. Not because he was afraid. Not at all. He was just cold. And he didn't want to touch anything. The baby in the old man's arms was crying, and the woman's eyes with no whites were gazing straight ahead. They all might have remained that way, frozen till Thursday, except one of the boys on the floor sighed. As if he were sunk in the pleasure of a deep sweet sleep, he sighed the sigh that flung the sheriff into action.

"I'll have to take you in. No trouble now. You've done enough to last you. Come on now."

She did not move.

"You come quiet, hear, and I won't have to tie you up."

She stayed still and he had made up his mind to go near her and some kind of way bind her wet red hands when a shadow behind him in the doorway made him turn. The nigger with the flower in her hat entered.

Baby Suggs noticed who breathed and who did not and went straight to the boys lying in the dirt. The old man moved to the woman gazing and said, "Sethe. You take my armload and gimme yours."

She turned to him, and glancing at the baby he was holding, made a low sound in her throat as though she'd made a mistake, left the salt out of the bread or something.

"I'm going out here and send for a wagon," the sheriff said and got into the sunlight at last.

But neither Stamp Paid nor Baby Suggs could make her put her crawling-already? girl down. Out of the shed, back in the house, she held on. Baby Suggs had got the boys inside and was bathing their heads, rubbing their hands, lifting their lids, whispering, "Beg your pardon, I beg your pardon," the whole time. She bound their wounds and made them breathe camphor before turning her attention to Sethe. She took the crying baby from Stamp Paid and carried it on her shoulder for a full two minutes, then stood in front of its mother.

"It's time to nurse your youngest," she said.

Sethe reached up for the baby without letting the dead one go.

Baby Suggs shook her head. "One at a time," she said and traded the living for the dead, which she carried into the keeping room. When she came back, Sethe was aiming a bloody nipple into the baby's mouth. Baby Suggs slammed her fist on the table and shouted, "Clean up! Clean your-self up!"

They fought then. Like rivals over the heart of the loved, they fought. Each struggling for the nursing child. Baby Suggs lost when she slipped in a red puddle and fell. So Denver took her mother's milk right along with the blood of her sister. And that's the way they were when the sheriff returned, having commandeered a neighbor's cart, and ordered Stamp to drive it.

Outside a throng, now, of black faces stopped murmuring. Holding the living child, Sethe walked past them in their silence and hers. She climbed into the cart, her profile knife-clean against a cheery blue sky. A profile that shocked them with its clarity. Was her head a bit too high? Her back a little too straight? Probably. Otherwise the singing would have begun at once, the moment she appeared in the doorway of the house on Bluestone Road. Some cape of sound would have quickly been wrapped around her, like arms to hold and steady her on the way. As it was, they waited till the cart turned about, headed west to town. And then no words. Humming. No words at all.

Baby Suggs meant to run, skip down the porch steps after the cart, screaming, No. No. Don't let her take that last one too. She meant to. Had started to, but when she got up from the floor and reached the yard the cart was gone and a wagon was rolling up. A red-haired boy and a yellow-haired girl jumped down and ran through the crowd toward her. The boy had a half-eaten sweet pepper in one hand and a pair of shoes in the other.

"Mama says Wednesday." He held them together by their tongues. "She says you got to have these fixed by Wednesday."

Baby Suggs looked at him, and then at the woman holding a twitching lead horse to the road.

"She says Wednesday, you hear? Baby? Baby?"

She took the shoes from him – high-topped and muddy – saying, "I beg your pardon. Lord, I beg your pardon. I sure do."

Out of sight, the cart creaked on down Bluestone Road. Nobody in it spoke. The wagon rock had put the baby to sleep. The hot sun dried Sethe's dress, stiff, like rigor mortis.

THAT AIN'T HER MOUTH.

Anybody who didn't know her, or maybe somebody who just got a glimpse of her through the peephole at the restaurant, might think it was hers, but Paul D knew better. Oh well, a little something around the forehead – a quietness – that kind of reminded you of her. But there was no way you could take that for her mouth and he said so. Told Stamp Paid, who was watching him carefully.

"I don't know, man. Don't look like it to me. I know Sethe's mouth and this ain't it." He smoothed the clipping with his fingers and peered at it, not at all disturbed. From the solemn air with which Stamp had unfolded the paper, the tenderness in the old man's fingers as he stroked its creases and flattened it out, first on his knees, then on the split top of the piling, Paul D knew that it ought to mess him up. That whatever was written on it should shake him.

Pigs were crying in the chute. All day Paul D, Stamp Paid and twenty more had pushed and prodded them from canal to shore to chute to slaughterhouse. Although, as grain farmers moved west, St. Louis and Chicago now ate up a lot of the business, Cincinnati was still pig port in the minds of Ohioans. Its main job was to receive, slaughter and ship up the river the hogs that Northerners did not want to live without. For a month or so in the winter any stray man had work, if he could breathe the stench of offal and stand up for twelve hours, skills in which Paul D was admirably trained.

A little pig shit, rinsed from every place he could touch, remained on his boots, and he was conscious of it as he stood there with a light smile of scorn curling his lips. Usually he left his boots in the shed and put his walking shoes on along with his day clothes in the corner before he went home. A route that took him smack dab through the middle of a cemetery as old as sky, rife with the agitation of dead Miami no longer content to rest in the mounds that covered them. Over their heads walked a strange people; through their earth pillows roads were cut; wells and houses nudged them out of eternal rest. Outraged more by their folly in believing land was holy than by the disturbances of their peace, they growled on the banks of Licking River, sighed in the trees on Catherine Street and rode the wind above the pig yards. Paul D heard them but he stayed on because all in all it wasn't a bad job, especially in winter when Cincinnati reassumed its status of slaughter and riverboat capital. The craving for pork was growing into a mania in every city in the country. Pig farmers were cashing in, provided they could raise enough and get them sold farther and farther away. And the Germans who flooded southern Ohio brought and developed swine cooking to its highest form. Pig boats jammed the Ohio River, and their captains' hollering at one another over the grunts of the stock was as common a water sound as that of the ducks flying over their heads. Sheep, cows and fowl too floated up and down that river, and all a Negro had to do was show up and there was work: poking, killing, cutting, skinning, case packing and saving offal.

A hundred yards from the crying pigs, the two men stood behind a shed on Western Row and it was clear why Stamp had been eyeing Paul D this last week of work; why he paused when the evening shift came on, to let Paul D's movements catch up to his own. He had made up his mind to show him this piece of paper – newspaper – with a picture drawing of a woman who favored Sethe except that was not her mouth. Nothing like it.

Paul D slid the clipping out from under Stamp's palm. The

print meant nothing to him so he didn't even glance at it. He simply looked at the face, shaking his head no. No. At the mouth, you see. And no at whatever it was those black scratches said, and no to whatever it was Stamp Paid wanted him to know. Because there was no way in hell a black face could appear in a newspaper if the story was about something anybody wanted to hear. A whip of fear broke through the heart chambers as soon as you saw a Negro's face in a paper, since the face was not there because the person had a healthy baby, or outran a street mob. Nor was it there because the person had been killed, or maimed or caught or burned or jailed or whipped or evicted or stomped or raped or cheated, since that could hardly qualify as news in a newspaper. It would have to be something out of the ordinary – something whitepeople would find interesting, truly different, worth a few minutes of teeth sucking if not gasps. And it must have been hard to find news about Negroes worth the breath catch of a white citizen of Cincinnati.

So who was this woman with a mouth that was not Sethe's, but whose eyes were almost as calm as hers? Whose head was turned on her neck in the manner he loved so well it watered his eye to see it.

And he said so. "This ain't her mouth. I know her mouth and this ain't it." Before Stamp Paid could speak he said it and even while he spoke Paul D said it again. Oh, he heard all the old man was saying, but the more he heard, the stranger the lips in the drawing became.

Stamp started with the party, the one Baby Suggs gave, but stopped and backed up a bit to tell about the berries – where they were and what was in the earth that made them grow like that.

"They open to the sun, but not the birds, 'cause snakes down in there and the birds know it, so they just grow – fat and sweet – with nobody to bother em 'cept me because don't nobody go in that piece of water but me and ain't too many legs willing to glide down that bank to get them. Me neither. But I was willing that day. Somehow or 'nother I was willing. And they whipped me, I'm telling you. Tore me up. But I filled two buckets anyhow. And took em over to Baby Suggs' house. It was on from then on. Such a cooking you never see no more. We baked, fried and stewed everything God put down here. Everybody came. Everybody stuffed. Cooked so much there wasn't a stick of kindlin left for the next day. I volunteered to do it. And next morning I come over, like I promised, to do it."

"But this ain't her mouth," Paul D said. "This ain't it at all."

Stamp Paid looked at him. He was going to tell him about how restless Baby Suggs was that morning, how she had a listening way about her; how she kept looking down past the corn to the stream so much he looked too. In between ax swings, he watched where Baby was watching. Which is why they both missed it: they were looking the wrong way – toward water – and all the while it was coming down the road. Four. Riding close together, bunched-up like, and righteous. He was going to tell him that, because he thought it was important: why he and Baby Suggs both missed it. And about the party too, because that explained why nobody ran on ahead; why nobody sent a fleet-footed son to cut 'cross a field soon as they saw the four horses in town hitched for watering while the riders asked questions. Not Ella, not John, not anybody ran down or to Bluestone Road, to say some new whitefolks with the Look just rode in. The right-eous Look every Negro learned to recognize along with his ma'am's tit. Like a flag hoisted, this righteousness telegraphed and announced the faggot, the whip, the fist, the lie, long before it went public. Nobody warned them, and he'd always believed it wasn't the exhaustion from a long day's gorging that dulled them, but some other thing – like, well, like meanness – that let them stand aside, or not pay attention, or tell themselves somebody else was probably bearing the news already to the house on Bluestone Road where a pretty woman had been living for almost a month. Young and deft with four children, one of which she delivered herself the day before she got there and who now had the full benefit of Baby Suggs' bounty and her big old heart. Maybe they just wanted to know if Baby really was special, blessed in some way they were not. He was going to tell him that, but Paul D was laughing, saying, "Uh uh. No way. A little semblance round the forehead maybe, but this ain't her mouth."

So Stamp Paid did not tell him how she flew, snatching up her children like a hawk on the wing; how her face beaked, how her hands worked like claws, how she collected them every which way: one on her shoulder, one under her arm, one by the hand, the other shouted forward into the woodshed filled with just sunlight and shavings now because there wasn't any wood. The party had used it all, which is why he was chopping some. Nothing was in that shed, he knew, having been there early that morning. Nothing but sunlight. Sunlight, shavings, a shovel. The ax he himself took out. Nothing else was in there except the shovel – and of course the saw.

"You forgetting I knew her before," Paul D was saying. "Back in Kentucky. When she was a girl. I didn't just make her acquaintance a few months ago. I been knowing her a long time. And I can tell you for sure: this ain't her mouth. May look like it, but it ain't."

So Stamp Paid didn't say it all. Instead he took a breath and leaned toward the mouth that was not hers and slowly read out the words Paul D couldn't. And when he finished, Paul D said with a vigor fresher than the first time, "I'm sorry, Stamp. It's a mistake somewhere 'cause that ain't her mouth."

Stamp looked into Paul D's eyes and the sweet conviction

in them almost made him wonder if it had happened at all, eighteen years ago, that while he and Baby Suggs were looking the wrong way, a pretty little slavegirl had recognized a hat, and split to the woodshed to kill her children.

"SHE WAS CRAWLING already when I got here. One week, less, and the baby who was sitting up and turning over when I put her on the wagon was crawling already. Devil of a time keeping her off the stairs. Nowadays babies get up and walk soon's you drop em, but twenty years ago when I was a girl, babies stayed babies longer. Howard didn't pick up his own head till he was nine months. Baby Suggs said it was the food, you know. If you ain't got nothing but milk to give em, well they don't do things so quick. Milk was all I ever had. I thought teeth meant they was ready to chew. Wasn't nobody to ask. Mrs. Garner never had no children and we was the only women there."

She was spinning. Round and round the room. Past the jelly cupboard, past the window, past the front door, another window, the sideboard, the keeping-room door, the dry sink, the stove – back to the jelly cupboard. Paul D sat at the table watching her drift into view then disappear behind his back, turning like a slow but steady wheel. Sometimes she crossed her hands behind her back. Other times she held her ears, covered her mouth or folded her arms across her breasts. Once in a while she rubbed her hips as she turned, but the wheel never stopped.

"Remember Aunt Phyllis? From out by Minnowville? Mr. Garner sent one a you all to get her for each and every one of my babies. That'd be the only time I saw her. Many's the time I wanted to get over to where she was. Just to talk. My plan was to ask Mrs. Garner to let me off at Minnowville whilst she went to meeting. Pick me up on her way back.

I believe she would a done that if I was to ask her. I never did, 'cause that's the only day Halle and me had with sunlight in it for the both of us to see each other by. So there wasn't nobody. To talk to, I mean, who'd know when it was time to chew up a little something and give it to em. Is that what make the teeth come on out, or should you wait till the teeth came and then solid food? Well, I know now, because Baby Suggs fed her right, and a week later, when I got here, she was crawling already. No stopping her either. She loved those steps so much we painted them so she could see her way to the top."

Sethe smiled then, at the memory of it. The smile broke in two and became a sudden suck of air, but she did not shudder or close her eyes. She wheeled.

"I wish I'd a known more, but, like I say, there wasn't nobody to talk to. Woman, I mean. So I tried to recollect what I'd seen back where I was before Sweet Home. How the women did there. Oh they knew all about it. How to make that thing you use to hang the babies in the trees – so you could see them out of harm's way while you worked the fields. Was a leaf thing too they gave em to chew on. Mint, I believe, or sassafras. Comfrey, maybe. I still don't know how they constructed that basket thing, but I didn't need it anyway, because all my work was in the barn and the house, but I forgot what the leaf was. I could have used that. I tied Buglar when we had all that pork to smoke. Fire everywhere and he was getting into everything. I liked to lost him so many times. Once he got up on the well, right on it. I flew. Snatched him just in time. So when I knew we'd be rendering and smoking and I couldn't see after him, well, I got a rope and tied it round his ankle. Just long enough to play round a little, but not long enough to reach the well or the fire. I didn't like the look of it, but I didn't know what else to do. It's hard, you know what I mean? by yourself and no woman to help you get through. Halle was good, but he was debt-working all over the place. And when he did get down to a little sleep, I didn't want to be bothering him with all that. Sixo was the biggest help. I don't 'spect you rememory this, but Howard got in the milk parlor and Red Cora I believe it was mashed his hand. Turned his thumb backwards. When I got to him, she was getting ready to bite it. I don't know to this day how I got him out. Sixo heard him screaming and come running. Know what he did? Turned the thumb right back and tied it cross his palm to his little finger. See, I never would have thought of that. Never. Taught me a lot, Sixo."

It made him dizzy. At first he thought it was her spinning. Circling him the way she was circling the subject. Round and round, never changing direction, which might have helped his head. Then he thought, No, it's the sound of her voice; it's too near. Each turn she made was at least three yards from where he sat, but listening to her was like having a child whisper into your ear so close you could feel its lips form the words you couldn't make out because they were too close. He caught only pieces of what she said – which was fine, because she hadn't gotten to the main part – the answer to the question he had not asked outright, but which lay in the clipping he showed her. And lay in the smile as well. Because he smiled too, when he showed it to her, so when she burst out laughing at the joke – the mix-up of her face put where some other coloredwoman's ought to be – well, he'd be ready to laugh right along with her. "Can you beat it?" he would ask. And "Stamp done lost his mind," she would giggle. "Plumb lost it."

But his smile never got a chance to grow. It hung there, small and alone, while she examined the clipping and then handed it back.

Perhaps it was the smile, or maybe the ever-ready love she saw in his eyes – easy and upfront, the way colts, evangelists and children look at you: with love you don't have to deserve

– that made her go ahead and tell him what she had not told Baby Suggs, the only person she felt obliged to explain anything to. Otherwise she would have said what the newspaper said she said and no more. Sethe could recognize only seventy-five printed words (half of which appeared in the newspaper clipping), but she knew that the words she did not understand hadn't any more power than she had to explain. It was the smile and the upfront love that made her try.

"I don't have to tell you about Sweet Home – what it was – but maybe you don't know what it was like for me to get away from there."

Covering the lower half of her face with her palms, she paused to consider again the size of the miracle; its flavor.

"I did it. I got us all out. Without Halle too. Up till then it was the only thing I ever did on my own. Decided. And it came off right, like it was supposed to. We was here. Each and every one of my babies and me too. I birthed them and I got em out and it wasn't no accident. I did that. I had help, of course, lots of that, but still it was me doing it; me saying, *Go on*, and *Now*. Me having to look out. Me using my own head. But it was more than that. It was a kind of selfishness I never knew nothing about before. It felt good. Good and right. I was big, Paul D, and deep and wide and when I stretched out my arms all my children could get in between. I was *that* wide. Look like I loved em more after I got here. Or maybe I couldn't love em proper in Kentucky because they wasn't mine to love. But when I got here, when I jumped down off that wagon – there wasn't nobody in the world I couldn't love if I wanted to. You know what I mean?"

Paul D did not answer because she didn't expect or want him to, but he did know what she meant. Listening to the doves in Alfred, Georgia, and having neither the right nor the permission to enjoy it because in that place mist, doves, sunlight, copper dirt, moon – everything belonged to the men who had the guns. Little men, some of them, big men too, each one of whom he could snap like a twig if he wanted to. Men who knew their manhood lay in their guns and were not even embarrassed by the knowledge that without gunshot fox would laugh at them. And these "men" who made even vixen laugh could, if you let them, stop you from hearing doves or loving moonlight. So you protected yourself and loved small. Picked the tiniest stars out of the sky to own; lay down with head twisted in order to see the loved one over the rim of the trench before you slept. Stole shy glances at her between the trees at chain-up. Grass blades, sala-manders, spiders, woodpeckers, beetles, a kingdom of ants. Anything bigger wouldn't do. A woman, a child, a brother – a big love like that would split you wide open in Alfred, Georgia. He knew exactly what she meant: to get to a place where you could love anything you chose – not to need permission for desire – well now, *that* was freedom.

Circling, circling, now she was gnawing something else instead of getting to the point.

"There was this piece of goods Mrs. Garner gave me. Calico. Stripes it had with little flowers in between. 'Bout a yard – not enough for more 'n a head tie. But I been wanting to make a shift for my girl with it. Had the prettiest colors. I don't even know what you call that color: a rose but with yellow in it. For the longest time I been meaning to make it for her and do you know like a fool I left it behind? No more than a yard, and I kept putting it off because I was tired or didn't have the time. So when I got here, even before they let me get out of bed, I stitched her a little something from a piece of cloth Baby Suggs had. Well, all I'm saying is that's a selfish pleasure I never had before. I couldn't let all that go back to where it was, and I couldn't let her nor any of em live under schoolteacher. That was out."

Sethe knew that the circle she was making around the room, him, the subject, would remain one. That she could never close in, pin it down for anybody who had to ask. If they didn't get it right off – she could never explain. Because the truth was simple, not a long-drawn-out record of flowered shifts, tree cages, selfishness, ankle ropes and wells. Simple: she was squatting in the garden and when she saw them coming and recognized schoolteacher's hat, she heard wings. Little hummingbirds stuck their needle beaks right through her headcloth into her hair and beat their wings. And if she thought anything, it was No. No. Nono. Nonono. Simple. She just flew. Collected every bit of life she had made, all the parts of her that were precious and fine and beautiful, and carried, pushed, dragged them through the veil, out, away, over there where no one could hurt them. Over there. Outside this place, where they would be safe. And the hummingbird wings beat on. Sethe paused in her circle again and looked out the window. She remembered when the yard had a fence with a gate that somebody was always latching and unlatching in the time when 124 was busy as a way station. She did not see the whiteboys who pulled it down, yanked up the posts and smashed the gate leaving 124 desolate and exposed at the very hour when everybody stopped dropping by. The shoulder weeds of Bluestone Road were all that came toward the house.

When she got back from the jail house, she was glad the fence was gone. That's where they had hitched their horses – where she saw, floating above the railing as she squatted in the garden, schoolteacher's hat. By the time she faced him, looked him dead in the eye, she had something in her arms that stopped him in his tracks. He took a backward step with each jump of the baby heart until finally there were none.

"I stopped him," she said, staring at the place where the fence used to be. "I took and put my babies where they'd be safe."

The roaring in Paul D's head did not prevent him from hearing the pat she gave to the last word, and it occurred to him that what she wanted for her children was exactly what was missing in 124: safety. Which was the very first message he got the day he walked through the door. He thought he had made it safe, had gotten rid of the danger; beat the shit out of it; run it off the place and showed it and everybody else the difference between a mule and a plow. And because she had not done it before he got there her own self, he thought it was because she could not do it. That she lived with 124 in helpless, apologetic resignation because she had no choice; that minus husband, sons, mother-in-law, she and her slow-witted daughter had to live there all alone making do. The prickly, mean-eyed Sweet Home girl he knew as Halle's girl was obedient (like Halle), shy (like Halle), and work-crazy (like Halle). He was wrong. This here Sethe was new. The ghost in her house didn't bother her for the very same reason a room-and-board witch with new shoes was welcome. This here Sethe talked about love like any other woman; talked about baby clothes like any other woman, but what she meant could cleave the bone. This here Sethe talked about safety with a handsaw. This here new Sethe didn't know where the world stopped and she began. Suddenly he saw what Stamp Paid wanted him to see: more important than what Sethe had done was what she claimed. It scared him.

"Your love is too thick," he said, thinking, That bitch is looking at me; she is right over my head looking down through the floor at me.

"Too thick?" she said, thinking of the Clearing where Baby Suggs' commands knocked the pods off horse chestnuts. "Love is or it ain't. Thin love ain't love at all."

"Yeah. It didn't work, did it? Did it work?" he asked.

"It worked," she said.

"How? Your boys gone you don't know where. One girl dead, the other won't leave the yard. How did it work?"

"They ain't at Sweet Home. Schoolteacher ain't got em."

"Maybe there's worse."

"It ain't my job to know what's worse. It's my job to

know what is and to keep them away from what I know is terrible. I did that."

"What you did was wrong, Sethe."

"I should have gone on back there? Taken my babies back there?"

"There could have been a way. Some other way."

"What way?"

"You got two feet, Sethe, not four," he said, and right then a forest sprang up between them; trackless and quiet.

Later he would wonder what made him say it. The calves of his youth? or the conviction that he was being observed through the ceiling? How fast he had moved from his shame to hers. From his cold-house secret straight to her too-thick love.

Meanwhile the forest was locking the distance between them, giving it shape and heft.

He did not put his hat on right away. First he fingered it, deciding how his going would be, how to make it an exit not an escape. And it was very important not to leave without looking. He stood up, turned and looked up the white stairs. She was there all right. Standing straight as a line with her back to him. He didn't rush to the door. He moved slowly and when he got there he opened it before asking Sethe to put supper aside for him because he might be a little late getting back. Only then did he put on his hat.

Sweet, she thought. He must think I can't bear to hear him say it. That after all I have told him and after telling me how many feet I have, "goodbye" would break me to pieces. Ain't that sweet.

"So long," she murmured from the far side of the trees.

II

124 WAS LOUD. Stamp Paid could hear it even from the road. He walked toward the house holding his head as high as possible so nobody looking could call him a sneak, although his worried mind made him feel like one. Ever since he showed that newspaper clipping to Paul D and learned that he'd moved out of 124 that very day, Stamp felt uneasy. Having wrestled with the question of whether or not to tell a man about his woman, and having convinced himself that he should, he then began to worry about Sethe. Had he stopped the one shot she had of the happiness a good man could bring her? Was she vexed by the loss, the free and unasked-for revival of gossip by the man who had helped her cross the river and who was her friend as well as Baby Suggs'?

"I'm too old," he thought, "for clear thinking. I'm too old and I seen too much." He had insisted on privacy during the revelation at the slaughter yard – now he wondered whom he was protecting. Paul D was the only one in town who didn't know. How did information that had been in the newspaper become a secret that needed to be whispered in a pig yard? A secret from whom? Sethe, that's who. He'd gone behind her back, like a sneak. But sneaking was his job – his life; though always for a clear and holy purpose. Before the War all he did was sneak: runaways into hidden places, secret information to public places. Underneath his legal vegetables were the contraband humans that he ferried across the river. Even the pigs he worked in the spring served his purposes. Whole families lived on the bones and guts he distributed to them. He wrote their letters and read to them the ones they received. He knew who had dropsy and who needed stovewood; which children had a gift and which needed correction. He knew the secrets of the Ohio River and its banks; empty houses and full; the best dancers, the worst speakers, those with beautiful voices and those who could not carry a tune. There was nothing interesting between his legs, but he remembered when there had been – when that drive drove the driven – and that was why he considered long and hard before opening his wooden box and searching for the eighteen-year-old clipping to show Paul D as proof.

Afterward – not before – he considered Sethe's feelings in the matter. And it was the lateness of this consideration that made him feel so bad. Maybe he should have left it alone; maybe Sethe would have gotten around to telling him herself; maybe he was not the high-minded Soldier of Christ he thought he was, but an ordinary, plain meddler who had interrupted something going along just fine for the sake of truth and forewarning, things he set much store by. Now 124 was back like it was before Paul D came to town – worrying Sethe and Denver with a pack of haunts he could hear from the road. Even if Sethe could deal with the return of the spirit, Stamp didn't believe her daughter could. Denver needed somebody normal in her life. By luck he had been there at her very birth almost – before she knew she was alive – and it made him partial to her. It was seeing her, alive, don't you know, and looking healthy four weeks later that pleased him so much he gathered all he could carry of the best blackberries in the county and stuck two in her mouth first, before he presented the difficult harvest to Baby Suggs. To this day he believed his berries (which sparked the feast and the wood chopping that followed) were the reason Denver was still alive. Had he not been there, chopping firewood, Sethe would have spread her baby brains on the planking. Maybe he should have thought of Denver, if not

Sethe, before he gave Paul D the news that ran him off, the one normal somebody in the girl's life since Baby Suggs died. And right there was the thorn.

Deeper and more painful than his belated concern for Denver or Sethe, scorching his soul like a silver dollar in a fool's pocket, was the memory of Baby Suggs – the mountain to his sky. It was the memory of her and the honor that was her due that made him walk straight-necked into the yard of 124, although he heard its voices from the road.

He had stepped foot in this house only once after the Misery (which is what he called Sethe's rough response to the Fugitive Bill) and that was to carry Baby Suggs, holy, out of it. When he picked her up in his arms, she looked to him like a girl, and he took the pleasure she would have knowing she didn't have to grind her hipbone anymore – that at last some-body carried her. Had she waited just a little she would have seen the end of the War, its short, flashy results. They could have celebrated together; gone to hear the great sermons preached on the occasion. As it was, he went alone from house to joyous house drinking what was offered. But she hadn't waited and he attended her funeral more put out with her than bereaved. Sethe and her daughter were dry-eyed on that occasion. Sethe had no instructions except "Take her to the Clearing," which he tried to do, but was prevented by some rule the whites had invented about where the dead should rest. Baby Suggs went down next to the baby with its throat cut – a neighborliness that Stamp wasn't sure had Baby Suggs' approval.

The setting-up was held in the yard because nobody besides himself would enter 124 – an injury Sethe answered with another by refusing to attend the service Reverend Pike presided over. She went instead to the gravesite, whose silence she competed with as she stood there not joining in the hymns the others sang with all their hearts. That insult spawned another by the mourners: back in the yard of 124, they ate the food they brought and did not touch Sethe's, who did not touch theirs and forbade Denver to. So Baby Suggs, holy, having devoted her freed life to harmony, was buried amid a regular dance of pride, fear, condemnation and spite. Just about everybody in town was longing for Sethe to come on difficult times. Her outrageous claims, her self-sufficiency seemed to demand it, and Stamp Paid, who had not felt a trickle of meanness his whole adult life, wondered if some of the "pride goeth before a fall" expectations of the townsfolk had rubbed off on him anyhow – which would explain why he had not considered Sethe's feelings or Denver's needs when he showed Paul D the clipping.

He hadn't the vaguest notion of what he would do or say when and if Sethe opened the door and turned her eyes on his. He was willing to offer her help, if she wanted any from him, or receive her anger, if she harbored any against him. Beyond that, he trusted his instincts to right what he may have done wrong to Baby Suggs' kin, and to guide him in and through the stepped-up haunting 124 was subject to, as evidenced by the voices he heard from the road. Other than that, he would rely on the power of Jesus Christ to deal with things older, but not stronger, than He Himself was.

What he heard, as he moved toward the porch, he didn't understand. Out on Bluestone Road he thought he heard a conflagration of hasty voices – loud, urgent, all speaking at once so he could not make out what they were talking about or to whom. The speech wasn't nonsensical, exactly, nor was it tongues. But something was wrong with the order of the words and he couldn't describe or cipher it to save his life. All he could make out was the word *mine*. The rest of it stayed outside his mind's reach. Yet he went on through. When he got to the steps, the voices drained suddenly to less than a whisper. It gave him pause. They had become an occasional mutter – like the interior sounds a woman makes when she believes she is alone and unobserved at her work:

a *sth* when she misses the needle's eye; a soft moan when she sees another chip in her one good platter; the low, friendly argument with which she greets the hens. Nothing fierce or startling. Just that eternal, private conversation that takes place between women and their tasks.

Stamp Paid raised his fist to knock on the door he had never knocked on (because it was always open to or for him) and could not do it. Dispensing with that formality was all the pay he expected from Negroes in his debt. Once Stamp Paid brought you a coat, got the message to you, saved your life, or fixed the cistern he took the liberty of walking in your door as though it were his own. Since all his visits were beneficial, his step or holler through a doorway got a bright welcome. Rather than forfeit the one privilege he claimed for himself, he lowered his hand and left the porch.

Over and over again he tried it: made up his mind to visit Sethe; broke through the loud hasty voices to the mumbling beyond it and stopped, trying to figure out what to do at the door. Six times in as many days he abandoned his normal route and tried to knock at 124. But the coldness of the gesture – its sign that he was indeed a stranger at the gate – overwhelmed him. Retracing his steps in the snow, he sighed. Spirit willing; flesh weak.

While Stamp Paid was making up his mind to visit 124 for Baby Suggs' sake, Sethe was trying to take her advice: *to lay it all down, sword and shield*. Not just to acknowledge the advice Baby Suggs gave her, but actually to take it. Four days after Paul D reminded her of how many feet she had, Sethe rummaged among the shoes of strangers to find the ice skates she was sure were there. Digging in the heap she despised herself for having been so trusting, so quick to surrender at the stove while Paul D kissed her back. She should have known that he would behave like everybody else in town once he knew. The twenty-eight days of having women friends, a mother-in-law, and all her children together; of being part of a neighborhood; of, in fact, having neighbors at all to call her own – all that was long gone and would never come back. No more dancing in the Clearing or happy feeds. No more discussions, stormy or quiet, about the true meaning of the Fugitive Bill, the Settlement Fee, God's Ways and Negro pews; antislavery, manumission, skin voting, Republicans, Dred Scott, book learning, Sojourner's high-wheeled buggy, the Colored Ladies of Delaware, Ohio, and the other weighty issues that held them in chairs, scraping the floorboards or pacing them in agony or exhilaration. No anxious wait for the *North Star* or news of a beat-off. No sighing at a new betrayal or handclapping at a small victory.

Those twenty-eight happy days were followed by eighteen years of disapproval and a solitary life. Then a few months of the sun-splashed life that the shadows holding hands on the road promised her; tentative greetings from other colored-people in Paul D's company; a bed life for herself. Except for Denver's friend, every bit of it had disappeared. Was that the pattern? she wondered. Every eighteen or twenty years her unlivable life would be interrupted by a short-lived glory?

Well, if that's the way it was – that's the way it was.

She had been on her knees, scrubbing the floor, Denver trailing her with the drying rags, when Beloved appeared saying, "What these do?" On her knees, scrub brush in hand, she looked at the girl and the skates she held up. Sethe couldn't skate a lick but then and there she decided to take Baby Suggs' advice: *lay it all down.* She left the bucket where it was. Told Denver to get out the shawls and started searching for the other skates she was certain were in that heap somewhere. Anybody feeling sorry for her, anybody wandering by to peep in and see how she was getting on (including Paul D) would discover that the woman junkheaped for the third time because she loved her children – that woman was sailing happily on a frozen creek.

Hurriedly, carelessly she threw the shoes about. She found one blade – a man's.

"Well," she said. "We'll take turns. Two skates on one; one skate on one; and shoe slide for the other."

Nobody saw them falling.

Holding hands, bracing each other, they swirled over the ice. Beloved wore the pair; Denver wore one, step-gliding over the treacherous ice. Sethe thought her two shoes would hold and anchor her. She was wrong. Two paces onto the creek, she lost her balance and landed on her behind. The girls, screaming with laughter, joined her on the ice. Sethe struggled to stand and discovered not only that she could do a split, but that it hurt. Her bones surfaced in unexpected places and so did laughter. Making a circle or a line, the three of them could not stay upright for one whole minute, but nobody saw them falling.

Each seemed to be helping the other two stay upright, yet every tumble doubled their delight. The live oak and sough-ing pine on the banks enclosed them and absorbed their laughter while they fought gravity for each other's hands. Their skirts flew like wings and their skin turned pewter in the cold and dying light.

Nobody saw them falling.

Exhausted finally they lay down on their backs to recover breath. The sky above them was another country. Winter stars, close enough to lick, had come out before sunset. For a moment, looking up, Sethe entered the perfect peace they offered. Then Denver stood up and tried for a long, independ-ent glide. The tip of her single skate hit an ice bump, and as she fell, the flapping of her arms was so wild and hopeless that all three – Sethe, Beloved and Denver herself – laughed till they coughed. Sethe rose to her hands and knees, laughter still shaking her chest, making her eyes wet. She stayed that way for a while, on all fours. But when her laughter died, the tears did not and it was some time before Beloved or Denver knew the difference. When they did they touched her lightly on the shoulders.

Walking back through the woods, Sethe put an arm around each girl at her side. Both of them had an arm around her waist. Making their way over hard snow, they stumbled and had to hold on tight, but nobody saw them fall.

Inside the house they found out they were cold. They took off their shoes, wet stockings, and put on dry woolen ones. Denver fed the fire. Sethe warmed a pan of milk and stirred cane syrup and vanilla into it. Wrapped in quilts and blankets before the cooking stove, they drank, wiped their noses, and drank again.

"We could roast some taters," said Denver.

"Tomorrow," said Sethe. "Time to sleep."

She poured them each a bit more of the hot sweet milk. The stovefire roared.

"You finished with your eyes?" asked Beloved.

Sethe smiled. "Yes, I'm finished with my eyes. Drink up. Time for bed."

But none of them wanted to leave the warmth of the blankets, the fire and the cups for the chill of an unheated bed. They went on sipping and watching the fire.

When the click came Sethe didn't know what it was. Afterward it was clear as daylight that the click came at the very beginning – a beat, almost, before it started; before she heard three notes; before the melody was even clear. Leaning forward a little, Beloved was humming softly.

It was then, when Beloved finished humming, that Sethe recalled the click – the settling of pieces into places designed and made especially for them. No milk spilled from her cup because her hand was not shaking. She simply turned her head and looked at Beloved's profile: the chin, mouth, nose, forehead, copied and exaggerated in the huge shadow the fire threw on the wall behind her. Her hair, which Denver had braided into twenty or thirty plaits, curved toward her shoulders like arms. From where she sat Sethe could not examine it, not the hairline, nor the eyebrows, the lips, nor...

"All I remember," Baby Suggs had said, "is how she loved the burned bottom of bread. Her little hands I wouldn't know em if they slapped me."

... the birthmark, nor the color of the gums, the shape of her ears, nor...

"Here. Look here. This is your ma'am. If you can't tell me by my face, look here."

... the fingers, nor their nails, nor even...

But there would be time. The click had clicked; things were where they ought to be or poised and ready to glide in.

"I made that song up," said Sethe. "I made it up and sang it to my children. Nobody knows that song but me and my children."

Beloved turned to look at Sethe. "I know it," she said.

A hobnail casket of jewels found in a tree hollow should be fondled before it is opened. Its lock may have rusted or broken away from the clasp. Still you should touch the nail heads, and test its weight. No smashing with an ax head before it is decently exhumed from the grave that has hidden it all this time. No gasp at a miracle that is truly miraculous because the magic lies in the fact that you knew it was there for you all along.

Sethe wiped the white satin coat from the inside of the pan, brought pillows from the keeping room for the girls' heads. There was no tremor in her voice as she instructed them to keep the fire — if not, come on upstairs.

With that, she gathered her blanket around her elbows and ascended the lily-white stairs like a bride. Outside, snow solidified itself into graceful forms. The peace of winter stars seemed permanent.

*

Fingering a ribbon and smelling skin, Stamp Paid approached 124 again.

"My marrow is tired," he thought. "I been tired all my days, bone-tired, but now it's in the marrow. Must be what Baby Suggs felt when she lay down and thought about color for the rest of her life." When she told him what her aim was, he thought she was ashamed and too shamed to say so. Her authority in the pulpit, her dance in the Clearing, her powerful Call (she didn't deliver sermons or preach – insisting she was too ignorant for that – she *called* and the hearing heard) – all that had been mocked and rebuked by the bloodspill in her backyard. God puzzled her and she was too ashamed of Him to say so. Instead she told Stamp she was going to bed to think about the colors of things. He tried to dissuade her. Sethe was in jail with her nursing baby, the one he had saved. Her sons were holding hands in the yard, terrified of letting go. Strangers and familiars were stopping by to hear how it went one more time, and suddenly Baby declared peace. She just up and quit. By the time Sethe was released she had exhausted blue and was well on her way to yellow.

At first he would see her in the yard occasionally, or delivering food to the jail, or shoes in town. Then less and less. He believed then that shame put her in the bed. Now, eight years after her contentious funeral and eighteen years after the Misery, he changed his mind. Her marrow was tired and it was a testimony to the heart that fed it that it took eight years to meet finally the color she was hankering after. The onslaught of her fatigue, like his, was sudden, but lasted for years. After sixty years of losing children to the people who chewed up her life and spit it out like a fish bone; after five years of freedom given to her by her last child, who bought her future with his, exchanged it, so to speak, so she could have one whether he did or not – to lose him too; to acquire a daughter and grandchildren and see that daughter slay the children (or try to); to belong to a community of other free

Negroes – to love and be loved by them, to counsel and be counseled, protect and be protected, feed and be fed – and then to have that community step back and hold itself at a distance – well, it could wear out even a Baby Suggs, holy.

"Listen here, girl," he told her, "you can't quit the Word. It's given to you to speak. You can't quit the Word, I don't care what all happen to you."

They were standing in Richmond Street, ankle deep in leaves. Lamps lit the downstairs windows of spacious houses and made the early evening look darker than it was. The odor of burning leaves was brilliant. Quite by chance, as he pocketed a penny tip for a delivery, he had glanced across the street and recognized the skipping woman as his old friend. He had not seen her in weeks. Quickly he crossed the street, scuffing red leaves as he went. When he stopped her with a greeting, she returned it with a face knocked clean of interest. She could have been a plate. A carpetbag full of shoes in her hand, she waited for him to begin, lead or share a conversation. If there had been sadness in her eyes he would have understood it; but indifference lodged where sadness should have been.

"You missed the Clearing three Saturdays running," he told her.

She turned her head away and scanned the houses along the street.

"Folks came," he said.

"Folks come; folks go," she answered.

"Here, let me carry that." He tried to take her bag from her but she wouldn't let him.

"I got a delivery someplace long in here," she said. "Name of Tucker."

"Yonder," he said. "Twin chestnuts in the yard. Sick, too."

They walked a bit, his pace slowed to accommodate her skip.

"Well?"

"Well, what?"

"Saturday coming. You going to Call or what?"

"If I call them and they come, what on earth I'm going to say?"

"Say the Word!" He checked his shout too late. Two whitemen burning leaves turned their heads in his direction. Bending low he whispered into her ear, "The Word. The Word."

"That's one other thing took away from me," she said, and that was when he exhorted her, pleaded with her not to quit, no matter what. The Word had been given to her and she had to speak it. Had to.

They had reached the twin chestnuts and the white house that stood behind them.

"See what I mean?" he said. "Big trees like that, both of em together ain't got the leaves of a young birch."

"I see what you mean," she said, but she peered instead at the white house.

"You got to do it," he said. "You got to. Can't nobody Call like you. You have to be there."

"What I have to do is get in my bed and lay down. I want to fix on something harmless in this world."

"What world you talking about? Ain't nothing harmless down here."

"Yes it is. Blue. That don't hurt nobody. Yellow neither."

"You getting in the bed to think about yellow?"

"I likes yellow."

"Then what? When you get through with blue and yellow, then what?"

"Can't say. It's something can't be planned."

"You blaming God," he said. "That's what you doing."

"No, Stamp. I ain't."

"You saying the whitefolks won? That what you saying?"

"I'm saying they came in my yard."

"You saying nothing counts."

"I'm saying they came in my yard."

"Sethe's the one did it."

"And if she hadn't?"

"You saying God give up? Nothing left for us but pour out our own blood?"

"I'm saying they came in my yard."

"You punishing Him, ain't you."

"Not like He punish me."

"You can't do that, Baby. It ain't right."

"Was a time I knew what that was."

"You still know."

"What I know is what I see: a nigger woman hauling shoes."

"Aw, Baby." He licked his lips searching with his tongue for the words that would turn her around, lighten her load. "We have to be steady. 'These things too will pass.' What you looking for? A miracle?"

"No," she said. "I'm looking for what I was put here to look for: the back door," and skipped right to it. They didn't let her in. They took the shoes from her as she stood on the steps and she rested her hip on the railing while the whitewoman went looking for the dime.

Stamp Paid rearranged his way. Too angry to walk her home and listen to more, he watched her for a moment and turned to go before the alert white face at the window next door had come to any conclusion.

Trying to get to 124 for the second time now, he regretted that conversation: the high tone he took; his refusal to see the effect of marrow weariness in a woman he believed was a mountain. Now, too late, he understood her. The heart that pumped out love, the mouth that spoke the Word, didn't count. They came in her yard anyway and she could not approve or condemn Sethe's rough choice. One or the other might have saved her, but beaten up by the claims of both, she went to bed. The whitefolks had tired her out at last.

And him. Eighteen seventy-four and whitefolks were still on the loose. Whole towns wiped clean of Negroes; eighty-seven lynchings in one year alone in Kentucky; four colored schools burned to the ground; grown men whipped like children; children whipped like adults; black women raped by the crew; property taken, necks broken. He smelled skin, skin and hot blood. The skin was one thing, but human blood cooked in a lynch fire was a whole other thing. The stench stank. Stank up off the pages of the *North Star*, out of the mouths of witnesses, etched in crooked handwriting in letters delivered by hand. Detailed in documents and petitions full of *whereas* and presented to any legal body who'd read it, it stank. But none of that had worn out his marrow. None of that. It was the ribbon. Tying his flatbed up on the bank of the Licking River, securing it the best he could, he caught sight of something red on its bottom. Reaching for it, he thought it was a cardinal feather stuck to his boat. He tugged and what came loose in his hand was a red ribbon knotted around a curl of wet woolly hair, clinging still to its bit of scalp. He untied the ribbon and put it in his pocket, dropped the curl in the weeds. On the way home, he stopped, short of breath and dizzy. He waited until the spell passed before continuing on his way. A moment later, his breath left him again. This time he sat down by a fence. Rested, he got to his feet, but before he took a step he turned to look back down the road he was traveling and said, to its frozen mud and the river beyond, "What *are* these people? You tell me, Jesus. What *are* they?"

When he got to his house he was too tired to eat the food his sister and nephews had prepared. He sat on the porch in the cold till way past dark and went to his bed only because his sister's voice calling him was getting nervous. He kept the ribbon; the skin smell nagged him, and his weakened marrow made him dwell on Baby Suggs' wish to consider what in the world was harmless. He hoped she stuck to blue, yellow, maybe green, and never fixed on red.

Mistaking her, upbraiding her, owing her, now he needed to let her know he knew, and to get right with her and her kin. So, in spite of his exhausted marrow, he kept on through the voices and tried once more to knock at the door of 124. This time, although he couldn't cipher but one word, he believed he knew who spoke them. The people of the broken necks, of fire-cooked blood and black girls who had lost their ribbons.

What a roaring.

Sethe had gone to bed smiling, eager to lie down and unravel the proof for the conclusion she had already leapt to. Fondle the day and circumstances of Beloved's arrival and the meaning of that kiss in the Clearing. She slept instead and woke, still smiling, to a snow-bright morning, cold enough to see her breath. She lingered a moment to collect the courage to throw off the blankets and hit a chilly floor. For the first time, she was going to be late for work.

Downstairs she saw the girls sleeping where she'd left them, but back to back now, each wrapped tight in blankets, breathing into their pillows. The pair and a half of skates were lying by the front door, the stockings hung on a nail behind the cooking stove to dry had not.

Sethe looked at Beloved's face and smiled.

Quietly, carefully she stepped around her to wake the fire. First a bit of paper, then a little kindlin – not too much – just a taste until it was strong enough for more. She fed its dance until it was wild and fast. When she went outside to collect more wood from the shed, she did not notice the man's frozen footprints. She crunched around to the back, to the cord piled high with snow. After scraping it clean, she filled her arms with as much dry wood as she could. She even looked straight at the shed, smiling, smiling at the things she would not have to remember now. Thinking, "She ain't even mad with me. Not a bit."

Obviously the hand-holding shadows she had seen on the road were not Paul D, Denver and herself, but "us three." The three holding on to each other skating the night before; the three sipping flavored milk. And since that was so – if her daughter could come back home from the timeless place – certainly her sons could, and would, come back from wherever they had gone to.

Sethe covered her front teeth with her tongue against the cold. Hunched forward by the burden in her arms, she walked back around the house to the porch – not once noticing the frozen tracks she stepped in.

Inside, the girls were still sleeping, although they had changed positions while she was gone, both drawn to the fire. Dumping the armload into the woodbox made them stir but not wake. Sethe started the cooking stove as quietly as she could, reluctant to wake the sisters, happy to have them asleep at her feet while she made breakfast. Too bad she would be late for work – too, too bad. Once in sixteen years? That's just too bad.

She had beaten two eggs into yesterday's hominy, formed it into patties and fried them with some ham pieces before Denver woke completely and groaned.

"Back stiff?"

"Ooh yeah."

"Sleeping on the floor's supposed to be good for you."

"Hurts like the devil," said Denver.

"Could be that fall you took."

Denver smiled. "That was fun." She turned to look down at Beloved snoring lightly. "Should I wake her?"

"No, let her rest."

"She likes to see you off in the morning."

"I'll make sure she does," said Sethe, and thought, Be nice to think first, before I talk to her, let her know I know.

Think about all I ain't got to remember no more. Do like Baby said: Think on it then lay it down – for good. Paul D convinced me there was a world out there and that I could live in it. Should have known better. *Did* know better. Whatever is going on outside my door ain't for me. The world is in this room. This here's all there is and all there needs to be.

They ate like men, ravenous and intent. Saying little, content with the company of the other and the opportunity to look in her eyes.

When Sethe wrapped her head and bundled up to go to town, it was already midmorning. And when she left the house she neither saw the prints nor heard the voices that ringed 124 like a noose.

Trudging in the ruts left earlier by wheels, Sethe was excited to giddiness by the things she no longer had to remember.

I don't have to remember nothing. I don't even have to explain. She understands it all. I can forget how Baby Suggs' heart collapsed; how we agreed it was consumption without a sign of it in the world. Her eyes when she brought my food, I can forget that, and how she told me that Howard and Buglar were all right but wouldn't let go each other's hands. Played that way: stayed that way especially in their sleep. She handed me the food from a basket; things wrapped small enough to get through the bars, whispering news: Mr. Bodwin going to see the judge – in chambers, she kept on saying, in chambers, like I knew what it meant or she did. The Colored Ladies of Delaware, Ohio, had drawn up a petition to keep me from being hanged. That two white preachers had come round and wanted to talk to me, pray for me. That a newspaperman came too. She told me the news and I told her I needed something for the rats. She wanted Denver out and slapped her palms when I wouldn't let her go. "Where your earrings?" she said. "I'll hold em for you." I told her the jailer took them, to protect me from myself. He thought I could do some harm with the wire. Baby Suggs covered her mouth with her hand. "Schoolteacher left town," she said. "Filed a claim and rode on off. They going to let you out for the burial," she said, "not the funeral, just the burial," and they did. The sheriff came with me and looked away when I fed Denver in the wagon. Neither Howard nor Buglar would let me near them, not even to touch their hair. I believe a lot of folks were there, but I just saw the box. Reverend Pike spoke in a real loud voice, but I didn't catch a word – except the first two, and three months later when Denver was ready for solid food and they let me out for good, I went and got you a gravestone, but I didn't have money enough for the carving so I exchanged (bartered, you might say) what I did have and I'm sorry to this day I never thought to ask him for the whole thing: all I heard of what Reverend Pike said. Dearly Beloved, which is what you are to me and I don't have to be sorry about getting only one word, and I don't have to remember the slaughterhouse and the Saturday girls who worked its yard. I can forget that what I did changed Baby Suggs' life. No Clearing, no company. Just laundry and shoes. I can forget it all now because as soon as I got the gravestone in place you made your presence known in the house and worried us all to distraction. I didn't understand it then. I thought you were mad with me. And now I know that if you was, you ain't now because you came back here to me and I was right all along: there is no world outside my door. I only need to know one thing. How bad is the scar?

As Sethe walked to work, late for the first time in sixteen years and wrapped in a timeless present, Stamp Paid fought fatigue and the habit of a lifetime. Baby Suggs refused to go to the Clearing because she believed *they* had won; he refused to acknowledge any such victory. Baby had no back door; so he braved the cold and a wall of talk to knock on the one she did have. He clutched the red ribbon in his pocket for strength. Softly at first, then harder. At the last he banged furiously – disbelieving it could happen. That the door of a house with coloredpeople in it did not fly open in his presence. He went to the window and wanted to cry. Sure enough, there they were, not a one of them heading for the door. Worrying his scrap of ribbon to shreds, the old man turned and went down the steps. Now curiosity joined his shame and his debt. Two backs curled away from him as he looked in the window. One had a head he recognized; the other troubled him. He didn't know her and didn't know anybody it could be. Nobody, but nobody visited that house.

After a disagreeable breakfast he went to see Ella and John to find out what they knew. Perhaps there he could find out if, after all these years of clarity, he had misnamed himself and there was yet another debt he owed. Born Joshua, he renamed himself when he handed over his wife to his master's son. Handed her over in the sense that he did not kill anybody, thereby himself, because his wife demanded he stay alive. Otherwise, she reasoned, where and to whom could she return when the boy was through? With that gift, he decided that he didn't owe anybody anything. Whatever his obligations were, that act paid them off. He thought it would make him rambunctious, renegade – a drunkard even, the debtlessness, and in a way it did. But there was nothing to do with it. Work well; work poorly. Work a little; work not at all. Make sense; make none. Sleep, wake up; like somebody, dislike others. It didn't seem much of a way to live and it brought him no satisfaction. So he extended this debtlessness to other people by helping them pay out and off whatever they owed in misery. Beaten runaways? He ferried them and rendered them paid for; gave them their own bill of sale, so to speak. "You paid it; now life owes you." And the receipt, as it were, was a welcome door that he never had to knock on, like John and Ella's in front of which he stood and said, "Who in there?" only once and she was pulling on the hinge.

"Where you been keeping yourself? I told John must be cold if Stamp stay inside."

"Oh, I been out." He took off his cap and massaged his scalp.

"Out where? Not by here." Ella hung two suits of underwear on a line behind the stove.

"Was over to Baby Suggs' this morning."

"What you want in there?" asked Ella. "Somebody invite you in?"

"That's Baby's kin. I don't need no invite to look after her people."

"Sth." Ella was unmoved. She had been Baby Suggs' friend and Sethe's too till the rough time. Except for a nod at the carnival, she hadn't given Sethe the time of day.

"Somebody new in there. A woman. Thought you might know who is she."

"Ain't no new Negroes in this town I don't know about," she said. "What she look like? You sure that wasn't Denver?"

"I know Denver. This girl's narrow."

"You sure?"

"I know what I see."

"Might see anything at all at 124."

"True."

"Better ask Paul D," she said.

"Can't locate him," said Stamp, which was the truth although his efforts to find Paul D had been feeble. He wasn't ready to confront the man whose life he had altered with his graveyard information.

"He's sleeping in the church," said Ella.

"The church!" Stamp was shocked and very hurt.

"Yeah. Asked Reverend Pike if he could stay in the cellar."

"It's cold as charity in there!"

"I expect he knows that."

"What he do that for?"

"He's a touch proud, seem like."

"He don't have to do that! Any number'll take him in."

Ella turned around to look at Stamp Paid. "Can't nobody read minds long distance. All he have to do is ask somebody."

"Why? Why he have to ask? Can't nobody offer? What's going on? Since when a blackman come to town have to sleep in a cellar like a dog?"

"Unrile yourself, Stamp."

"Not me. I'm going to stay riled till somebody gets some sense and leastway act like a Christian."

"It's only a few days he been there."

"Shouldn't be no days! You know all about it and don't give him a hand? That don't sound like you, Ella. Me and you been pulling coloredfolk out the water more'n twenty years. Now you tell me you can't offer a man a bed? A working man, too! A man what can pay his own way."

"He ask, I give him anything."

"Why's that necessary all of a sudden?"

"I don't know him all that well."

"You know he's colored!"

"Stamp, don't tear me up this morning. I don't feel like it."

"It's her, ain't it?"

"Her who?"

"Sethe. He took up with her and stayed in there and you don't want nothing to —"

"Hold on. Don't jump if you can't see bottom."

"Girl, give it up. We been friends too long to act like this."

"Well, who can tell what all went on in there? Look here, I don't know who Sethe is or none of her people."

"What?!"

"All I know is she married Baby Suggs' boy and I ain't sure I know that. Where is *he*, huh? Baby never laid eyes on her till John carried her to the door with a baby I strapped on her chest.''

"*I* strapped that baby! And you way off the track with that wagon. Her children know who she was even if you don't.''

"So what? I ain't saying she wasn't their ma'ammy, but who's to say they was Baby Suggs' grandchildren? How she get on board and her husband didn't? And tell me this, how she have that baby in the woods by herself? Said a whitewoman come out the trees and helped her. Shoot. You believe that? A *white* woman? Well, I know what kind of white that was.''

"Aw, no, Ella.''

"Anything white floating around in the woods – if it ain't got a shotgun, it's something I don't want *no* part of!''

"You all was friends.''

"Yeah, till she showed herself.''

"Ella.''

"I ain't got no friends take a handsaw to their own children.''

"You in deep water, girl.''

"Uh uh. I'm on dry land and I'm going to stay there. You the one wet.''

"What's any of what you talking got to do with Paul D?''

"What run him off? Tell me that.''

"I run him off.''

"You?''

"I told him about – I showed him the newspaper, about the – what Sethe did. Read it to him. He left that very day.''

"You didn't tell me that. I thought he knew.''

"He didn't know nothing. Except her, from when they was at that place Baby Suggs was at.''

"He knew Baby Suggs?''

"Sure he knew her. Her boy Halle too.''

"And left when he found out what Sethe did?''

"Look like he might have a place to stay after all.''

"What you say casts a different light. I thought –"

But Stamp Paid knew what she thought.

"You didn't come here asking about him," Ella said. "You came about some new girl."

"That's so."

"Well, Paul D must know who she is. Or *what* she is."

"Your mind is loaded with spirits. Everywhere you look you see one."

"You know as well as I do that people who die bad don't stay in the ground."

He couldn't deny it. Jesus Christ Himself didn't, so Stamp ate a piece of Ella's head cheese to show there were no bad feelings and set out to find Paul D. He found him on the steps of Holy Redeemer, holding his wrists between his knees and looking red-eyed.

Sawyer shouted at her when she entered the kitchen, but she just turned her back and reached for her apron. There was no entry now. No crack or crevice available. She had taken pains to keep them out, but knew full well that at any moment they could rock her, rip her from her moorings, send the birds twittering back into her hair. Drain her mother's milk, they had already done. Divided her back into plant life – that too. Driven her fat-bellied into the woods – they had done that. All news of them was rot. They buttered Halle's face; gave Paul D iron to eat; crisped Sixo; hanged her own mother. She didn't want any more news about whitefolks; didn't want to know what Ella knew and John and Stamp Paid, about the world done up the way whitefolks loved it. All news of them should have stopped with the birds in her hair.

Once, long ago, she was soft, trusting. She trusted Mrs. Garner and her husband too. She knotted the earrings into her underskirt to take along, not so much to wear but to hold. Earrings that made her believe she could discriminate among them. That for every schoolteacher there would be an Amy; that for every pupil there was a Garner, or Bodwin, or even a sheriff, whose touch at her elbow was gentle and who looked away when she nursed. But she had come to believe every one of Baby Suggs' last words and buried all recollection of them and luck. Paul D dug it up, gave her back her body, kissed her divided back, stirred her rememory and brought her more news: of clabber, of iron, of roosters' smiling, but when he heard *her* news, he counted her feet and didn't even say goodbye.

"Don't talk to me, Mr. Sawyer. Don't say nothing to me this morning."

"What? What? What? You talking back to me?"

"I'm telling you don't say nothing to me."

"You better get them pies made."

Sethe touched the fruit and picked up the paring knife.

When pie juice hit the bottom of the oven and hissed, Sethe was well into the potato salad. Sawyer came in and said, "Not too sweet. You make it too sweet they don't eat it."

"Make it the way I always did."

"Yeah. Too sweet."

None of the sausages came back. The cook had a way with them and Sawyer's Restaurant never had leftover sausage. If Sethe wanted any, she put them aside soon as they were ready. But there was some passable stew. Problem was, all her pies were sold too. Only rice pudding left and half a pan of gingerbread that didn't come out right. Had she been paying attention instead of daydreaming all morning, she wouldn't be picking around looking for her dinner like a crab. She couldn't read clock time very well, but she knew when the hands were closed in prayer at the top of the face she was through for the day. She got a metal-top jar, filled it with stew and wrapped the gingerbread in butcher paper. These she dropped in her outer skirt pockets and began washing up. None of it was anything like what the cook and the two waiters walked off with. Mr. Sawyer included midday dinner in the terms of the job – along with $3.40 a week – and she made him understand from the beginning she would take her dinner home. But matches, sometimes a bit of kerosene, a little salt, butter too – these things she took also, once in a while, and felt ashamed because she could afford to buy them; she just didn't want the embarrassment of waiting out back of Phelps store with the others till every white in Ohio was served before the keeper turned to the cluster of Negro faces looking through a hole in his back door. She was ashamed, too, because it was stealing and Sixo's argument on the subject amused her but didn't change the way she felt; just as it didn't change schoolteacher's mind.

"Did you steal that shoat? You stole that shoat." School-teacher was quiet but firm, like he was just going through the motions – not expecting an answer that mattered. Sixo sat there, not even getting up to plead or deny. He just sat there, the streak-of-lean in his hand, the gristle clustered in the tin plate like gemstones – rough, unpolished, but loot nevertheless.

"You stole that shoat, didn't you?"

"No. Sir," said Sixo, but he had the decency to keep his eyes on the meat.

"You telling me you didn't steal it, and I'm looking right at you?"

"No, sir. I didn't steal it."

Schoolteacher smiled. "Did you kill it?"

"Yes, sir. I killed it."

"Did you butcher it?"

"Yes, sir."

"Did you cook it?"

"Yes, sir."

"Well, then. Did you eat it?"

"Yes, sir. I sure did."

"And you telling me that's not stealing?"

"No, sir. It ain't."

"What is it then?"

"Improving your property, sir."

"What?"

"Sixo plant rye to give the high piece a better chance. Sixo take and feed the soil, give you more crop. Sixo take and feed Sixo give you more work."

Clever, but schoolteacher beat him anyway to show him that definitions belonged to the definers – not the defined. After Mr. Garner died with a hole in his ear that Mrs. Garner said was an exploded ear drum brought on by stroke and Sixo said was gunpowder, everything they touched was looked on as stealing. Not just a rifle of corn, or two yard eggs the hen herself didn't even remember, everything. Schoolteacher took away the guns from the Sweet Home men and, deprived of game to round out their diet of bread, beans, hominy, vegetables and a little extra at slaughter time, they began to pilfer in earnest, and it became not only their right but their obligation.

Sethe understood it then, but now with a paying job and an employer who was kind enough to hire an ex-convict, she despised herself for the pride that made pilfering better than standing in line at the window of the general store with all the other Negroes. She didn't want to jostle them or be jostled by them. Feel their judgment or their pity, especially now. She touched her forehead with the back of her wrist and blotted the perspiration. The workday had come to a close and already she was feeling the excitement. Not since that other escape had she felt so alive. Slopping the alley dogs, watching their frenzy, she pressed her lips. Today would be a day she would accept a lift, if anybody on a wagon offered it. No one would, and for sixteen years her pride had not let her ask. But today. Oh, today. Now she wanted speed, to skip over the long walk home and *be* there.

When Sawyer warned her about being late again, she barely heard him. He used to be a sweet man. Patient, tender in his dealings with his help. But each year, following the death of his son in the War, he grew more and more crotchety. As though Sethe's dark face was to blame.

"Un huh," she said, wondering how she could hurry time along and get to the no-time waiting for her.

She needn't have worried. Wrapped tight, hunched forward, as she started home her mind was busy with the things she could forget.

Thank God I don't have to rememory or say a thing because you know it. All. You know I never would a left you. Never. It was all I could think of to do. When the train came I had to be ready. Schoolteacher was teaching us things we couldn't learn. I didn't care nothing about the measuring string. We all laughed about that – except Sixo. He didn't laugh at nothing. But I didn't care. Schoolteacher'd wrap that string all over my head, 'cross my nose, around my behind. Number my teeth. I thought he was a fool. And the questions he asked was the biggest foolishness of all.

Then me and your brothers come up from the second patch. The first one was close to the house where the quick things grew: beans, onions, sweet peas. The other one was further down for long-lasting things, potatoes, pumpkin, okra, pork salad. Not much was up yet down there. It was early still. Some young salad maybe, but that was all. We pulled weeds and hoed a little to give everything a good start. After that we hit out for the house. The ground raised up from the second patch. Not a hill exactly but kind of. Enough for Buglar and Howard to run up and roll down, run up and roll down. That's the way I used to see them in my dreams, laughing, their short fat legs running up the hill. Now all I see is their backs walking down the railroad tracks. Away from me. Always away from me. But that day they was happy, running up and rolling down. It was early still –

the growing season had took hold but not much was up. I remember the peas still had flowers. The grass was long though, full of white buds and those tall red blossoms people call Diane and something there with the leastest little bit of blue – light, like a cornflower but pale, pale. Real pale. I maybe should have hurried because I left you back at the house in a basket in the yard. Away from where the chickens scratched but you never know. Anyway I took my time getting back but your brothers didn't have patience with me staring at flowers and sky every two or three steps. They ran on ahead and I let em. Something sweet lives in the air that time of year, and if the breeze is right, it's hard to stay indoors. When I got back I could hear Howard and Buglar laughing down by the quarters. I put my hoe down and cut across the side yard to get to you. The shade moved so by the time I got back the sun was shining right on you. Right in your face, but you wasn't woke at all. Still asleep. I wanted to pick you up in my arms and I wanted to look at you sleeping too. Didn't know which; you had the sweetest face. Yonder, not far, was a grape arbor Mr. Garner made. Always full of big plans, he wanted to make his own wine to get drunk off. Never did get more than a kettle of jelly from it. I don't think the soil was right for grapes. Your daddy believed it was the rain, not the soil. Sixo said it was bugs. The grapes so little and tight. Sour as vinegar too. But there was a little table in there. So I picked up your basket and carried you over to the grape arbor. Cool in there and shady. I set you down on the little table and figured if I got a piece of muslin the bugs and things wouldn't get to you. And if Mrs. Garner didn't need me right there in the kitchen, I could get a chair and you and me could set out there while I did the vegetables. I headed for the back door to get the clean muslin we kept in the kitchen press. The grass felt good on my feet. I got near the door and I heard voices. Schoolteacher made his pupils sit and learn books for a spell every afternoon. If it was nice enough weather, they'd sit on the side porch. All three of em. He'd talk and they'd write. Or he would read and they would write down what he said. I never told nobody this. Not your pap, not nobody. I almost told Mrs. Garner, but she was so weak then and getting weaker. This is the first time I'm telling it and I'm telling it to you because it might help explain something to you although I know you don't need me to do it. To tell it or even think over it. You don't have to listen either, if you don't want to. But I couldn't help listening to what I heard that day. He was talking to his pupils and I heard him say, "Which one are you doing?" And one of the boys said, "Sethe." That's when I stopped because I heard my name, and then I took a few steps to where I could see what they was doing. School-teacher was standing over one of them with one hand behind his back. He licked a forefinger a couple of times and turned a few pages. Slow. I was about to turn around and keep on my way to where the muslin was, when I heard him say, "No, no. That's not the way. I told you to put her human characteristics on the left; her animal ones on the right. And don't forget to line them up." I commenced to walk backward, didn't even look behind me to find out where I was headed. I just kept lifting my feet and pushing back. When I bumped up against a tree my scalp was prickly. One of the dogs was licking out a pan in the yard. I got to the grape arbor fast enough, but I didn't have the muslin. Flies settled all over your face, rubbing their hands. My head itched like the devil. Like somebody was sticking fine needles in my scalp. I never told Halle or nobody. But that very day I asked Mrs. Garner a part of it. She was low then. Not as low as she ended up, but failing. A kind of bag grew under her jaw. It didn't seem to hurt her, but it made her weak. First she'd be up and spry in the morning and by the second milking she couldn't stand up. Next she took to sleeping late. The day I went up there she was in bed the whole day, and I thought to carry her some bean soup and ask her then. When I opened the bedroom door she looked at me from underneath her nightcap. Already it was hard to catch life in her eyes. Her shoes and stockings were on the floor so I knew she had tried to get dressed.

"I brung you some bean soup," I said.

She said, "I don't think I can swallow that."

"Try a bit," I told her.

"Too thick. I'm sure it's too thick."

"Want me to loosen it up with a little water?"

"No. Take it away. Bring me some cool water, that's all."

"Yes, ma'am. Ma'am? Could I ask you something?"

"What is it, Sethe?"

"What do characteristics mean?"

"What?"

"A word. Characteristics."

"Oh." She moved her head around on the pillow. "Features. Who taught you that?"

"I heard the schoolteacher say it."

"Change the water, Sethe. This is warm."

"Yes, ma'am. Features?"

"Water, Sethe. Cool water."

I put the pitcher on the tray with the white bean soup and went downstairs. When I got back with the fresh water I held her head while she drank. It took her a while because that lump made it hard to swallow. She laid back and wiped her mouth. The drinking seemed to satisfy her but she frowned and said, "I don't seem able to wake up, Sethe. All I seem to want is sleep."

"Then do it," I told her. "I'm take care of things."

Then she went on: what about this? what about that? Said she knew Halle was no trouble, but she wanted to know if schoolteacher was handling the Pauls all right and Sixo.

"Yes, ma'am," I said. "Look like it."

"Do they do what he tells them?"

"They don't need telling."

"Good. That's a mercy. I should be back downstairs in a day or two. I just need more rest. Doctor's due back. Tomorrow, is it?"

"You said features, ma'am?"

"What?"

"Features?"

"Umm. Like, a feature of summer is heat. A characteristic is a feature. A thing that's natural to a thing."

"Can you have more than one?"

"You can have quite a few. You know. Say a baby sucks its thumb. That's one, but it has others too. Keep Billy away from Red Cora. Mr. Garner never let her calve every other year. Sethe, you hear me? Come away from that window and listen."

"Yes, ma'am."

"Ask my brother-in-law to come up after supper."

"Yes, ma'am."

"If you'd wash your hair you could get rid of that lice."

"Ain't no lice in my head, ma'am."

"Whatever it is, a good scrubbing is what it needs, not scratching. Don't tell me we're out of soap."

"No, ma'am."

"All right now. I'm through. Talking makes me tired."

"Yes, ma'am."

"And thank you, Sethe."

"Yes, ma'am."

You was too little to remember the quarters. Your brothers slept under the window. Me, you and your daddy slept by the wall. The night after I heard why schoolteacher measured me, I had trouble sleeping. When Halle came in I asked him what he thought about schoolteacher. He said there wasn't nothing to think about. Said, He's white, ain't he? I said, But I mean is he like Mr. Garner?

"What you want to know, Sethe?"

"Him and her," I said, "they ain't like the whites I seen before. The ones in the big place I was before I came here."

"How these different?" he asked me.

"Well," I said, "they talk soft for one thing."

"It don't matter, Sethe. What they say is the same. Loud or soft."

"Mr. Garner let you buy out your mother," I said.

"Yep. He did."

"Well?"

"If he hadn't of, she would of dropped in his cooking stove."

"Still, he did it. Let you work it off."

"Uh huh."

"Wake up, Halle."

"I said, Uh huh."

"He could of said no. He didn't tell you no."

"No, he didn't tell me no. She worked here for ten years. If she worked another ten you think she would've made it out? I pay him for her last years and in return he got you, me and three more coming up. I got one more year of debt work; one more. Schoolteacher in there told me to quit it. Said the reason for doing it don't hold. I should do the extra but here at Sweet Home."

"Is he going to pay you for the extra?"

"Nope."

"Then how you going to pay it off? How much is it?"

"$123.70."

"Don't he want it back?"

"He want something."

"What?"

"I don't know. Something. But he don't want me off Sweet Home no more. Say it don't pay to have my labor somewhere else while the boys is small."

"What about the money you owe?"

"He must have another way of getting it."

"What way?"

"I don't know, Sethe."

"Then the only question is how? How he going get it?"

"No. That's one question. There's one more."

"What's that?"

He leaned up and turned over, touching my cheek with his knuckles. "The question now is, Who's going buy you out? Or me? Or her?" He pointed over to where you was laying.

"What?"

"If all my labor is Sweet Home, including the extra, what I got left to sell?"

He turned over then and went back to sleep and I thought I wouldn't but I did too for a while. Something he said, maybe, or something he didn't say woke me. I sat up like somebody hit me, and you woke up too and commenced to cry. I rocked you some, but there wasn't much room, so I stepped outside the door to walk you. Up and down I went. Up and down. Everything dark but lamplight in the top window of the house. She must've been up still. I couldn't get out of my head the thing that woke me up: "While the boys is small." That's what he said and it snapped me awake. They tagged after me the whole day weeding, milking, getting firewood. For now. For now.

That's when we should have begun to plan. But we didn't. I don't know what we thought – but getting away was a money thing to us. Buy out. Running was nowhere on our minds. All of us? Some? Where to? How to go? It was Sixo who brought it up, finally, after Paul F. Mrs. Garner sold him, trying to keep things up. Already she lived two years off his price. But it ran out, I guess, so she wrote schoolteacher to come take over. Four Sweet Home men and she still believed she needed her brother-in-law and two boys 'cause people said she shouldn't be alone out there with nothing but Negroes. So he came with a big hat and spectacles and a coach box full of paper. Talking soft and watching hard. He beat Paul A. Not hard and not long, but it was the first time anyone had, because Mr. Garner disallowed it. Next time I saw him he had company in the prettiest trees you ever saw. Sixo started watching the sky. He was the only one who crept at night and Halle said that's how he learned about the train.

"That way." Halle was pointing over the stable. "Where he took my ma'am. Sixo say freedom is that way. A whole train is going and if we can get there, don't need to be no buy-out."

"Train? What's that?" I asked him.

They stopped talking in front of me then. Even Halle. But they whispered among themselves and Sixo watched the sky. Not the high part, the low part where it touched the trees. You could tell his mind was gone from Sweet Home.

The plan was a good one, but when it came time, I was big with Denver. So we changed it a little. A little. Just enough to butter Halle's face, so Paul D tells me, and make Sixo laugh at last.

But I got you out, baby. And the boys too. When the signal for the train come, you all was the only ones ready. I couldn't find Halle or nobody. I didn't know Sixo was burned up and Paul D dressed in a collar you wouldn't believe. Not till later. So I sent you all to the wagon with the woman who waited in the corn. Ha ha. No notebook for my babies and no measuring string neither. What I had to get through later I got through because of you. Passed right by those boys hanging in the trees. One had Paul A's shirt on but not his feet or his head. I walked right on by because only me had your milk, and God do what He would, I was going to get it to you. You remember that, don't you; that I did? That when I got here I had milk enough for all?

*

228

One more curve in the road, and Sethe could see her chimney; it wasn't lonely-looking anymore. The ribbon of smoke was from a fire that warmed a body returned to her — just like it never went away, never needed a headstone. And the heart that beat inside it had not for a single moment stopped in her hands.

She opened the door, walked in and locked it tight behind her.

The day Stamp Paid saw the two backs through the window and then hurried down the steps, he believed the undecipherable language clamoring around the house was the mumbling of the black and angry dead. Very few had died in bed, like Baby Suggs, and none that he knew of, including Baby, had lived a livable life. Even the educated colored: the long-school people, the doctors, the teachers, the paper-writers and businessmen had a hard row to hoe. In addition to having to use their heads to get ahead, they had the weight of the whole race sitting there. You needed two heads for that. Whitepeople believed that whatever the manners, under every dark skin was a jungle. Swift unnavigable waters, swinging screaming baboons, sleeping snakes, red gums ready for their sweet white blood. In a way, he thought, they were right. The more coloredpeople spent their strength trying to convince them how gentle they were, how clever and loving, how human, the more they used themselves up to persuade whites of something Negroes believed could not be questioned, the deeper and more tangled the jungle grew inside. But it wasn't the jungle blacks brought with them to this place from the other (livable) place. It was the jungle whitefolks planted in them. And it grew. It spread. In, through and after life, it spread, until it invaded the whites who had made it. Touched them every one. Changed and altered them. Made them bloody, silly, worse than even they wanted to be, so scared were they of the jungle they had made. The screaming baboon lived under their own white skin; the red gums were their own.

Meantime, the secret spread of this new kind of whitefolks' jungle was hidden, silent, except once in a while when you could hear its mumbling in places like 124.

Stamp Paid abandoned his efforts to see about Sethe, after the pain of knocking and not gaining entrance, and when he did, 124 was left to its own devices. When Sethe locked the door, the women inside were free at last to be what they liked, see whatever they saw and say whatever was on their minds.

Almost. Mixed in with the voices surrounding the house, recognizable but undecipherable to Stamp Paid, were the thoughts of the women of 124, unspeakable thoughts, unspoken.

BELOVED, SHE MY daughter. She mine. See. She come back to me of her own free will and I don't have to explain a thing. I didn't have time to explain before because it had to be done quick. Quick. She had to be safe and I put her where she would be. But my love was tough and she back now. I knew she would be. Paul D ran her off so she had no choice but to come back to me in the flesh. I bet you Baby Suggs, on the other side, helped. I won't never let her go. I'll explain to her, even though I don't have to. Why I did it. How if I hadn't killed her she would have died and that is something I could not bear to happen to her. When I explain it she'll understand, because she understands everything already. I'll tend her as no mother ever tended a child, a daughter. Nobody will ever get my milk no more except my own children. I never had to give it to nobody else – and the one time I did it was took from me – they held me down and took it. Milk that belonged to my baby. Nan had to nurse whitebabies and me too because Ma'am was in the rice. The little whitebabies got it first and I got what was left. Or none. There was no nursing milk to call my own. I know what it is to be without the milk that belongs to you; to have to fight and holler for it, and to have so little left. I'll tell Beloved about that; she'll understand. She my daughter. The one I managed to have milk for and to get it to her even after they stole it; after they handled me like I was the cow, no, the goat, back behind the stable because it was too nasty to stay in with the horses. But I wasn't too nasty to cook their food or take care of Mrs. Garner. I tended her like

I would have tended my own mother if she needed me. If they had let her out the rice field, because I was the one she didn't throw away. I couldn't have done more for that woman than I would my own ma'am if she was to take sick and need me and I'd have stayed with her till she got well or died. And I would have stayed after that except Nan snatched me back. Before I could check for the sign. It was her all right, but for a long time I didn't believe it. I looked everywhere for that hat. Stuttered after that. Didn't stop it till I saw Halle. Oh, but that's all over now. I'm here. I lasted. And my girl come home. Now I can look at things again because she's here to see them too. After the shed, I stopped. Now, in the morning, when I light the fire I mean to look out the window to see what the sun is doing to the day. Does it hit the pump handle first or the spigot? See if the grass is gray-green or brown or what. Now I know why Baby Suggs pondered color her last years. She never had time to see, let alone enjoy it before. Took her a long time to finish with blue, then yellow, then green. She was well into pink when she died. I don't believe she wanted to get to red and I understand why because me and Beloved outdid ourselves with it. Matter of fact, that and her pinkish headstone was the last color I recall. Now I'll be on the lookout. Think what spring will be for us! I'll plant carrots just so she can see them, and turnips. Have you ever seen one, baby? A prettier thing God never made. White and purple with a tender tail and a hard head. Feels good when you hold it in your hand and smells like the creek when it floods, bitter but happy. We'll smell them together, Beloved. Beloved. Because you mine and I have to show you these things, and teach you what a mother should. Funny how you lose sight of some things and memory others. I never will forget that whitegirl's hands. Amy. But I forget the color of all that hair on her head. Eyes must have been gray, though. Seem like I do rememory that. Mrs. Garner's was light brown – while she was well. Got dark when she took sick. A strong woman, used to be. And when she talked off her head, she'd say it. "I used to be strong as a mule, Jenny." Called me "Jenny" when she was babbling, and I can bear witness to that. Tall and strong. The two of us on a cord of wood was as good as two men. Hurt her like the devil not to be able to raise her head off the pillow. Still can't figure why she thought she needed schoolteacher, though. I wonder if she lasted, like I did. Last time I saw her she couldn't do nothing but cry, and I couldn't do a thing for her but wipe her face when I told her what they done to me. Somebody had to know it. Hear it. Somebody. Maybe she lasted. Schoolteacher wouldn't treat her the way he treated me. First beating I took was the last. Nobody going to keep me from my children. Hadn't been for me taking care of her maybe I would have known what happened. Maybe Halle was trying to get to me. I stood by her bed waiting for her to finish with the slop jar. When I got her back in the bed she said she was cold. Hot as blazes and she wanted quilts. Said to shut the window. I told her no. She needed the cover; I needed the breeze. Long as those yellow curtains flapped, I was all right. Should have heeded her. Maybe what sounded like shots really was. Maybe I would have seen somebody or something. Maybe. Anyhow I took my babies to the corn, Halle or no. Jesus. When I heard that woman's rattle. She said, Any more? I told her I didn't know. She said, I been here all night. Can't wait. I tried to make her. She said, Can't do it. Come on. Hoo! Not a man around. Boys scared. You asleep on my back. Denver sleep in my stomach. Felt like I was split in two. I told her to take you all; I had to go back. In case. She just looked at me. Said, Woman? Bit a piece of my tongue off when they opened my back. It was hanging by a shred. I didn't mean to. Clamped down on it, it come right off. I thought, Good God, I'm going to eat myself up. They dug a hole for my stomach so as not to hurt the baby. Denver don't like for me to talk about it. She hates anything about Sweet Home except how she was born. But you was there and even if you too young to memory it, I can tell it to you. The grape arbor. You memory that? I ran so fast. Flies beat me to you. I would have known right away who you was when the sun blotted out your face the way it did when I took you to the grape arbor. I would have known at once when my water broke. The minute I saw you sitting on the stump, it broke. And when I did see your face it had more than a hint of what you would look like after all these years. I would have known who you were right away because the cup after cup of water you drank proved and connected to the fact that you dribbled clear spit on my face the day I got to 124. I would have known right off, but Paul D distracted me. Otherwise I would have seen my fingernail prints right there on your forehead for all the world see. From when I held your head up, out in the shed. And later on, when you asked me about the earrings I used to dangle for you to play with, I would have recognized you right off, except for Paul D. Seems to me he wanted you out from the beginning, but I wouldn't let him. What you think? And look how he ran when he found out about me and you in the shed. Too rough for him to listen to. Too thick, he said. My love was too thick. What he know about it? Who in the world is he willing to die for? Would he give his privates to a stranger in return for a carving? Some other way, he said. There must have been some other way. Let schoolteacher haul us away, I guess, to measure your behind before he tore it up? I have felt what it felt like and nobody walking or stretched out is going to make you feel it too. Not you, not none of mine, and when I tell you you mine, I also mean I'm yours. I wouldn't draw breath without my children. I told Baby Suggs that and she got down on her knees to beg God's pardon for me. Still, it's so. My plan was to take us all to the other side where my own ma'am is. They stopped me from getting us there, but they didn't stop you from getting here. Ha ha. You came right on back like a good girl, like a daughter, which is what I wanted to be and would have been if my ma'am had been able to get out of the rice long enough before they hanged her and let me be one. You know what? She'd had the bit so many times she smiled. When she wasn't smiling she smiled, and I never saw her own smile. I wonder what they was doing when they was caught. Running, you think? No. Not that. Because she was my ma'am and nobody's ma'am would run off and leave her daughter, would she? Would she, now? Leave her in the yard with a one-armed woman? Even if she hadn't been able to suckle the daughter for more than a week or two and had to turn her over to another woman's tit that never had enough for all. They said it was the bit that made her smile when she didn't want to. Like the Saturday girls working the slaughterhouse yard. When I came out of jail I saw them plain. They came when the shift changed on Saturday when the men got paid and worked behind the fences, back of the outhouse. Some worked standing up, leaning on the toolhouse door. They gave some of their nickels and dimes to the foreman as they left but by then their smiles was over. Some of them drank liquor to keep from feeling what they felt. Some didn't drink a drop – just beat it on over to Phelps to pay for what their children needed, or their ma'ammies. Working a pig yard. That has got to be something for a woman to do, and I got close to it myself when I got out of jail and bought, so to speak, your name. But the Bodwins got me the cooking job at Sawyer's and left me able to smile on my own like now when I think about you.

But you know all that because you smart like everybody said because when I got here you was crawling already. Trying to get up the stairs. Baby Suggs had them painted white so you could see your way to the top in the dark where lamplight didn't reach. Lord, you loved the stairsteps.

I got close. I got close. To being a Saturday girl. I had

already worked a stone mason's shop. A step to the slaughter-house would have been a short one. When I put that head-stone up I wanted to lay in there with you, put your head on my shoulder and keep you warm, and I would have if Buglar and Howard and Denver didn't need me, because my mind was homeless then. I couldn't lay down with you then. No matter how much I wanted to. I couldn't lay down nowhere in peace, back then. Now I can. I can sleep like the drowned, have mercy. She come back to me, my daughter, and she is mine.

BELOVED IS MY SISTER. I swallowed her blood right along with my mother's milk. The first thing I heard after not hearing anything was the sound of her crawling up the stairs. She was my secret company until Paul D came. He threw her out. Ever since I was little she was my company and she helped me wait for my daddy. Me and her waited for him. I love my mother but I know she killed one of her own daughters, and tender as she is with me, I'm scared of her because of it. She missed killing my brothers and they knew it. They told me die-witch! stories to show me the way to do it, if ever I needed to. Maybe it was getting that close to dying made them want to fight the War. That's what they told me they were going to do. I guess they rather be around killing men than killing women, and there sure is something in her that makes it all right to kill her own. All the time, I'm afraid the thing that happened that made it all right for my mother to kill my sister could happen again. I don't know what it is, I don't know who it is, but maybe there is something else terrible enough to make her do it again. I need to know what that thing might be, but I don't want to. Whatever it is, it comes from outside this house, outside the yard, and it can come right on in the yard if it wants to. So I never leave this house and I watch over the yard, so it can't happen again and my mother won't have to kill me too. Not since Miss Lady Jones' house have I left 124 by myself. Never. The only other times – two times in all – I was with my mother. Once to see Grandma Baby put down next to Beloved, she's my sister. The other time Paul D went

237

too and when we came back I thought the house would still be empty from when he threw my sister's ghost out. But no. When I came back to 124, there she was. Beloved. Waiting for me. Tired from her long journey back. Ready to be taken care of; ready for me to protect her. This time I have to keep my mother away from her. That's hard, but I have to. It's all on me. I've seen my mother in a dark place, with scratching noises. A smell coming from her dress. I have been with her where something little watched us from the corners. And touched. Sometimes they touched. I didn't remember it for a long time until Nelson Lord made me. I asked her if it was true but couldn't hear what she said and there was no point in going back to Lady Jones if you couldn't hear what anybody said. So quiet. Made me have to read faces and learn how to figure out what people were thinking, so I didn't need to hear what they said. That's how come me and Beloved could play together. Not talking. On the porch. By the creek. In the secret house. It's all on me, now, but she can count on me. I thought she was trying to kill her that day in the Clearing. Kill her back. But then she kissed her neck and I have to warn her about that. Don't love her too much. Don't. Maybe it's still in her the thing that makes it all right to kill her children. I have to tell her. I have to protect her.

She cut my head off every night. Buglar and Howard told me she would and she did. Her pretty eyes looking at me like I was a stranger. Not mean or anything, but like I was somebody she found and felt sorry for. Like she didn't want to do it but she had to and it wasn't going to hurt. That it was just a thing grown-up people do – like pull a splinter out your hand; touch the corner of a towel in your eye if you get a cinder in it. She looks over at Buglar and Howard – see if they all right. Then she comes over to my side. I know she'll be good at it, careful. That when she cuts it off it'll be done right; it won't hurt. After she does it I lie there for a minute with just my head. Then she carries it downstairs to braid my hair. I try not to cry but it hurts so much to comb it. When she finishes the combing and starts the braiding, I get sleepy. I want to go to sleep but I know if I do I won't wake up. So I have to stay awake while she finishes my hair, then I can sleep. The scary part is waiting for her to come in and do it. Not when she does it, but when I wait for her to. Only place she can't get to me in the night is Grandma Baby's room. The room we sleep in upstairs used to be where the help slept when whitepeople lived here. They had a kitchen outside, too. But Grandma Baby turned it into a woodshed and toolroom when she moved in. And she boarded up the back door that led to it because she said she didn't want to make that journey no more. She built around it to make a storeroom, so if you want to get in 124 you have to come by her. Said she didn't care what folks said about her fixing a two-story house up like a cabin where you cook inside. She said they told her visitors with nice dresses don't want to sit in the same room with the cook stove and the peelings and the grease and the smoke. She wouldn't pay them no mind, she said. I was safe at night in there with her. All I could hear was me breathing but sometimes in the day I couldn't tell whether it was me breathing or somebody next to me. I used to watch Here Boy's stomach go in and out, in and out, to see if it matched mine, holding my breath to get off his rhythm, releasing it to get on. Just to see whose it was – that sound like when you blow soft in a bottle only regular, regular. Am I making that sound? Is Howard? Who is? That was when everybody was quiet and I couldn't hear anything they said. I didn't care either because the quiet let me dream my daddy better. I always knew he was coming. Something was holding him up. He had a problem with the horse. The river flooded; the boat sank and he had to make a new one. Sometimes it was a lynch mob or a windstorm. He was coming and it was a secret. I spent all of my outside self loving Ma'am so she wouldn't kill me, loving her even when she braided my head at night. I never let her know my daddy was coming for me. Grandma Baby thought he was coming, too. For a while she thought so, then she stopped. I never did. Even when Buglar and Howard ran away. Then Paul D came in here. I heard his voice downstairs, and Ma'am laughing, so I thought it was him, my daddy. Nobody comes to this house anymore. But when I got downstairs it was Paul D and he didn't come for me; he wanted my mother. At first. Then he wanted my sister, too, but she got him out of here and I'm so glad he's gone. Now it's just us and I can protect her till my daddy gets here to help me watch out for Ma'am and anything come in the yard.

My daddy do anything for runny fried eggs. Dip his bread in it. Grandma used to tell me his things. She said anytime she could make him a plate of soft fried eggs was Christmas, made him so happy. She said she was always a little scared of my daddy. He was too good, she said. From the beginning, she said, he was too good for the world. Scared her. She thought, He'll never make it through nothing. Whitepeople must have thought so too, because they never got split up. So she got the chance to know him, look after him, and he scared her the way he loved things. Animals and tools and crops and the alphabet. He could count on paper. The boss taught him. Offered to teach the other boys but only my daddy wanted it. She said the other boys said no. One of them with a number for a name said it would change his mind – make him forget things he shouldn't and memorize things he shouldn't and he didn't want his mind messed up. But my daddy said, If you can't count they can cheat you. If you can't read they can beat you. They thought that was funny. Grandma said she didn't know, but it was because my daddy could count on paper and figure that he bought her away from there. And she said she always wished she could read the Bible like real preachers. So it was good for me to learn how, and I did until it got quiet and all I could hear was my own breathing and one other who knocked over the milk jug while it was sitting on the table. Nobody near it. Ma'am whipped Buglar but he didn't touch it. Then it messed up all the ironed clothes and put its hands in the cake. Look like I was the only one who knew right away who it was. Just like when she came back I knew who she was too. Not right away, but soon as she spelled her name – not her given name, but the one Ma'am paid the stonecutter for – I knew. And when she wondered about Ma'am's earrings – something I didn't know about – well, that just made the cheese more binding: my sister come to help me wait for my daddy.

My daddy was an angel man. He could look at you and tell where you hurt and he could fix it too. He made a hanging thing for Grandma Baby, so she could pull herself up from the floor when she woke up in the morning, and he made a step so when she stood up she was level. Grandma said she was always afraid a whiteman would knock her down in front of her children. She behaved and did everything right in front of her children because she didn't want them to see her knocked down. She said it made children crazy to see that. At Sweet Home nobody did or said they would, so my daddy never saw it there and never went crazy and even now I bet he's trying to get here. If Paul D could do it my daddy could too. Angel man. We should all be together. Me, him and Beloved. Ma'am could stay or go off with Paul D if she wanted to. Unless Daddy wanted her himself, but I don't think he would now, since she let Paul D in her bed. Grandma Baby said people look down on her because she had eight children with different men. Coloredpeople and whitepeople both look down on her for that. Slaves not supposed to have pleasurable feelings on their own; their bodies not supposed to be like that, but they have to have as many children as they can to please whoever owned them. Still, they were not supposed to have pleasure deep down. She said for me not to listen to all that. That I should always listen to my body and love it.

The secret house. When she died I went there. Ma'am wouldn't let me go outside in the yard and eat with the others. We stayed inside. That hurt. I know Grandma Baby would have liked the party and the people who came to it, because she got low not seeing anybody or going anywhere – just grieving and thinking about colors and how she made a mistake. That what she thought about what the heart and the body could do was wrong. The whitepeople came anyway. In her yard. She had done everything right and they came in her yard anyway. And she didn't know what to think. All she had left was her heart and they busted it so even the War couldn't rouse her.

She told me all my daddy's things. How hard he worked to buy her. After the cake was ruined and the ironed clothes all messed up, and after I heard my sister crawling up the stairs to get back to her bed, she told me my things too. That I was charmed. My birth was and I got saved all the time. And that I shouldn't be afraid of the ghost. It wouldn't harm me because I tasted its blood when Ma'am nursed me. She said the ghost was after Ma'am and her too for not doing anything to stop it. But it would never hurt me. I just had to watch out for it because it was a greedy ghost and needed a lot of love, which was only natural, considering. And I do. Love her. I do. She played with me and always came to be with me whenever I needed her. She's mine, Beloved. She's mine.

I AM BELOVED and she is mine. I see her take flowers away
from leaves   she puts them in a round basket   the leaves are
not for her   she fills the basket   she opens the grass
I would help her but the clouds are in the way   how can
I say things that are pictures   I am not separate from her
there is no place where I stop   her face is my own and I want
to be there in the place where her face is and to be looking
at it too   a hot thing

All of it is now   it is always now   there will never be a time
when I am not crouching and watching others who are
crouching too   I am always crouching   the man on my face
is dead   his face is not mine   his mouth smells sweet but
his eyes are locked
        some who eat nasty themselves   I do not eat   the men
without skin bring us their morning water to drink   we
have none   at night I cannot see the dead man on my
face   daylight comes through the cracks and I can see his
locked eyes   I am not big   small rats do not wait for us to
sleep   someone is thrashing but there is no room to do it
in   if we had more to drink we could make tears   we cannot
make sweat or morning water so the men without skin bring
us theirs   one time they bring us sweet rocks to suck   we
are all trying to leave our bodies behind   the man on my
face has done it   it is hard to make yourself die forever   you
sleep short and then return   in the beginning we could
vomit   now we do not
        now we cannot   his teeth are pretty white points

243

someone is trembling   I can feel it over here   he is fighting
hard to leave his body which is a small bird trembling   there
is no room to tremble so he is not able to die   my own dead
man is pulled away from my face   I miss his pretty white
points

We are not crouching now   we are standing but my legs are
like my dead man's eyes   I cannot fall because there is no
room to   the men without skin are making loud noises
I am not dead   the bread is sea-colored   I am too hungry
to eat it   the sun closes my eyes   those able to die are in a
pile   I cannot find my man   the one whose teeth I have
loved   a hot thing   the little hill of dead people   a hot
thing   the men without skin push them through with
poles   the woman is there with the face I want   the face
that is mine   they fall into the sea which is the color of the
bread   she has nothing in her ears   if I had the teeth of the
man who died on my face I would bite the circle around her
neck   bite it away   I know she does not like it   now there
is room to crouch and to watch the crouching others   it is
the crouching that is now always now   inside   the woman
with my face is in the sea   a hot thing

In the beginning I could see her   I could not help her
because the clouds were in the way   in the beginning I could
see her   the shining in her ears   she does not like the circle
around her neck   I know this   I look hard at her so she
will know that the clouds are in the way   I am sure she
saw me   I am looking at her see me   she empties out her
eyes   I am there in the place where her face is and telling her
the noisy clouds were in my way   she wants her earrings
she wants her round basket   I want her face   a hot thing
       in the beginning the women are away from the men
and the men are away from the women   storms rock us

and mix the men into the women and the women into the men   that is when I begin to be on the back of the man   for a long time I see only his neck and his wide shoulders above me   I am small   I love him because he has a song   when he turned around to die I see the teeth he sang through   his singing was soft   his singing is of the place where a woman takes flowers away from their leaves and puts them in a round basket   before the clouds   she is crouching near us   but I do not see her until he locks his eyes and dies on my face   we are that way   there is no breath coming from his mouth and the place where breath should be is sweet-smelling   the others do not know he is dead   I know   his song is gone   now I love his pretty little teeth instead

I cannot lose her again   my dead man was in the way like the noisy clouds   when he dies on my face I can see hers   she is going to smile at me   she is going to   her sharp earrings are gone   the men without skin are making loud noises they push my own man through   they do not push the woman with my face through   she goes in   they do not push her   she goes in   the little hill is gone   she was going to smile at me   she was going to   a hot thing

They are not crouching now   we are   they are floating on the water   they break up the little hill and push it through   I cannot find my pretty teeth   I see the dark face that is going to smile at me   it is my dark face that is going to smile at me   the iron circle is around our neck   she does not have sharp earrings in her ears or a round basket   she goes in the water   with my face

I am standing in the rain falling   the others are taken   I am not taken   I am falling like the rain is   I watch him eat inside I am crouching to keep from falling with the rain

I am going to be in pieces   he hurts where I sleep   he puts his finger there   I drop the food and break into pieces   she took my face away

there is no one to want me   to say me my name   I wait on the bridge because she is under it   there is night and there is day

again   again   night day   night day   I am waiting no iron circle is around my neck   no boats go on this water   no men without skin   my dead man is not floating here   his teeth are down there where the blue is and the grass   so is the face I want   the face that is going to smile at me   it is going to   in the day diamonds are in the water where she is and turtles   in the night I hear chewing and swallowing and laughter   it belongs to me   she is the laugh I am the laugher   I see her face which is mine   it is the face that was going to smile at me in the place where we crouched   now she is going to   her face comes through the water   a hot thing   her face is mine   she is not smiling she is chewing and swallowing   I have to have my face   I go in   the grass opens   she opens it   I am in the water and she is coming   there is no round basket   no iron circle around her neck   she goes up where the diamonds are   I follow her   we are in the diamonds which are her earrings now   my face is coming   I have to have it   I am looking for the join   I am loving my face so much   my dark face is close to me   I want to join   she whispers to me   she whispers   I reach for her   chewing and swallowing   she touches me   she knows I want to join   she chews and swallows me   I am gone   now I am her face   my own face has left me   I see me swim away   a hot thing   I see the bottoms of my feet   I am alone   I want to be the two of us   I want the join

I come out of blue water   after the bottoms of my feet swim   away from me I come up   I need to find a place to be   the air is heavy   I am not dead   I am not   there is

a house   there is what she whispered to me   I am where
she told me   I am not dead   I sit   the sun closes my
eyes   when I open them I see the face I lost   Sethe's is the
face that left me   Sethe sees me see her and I see the
smile   her smiling face is the place for me   it is the face
I lost   she is my face smiling at me   doing it at last   a hot
thing   now we can join   a hot thing

I AM BELOVED and she is mine. Sethe is the one that picked flowers, yellow flowers in the place before the crouching. Took them away from their green leaves. They are on the quilt now where we sleep. She was about to smile at me when the men without skin came and took us up into the sunlight with the dead and shoved them into the sea. Sethe went into the sea. She went there. They did not push her. She went there. She was getting ready to smile at me and when she saw the dead people pushed into the sea she went also and left me there with no face or hers. Sethe is the face I found and lost in the water under the bridge. When I went in, I saw her face coming to me and it was my face too. I wanted to join. I tried to join, but she went up into the pieces of light at the top of the water. I lost her again, but I found the house she whispered to me and there she was, smiling at last. It's good, but I cannot lose her again. All I want to know is why did she go in the water in the place where we crouched? Why did she do that when she was just about to smile at me? I wanted to join her in the sea but I could not move; I wanted to help her when she was picking the flowers, but the clouds of gunsmoke blinded me and I lost her. Three times I lost her: once with the flowers because of the noisy clouds of smoke; once when she went into the sea instead of smiling at me; once under the bridge when I went in to join her and she came toward me but did not smile. She whispered to me, chewed me, and swam away. Now I have found her in this house. She smiles at me and it is my own face smiling. I will not lose her again. She is mine.

*

Tell me the truth. Didn't you come from the other side?
Yes. I was on the other side.
You came back because of me?
Yes.
You rememory me?
Yes. I remember you.
You never forgot me?
Your face is mine.
Do you forgive me? Will you stay? You safe here now.
Where are the men without skin?
Out there. Way off.
Can they get in here?
No. They tried that once, but I stopped them. They won't
   ever come back.
One of them was in the house I was in. He hurt me.
They can't hurt us no more.
Where are your earrings?
They took them from me.
The men without skin took them?
Yes.
I was going to help you but the clouds got in the way.
There're no clouds here.
If they put an iron circle around your neck I will bite it away.
Beloved.
I will make you a round basket.
You're back. You're back.
Will we smile at me?
Can't you see I'm smiling?
I love your face.

We played by the creek.
I was there in the water.
In the quiet time, we played.
The clouds were noisy and in the way.
When I needed you, you came to be with me.

I needed her face to smile.
I could only hear breathing.
The breathing is gone; only the teeth are left.
She said you wouldn't hurt me.
She hurt me.
I will protect you.
I want her face.
Don't love her too much.
I am loving her too much.
Watch out for her; she can give you dreams.
She chews and swallows.
Don't fall asleep when she braids your hair.
She is the laugh; I am the laughter.
I watch the house; I watch the yard.
She left me.
Daddy is coming for us.
A hot thing.

Beloved
You are my sister
You are my daughter
You are my face; you are me
I have found you again; you have come back to me
You are my Beloved
You are mine
You are mine
You are mine

I have your milk
I have your smile
I will take care of you

You are my face; I am you. Why did you leave me who
    am you?
I will never leave you again

BELOVED

Don't ever leave me again
You will never leave me again
You went in the water
I drank your blood
I brought your milk
You forgot to smile
I loved you
You hurt me
You came back to me
You left me

I waited for you
You are mine
You are mine
You are mine

IT WAS A TINY church no bigger than a rich man's parlor. The pews had no backs, and since the congregation was also the choir, it didn't need a stall. Certain members had been assigned the construction of a platform to raise the preacher a few inches above his congregation, but it was a less than urgent task, since the major elevation, a white oak cross, had already taken place. Before it was the Church of the Holy Redeemer, it was a dry-goods shop that had no use for side windows, just front ones for display. These were papered over while members considered whether to paint or curtain them – how to have privacy without losing the little light that might want to shine on them. In the summer the doors were left open for ventilation. In winter an iron stove in the aisle did what it could. At the front of the church was a sturdy porch where customers used to sit, and children laughed at the boy who got his head stuck between the railings. On a sunny and windless day in January it was actually warmer out there than inside, if the iron stove was cold. The damp cellar was fairly warm, but there was no light lighting the pallet or the washbasin or the nail from which a man's clothes could be hung. And an oil lamp in a cellar was sad, so Paul D sat on the porch steps and got additional warmth from a bottle of liquor jammed in his coat pocket. Warmth and red eyes. He held his wrist between his knees, not to keep his hands still but because he had nothing else to hold on to. His tobacco tin, blown open, spilled contents that floated freely and made him their play and prey.

He couldn't figure out why it took so long. He may as well have jumped in the fire with Sixo and they both could have had a good laugh. Surrender was bound to come anyway, why not meet it with a laugh, shouting Seven-O! Why not? Why the delay? He had already seen his brother wave goodbye from the back of a dray, fried chicken in his pocket, tears in his eyes. Mother. Father. Didn't remember the one. Never saw the other. He was the youngest of three half-brothers (same mother – different fathers) sold to Garner and kept there, forbidden to leave the farm, for twenty years. Once, in Maryland, he met four families of slaves who had all been together for a hundred years: great-grands, grands, mothers, fathers, aunts, uncles, cousins, children. Half white, part white, all black, mixed with Indian. He watched them with awe and envy, and each time he discovered large families of black people he made them identify over and over who each was, what relation, who, in fact, belonged to who.

"That there's my auntie. This here's her boy. Yonder is my pap's cousin. My ma'am was married twice – this my half-sister and these her two children. Now, my wife . . ."

Nothing like that had ever been his and growing up at Sweet Home he didn't miss it. He had his brothers, two friends, Baby Suggs in the kitchen, a boss who showed them how to shoot and listened to what they had to say. A mistress who made their soap and never raised her voice. For twenty years they had all lived in that cradle, until Baby left, Sethe came, and Halle took her. He made a family with her, and Sixo was hell-bent to make one with the Thirty-Mile Woman. When Paul D waved goodbye to his oldest brother, the boss was dead, the mistress nervous and the cradle already split. Sixo said the doctor made Mrs. Garner sick. Said he was giving her to drink what stallions got when they broke a leg and no gunpowder could be spared, and had it not been for schoolteacher's new rules, he would have told her so. They laughed at him. Sixo had a knowing tale about everything.

Including Mr. Garner's stroke, which he said was a shot in his ear put there by a jealous neighbor.

"Where's the blood?" they asked him.

There was no blood. Mr. Garner came home bent over his mare's neck, sweating and blue-white. Not a drop of blood. Sixo grunted, the only one of them not sorry to see him go. Later, however, he was mighty sorry; they all were.

"Why she call on him?" Paul D asked. "Why she need the schoolteacher?"

"She need somebody can figure," said Halle.

"You can do figures."

"Not like that."

"No, man," said Sixo. "She need another white on the place."

"What for?"

"What you think? What you think?"

Well, that's the way it was. Nobody counted on Garner dying. Nobody thought he could. How 'bout that? Everything rested on Garner being alive. Without his life each of theirs fell to pieces. Now ain't that slavery or what is it? At the peak of his strength, taller than tall men, and stronger than most, they clipped him, Paul D. First his shotgun, then his thoughts, for schoolteacher didn't take advice from Negroes. The information they offered he called backtalk and developed a variety of corrections (which he recorded in his notebook) to reeducate them. He complained they ate too much, rested too much, talked too much, which was certainly true compared to him, because schoolteacher ate little, spoke less and rested not at all. Once he saw them playing – a pitching game – and his look of deeply felt hurt was enough to make Paul D blink. He was as hard on his pupils as he was on them – except for the corrections.

For years Paul D believed schoolteacher broke into children what Garner had raised into men. And it was that that made them run off. Now, plagued by the contents of his tobacco tin, he wondered how much difference there really was between before schoolteacher and after. Garner called and announced them men – but only on Sweet Home, and by his leave. Was he naming what he saw or creating what he did not? That was the wonder of Sixo, and even Halle; it was always clear to Paul D that those two were men whether Garner said so or not. It troubled him that, concerning his own manhood, he could not satisfy himself on that point. Oh, he did manly things, but was that Garner's gift or his own will? What would he have been anyway – before Sweet Home – without Garner? In Sixo's country, or his mother's? Or, God help him, on the boat? Did a whiteman saying it make it so? Suppose Garner woke up one morning and changed his mind? Took the word away. Would they have run then? And if he didn't, would the Pauls have stayed there all their lives? Why did the brothers need the one whole night to decide? To discuss whether they would join Sixo and Halle. Because they had been isolated in a wonderful lie, dismissing Halle's and Baby Suggs' life before Sweet Home as bad luck. Ignorant of or amused by Sixo's dark stories. Protected and convinced they were special. Never suspecting the problem of Alfred, Georgia; being so in love with the look of the world, putting up with anything and everything, just to stay alive in a place where a moon he had no right to was nevertheless there. Loving small and in secret. His little love was a tree, of course, but not like Brother – old, wide and beckoning.

In Alfred, Georgia, there was an aspen too young to call sapling. Just a shoot no taller than his waist. The kind of thing a man would cut to whip his horse. Song-murder and the aspen. He stayed alive to sing songs that murdered life, and watched an aspen that confirmed it, and never for a minute did he believe he could escape. Until it rained. Afterward, after the Cherokee pointed and sent him running toward blossoms, he wanted simply to move, go, pick up one day and be somewhere else the next. Resigned to life without aunts, cousins, children. Even a woman, until Sethe.

And then she moved him. Just when doubt, regret and every single unasked question was packed away, long after he believed he had willed himself into being, at the very time and place he wanted to take root – she moved him. From room to room. Like a rag doll.

Sitting on the porch of a dry-goods church, a little bit drunk and nothing much to do, he could have these thoughts. Slow, what-if thoughts that cut deep but struck nothing solid a man could hold on to. So he held his wrists. Passing by that woman's life, getting in it and letting it get in him had set him up for this fall. Wanting to live out his life with a whole woman was new, and losing the feeling of it made him want to cry and think deep thoughts that struck nothing solid. When he was drifting, thinking only about the next meal and night's sleep, when everything was packed tight in his chest, he had no sense of failure, of things not working out. Anything that worked at all worked out. Now he wondered what all went wrong, and starting with the Plan, everything had. It was a good plan, too. Worked out in detail with every possibility of error eliminated.

Sixo, hitching up the horses, is speaking English again and tells Halle what his Thirty-Mile Woman told him. That seven Negroes on her place were joining two others going North. That the two others had done it before and knew the way. That one of the two, a woman, would wait for them in the corn when it was high – one night and half of the next day she would wait, and if they came she would take them to the caravan, where the others would be hidden. That she would rattle, and that would be the sign. Sixo was going, his woman was going, and Halle was taking his whole family. The two Pauls say they need time to think about it. Time to wonder where they will end up; how they will live. What work; who will take them in; should they try to get to Paul F, whose owner, they remember, lived in something called the "trace"? It takes them one evening's conversation to decide.

Now all they have to do is wait through the spring, till the corn is as high as it ever got and the moon as fat.

And plan. Is it better to leave in the dark to get a better start, or go at daybreak to be able to see the way better? Sixo spits at the suggestion. Night gives them more time and the protection of color. He does not ask them if they are afraid. He manages some dry runs to the corn at night, burying blankets and two knives near the creek. Will Sethe be able to swim the creek? they ask him. It will be dry, he says, when the corn is tall. There is no food to put by, but Sethe says she will get a jug of cane syrup or molasses, and some bread when it is near the time to go. She only wants to be sure the blankets are where they should be, for they will need them to tie her baby on her back and to cover them during the journey. There are no clothes other than what they wear. And of course no shoes. The knives will help them eat, but they bury rope and a pot as well. A good plan.

They watch and memorize the comings and goings of schoolteacher and his pupils: what is wanted when and where; how long it takes. Mrs. Garner, restless at night, is sunk in sleep all morning. Some days the pupils and their teacher do lessons until breakfast. One day a week they skip breakfast completely and travel ten miles to church, expecting a large dinner upon their return. Schoolteacher writes in his notebook after supper; the pupils clean, mend or sharpen tools. Sethe's work is the most uncertain because she is on call for Mrs. Garner anytime, including nighttime when the pain or the weakness or the downright loneliness is too much for her. So: Sixo and the Pauls will go after supper and wait in the creek for the Thirty-Mile Woman. Halle will bring Sethe and the three children before dawn – before the sun, before the chickens and the milking cow need attention, so by the time smoke should be coming from the cooking stove, they will be in or near the creek with the others. That way, if Mrs. Garner needs Sethe in the night and calls her, Sethe will be there to answer. They only have to wait through the spring.

But. Sethe was pregnant in the spring and by August is so heavy with child she may not be able to keep up with the men, who can carry the children but not her.

But. Neighbors discouraged by Garner when he was alive now feel free to visit Sweet Home and might appear in the right place at the wrong time.

But. Sethe's children cannot play in the kitchen anymore, so she is dashing back and forth between house and quarters – fidgety and frustrated trying to watch over them. They are too young for men's work and the baby girl is nine months old. Without Mrs. Garner's help her work increases as do schoolteacher's demands.

But. After the conversation about the shoat, Sixo is tied up with the stock at night, and locks are put on bins, pens, sheds, coops, the tackroom and the barn door. There is no place to dart into or congregate. Sixo keeps a nail in his mouth now, to help him undo the rope when he has to.

But. Halle is told to work his extra on Sweet Home and has no call to be anywhere other than where schoolteacher tells him. Only Sixo, who has been stealing away to see his woman, and Halle, who has been hired away for years, know what lies outside Sweet Home and how to get there.

It is a good plan. It can be done right under the watchful pupils and their teacher.

But. They had to alter it – just a little. First they change the leaving. They memorize the directions Halle gives them. Sixo, needing time to untie himself, break open the door and not disturb the horses, will leave later, joining them at the creek with the Thirty-Mile Woman. All four will go straight to the corn. Halle, who also needs more time now, because of Sethe, decides to bring her and the children at night; not wait till first light. They will go straight to the corn and not assemble at the creek. The corn stretches to their shoulders – it will never be higher. The moon is swelling. They can hardly harvest, or chop, or clear, or pick, or haul for listening for a rattle that is not bird or snake. Then one midmorning, they hear it. Or Halle does and begins to sing it to the others: "Hush, hush. Somebody's calling my name. Hush, hush. Somebody's calling my name. O my Lord, O my Lord, what shall I do?"

On his dinner break he leaves the field. He has to. He has to tell Sethe that he has heard the sign. For two successive nights she has been with Mrs. Garner and he can't chance it that she will not know that this night she cannot be. The Pauls see him go. From underneath Brother's shade where they are chewing corn cake, they see him, swinging along. The bread tastes good. They lick sweat from their lips to give it a saltier flavor. Schoolteacher and his pupils are already at the house eating dinner. Halle swings along. He is not singing now.

Nobody knows what happened. Except for the churn, that was the last anybody ever saw of Halle. What Paul D knew was that Halle disappeared, never told Sethe anything, and was next seen squatting in butter. Maybe when he got to the gate and asked to see Sethe, schoolteacher heard a tint of anxiety in his voice – the tint that would make him pick up his ever-ready shotgun. Maybe Halle made the mistake of saying "my wife" in some way that would put a light in schoolteacher's eye. Sethe says now that she heard shots, but did not look out the window of Mrs. Garner's bedroom. But Halle was not killed or wounded that day because Paul D saw him later, after she had run off with no one's help; after Sixo laughed and his brother disappeared. Saw him greased and flat-eyed as a fish. Maybe schoolteacher shot after him, shot at his feet, to remind him of the trespass. Maybe Halle got in the barn, hid there and got locked in with the rest of schoolteacher's stock. Maybe anything. He disappeared and everybody was on his own.

Paul A goes back to moving timber after dinner. They are to meet at quarters for supper. He never shows up. Paul D leaves for the creek on time, believing, hoping, Paul A has gone on ahead; certain schoolteacher has learned something. Paul D gets to the creek and it is as dry as Sixo promised. He waits there with the Thirty-Mile Woman for Sixo and Paul A. Only Sixo shows up, his wrists bleeding, his tongue licking his lips like a flame.

"You see Paul A?"

"No."

"Halle?"

"No."

"No sign of them?"

"No sign. Nobody in quarters but the children."

"Sethe?"

"Her children sleep. She must be there still."

"I can't leave without Paul A."

"I can't help you."

"Should I go back and look for them?"

"I can't help you."

"What you think?"

"I think they go straight to the corn."

Sixo turns, then, to the woman and they clutch each other and whisper. She is lit now with some glowing, some shining that comes from inside her. Before when she knelt on creek pebbles with Paul D, she was nothing, a shape in the dark breathing lightly.

Sixo is about to crawl out to look for the knives he buried. He hears something. He hears nothing. Forget the knives. Now. The three of them climb up the bank and school-teacher, his pupils and four other whitemen move toward them. With lamps. Sixo pushes the Thirty-Mile Woman and she runs further on in the creekbed. Paul D and Sixo run the other way toward the woods. Both are surrounded and tied.

The air gets sweet then. Perfumed by the things honeybees love. Tied like a mule, Paul D feels how dewy and inviting the grass is. He is thinking about that and where Paul A might be when Sixo turns and grabs the mouth of the nearest pointing rifle. He begins to sing. Two others shove Paul D and tie him to a tree. Schoolteacher is saying, "Alive. Alive. I want him alive." Sixo swings and cracks the ribs of one, but with bound hands cannot get the weapon in position to use it in any other way. All the whitemen have to do is wait. For his song, perhaps, to end? Five guns are trained on him while they listen. Paul D cannot see them when they step away from lamplight. Finally one of them hits Sixo in the head with his rifle, and when he comes to, a hickory fire is in front of him and he is tied at the waist to a tree. School-teacher has changed his mind: "This one will never be suitable." The song must have convinced him.

The fire keeps failing and the whitemen are put out with themselves at not being prepared for this emergency. They came to capture, not kill. What they can manage is only enough for cooking hominy. Dry faggots are scarce and the grass is slick with dew.

By the light of the hominy fire Sixo straightens. He is through with his song. He laughs. A rippling sound like Sethe's sons make when they tumble in hay or splash in rainwater. His feet are cooking; the cloth of his trousers smokes. He laughs. Something is funny. Paul D guesses what it is when Sixo interrupts his laughter to call out, "Seven-O! Seven-O!"

Smoky, stubborn fire. They shoot him to shut him up. Have to.

Shackled, walking through the perfumed things honeybees love, Paul D hears the men talking and for the first time learns his worth. He has always known, or believed he did, his value – as a hand, a laborer who could make profit on a farm – but now he discovers his worth, which is to say he learns his price. The dollar value of his weight, his strength, his heart, his brain, his penis, and his future.

As soon as the whitemen get to where they have tied their horses and mount them, they are calmer, talking among themselves about the difficulty they face. The problems. Voices remind schoolteacher about the spoiling these particular slaves have had at Garner's hands. There's laws against what he done: letting niggers hire out their own time to buy themselves. He even let em have guns! And you think he mated them niggers to get him some more? Hell no! He planned for them to marry! if that don't beat all! School-teacher sighs, and says doesn't he know it? He had come to put the place aright. Now it faced greater ruin than what Garner left for it, because of the loss of two niggers, at the least, and maybe three because he is not sure they will find the one called Halle. The sister-in-law is too weak to help out and doggone if now there ain't a full-scale stampede on his hands. He would have to trade this here one for $900 if he could get it, and set out to secure the breeding one, her foal and the other one, if he found him. With the money from "this here one" he could get two young ones, twelve or fifteen years old. And maybe with the breeding one, her three pickaninnies and whatever the foal might be, he and his nephews would have seven niggers and Sweet Home would be worth the trouble it was causing him.

"Look to you like Lillian gonna make it?"

"Touch and go. Touch and go."

"You was married to her sister-in-law, wasn't you?"

"I was."

"She frail too?"

"A bit. Fever took her."

"Well, you don't need to stay no widower in these parts."

"My cogitation right now is Sweet Home."

"Can't say as I blame you. That's some spread."

They put a three-spoke collar on him so he can't lie down and they chain his ankles together. The number he heard with his ear is now in his head. Two. Two? Two niggers lost? Paul D thinks his heart is jumping. They are going to look for Halle, not Paul A. They must have found Paul A and if a whiteman finds you it means you are surely lost.

Schoolteacher looks at him for a long time before he closes the door of the cabin. Carefully, he looks. Paul D does not look back. It is sprinkling now. A teasing August rain that raises expectations it cannot fill. He thinks he should have sung along. Loud, something loud and rolling to go with Sixo's tune, but the words put him off – he didn't understand the words. Although it shouldn't have mattered because he understood the sound: hatred so loose it was juba.

The warm sprinkle comes and goes, comes and goes. He thinks he hears sobbing that seems to come from Mrs. Garner's window, but it could be anything, anyone, even a she-cat making her yearning known. Tired of holding his head up, he lets his chin rest on the collar and speculates on how he can hobble over to the grate, boil a little water and throw in a handful of meal. That's what he is doing when Sethe comes in, rain-wet and big-bellied, saying she is going to cut. She has just come back from taking her children to the corn. The whites were not around. She couldn't find Halle. Who was caught? Did Sixo get away? Paul A?

He tells her what he knows: Sixo is dead; the Thirty-Mile Woman ran, and he doesn't know what happened to Paul A or Halle. "Where could he be?" she asks.

Paul D shrugs because he can't shake his head.

"You saw Sixo die? You sure?"

"I'm sure."

"Was he woke when it happened? Did he see it coming?"

"He was woke. Woke and laughing."

"Sixo laughed?"

"You should have heard him, Sethe."

Sethe's dress steams before the little fire over which he is boiling water. It is hard to move about with shackled ankles and the neck jewelry embarrasses him. In his shame he avoids her eyes, but when he doesn't he sees only black in them – no whites. She says she is going, and he thinks she will never make it to the gate, but he doesn't dissuade her. He knows he will never see her again, and right then and there his heart stopped.

The pupils must have taken her to the barn for sport right afterward, and when she told Mrs. Garner, they took down the cowhide. Who in hell or on this earth would have thought that she would cut anyway? They must have believed, what with her belly and her back, that she wasn't going anywhere. He wasn't surprised to learn that they had tracked her down in Cincinnati, because, when he thought about it now, her price was greater than his; property that reproduced itself without cost.

Remembering his own price, down to the cent, that schoolteacher was able to get for him, he wondered what Sethe's would have been. What had Baby Suggs' been? How much did Halle owe, still, besides his labor? What did Mrs. Garner get for Paul F? More than nine hundred dollars? How much more? Ten dollars? Twenty? Schoolteacher would know. He knew the worth of everything. It accounted for the real sorrow in his voice when he pronounced Sixo unsuitable. Who could be fooled into buying a singing nigger with a gun? Shouting Seven-O! Seven-O! because his Thirty-Mile Woman got away with his blossoming seed. What a laugh. So rippling and full of glee it put out the fire. And it was Sixo's laughter that was on his mind, not the bit in his mouth, when they hitched him to the buckboard. Then he saw Halle, then the rooster, smiling as if to say, You ain't seen nothing yet. How could a rooster know about Alfred, Georgia?

"HOWDY."

Stamp Paid was still fingering the ribbon and it made a little motion in his pants pocket.

Paul D looked up, noticed the side pocket agitation and snorted. "I can't read. You got any more newspaper for me, just a waste of time."

Stamp withdrew the ribbon and sat down on the steps.

"No. This here's something else." He stroked the red cloth between forefinger and thumb. "Something else."

Paul D didn't say anything so the two men sat in silence for a few moments.

"This is hard for me," said Stamp. "But I got to do it. Two things I got to say to you. I'm a take the easy one first."

Paul D chuckled. "If it's hard for you, might kill me dead."

"No, no. Nothing like that. I come looking for you to ask your pardon. Apologize."

"For what?" Paul D reached in his coat pocket for his bottle.

"You pick any house, any house where colored live. In all of Cincinnati. Pick any one and you welcome to stay there. I'm apologizing because they didn't offer or tell you. But you welcome anywhere you want to be. My house is your house too. John and Ella, Miss Lady, Able Woodruff, Willie Pike – anybody. You choose. You ain't got to sleep in no cellar, and I apologize for each and every night you did. I don't know how that preacher let you do it. I knowed him since he was a boy."

"Whoa, Stamp. He offered."

"Did? Well?"

"Well. I wanted, I didn't want to, I just wanted to be off by myself a spell. He offered. Every time I see him he offers again."

"That's a load off. I thought everybody gone crazy."

Paul D shook his head. "Just me."

"You planning to do anything about it?"

"Oh, yeah. I got big plans." He swallowed twice from the bottle.

Any planning in a bottle is short, thought Stamp, but he knew from personal experience the pointlessness of telling a drinking man not to. He cleared his sinuses and began to think how to get to the second thing he had come to say. Very few people were out today. The canal was frozen so that traffic too had stopped. They heard the clop of a horse approaching. Its rider sat a high Eastern saddle but everything else about him was Ohio Valley. As he rode by he looked at them and suddenly reined his horse, and came up to the path leading to the church. He leaned forward.

"Hey," he said.

Stamp put his ribbon in his pocket. "Yes, sir?"

"I'm looking for a gal name of Judy. Works over by the slaughterhouse."

"Don't believe I know her. No, sir."

"Said she lived on Plank Road."

"Plank Road. Yes, sir. That's up a ways. Mile, maybe."

"You don't know her? Judy. Works in the slaughterhouse."

"No, sir, but I know Plank Road. 'Bout a mile up thataway."

Paul D lifted his bottle and swallowed. The rider looked at him and then back at Stamp Paid. Loosening the right rein, he turned his horse toward the road, then changed his mind and came back.

"Look here," he said to Paul D. "There's a cross up there,

266

so I guess this here's a church or used to be. Seems to me like you ought to show it some respect, you follow me?"

"Yes, sir," said Stamp. "You right about that. That's just what I come over to talk to him about. Just that."

The rider clicked his tongue and trotted off. Stamp made small circles in the palm of his left hand with two fingers of his right. "You got to choose," he said. "Choose anyone. They let you be if you want em to. My house. Ella. Willie Pike. None of us got much, but all of us got room for one more. Pay a little something when you can, don't when you can't. Think about it. You grown. I can't make you do what you won't, but think about it."

Paul D said nothing.

"If I did you harm, I'm here to rectify it."

"No need for that. No need at all."

A woman with four children walked by on the other side of the road. She waved, smiling. "Hoo-oo. I can't stop. See you at meeting."

"I be there," Stamp returned her greeting. "There's another one," he said to Paul D. "Scripture Woodruff, Able's sister. Works at the brush and tallow factory. You'll see. Stay around here long enough, you'll see ain't a sweeter bunch of colored anywhere than what's right here. Pride, well, that bothers em a bit. They can get messy when they think somebody's too proud, but when it comes right down to it, they good people and anyone will take you in."

"What about Judy? She take me in?"

"Depends. What you got in mind?"

"You know Judy?"

"Judith. I know everybody."

"Out on Plank Road?"

"Everybody."

"Well? She take me in?"

Stamp leaned down and untied his shoe. Twelve black buttonhooks, six on each side at the bottom, led to four pairs of eyes at the top. He loosened the laces all the way down, adjusted the tongue carefully and wound them back again. When he got to the eyes he rolled the lace tips with his fingers before inserting them.

"Let me tell you how I got my name." The knot was tight and so was the bow. "They called me Joshua," he said. "I re-named myself," he said, "and I'm going to tell you why I did it," and he told him about Vashti. "I never touched her all that time. Not once. Almost a year. We was planting when it started and picking when it stopped. Seemed longer. I should have killed him. She said no, but I should have. I didn't have the patience I got now, but I figured maybe somebody else didn't have much patience either – his own wife. Took it in my head to see if she was taking it any better than I was. Vashti and me was in the fields together in the day and every now and then she be gone all night. I never touched her and damn me if I spoke three words to her a day. I took any chance I had to get near the great house to see her, the young master's wife. Nothing but a boy. Seventeen, twenty maybe. I caught sight of her finally, standing in the backyard by the fence with a glass of water. She was drinking out of it and just gazing out over the yard. I went over. Stood back a ways and took off my hat. I said, 'Scuse me, miss. Scuse me?' She turned to look. I'm smiling. 'Scuse me. You seen Vashti? My wife Vashti?' A little bitty thing, she was. Black hair. Face no bigger than my hand. She said, 'What? Vashti?' I say, 'Yes'm, Vashti. My wife. She say she owe you all some eggs. You know if she brung em? You know her if you see her. Wear a black ribbon on her neck.' She got rosy then and I knowed she knowed. He give Vashti that to wear. A cameo on a black ribbon. She used to put it on every time she went to him. I put my hat back on. 'You see her tell her I need her. Thank you. Thank you, ma'am.' I backed off before she could say something. I didn't dare look back till I got behind some trees. She was standing just as I left her, looking in her water glass. I thought it would give me more satisfaction than it did. I also thought she might stop it, but it went right on. Till one morning Vashti came in and sat by the window. A Sunday. We worked our own patches on Sunday. She sat by the window looking out of it. 'I'm back,' she said. 'I'm back, Josh.' I looked at the back of her neck. She had a real small neck. I decided to break it. You know, like a twig – just snap it. I been low but that was as low as I ever got."

"Did you? Snap it?"

"Uh uh. I changed my name."

"How you get out of there? How you get up here?"

"Boat. On up the Mississippi to Memphis. Walked from Memphis to Cumberland."

"Vashti too?"

"No. She died."

"Aw, man. Tie your other shoe!"

"What?"

"Tie your goddamn shoe! It's sitting right in front of you! Tie it!"

"That make you feel better?"

"No." Paul D tossed the bottle on the ground and stared at the golden chariot on its label. No horses. Just a golden coach draped in blue cloth.

"I said I had two things to say to you. I only told you one. I have to tell you the other."

"I don't want to know it. I don't want to know nothing. Just if Judy will take me in or won't she."

"I was there, Paul D."

"You was where?"

"There in the yard. When she did it."

"Judy?"

"Sethe."

"Jesus."

"It ain't what you think."

"You don't know what I think."

269

"She ain't crazy. She love those children. She was trying to out-hurt the hurter."

"Leave off."

"And spread it."

"Stamp, let me off. I knew her when she was a girl. She scares me and I knew her when she was a girl."

"You ain't scared of Sethe. I don't believe you."

"Sethe scares me. I scare me. And that girl in her house scares me the most."

"Who is that girl? Where she come from?"

"I don't know. Just shot up one day sitting on a stump."

"Huh. Look like you and me the only ones outside 124 lay eyes on her."

"She don't go nowhere. Where'd you see her?"

"Sleeping on the kitchen floor. I peeped in."

"First minute I saw her I didn't want to be nowhere around her. Something funny about her. Talks funny. Acts funny." Paul D dug his fingers underneath his cap and rubbed the scalp over his temple. "She reminds me of something. Something, look like, I'm supposed to remember."

"She never say where she was from? Where's her people?"

"She don't know, or says she don't. All I ever heard her say was something about stealing her clothes and living on a bridge."

"What kind of bridge?"

"Who you asking?"

"No bridges around here I don't know about. But don't nobody live on em. Under em neither. How long she been over there with Sethe?"

"Last August. Day of the carnival."

"That's a bad sign. Was she at the carnival?"

"No. When we got back, there she was – 'sleep on a stump. Silk dress. Brand-new shoes. Black as oil."

"You don't say? Huh. Was a girl locked up in the house with a whiteman over by Deer Creek. Found him dead last summer and the girl gone. Maybe that's her. Folks say he had her in there since she was a pup."

"Well, now she's a bitch."

"Is she what run you off? Not what I told you 'bout Sethe?"

A shudder ran through Paul D. A bone-cold spasm that made him clutch his knees. He didn't know if it was bad whiskey, nights in the cellar, pig fever, iron bits, smiling roosters, fired feet, laughing dead men, hissing grass, rain, apple blossoms, neck jewelry, Judy in the slaughterhouse, Halle in the butter, ghost-white stairs, chokecherry trees, cameo pins, aspens, Paul A's face, sausage or the loss of a red, red heart.

"Tell me something, Stamp." Paul D's eyes were rheumy. "Tell me this one thing. How much is a nigger supposed to take? Tell me. How much?"

"All he can," said Stamp Paid. "All he can."

"Why? Why? Why? Why? Why?"

III

124 WAS QUIET. Denver, who thought she knew all about silence, was surprised to learn hunger could do that: quiet you down and wear you out. Neither Sethe nor Beloved knew or cared about it one way or another. They were too busy rationing their strength to fight each other. So it was she who had to step off the edge of the world and die because if she didn't, they all would. The flesh between her mother's forefinger and thumb was thin as china silk and there wasn't a piece of clothing in the house that didn't sag on her. Beloved held her head up with the palms of her hands, slept wherever she happened to be, and whined for sweets although she was getting bigger, plumper by the day. Everything was gone except two laying hens, and somebody would soon have to decide whether an egg every now and then was worth more than two fried chickens. The hungrier they got, the weaker; the weaker they got, the quieter they were – which was better than the furious arguments, the poker slammed up against the wall, all the shouting and crying that followed that one happy January when they played. Denver had joined in the play, holding back a bit out of habit, even though it was the most fun she had ever known. But once Sethe had seen the scar, the tip of which Denver had been looking at whenever Beloved undressed – the little curved shadow of a smile in the kootchy-kootchy-coo place under her chin – once Sethe saw it, fingered it and closed her eyes for a long time, the two of them cut Denver out of the games. The cooking games, the sewing games, the hair and dressing-up games. Games her mother loved so well she took

to going to work later and later each day until the predictable happened: Sawyer told her not to come back. And instead of looking for another job, Sethe played all the harder with Beloved, who never got enough of anything: lullabies, new stitches, the bottom of the cake bowl, the top of the milk. If the hen had only two eggs, she got both. It was as though her mother had lost her mind, like Grandma Baby calling for pink and not doing the things she used to. But different because, unlike Baby Suggs, she cut Denver out completely. Even the song that she used to sing to Denver she sang for Beloved alone: "High Johnny, wide Johnny, don't you leave my side, Johnny."

At first they played together. A whole month and Denver loved it. From the night they ice-skated under a star-loaded sky and drank sweet milk by the stove, to the string puzzles Sethe did for them in afternoon light, and shadow pictures in the gloaming. In the very teeth of winter and Sethe, her eyes fever bright, was plotting a garden of vegetables and flowers – talking, talking about what colors it would have. She played with Beloved's hair, braiding, puffing, tying, oiling it until it made Denver nervous to watch her. They changed beds and exchanged clothes. Walked arm in arm and smiled all the time. When the weather broke, they were on their knees in the backyard designing a garden in dirt too hard to chop. The thirty-eight dollars of life savings went to feed themselves with fancy food and decorate themselves with ribbon and dress goods, which Sethe cut and sewed like they were going somewhere in a hurry. Bright clothes – with blue stripes and sassy prints. She walked the four miles to John Shillito's to buy yellow ribbon, shiny buttons and bits of black lace. By the end of March the three of them looked like carnival women with nothing to do. When it became clear that they were only interested in each other, Denver began to drift from the play, but she watched it, alert for any sign that Beloved was in danger. Finally convinced there was none, and seeing her mother that happy, that smiling – how could it go wrong? – she let down her guard and it did. Her problem at first was trying to find out who was to blame. Her eye was on her mother, for a signal that the thing that was in her was out, and she would kill again. But it was Beloved who made demands. Anything she wanted she got, and when Sethe ran out of things to give her, Beloved invented desire. She wanted Sethe's company for hours to watch the layer of brown leaves waving at them from the bottom of the creek, in the same place where, as a little girl, Denver played in the silence with her. Now the players were altered. As soon as the thaw was complete Beloved gazed at her gazing face, rippling, folding, spreading, disappearing into the leaves below. She flattened herself on the ground, dirtying her bold stripes, and touched the rocking faces with her own. She filled basket after basket with the first things warmer weather let loose in the ground – dandelions, violets, forsythia – presenting them to Sethe, who arranged them, stuck them, wound them all over the house. Dressed in Sethe's dresses, she stroked her skin with the palm of her hand. She imitated Sethe, talked the way she did, laughed her laugh and used her body the same way down to the walk, the way Sethe moved her hands, sighed through her nose, held her head. Sometimes coming upon them making men and women cookies or tacking scraps of cloth on Baby Suggs' old quilt, it was difficult for Denver to tell who was who.

Then the mood changed and the arguments began. Slowly at first. A complaint from Beloved, an apology from Sethe. A reduction of pleasure at some special effort the older woman made. Wasn't it too cold to stay outside? Beloved gave a look that said, So what? Was it past bedtime, the light no good for sewing? Beloved didn't move; said, "Do it," and Sethe complied. She took the best of everything – first. The best chair, the biggest piece, the prettiest plate, the brightest ribbon for her hair, and the more she took, the more Sethe began to talk, explain, describe how much she had suffered, been through, for her children, waving away flies in grape arbors, crawling on her knees to a lean-to. None of which made the impression it was supposed to. Beloved accused her of leaving her behind. Of not being nice to her, not smiling at her. She said they were the same, had the same face, how could she have left her? And Sethe cried, saying she never did, or meant to – that she had to get them out, away, that she had the milk all the time and had the money too for the stone but not enough. That her plan was always that they would all be together on the other side, forever. Beloved wasn't interested. She said when she cried there was no one. That dead men lay on top of her. That she had nothing to eat. Ghosts without skin stuck their fingers in her and said beloved in the dark and bitch in the light. Sethe pleaded for forgiveness, counting, listing again and again her reasons: that Beloved was more important, meant more to her than her own life. That she would trade places any day. Give up her life, every minute and hour of it, to take back just one of Beloved's tears. Did she know it hurt her when mosquitoes bit her baby? That to leave her on the ground to run into the big house drove her crazy? That before leaving Sweet Home Beloved slept every night on her chest or curled on her back? Beloved denied it. Sethe never came to her, never said a word to her, never smiled and worst of all never waved goodbye or even looked her way before running away from her.

When once or twice Sethe tried to assert herself – be the unquestioned mother whose word was law and who knew what was best – Beloved slammed things, wiped the table clean of plates, threw salt on the floor, broke a windowpane.

She was not like them. She was wild game, and nobody said, Get on out of here, girl, and come back when you get some sense. Nobody said, You raise your hand to me and I will knock you into the middle of next week. Ax the trunk, the limb will die. Honor thy mother and father that thy days may be long upon the land which the Lord thy God giveth thee. I will wrap you round that doorknob, don't nobody work for you and God don't love ugly ways.

No, no. They mended the plates, swept the salt, and little by little it dawned on Denver that if Sethe didn't wake up one morning and pick up a knife, Beloved might. Frightened as she was by the thing in Sethe that could come out, it shamed her to see her mother serving a girl not much older than herself. When she saw her carrying out Beloved's night bucket, Denver raced to relieve her of it. But the pain was unbearable when they ran low on food, and Denver watched her mother go without – pick-eating around the edges of the table and stove: the hominy that stuck on the bottom; the crusts and rinds and peelings of things. Once she saw her run her longest finger deep in an empty jam jar before rinsing and putting it away.

They grew tired, and even Beloved, who was getting bigger, seemed nevertheless as exhausted as they were. In any case she substituted a snarl or a tooth-suck for waving a poker around and 124 was quiet. Listless and sleepy with hunger Denver saw the flesh between her mother's forefinger and thumb fade. Saw Sethe's eyes bright but dead, alert but vacant, paying attention to everything about Beloved – her lineless palms, her forehead, the smile under her jaw, crooked and much too long – everything except her basket-fat stomach. She also saw the sleeves of her own carnival shirtwaist cover her fingers; hems that once showed her ankles now swept the floor. She saw themselves beribboned, decked-out, limp and starving but locked in a love that wore everybody out. Then Sethe spit up something she had not eaten and it rocked Denver like gunshot. The job she started out with, protecting Beloved from Sethe, changed to protecting her mother from Beloved. Now it was obvious that her mother could die and leave them both and what would

Beloved do then? Whatever was happening, it only worked with three – not two – and since neither Beloved nor Sethe seemed to care what the next day might bring (Sethe happy when Beloved was; Beloved lapping devotion like cream), Denver knew it was on her. She would have to leave the yard; step off the edge of the world, leave the two behind and go ask somebody for help.

Who would it be? Who could she stand in front of who wouldn't shame her on learning that her mother sat around like a rag doll, broke down, finally, from trying to take care of and make up for. Denver knew *about* several people, from hearing her mother and grandmother talk. But she knew, personally, only two: an old man with white hair called Stamp and Lady Jones. Well, Paul D, of course. And that boy who told her about Sethe. But they wouldn't do at all. Her heart kicked and an itchy burning in her throat made her swallow all her saliva away. She didn't even know which way to go. When Sethe used to work at the restaurant and when she still had money to shop, she turned right. Back when Denver went to Lady Jones' school, it was left.

The weather was warm; the day beautiful. It was April and everything alive was tentative. Denver wrapped her hair and her shoulders. In the brightest of the carnival dresses and wearing a stranger's shoes, she stood on the porch of 124 ready to be swallowed up in the world beyond the edge of the porch. Out there where small things scratched and sometimes touched. Where words could be spoken that would close your ears shut. Where, if you were alone, feeling could overtake you and stick to you like a shadow. Out there where there were places in which things so bad had happened that when you went near them it would happen again. Like Sweet Home where time didn't pass and where, like her mother said, the bad was waiting for her as well. How would she know these places? What was more – much more – out there were whitepeople and how could you tell about them?

Sethe said the mouth and sometimes the hands. Grandma Baby said there was no defense – they could prowl at will, change from one mind to another, and even when they thought they were behaving, it was a far cry from what real humans did.

"They got me out of jail," Sethe once told Baby Suggs.

"They also put you in it," she answered.

"They drove you 'cross the river."

"On my son's back."

"They gave you this house."

"Nobody *gave* me nothing."

"I got a job from them."

"He got a cook from them, girl."

"Oh, some of them do all right by us."

"And every time it's a surprise, ain't it?"

"You didn't used to talk this way."

"Don't box with me. There's more of us they drowned than there is all of them ever lived from the start of time. Lay down your sword. This ain't a battle; it's a rout."

Remembering those conversations and her grandmother's last and final words, Denver stood on the porch in the sun and couldn't leave it. Her throat itched; her heart kicked – and then Baby Suggs laughed, clear as anything. "You mean I never told you nothing about Carolina? About your daddy? You don't remember nothing about how come I walk the way I do and about your mother's feet, not to speak of her back? I never told you all that? Is that why you can't walk down the steps? My Jesus my."

But you said there was no defense.

"There ain't."

Then what do I do?

"Know it, and go on out the yard. Go on."

It came back. A dozen years had passed and the way came back. Four houses on the right, sitting close together in a line like wrens. The first house had two steps and a rocking chair on the porch; the second had three steps, a broom propped on the porch beam, two broken chairs and a clump of forsythia at the side. No window at the front. A little boy sat on the ground chewing a stick. The third house had yellow shutters on its two front windows and pot after pot of green leaves with white hearts or red. Denver could hear chickens and the knock of a badly hinged gate. At the fourth house the buds of a sycamore tree had rained down on the roof and made the yard look as though grass grew there. A woman, standing at the open door, lifted her hand halfway in greeting, then froze it near her shoulder as she leaned forward to see whom she waved to. Denver lowered her head. Next was a tiny fenced plot with a cow in it. She remembered the plot but not the cow. Under her headcloth her scalp was wet with tension. Beyond her, voices, male voices, floated, coming closer with each step she took. Denver kept her eyes on the road in case they were whitemen; in case she was walking where they wanted to; in case they said something and she would have to answer them. Suppose they flung out at her, grabbed her, tied her. They were getting closer. Maybe she should cross the road – now. Was the woman who half waved at her still there in the open door? Would she come to her rescue, or, angry at Denver for not waving back, would she withhold her help? Maybe she should turn around, get closer to the waving woman's house. Before she could make up her mind, it was too late – they were right in front of her. Two men, Negro. Denver breathed. Both men touched their caps and murmured, "Morning. Morning." Denver believed her eyes spoke gratitude but she never got her mouth open in time to reply. They moved left of her and passed on.

Braced and heartened by that easy encounter, she picked up speed and began to look deliberately at the neighborhood surrounding her. She was shocked to see how small the big things were: the boulder by the edge of the road she once couldn't see over was a sitting-on rock. Paths leading to houses weren't miles long. Dogs didn't even reach her knees. Letters cut into beeches and oaks by giants were eye level now.

She would have known it anywhere. The post and scrap-lumber fence was gray now, not white, but she would have known it anywhere. The stone porch sitting in a skirt of ivy, pale yellow curtains at the windows; the laid brick path to the front door and wood planks leading around to the back, passing under the windows where she had stood on tiptoe to see above the sill. Denver was about to do it again, when she realized how silly it would be to be found once more staring into the parlor of Mrs. Lady Jones. The pleasure she felt at having found the house dissolved, suddenly, in doubt. Suppose she didn't live there anymore? Or remember her former student after all this time? What would she say? Denver shivered inside, wiped the perspiration from her forehead and knocked.

Lady Jones went to the door expecting raisins. A child, probably, from the softness of the knock, sent by its mother with the raisins she needed if her contribution to the supper was to be worth the trouble. There would be any number of plain cakes, potato pies. She had reluctantly volunteered her own special creation, but said she didn't have raisins, so raisins is what the president said would be provided – early enough so there would be no excuses. Mrs. Jones, dreading the fatigue of beating batter, had been hoping she had forgotten. Her bake oven had been cold all week – getting it to the right temperature would be awful. Since her husband died and her eyes grew dim, she had let up-to-snuff housekeeping fall away. She was of two minds about baking something for the church. On the one hand, she wanted to remind everybody of what she was able to do in the cooking line; on the other, she didn't want to have to. When she heard the tapping at the door, she sighed and went to it hoping the raisins had at least been cleaned.

She was older, of course, and dressed like a chippy, but the girl was immediately recognizable to Lady Jones. Everybody's child was in that face: the nickel-round eyes, bold yet mistrustful; the large powerful teeth between dark sculptured lips that did not cover them. Some vulnerability lay across the bridge of the nose, above the cheeks. And then the skin. Flawless, economical – just enough of it to cover the bone and not a bit more. She must be eighteen or nineteen by now, thought Lady Jones, looking at the face young enough to be twelve. Heavy eyebrows, thick baby lashes and the unmistakable love call that shimmered around children until they learned better.

"Why, Denver," she said. "Look at you."

Lady Jones had to take her by the hand and pull her in, because the smile seemed all the girl could manage. Other people said this child was simple, but Lady Jones never believed it. Having taught her, watched her eat up a page, a rule, a figure, she knew better. When suddenly she had stopped coming, Lady Jones thought it was the nickel. She approached the ignorant grandmother one day on the road, a woods preacher who mended shoes, to tell her it was all right if the money was owed. The woman said that wasn't it; the child was deaf, and deaf Lady Jones thought she still was until she offered her a seat and Denver heard that.

"It's nice of you to come see me. What brings you?"

Denver didn't answer.

"Well, nobody needs a reason to visit. Let me make us some tea."

Lady Jones was mixed. Gray eyes and yellow woolly hair, every strand of which she hated – though whether it was the color or the texture even she didn't know. She had married the blackest man she could find, had five rainbow-colored children and sent them all to Wilberforce, after teaching them all she knew right along with the others who sat in her parlor. Her light skin got her picked for a coloredgirls' normal school in Pennsylvania and she paid it back by teaching the unpicked. The children who played in dirt until they were old enough for chores, these she taught. The colored population of Cincinnati had two graveyards and six churches, but since no school or hospital was obliged to serve them, they learned and died at home. She believed in her heart that, except for her husband, the whole world (including her children) despised her and her hair. She had been listening to "all that yellow gone to waste" and "white nigger" since she was a girl in a houseful of silt-black children, so she disliked everybody a little bit because she believed they hated her hair as much as she did. With that education pat and firmly set, she dispensed with rancor, was indiscriminately polite, saving her real affection for the unpicked children of Cincinnati, one of whom sat before her in a dress so loud it embarrassed the needlepoint chair seat.

"Sugar?"

"Yes. Thank you." Denver drank it all down.

"More?"

"No, ma'am."

"Here. Go ahead."

"Yes, ma'am."

"How's your family, honey?"

Denver stopped in the middle of a swallow. There was no way to tell her how her family was, so she said what was at the top of her mind.

"I want work, Miss Lady."

"Work?"

"Yes, ma'am. Anything."

Lady Jones smiled. "What can you do?"

"I can't do anything, but I would learn it for you if you have a little extra."

"Extra?"

"Food. My ma'am, she doesn't feel good."

"Oh, baby," said Mrs. Jones. "Oh, baby."

Denver looked up at her. She did not know it then, but it was the word "baby," said softly and with such kindness, that inaugurated her life in the world as a woman. The trail she followed to get to that sweet thorny place was made up of paper scraps containing the handwritten names of others. Lady Jones gave her some rice, four eggs and some tea. Denver said she couldn't be away from home long because of her mother's condition. Could she do chores in the morning? Lady Jones told her that no one, not herself, not anyone she knew, could pay anybody anything for work they did themselves. "But if you all need to eat until your mother is well, all you have to do is say so." She mentioned her church's committee invented so nobody had to go hungry. That agitated her guest who said, "No, no," as though asking for help from strangers was worse than hunger. Lady Jones said goodbye to her and asked her to come back anytime. "Anytime at all."

Two days later Denver stood on the porch and noticed something lying on the tree stump at the edge of the yard. She went to look and found a sack of white beans. Another time a plate of cold rabbit meat. One morning a basket of eggs sat there. As she lifted it, a slip of paper fluttered down. She picked it up and looked at it. "M. Lucille Williams" was written in big crooked letters. On the back was a blob of flour-water paste. So Denver paid a second visit to the world outside the porch, although all she said when she returned the basket was "Thank you."

"Welcome," said M. Lucille Williams.

Every now and then, all through the spring, names appeared near or in gifts of food. Obviously for the return of the pan or plate or basket; but also to let the girl know, if she cared to, who the donor was, because some of the parcels were wrapped in paper, and though there was nothing to return, the name was nevertheless there. Many had X's with designs about them, and Lady Jones tried to identify the plate or pan or the covering towel. When she could only guess, Denver followed her directions and went to say thank you anyway – whether she had the right benefactor or not. When she was wrong, when the person said, "No, darling. That's not my bowl. Mine's got a blue ring on it," a small conversation took place. All of them knew her grandmother and some had even danced with her in the Clearing. Others remembered the days when 124 was a way station, the place they assembled to catch news, taste oxtail soup, leave their children, cut out a skirt. One remembered the tonic mixed there that cured a relative. One showed her the border of a pillowslip, the stamens of its pale blue flowers French-knotted in Baby Suggs' kitchen by the light of an oil lamp while arguing the Settlement Fee. They remembered the party with twelve turkeys and tubs of strawberry smash. One said she wrapped Denver when she was a single day old and cut shoes to fit her mother's blasted feet. Maybe they were sorry for her. Or for Sethe. Maybe they were sorry for the years of their own disdain. Maybe they were simply nice people who could hold meanness toward each other for just so long and when trouble rode bareback among them, quickly, easily they did what they could to trip him up. In any case, the personal pride, the arrogant claim staked out at 124 seemed to them to have run its course. They whispered, naturally, wondered, shook their heads. Some even laughed outright at Denver's clothes of a hussy, but it didn't stop them caring whether she ate and it didn't stop the pleasure they took in her soft "Thank you."

At least once a week, she visited Lady Jones, who perked up enough to do a raisin loaf especially for her, since Denver was set on sweet things. She gave her a book of Bible verse and listened while she mumbled words or fairly shouted them. By June Denver had read and memorized all fifty-two pages – one for each week of the year.

As Denver's outside life improved, her home life deteriorated. If the whitepeople of Cincinnati had allowed Negroes into their lunatic asylum they could have found candidates in 124. Strengthened by the gifts of food, the source of which neither Sethe nor Beloved questioned, the women had arrived at a doomsday truce designed by the devil. Beloved sat around, ate, went from bed to bed. Sometimes she screamed, "Rain! Rain!" and clawed her throat until rubies of blood opened there, made brighter by her midnight skin. Then Sethe shouted, "No!" and knocked over chairs to get to her and wipe the jewels away. Other times Beloved curled up on the floor, her wrists between her knees, and stayed there for hours. Or she would go to the creek, stick her feet in the water and whoosh it up her legs. Afterward she would go to Sethe, run her fingers over the woman's teeth while tears slid from her wide black eyes. Then it seemed to Denver the thing was done: Beloved bending over Sethe looked the mother, Sethe the teething child, for other than those times when Beloved needed her, Sethe confined herself to a corner chair. The bigger Beloved got, the smaller Sethe became; the brighter Beloved's eyes, the more those eyes that used never to look away became slits of sleeplessness. Sethe no longer combed her hair or splashed her face with water. She sat in the chair licking her lips like a chastised child while Beloved ate up her life, took it, swelled up with it, grew taller on it. And the older woman yielded it up without a murmur.

Denver served them both. Washing, cooking, forcing, cajoling her mother to eat a little now and then, providing sweet things for Beloved as often as she could to calm her down. It was hard to know what she would do from minute to minute. When the heat got hot, she might walk around the house naked or wrapped in a sheet, her belly protruding like a winning watermelon.

Denver thought she understood the connection between her mother and Beloved: Sethe was trying to make up for the handsaw; Beloved was making her pay for it. But there would never be an end to that, and seeing her mother diminished shamed and infuriated her. Yet she knew Sethe's greatest fear was the same one Denver had in the beginning – that Beloved might leave. That before Sethe could make her understand what it meant – what it took to drag the teeth of that saw under the little chin; to feel the baby blood pump like oil in her hands; to hold her face so her head would stay on; to squeeze her so she could absorb, still, the death spasms that shot through that adored body, plump and sweet with life – Beloved might leave. Leave before Sethe could make her realize that worse than that – far worse – was what Baby Suggs died of, what Ella knew, what Stamp saw and what made Paul D tremble. That anybody white could take your whole self for anything that came to mind. Not just work, kill, or maim you, but dirty you. Dirty you so bad you couldn't like yourself anymore. Dirty you so bad you forgot who you were and couldn't think it up. And though she and others lived through and got over it, she could never let it happen to her own. The best thing she was, was her children. Whites might dirty *her* all right, but not her best thing, her beautiful, magical best thing – the part of her that was clean. No undreamable dreams about whether the headless, feetless torso hanging in the tree with a sign on it was her husband or Paul A; whether the bubbling-hot girls in the colored-school fire set by patriots included her daughter; whether a gang of whites invaded her daughter's private parts, soiled her daughter's thighs and threw her daughter out of the wagon. *She* might have to work the slaughterhouse yard, but not her daughter.

And no one, nobody on this earth, would list her daughter's characteristics on the animal side of the paper. No. Oh no. Maybe Baby Suggs could worry about it, live with the likelihood of it; Sethe had refused – and refused still.

This and much more Denver heard her say from her corner chair, trying to persuade Beloved, the one and only person she felt she had to convince, that what she had done was right because it came from true love.

Beloved, her fat new feet propped on the seat of a chair in front of the one she sat in, her unlined hands resting on her stomach, looked at her. Uncomprehending everything except that Sethe was the woman who took her face away, leaving her crouching in a dark, dark place, forgetting to smile.

Her father's daughter after all, Denver decided to do the necessary. Decided to stop relying on kindness to leave something on the stump. She would hire herself out somewhere, and although she was afraid to leave Sethe and Beloved alone all day not knowing what calamity either one of them would create, she came to realize that her presence in that house had no influence on what either woman did. She kept them alive and they ignored her. Growled when they chose; sulked, explained, demanded, strutted, cowered, cried and provoked each other to the edge of violence, then over. She had begun to notice that even when Beloved was quiet, dreamy, minding her own business, Sethe got her going again. Whispering, muttering some justification, some bit of clarifying information to Beloved to explain what it had been like, and why, and how come. It was as though Sethe didn't really want forgiveness given; she wanted it refused. And Beloved helped her out.

Somebody had to be saved, but unless Denver got work, there would be no one to save, no one to come home to, and no Denver either. It was a new thought, having a self to look out for and preserve. And it might not have occurred to her if she hadn't met Nelson Lord leaving his grandmother's house as Denver entered it to pay a thank you for half a pie. All he did was smile and say, "Take care of yourself, Denver," but she heard it as though it were what language was made for. The last time he spoke to her his words blocked up her ears. Now they opened her mind.

Weeding the garden, pulling vegetables, cooking, washing, she plotted what to do and how. The Bodwins were most likely to help since they had done it twice. Once for Baby Suggs and once for her mother. Why not the third generation as well?

She got lost so many times in the streets of Cincinnati it was noon before she arrived, though she started out at sunrise. The house sat back from the sidewalk with large windows looking out on a noisy, busy street. The Negro woman who answered the front door said, "Yes?"

"May I come in?"

"What you want?"

"I want to see Mr. and Mrs. Bodwin."

"Miss Bodwin. They brother and sister."

"Oh."

"What you want em for?"

"I'm looking for work. I was thinking they might know of some."

"You Baby Suggs' kin, ain't you?"

"Yes, ma'am."

"Come on in. You letting in flies." She led Denver toward the kitchen, saying, "First thing you have to know is what door to knock on." But Denver only half heard her because she was stepping on something soft and blue. All around her was thick, soft and blue. Glass cases crammed full of glistening things. Books on tables and shelves. Pearl-white lamps with shiny metal bottoms. And a smell like the cologne she poured in the emerald house, only better.

"Sit down," the woman said. "You know my name?"

"No, ma'am."

"Janey. Janey Wagon."

"How do you do?"

"Fairly. I heard your mother took sick, that so?"

"Yes, ma'am."

"Who's looking after her?"

"I am. But I have to find work."

Janey laughed. "You know what? I've been here since I was fourteen, and I remember like yesterday when Baby Suggs, holy, came here and sat right there where you are. Whiteman brought her. That's how she got that house you all live in. Other things, too."

"Yes, ma'am."

"What's the trouble with Sethe?" Janey leaned against an indoor sink and folded her arms.

It was a little thing to pay, but it seemed big to Denver. Nobody was going to help her unless she told it – told all of it. It was clear Janey wouldn't and wouldn't let her see the Bodwins otherwise. So Denver told this stranger what she hadn't told Lady Jones, in return for which Janey admitted the Bodwins needed help, although they didn't know it. She was alone there, and now that her employers were getting older, she couldn't take care of them like she used to. More and more she was required to sleep the night there. Maybe she could talk them into letting Denver do the night shift, come right after supper, say, maybe get the breakfast. That way Denver could care for Sethe in the day and earn a little something at night, how's that?

Denver had explained the girl in her house who plagued her mother as a cousin come to visit, who got sick too and bothered them both. Janey seemed more interested in Sethe's condition, and from what Denver told her it seemed the woman had lost her mind. That wasn't the Sethe she remembered. This Sethe had lost her wits, finally, as Janey knew she would – trying to do it all alone with her nose in the air. Denver squirmed under the criticism of her mother, shifting in the chair and keeping her eyes on the inside sink. Janey Wagon went on about pride until she got to Baby Suggs, for whom she had nothing but sweet words. "I never went to those woodland services she had, but she was always nice to me. Always. Never be another like her."

"I miss her too," said Denver.

"Bet you do. Everybody miss her. That was a good woman."

Denver didn't say anything else and Janey looked at her face for a while. "Neither one of your brothers ever come back to see how you all was?"

"No, ma'am."

"Ever hear from them?"

"No, ma'am. Nothing."

"Guess they had a rough time in that house. Tell me, this here woman in your house. The cousin. She got any lines in her hands?"

"No," said Denver.

"Well," said Janey. "I guess there's a God after all."

The interview ended with Janey telling her to come back in a few days. She needed time to convince her employers what they needed: night help because Janey's own family needed her. "I don't want to quit these people, but they can't have all my days and nights too."

What did Denver have to do at night?

"Be here. In case."

In case what?

Janey shrugged. "In case the house burn down." She smiled then. "Or bad weather slop the roads so bad I can't get here early enough for them. Case late guests need serving or cleaning up after. Anything. Don't ask me what whitefolks need at night."

"They used to be good whitefolks."

"Oh, yeah. They good. Can't say they ain't good. I wouldn't trade them for another pair, tell you that."

With those assurances, Denver left, but not before she had seen, sitting on a shelf by the back door, a blackboy's mouth full of money. His head was thrown back farther than a head could go, his hands were shoved in his pockets. Bulging like moons, two eyes were all the face he had above the gaping red mouth. His hair was a cluster of raised, widely spaced dots made of nail heads. And he was on his knees. His mouth, wide as a cup, held the coins needed to pay for a delivery or some other small service, but could just as well have held buttons, pins or crab-apple jelly. Painted across the pedestal he knelt on were the words "At Yo Service."

The news that Janey got hold of she spread among the other coloredwomen. Sethe's dead daughter, the one whose throat she cut, had come back to fix her. Sethe was worn down, speckled, dying, spinning, changing shapes and generally bedeviled. That this daughter beat her, tied her to the bed and pulled out all her hair. It took them days to get the story properly blown up and themselves agitated and then to calm down and assess the situation. They fell into three groups: those that believed the worst; those that believed none of it; and those, like Ella, who thought it through.

"Ella. What's all this I'm hearing about Sethe?"

"Tell me it's in there with her. That's all I know."

"The daughter? The killed one?"

"That's what they tell me."

"How they know that's her?"

"It's sitting there. Sleeps, eats and raises hell. Whipping Sethe every day."

"I'll be. A baby?"

"No. Grown. The age it would have been had it lived."

"You talking about flesh?"

"I'm talking about flesh."

"Whipping her?"

"Like she was batter."

"Guess she had it coming."

"Nobody got that coming."

"But, Ella —"

"But nothing. What's fair ain't necessarily right."

"You can't just up and kill your children."

"No, and the children can't just up and kill the mama."

It was Ella more than anyone who convinced the others that rescue was in order. She was a practical woman who believed there was a root either to chew or avoid for every ailment. Cogitation, as she called it, clouded things and prevented action. Nobody loved her and she wouldn't have liked it if they had, for she considered love a serious disability. Her puberty was spent in a house where she was shared by father and son, whom she called "the lowest yet." It was "the lowest yet" who gave her a disgust for sex and against whom she measured all atrocities. A killing, a kidnap, a rape – whatever, she listened and nodded. Nothing compared to "the lowest yet." She understood Sethe's rage in the shed twenty years ago, but not her reaction to it, which Ella thought was prideful, misdirected, and Sethe herself too complicated. When she got out of jail and made no gesture toward anybody, and lived as though she were alone, Ella junked her and wouldn't give her the time of day.

The daughter, however, appeared to have some sense after all. At least she had stepped out the door, asked for the help she needed and wanted work. When Ella heard 124 was occupied by something-or-other beating up on Sethe, it infuriated her and gave her another opportunity to measure what could very well be the devil himself against "the lowest yet." There was also something very personal in her fury. Whatever Sethe had done, Ella didn't like the idea of past errors taking possession of the present. Sethe's crime was staggering and her pride outstripped even that; but she could not countenance the possibility of sin moving on in the house, unleashed and sassy. Daily life took as much as she had. The future was sunset; the past something to leave behind. And if it didn't stay behind, well, you might have to stomp it out. Slave life; freed life – every day was a test and a trial. Nothing could be counted on in a world where even when you were a solution you were a problem. "Sufficient unto the day is the evil thereof," and nobody needed more;

nobody needed a grown-up evil sitting at the table with a grudge. As long as the ghost showed out from its ghostly place – shaking stuff, crying, smashing and such – Ella respected it. But if it took flesh and came in her world, well, the shoe was on the other foot. She didn't mind a little communication between the two worlds, but this was an invasion.

"Shall we pray?" asked the women.

"Uh huh," said Ella. "First. Then we got to get down to business."

The day Denver was to spend her first night at the Bodwins', Mr. Bodwin had some business on the edge of the city and told Janey he would pick the new girl up before supper. Denver sat on the porch steps with a bundle in her lap, her carnival dress sun-faded to a quieter rainbow. She was looking to the right, in the direction Mr. Bodwin would be coming from. She did not see the women approaching, accumulating slowly in groups of twos and threes from the left. Denver was looking to the right. She was a little anxious about whether she would prove satisfactory to the Bodwins, and uneasy too because she woke up crying from a dream about a running pair of shoes. The sadness of the dream she hadn't been able to shake, and the heat oppressed her as she went about the chores. Far too early she wrapped a nightdress and hairbrush into a bundle. Nervous, she fidgeted the knot and looked to the right.

Some brought what they could and what they believed would work. Stuffed in apron pockets, strung around their necks, lying in the space between their breasts. Others brought Christian faith – as shield and sword. Most brought a little of both. They had no idea what they would do once they got there. They just started out, walked down Bluestone Road and came together at the agreed-upon time. The heat kept a few women who promised to go at home. Others who believed the story didn't want any part of the confrontation and wouldn't have come no matter what the weather.

And there were those like Lady Jones who didn't believe the story and hated the ignorance of those who did. So thirty women made up that company and walked slowly, slowly toward 124.

It was three in the afternoon on a Friday so wet and hot Cincinnati's stench had traveled to the country: from the canal, from hanging meat and things rotting in jars; from small animals dead in the fields, town sewers and factories. The stench, the heat, the moisture – trust the devil to make his presence known. Otherwise it looked almost like a regular workday. They could have been going to do the laundry at the orphanage or the insane asylum; corn shucking at the mill; or to clean fish, rinse offal, cradle whitebabies, sweep stores, scrape hog skin, press lard, case-pack sausage or hide in tavern kitchens so whitepeople didn't have to see them handle their food.

But not today.

When they caught up with each other, all thirty, and arrived at 124, the first thing they saw was not Denver sitting on the steps, but themselves. Younger, stronger, even as little girls lying in the grass asleep. Catfish was popping grease in the pan and they saw themselves scoop German potato salad onto the plate. Cobbler oozing purple syrup colored their teeth. They sat on the porch, ran down to the creek, teased the men, hoisted children on their hips or, if they were the children, straddled the ankles of old men who held their little hands while giving them a horsey ride. Baby Suggs laughed and skipped among them, urging more. Mothers, dead now, moved their shoulders to mouth harps. The fence they had leaned on and climbed over was gone. The stump of the butternut had split like a fan. But there they were, young and happy, playing in Baby Suggs' yard, not feeling the envy that surfaced the next day.

Denver heard mumbling and looked to the left. She stood when she saw them. They grouped, murmuring and whispering, but did not step foot in the yard. Denver waved. A few waved back but came no closer. Denver sat back down wondering what was going on. A woman dropped to her knees. Half of the others did likewise. Denver saw lowered heads, but could not hear the lead prayer – only the earnest syllables of agreement that backed it: Yes, yes, yes, oh yes. Hear me. Hear me. Do it, Maker, do it. Yes. Among those not on their knees, who stood holding 124 in a fixed glare, was Ella, trying to see through the walls, behind the door, to what was really in there. Was it true the dead daughter come back? Or a pretend? Was it whipping Sethe? Ella had been beaten every way but down. She remembered the bottom teeth she had lost to the brake and the scars from the belt were thick as rope around her waist. She had delivered, but would not nurse, a hairy white thing, fathered by "the lowest yet." It lived five days never making a sound. The idea of that pup coming back to whip her too set her jaw working, and then Ella hollered.

Instantly the kneelers and the standers joined her. They stopped praying and took a step back to the beginning. In the beginning there were no words. In the beginning was the sound, and they all knew what that sound sounded like.

Edward Bodwin drove a cart down Bluestone Road. It displeased him a bit because he preferred his figure astride Princess. Curved over his own hands, holding the reins made him look the age he was. But he had promised his sister a detour to pick up a new girl. He didn't have to think about the way – he was headed for the house he was born in. Perhaps it was his destination that turned his thoughts to time – the way it dripped or ran. He had not seen the house for thirty years. Not the butternut in front, the stream at the rear nor the block house in between. Not even the meadow across the road. Very few of the interior details did he remember because he was three years old when his family moved into town. But he did remember that the cooking was done behind the house, the well was forbidden to play near, and that women died there: his mother, grandmother, an aunt and an older sister before he was born. The men (his father and grandfather) moved with himself and his baby sister to Court Street sixty-seven years ago. The land, of course, eighty acres of it on both sides of Bluestone, was the central thing, but he felt something sweeter and deeper about the house which is why he rented it for a little something if he could get it, but it didn't trouble him to get no rent at all since the tenants at least kept it from the disrepair total abandonment would permit.

There was a time when he buried things there. Precious things he wanted to protect. As a child every item he owned was available and accountable to his family. Privacy was an adult indulgence, but when he got to be one, he seemed not to need it.

The horse trotted along and Edward Bodwin cooled his beautiful mustache with his breath. It was generally agreed upon by the women in the Society that, except for his hands, it was the most attractive feature he had. Dark, velvety, its beauty was enhanced by his strong clean-shaven chin. But his hair was white, like his sister's – and had been since he was a young man. It made him the most visible and memorable person at every gathering, and cartoonists had fastened onto the theatricality of his white hair and big black mustache whenever they depicted local political antagonism. Twenty years ago when the Society was at its height in opposing slavery, it was as though his coloring was itself the heart of the matter. The "bleached nigger" was what his enemies called him, and on a trip to Arkansas, some Mississippi rivermen, enraged by the Negro boatmen they competed with, had caught him and shoe-blackened his face and his hair. Those heady days were gone now; what remained was the sludge of ill will; dashed hopes and difficulties beyond repair. A tranquil Republic? Well, not in his lifetime.

Even the weather was getting to be too much for him. He was either too hot or freezing, and this day was a blister. He pressed his hat down to keep the sun from his neck, where heatstroke was a real possibility. Such thoughts of mortality were not new to him (he was over seventy now), but they still had the power to annoy. As he drew closer to the old homestead, the place that continued to surface in his dreams, he was even more aware of the way time moved. Measured by the wars he had lived through but not fought in (against the Miami, the Spaniards, the Secessionists), it was slow. But measured by the burial of his private things it was the blink of an eye. Where, exactly, was the box of tin soldiers? The watch chain with no watch? And who was he hiding them from? His father, probably, a deeply religious man who knew what God knew and told everybody what it was. Edward Bodwin thought him an odd man, in so many ways, yet he had one clear directive: human life is holy, all of it. And that his son still believed, although he had less and less reason to. Nothing since was as stimulating as the old days of letters, petitions, meetings, debates, recruitment, quarrels, rescue and downright sedition. Yet it had worked, more or less, and when it had not, he and his sister made themselves available to circumvent obstacles. As they had when a runaway slavewoman lived in his homestead with her mother-in-law and got herself into a world of trouble. The Society managed to turn infanticide and the cry of savagery around, and build a further case for abolishing slavery. Good years, they were, full of spit and conviction. Now he just wanted to know where his soldiers were and his watchless chain. That would be enough for this day of unbearable heat: bring back the new girl and recall exactly where his treasure lay. Then home, supper, and God willing, the sun would drop once more to give him the blessing of a good night's sleep.

The road curved like an elbow, and as he approached it he heard the singers before he saw them.

When the women assembled outside 124, Sethe was breaking a lump of ice into chunks. She dropped the ice pick into
her apron pocket to scoop the pieces into a basin of water.
When the music entered the window she was wringing a
cool cloth to put on Beloved's forehead. Beloved, sweating
profusely, was sprawled on the bed in the keeping room, a
salt rock in her hand. Both women heard it at the same
time and both lifted their heads. As the voices grew louder,
Beloved sat up, licked the salt and went into the bigger room.
Sethe and she exchanged glances and started toward the
window. They saw Denver sitting on the steps and beyond
her, where the yard met the road, they saw the rapt faces of
thirty neighborhood women. Some had their eyes closed;
others looked at the hot, cloudless sky. Sethe opened the
door and reached for Beloved's hand. Together they stood
in the doorway. For Sethe it was as though the Clearing had
come to her with all its heat and simmering leaves, where
the voices of women searched for the right combination, the
key, the code, the sound that broke the back of words. Building voice upon voice until they found it, and when they did
it was a wave of sound wide enough to sound deep water
and knock the pods off chestnut trees. It broke over Sethe
and she trembled like the baptized in its wash.

The singing women recognized Sethe at once and surprised themselves by their absence of fear when they saw
what stood next to her. The devil-child was clever, they
thought. And beautiful. It had taken the shape of a pregnant
woman, naked and smiling in the heat of the afternoon sun.
Thunder-black and glistening, she stood on long straight
legs, her belly big and tight. Vines of hair twisted all over
her head. Jesus. Her smile was dazzling.

Sethe feels her eyes burn and it may have been to keep
them clear that she looks up. The sky is blue and clear. Not
one touch of death in the definite green of the leaves. It is
when she lowers her eyes to look again at the loving faces

before her that she sees him. Guiding the mare, slowing down, his black hat wide-brimmed enough to hide his face but not his purpose. He is coming into her yard and he is coming for her best thing. She hears wings. Little humming-birds stick needle beaks right through her headcloth into her hair and beat their wings. And if she thinks anything, it is no. No no. Nonono. She flies. The ice pick is not in her hand; it is her hand.

Standing alone on the porch, Beloved is smiling. But now her hand is empty. Sethe is running away from her, running, and she feels the emptiness in the hand Sethe has been hold-ing. Now she is running into the faces of the people out there, joining them and leaving Beloved behind. Alone. Again. Then Denver, running too. Away from her to the pile of people out there. They make a hill. A hill of black people, falling. And above them all, rising from his place with a whip in his hand, the man without skin, looking. He is looking at her.

Bare feet and chamomile sap.
Took off my shoes; took off my hat.
Bare feet and chamomile sap.
Gimme back my shoes; gimme back my hat.

Lay my head on a potato sack,
Devil sneak up behind my back.
Steam engine got a lonesome whine;
Love that woman till you go stone blind.

Stone blind; stone blind.
Sweet Home gal make you lose your mind.

HIS COMING IS the reverse route of his going. First the cold house, the storeroom, then the kitchen before he tackles the beds. Here Boy, feeble and shedding his coat in patches, is asleep by the pump, so Paul D knows Beloved is truly gone. Disappeared, some say, exploded right before their eyes. Ella is not so sure. "Maybe," she says, "maybe not. Could be hiding in the trees waiting for another chance." But when Paul D sees the ancient dog, eighteen years if a day, he is certain 124 is clear of her. But he opens the door to the cold house halfway expecting to hear her. "Touch me. Touch me. On the inside part and call me my name."

There is the pallet spread with old newspapers gnawed at the edges by mice. The lard can. The potato sacks too, but empty now, they lie on the dirt floor in heaps. In daylight he can't imagine it in darkness with moonlight seeping through the cracks. Nor the desire that drowned him there and forced him to struggle up, up into that girl like she was the clear air at the top of the sea. Coupling with her wasn't even fun. It was more like a brainless urge to stay alive. Each time she came, pulled up her skirts, a life hunger overwhelmed him and he had no more control over it than over his lungs. And afterward, beached and gobbling air, in the midst of repulsion and personal shame, he was thankful too for having been escorted to some ocean-deep place he once belonged to.

Sifting daylight dissolves the memory, turns it into dust motes floating in light. Paul D shuts the door. He looks toward the house and, surprisingly, it does not look back at him. Unloaded, 124 is just another weathered house needing repair. Quiet, just as Stamp Paid said.

"Used to be voices all round that place. Quiet, now," Stamp said. "I been past it a few times and I can't hear a thing. Chastened, I reckon, 'cause Mr. Bodwin say he selling it soon's he can."

"That the name of the one she tried to stab? That one?"

"Yep. His sister say it's full of trouble. Told Janey she was going to get rid of it."

"And him?" asked Paul D.

"Janey say he against it but won't stop it."

"Who they think want a house out there? Anybody got the money don't want to live out there."

"Beats me," Stamp answered. "It'll be a spell, I guess, before it get took off his hands."

"He don't plan on taking her to the law?"

"Don't seem like it. Janey say all he wants to know is who was the naked blackwoman standing on the porch. He was looking at her so hard he didn't notice what Sethe was up to. All he saw was some coloredwomen fighting. He thought Sethe was after one of them, Janey say."

"Janey tell him any different?"

"No. She say she so glad her boss ain't dead. If Ella hadn't clipped her, she say she would have. Scared her to death have that woman kill her boss. She *and* Denver be looking for a job."

"Who Janey tell him the naked woman was?"

"Told him she didn't see none."

"You believe they saw it?"

"Well, they saw something. I trust Ella anyway, and she say she looked it in the eye. It was standing right next to Sethe. But from the way they describe it, don't seem like it was the girl I saw in there. The girl I saw was narrow. This one was big. She say they was holding hands and Sethe looked like a little girl beside it."

"Little girl with a ice pick. How close she get to him?"

"Right up on him, they say. Before Denver and them grabbed her and Ella put her fist in her jaw."

"He got to know Sethe was after him. He got to."

"Maybe. I don't know. If he did think it, I reckon he decided not to. That be just like him, too. He's somebody never turned us down. Steady as a rock. I tell you something, if she had got to him, it'd be the worst thing in the world for us. You know, don't you, he's the main one kept Sethe from the gallows in the first place."

"Yeah. Damn. That woman is crazy. Crazy."

"Yeah, well, ain't we all?"

They laughed then. A rusty chuckle at first and then more, louder and louder until Stamp took out his pocket handkerchief and wiped his eyes while Paul D pressed the heel of his hand in his own. As the scene neither one had witnessed took shape before them, its seriousness and its embarrassment made them shake with laughter.

"Every time a whiteman come to the door she got to kill somebody?"

"For all she know, the man could be coming for the rent."

"Good thing they don't deliver mail out that way."

"Wouldn't nobody get no letter."

"Except the postman."

"Be a mighty hard message."

"And his last."

When their laughter was spent, they took deep breaths and shook their heads.

"And he still going to let Denver spend the night in his house? Ha!"

"Aw no. Hey. Lay off Denver, Paul D. That's my heart. I'm proud of that girl. She was the first one wrestle her mother down. Before anybody knew what the devil was going on."

"She saved his life then, you could say."

"You could. You could," said Stamp, thinking suddenly of the leap, the wide swing and snatch of his arm as he rescued the little curly-headed baby from within inches of a split skull. "I'm proud of her. She turning out fine. Fine."

It was true. Paul D saw her the next morning when he was on his way to work and she was leaving hers. Thinner, steady in the eyes, she looked more like Halle than ever.

She was the first to smile. "Good morning, Mr. D."

"Well, it is now." Her smile, no longer the sneer he remembered, had welcome in it and strong traces of Sethe's mouth. Paul D touched his cap. "How you getting along?"

"Don't pay to complain."

"You on your way home?"

She said no. She had heard about an afternoon job at the shirt factory. She hoped that with her night work at the Bodwins' and another one, she could put away something and help her mother too. When he asked her if they treated her all right over there, she said more than all right. Miss Bodwin taught her stuff. He asked her what stuff and she laughed and said book stuff. "She says I might go to Oberlin. She's experimenting on me." And he didn't say, "Watch out.

Watch out. Nothing in the world more dangerous than a white schoolteacher." Instead he nodded and asked the question he wanted to.

"Your mother all right?"

"No," said Denver. "No. No, not a bit all right."

"You think I should stop by? Would she welcome it?"

"I don't know," said Denver. "I think I've lost my mother, Paul D."

They were both silent for a moment and then he said, "Uh, that girl. You know. Beloved?"

"Yes?"

"You think she sure 'nough your sister?"

Denver looked at her shoes. "At times. At times I think she was – more." She fiddled with her shirtwaist, rubbing a spot of something. Suddenly she leveled her eyes at his. "But who would know that better than you, Paul D? I mean, you sure 'nough knew her."

He licked his lips. "Well, if you want my opinion –"

"I don't," she said. "I have my own."

"You grown," he said.

"Yes, sir."

"Well. Well, good luck with the job."

"Thank you. And, Paul D, you don't have to stay 'way, but be careful how you talk to my ma'am, hear?"

"Don't worry," he said and left her then, or rather she left him because a young man was running toward her, saying, "Hey, Miss Denver. Wait up."

She turned to him, her face looking like someone had turned up the gas jet.

He left her unwillingly because he wanted to talk more, make sense out of the stories he had been hearing: white-man came to take Denver to work and Sethe cut him. Baby ghost came back evil and sent Sethe out to get the man who kept her from hanging. One point of agreement is: first they saw it and then they didn't. When they got Sethe down on the ground and the ice pick out of her hands and looked back to the house, it was gone. Later, a little boy put it out how he had been looking for bait back of 124, down by the stream, and saw, cutting through the woods, a naked woman with fish for hair.

As a matter of fact, Paul D doesn't care how It went or even why. He cares about how he left and why. When he looks at himself through Garner's eyes, he sees one thing. Through Sixo's, another. One makes him feel righteous. One makes him feel ashamed. Like the time he worked both sides of the War. Running away from the Northpoint Bank and Railway to join the 44th Colored Regiment in Tennessee, he thought he had made it, only to discover he had arrived at another colored regiment forming under a commander in New Jersey. He stayed there four weeks. The regiment fell apart before it got started on the question of whether the soldiers should have weapons or not. Not, it was decided, and the white commander had to figure out what to command them to do instead of kill other whitemen. Some of the ten thousand stayed there to clean, haul and build things; others drifted away to another regiment; most were abandoned, left to their own devices with bitterness for pay. He was trying to make up his mind what to do when an agent from Northpoint Bank caught up with him and took him back to Delaware, where he slave-worked a year. Then Northpoint took $300 in exchange for his services in Alabama, where he worked for the Rebellers, first sorting the dead and then smelting iron. When he and his group combed the battlefields, their job was to pull the Confederate wounded away from the Confederate dead. Care, they told them. Take good care. Coloredmen and white, their faces wrapped to their eyes, picked their way through the meadows with lamps, listening in the dark for groans of life in the indifferent silence of the dead. Mostly young men, some children, and it shamed him a little to feel pity for what he imagined were the sons of the guards in Alfred, Georgia.

In five tries he had not had one permanent success. Every one of his escapes (from Sweet Home, from Brandywine, from Alfred, Georgia, from Wilmington, from Northpoint) had been frustrated. Alone, undisguised, with visible skin, memorable hair and no whiteman to protect him, he never stayed uncaught. The longest had been when he ran with the convicts, stayed with the Cherokee, followed their advice and lived in hiding with the weaver woman in Wilmington, Delaware: three years. And in all those escapes he could not help being astonished by the beauty of this land that was not his. He hid in its breast, fingered its earth for food, clung to its banks to lap water and tried not to love it. On nights when the sky was personal, weak with the weight of its own stars, he made himself not love it. Its graveyards and low-lying rivers. Or just a house – solitary under a chinaberry tree; maybe a mule tethered and the light hitting its hide just so. Anything could stir him and he tried hard not to love it.

After a few months on the battlefields of Alabama, he was impressed to a foundry in Selma along with three hundred captured, lent or taken coloredmen. That's where the War's end found him, and leaving Alabama when he had been declared free should have been a snap. He should have been able to walk from the foundry in Selma straight to Philadelphia, taking the main roads, a train if he wanted to, or passage on a boat. But it wasn't like that. When he and two colored soldiers (who had been captured from the 44th he had looked for) walked from Selma to Mobile, they saw twelve dead blacks in the first eighteen miles. Two were women, four were little boys. He thought this, for sure, would be the walk of his life. The Yankees in control left the Rebels out of control. They got to the outskirts of Mobile, where blacks were putting down tracks for the Union that, earlier, they had torn up for the Rebels. One of the men with him, a private called

Keane, had been with the Massachusetts 54th. He told Paul D they had been paid less than white soldiers. It was a sore point with him that, as a group, they had refused the offer Massachusetts made to make up the difference in pay. Paul D was so impressed by the idea of being paid money to fight he looked at the private with wonder and envy.

Keane and his friend, a Sergeant Rossiter, confiscated a skiff and the three of them floated in Mobile Bay. There the private hailed a Union gunboat, which took all three aboard. Keane and Rossiter disembarked at Memphis to look for their commanders. The captain of the gunboat let Paul D stay aboard all the way to Wheeling, West Virginia. He made his own way to New Jersey.

By the time he got to Mobile, he had seen more dead people than living ones, but when he got to Trenton the crowds of alive people, neither hunting nor hunted, gave him a measure of free life so tasty he never forgot it. Moving down a busy street full of whitepeople who needed no explanation for his presence, the glances he got had to do with his disgusting clothes and unforgivable hair. Still, nobody raised an alarm. Then came the miracle. Standing in a street in front of a row of brick houses, he heard a whiteman call him ("Say there! Yo!") to help unload two trunks from a coach cab. Afterward the whiteman gave him a coin. Paul D walked around with it for hours – not sure what it could buy (a suit? a meal? a horse?) and if anybody would sell him anything. Finally he saw a greengrocer selling vegetables from a wagon. Paul D pointed to a bunch of turnips. The grocer handed them to him, took his one coin and gave him several more. Stunned, he backed away. Looking around, he saw that nobody seemed interested in the "mistake" or him, so he walked along, happily chewing turnips. Only a few women looked vaguely repelled as they passed. His first earned purchase made him glow, never mind the turnips were withered dry. That was when he decided that to eat, walk and sleep anywhere was life as good as it got. And he did it for seven years till he found himself in southern Ohio, where an old woman and a girl he used to know had gone.

Now his coming is the reverse of his going. First he stands in the back, near the cold house, amazed by the riot of late-summer flowers where vegetables should be growing. Sweet william, morning glory, chrysanthemums. The odd placement of cans jammed with the rotting stems of things, the blossoms shriveled like sores. Dead ivy twines around bean poles and door handles. Faded newspaper pictures are nailed to the outhouse and on trees. A rope too short for anything but skip-jumping lies discarded near the washtub; and jars and jars of dead lightning bugs. Like a child's house; the house of a very tall child.

He walks to the front door and opens it. It is stone quiet. In the place where once a shaft of sad red light had bathed him, locking him where he stood, is nothing. A bleak and minus nothing. More like absence, but an absence he had to get through with the same determination he had when he trusted Sethe and stepped through the pulsing light. He glances quickly at the lightning-white stairs. The entire railing is wound with ribbons, bows, bouquets. Paul D steps inside. The outdoor breeze he brings with him stirs the ribbons. Carefully, not quite in a hurry but losing no time, he climbs the luminous stairs. He enters Sethe's room. She isn't there and the bed looks so small he wonders how the two of them had lain there. It has no sheets, and because the roof windows do not open the room is stifling. Brightly colored clothes lie on the floor. Hanging from a wall peg is the dress Beloved wore when he first saw her. A pair of ice skates nestles in a basket in the corner. He turns his eyes back to the bed and keeps looking at it. It seems to him a place he is not. With an effort that makes him sweat he forces a picture of himself lying there, and when he sees it, it lifts his spirit. He goes to the other bedroom. Denver's is as neat as the other is messy. But still no Sethe. Maybe she has gone back to work, gotten better in the days since he talked to Denver. He goes back down the stairs, leaving the image of himself firmly in place on the narrow bed. At the kitchen table he sits down. Something is missing from 124. Something larger than the people who lived there. Something more than Beloved or the red light. He can't put his finger on it, but it seems, for a moment, that just beyond his knowing is the glare of an outside thing that embraces while it accuses.

To the right of him, where the door to the keeping room is ajar, he hears humming. Someone is humming a tune. Something soft and sweet, like a lullaby. Then a few words. Sounds like "high Johnny, wide Johnny. Sweet William bend down low." Of course, he thinks. That's where she is — and she is. Lying under a quilt of merry colors. Her hair, like the dark delicate roots of good plants, spreads and curves on the pillow. Her eyes, fixed on the window, are so expressionless he is not sure she will know who he is. There is too much light here in this room. Things look sold.

"Jackweed raise up high," she sings. "Lambswool over my shoulder, buttercup and clover fly." She is fingering a long clump of her hair.

Paul D clears his throat to interrupt her. "Sethe?"

She turns her head. "Paul D."

"Aw, Sethe."

"I made the ink, Paul D. He couldn't have done it if I hadn't made the ink."

"What ink? Who?"

"You shaved."

"Yeah. Look bad?"

"No. You looking good."

"Devil's confusion. What's this I hear about you not getting out of bed?"

She smiles, lets it fade and turns her eyes back to the window.

"I need to talk to you," he tells her.

She doesn't answer.

"I saw Denver. She tell you?"

"She comes in the daytime. Denver. She's still with me, my Denver."

"You got to get up from here, girl." He is nervous. This reminds him of something.

"I'm tired, Paul D. So tired. I have to rest a while."

Now he knows what he is reminded of and he shouts at her, "Don't you die on me! This is Baby Suggs' bed! Is that what you planning?" He is so angry he could kill her. He checks himself, remembering Denver's warning, and whispers, "What you planning, Sethe?"

"Oh, I don't have no plans. No plans at all."

"Look," he says, "Denver be here in the day. I be here in the night. I'm a take care of you, you hear? Starting now. First off, you don't smell right. Stay there. Don't move. Let me heat up some water." He stops. "Is it all right, Sethe, if I heat up some water?"

"And count my feet?" she asks him.

He steps closer. "Rub your feet."

Sethe closes her eyes and presses her lips together. She is thinking: No. This little place by a window is what I want. And rest. There's nothing to rub now and no reason to. Nothing left to bathe, assuming he even knows how. Will he do it in sections? First her face, then her hands, her thighs, her feet, her back? Ending with her exhausted breasts? And if he bathes her in sections, will the parts hold? She opens her eyes, knowing the danger of looking at him. She looks at him. The peachstone skin, the crease between his ready, waiting eyes and sees it – the thing in him, the blessedness, that has made him the kind of man who can walk in a house and make the women cry. Because with him, in his presence, they could. Cry and tell him things they only told each other: that time didn't stay put; that she called, but Howard and

Buglar walked on down the railroad track and couldn't hear her; that Amy was scared to stay with her because her feet were ugly and her back looked so bad; that her ma'am had hurt her feelings and she couldn't find her hat anywhere and "Paul D?"

"What, baby?"

"She left me."

"Aw, girl. Don't cry."

"She was my best thing."

Paul D sits down in the rocking chair and examines the quilt patched in carnival colors. His hands are limp between his knees. There are too many things to feel about this woman. His head hurts. Suddenly he remembers Sixo trying to describe what he felt about the Thirty-Mile Woman. "She is a friend of my mind. She gather me, man. The pieces I am, she gather them and give them back to me in all the right order. It's good, you know, when you got a woman who is a friend of your mind."

He is staring at the quilt but he is thinking about her wrought-iron back; the delicious mouth still puffy at the corner from Ella's fist. The mean black eyes. The wet dress steaming before the fire. Her tenderness about his neck jewelry – its three wands, like attentive baby rattlers, curving two feet into the air. How she never mentioned or looked at it, so he did not have to feel the shame of being collared like a beast. Only this woman Sethe could have left him his manhood like that. He wants to put his story next to hers.

"Sethe," he says, "me and you, we got more yesterday than anybody. We need some kind of tomorrow."

He leans over and takes her hand. With the other he touches her face. "You your best thing, Sethe. You are." His holding fingers are holding hers.

"Me? Me?"

THERE IS A LONELINESS that can be rocked. Arms crossed, knees drawn up; holding, holding on, this motion, unlike a ship's, smooths and contains the rocker. It's an inside kind – wrapped tight like skin. Then there is a loneliness that roams. No rocking can hold it down. It is alive, on its own. A dry and spreading thing that makes the sound of one's own feet going seem to come from a far-off place.

Everybody knew what she was called, but nobody anywhere knew her name. Disremembered and unaccounted for, she cannot be lost because no one is looking for her, and even if they were, how can they call her if they don't know her name? Although she has claim, she is not claimed. In the place where long grass opens, the girl who waited to be loved and cry shame erupts into her separate parts, to make it easy for the chewing laughter to swallow her all away.

It was not a story to pass on.

They forgot her like a bad dream. After they made up their tales, shaped and decorated them, those that saw her that day on the porch quickly and deliberately forgot her. It took longer for those who had spoken to her, lived with her, fallen in love with her, to forget, until they realized they couldn't remember or repeat a single thing she said, and began to believe that, other than what they themselves were thinking, she hadn't said anything at all. So, in the end, they forgot her too. Remembering seemed unwise. They never knew

TONI MORRISON

where or why she crouched, or whose was the underwater
face she needed like that. Where the memory of the smile
under her chin might have been and was not, a latch latched
and lichen attached its apple-green bloom to the metal. What
made her think her fingernails could open locks the rain
rained on?

It was not a story to pass on.

So they forgot her. Like an unpleasant dream during a troub-
ling sleep. Occasionally, however, the rustle of a skirt hushes
when they wake, and the knuckles brushing a cheek in sleep
seem to belong to the sleeper. Sometimes the photograph of
a close friend or relative – looked at too long – shifts, and
something more familiar than the dear face itself moves there.
They can touch it if they like, but don't, because they know
things will never be the same if they do.

This is not a story to pass on.

Down by the stream in back of 124 her footprints come
and go, come and go. They are so familiar. Should a child,
an adult place his feet in them, they will fit. Take them out
and they disappear again as though nobody ever walked there.

By and by all trace is gone, and what is forgotten is not
only the footprints but the water too and what it is down
there. The rest is weather. Not the breath of the disremembered and unaccounted for, but wind in the eaves, or spring
ice thawing too quickly. Just weather. Certainly no clamor
for a kiss.

Beloved.

ABOUT THE INTRODUCER

A. S. BYATT was Senior Lecturer in English and American Literature at University College, London, before becoming a full-time writer. Her novels include *The Virgin in the Garden*, *Possession* (for which she won the Booker Prize in 1990), *Babel Tower* and *The Whistling Woman*; her short-story collections include *The Matisse Stories* and *Elementals*. Her critical work includes studies of Wordsworth, Coleridge and Iris Murdoch. She was appointed CBE in 1990 and DBE in 1999.

CHINUA ACHEBE
Things Fall Apart

AESCHYLUS
The Oresteia

ISABEL ALLENDE
The House of the Spirits

THE ARABIAN NIGHTS
(in 2 vols, tr. Husain Haddawy)

JOHN JAMES AUDUBON
The Audubon Reader

AUGUSTINE
The Confessions

JANE AUSTEN
Emma
Mansfield Park
Northanger Abbey
Persuasion
Pride and Prejudice
Sanditon and Other Stories
Sense and Sensibility

HONORÉ DE BALZAC
Cousin Bette
Eugénie Grandet
Old Goriot

GIORGIO BASSANI
The Garden of the Finzi-Continis

SIMONE DE BEAUVOIR
The Second Sex

SAMUEL BECKETT
Molloy, Malone Dies,
The Unnamable
(US only)

SAUL BELLOW
The Adventures of Augie March

HECTOR BERLIOZ
The Memoirs of Hector Berlioz

WILLIAM BLAKE
Poems and Prophecies

JORGE LUIS BORGES
Ficciones

JAMES BOSWELL
The Life of Samuel Johnson
The Journal of a Tour to
the Hebrides

CHARLOTTE BRONTË
Jane Eyre
Villette

EMILY BRONTË
Wuthering Heights

MIKHAIL BULGAKOV
The Master and Margarita

SAMUEL BUTLER
The Way of all Flesh

JAMES M. CAIN
The Postman Always Rings Twice
Double Indemnity
Mildred Pierce
Selected Stories
(in 1 vol. US only)

ITALO CALVINO
If on a winter's night a traveler

ALBERT CAMUS
The Outsider (UK)
The Stranger (US)
The Plague, The Fall,
Exile and the Kingdom,
and Selected Essays
(in 1 vol.)

WILLA CATHER
Death Comes for the Archbishop
My Ántonia (US only)

MIGUEL DE CERVANTES
Don Quixote

RAYMOND CHANDLER
The novels (in 2 vols)
Collected Stories

GEOFFREY CHAUCER
Canterbury Tales

ANTON CHEKHOV
The Complete Short Novels
My Life and Other Stories
The Steppe and Other Stories

KATE CHOPIN
The Awakening

CARL VON CLAUSEWITZ
On War

S. T. COLERIDGE
Poems

This book is set in BEMBO which was cut
by the punch-cutter Francesco Griffo
for the Venetian printer-publisher
Aldus Manutius in early 1495
and first used in a pamphlet
by a young scholar
named Pietro
Bembo.